SAMSON OCCOM
AND THE CHRISTIAN INDIANS
OF NEW ENGLAND

WITHDRAWN

Laurence M. Hauptman, *Series Editor*

Samson Occom The Indian
of mohegan Ejus manus

SAMSON OCCOM

AND

THE CHRISTIAN INDIANS OF NEW ENGLAND

BY

W. DeLOSS LOVE, Ph.D.

AUTHOR OF "THE FAST AND THANKSGIVING DAYS OF NEW ENGLAND"

WITH AN INTRODUCTION BY
MARGARET CONNELL SZASZ

SYRACUSE UNIVERSITY PRESS

Introduction copyright © 2000 by Margaret Connell Szasz

First Syracuse University Press Edition 2000

00   01   02   03   04   05   6   5   4   3   2   1

Originally published in 1899 by the Pilgrim Press.

The paper used in this publication meets the minimum requirements of American National Standard for Information Sciences—Permanence of Paper for Printed Library Materials, ANSI Z39.48–1984. ∞™

Library of Congress Cataloging-in-Publication Data

Love, William DeLoss, 1851–1918.
  Samson Occom and the Christian Indians of New England / by W. DeLoss Love; with an introduction by Margaret Connell Szasz. —1st Syracuse University Press ed.
      p.   cm. —(The Iroquois and their neighbors)
  Originally published: Boston: Pilgrim Press, 1899.
  Includes Index.
  ISBN 0-8156-2728-9 (cloth: alk. paper). —ISBN 0-8156-0436-X (paperback: alk. paper)
      1. Occom, Samson, 1723–1792.   2. Mohegan Indians—Biography.
  3. Missionaries—New England—Biography.   4. Algonquian Indians—Missions.   5. Algonquian Indians—Relocation.   6. Algonquian Indians—Government relations.   7. Presbyterian Church—Missions—New England—History.   8. Brotherton Indians—History.
  9. Brotherton Indians—Land tenure.   I. Title.   II. Series.
  E99.M830255 1997
  974'.004973
  [B]—DC20   96-17929

Manufactured in the United States of America

 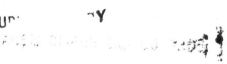

TO

PROFESSOR EDWARD NORTH, L. H. D.

HONORED AND BELOVED

IN REMEMBRANCE OF THE TWENTIETH REUNION

OF THE

CLASS OF 1873

HAMILTON COLLEGE

THIS VOLUME IS INSCRIBED

CONTENTS

CHAPTER XII

THE PLAN OF EMIGRATION TO ONEIDA

1771–1776

CHAPTER XIII

INDIAN FRIENDS AT STOCKBRIDGE

1734–1783

CHAPTER XIV

THE MISSIONARY OF THE WILDERNESS

1783–1789

CHAPTER XV

THE TRIALS OF OCCOM'S LAST DAYS

1785–1792

CHAPTER XVI

INDIAN TOWN GOVERNMENT

1785–1842

CHAPTER XVII

THE LAST REMOVE

1809–1898

APPENDIX

ILLUSTRATIONS

INTRODUCTION

MARGARET CONNELL SZASZ

Samson Occom was one of the most unusual actors to step on stage in the eighteenth-century American colonies. Mohegan yet Christian, raised in a wigwam yet comfortable in a two-story home, a native speaker of Mohegan yet fluent in English and literate in Greek, Latin, French, and probably Hebrew, Occom strode across the cultures of his time and place. As a cultural intermediary, he earned a strong following within Native and Euroamerican communities and in England and Scotland, where he lived during a 1760s fund-raising trip. Simultaneously, he incurred the antagonism of tribespeople and Euroamericans, and some English who refused support of the fund-raising tour. Hero to his followers and enemy to his opponents, Occom played a complex role in the eighteenth-century world bounded by the Great Awakening of the 1740s, the War for Independence, and the emergence of the Young Republic.[1]

Occom was a spiritual and educational broker among cultures engaged in an era of tumultuous change.[2] Consequently, he left a multifaceted heritage. He guided the Mohegans and other New England Algonquian groups through his leadership and broker-

---

[1] The author would like to thank Kate Lugar, University of New Mexico reference librarian and History specialist, John Simon, Congregational Library, Boston, Frank K. Lorenz, curator of archives and special collections at Hamilton College Library, and Ferenc M. Szasz, who has offered valuable suggestions on this essay.

[2] Margaret Connell Szasz, "Samson Occom: Mohegan as Spiritual Intermediary." In *Between Indian and White Worlds: The Cultural Broker,* ed. Margaret Connell Szasz (Norman: Univ. of Oklahoma Press, 1994), 61–78.

age skills; he offered spiritual sustenance to Algonquians, as well as Euroamericans and African Americans; he secured the funding necessary for the creation of Dartmouth College (although his goal of significant Indian enrollment was not attained until recently); and he published a hymnal that included some of his own hymns.

Despite a number of more recent works that focus on Occom, including a biography, none has superseded W. DeLoss Love's biography, *Samson Occom and the Christian Indians of New England*.[3] Long out of print, it is fitting that it be reprinted a century after its first appearance in 1899.

Love's biography reflects the fin de siècle milieu: it is a work of its time. The approach and methodology of the author suggest his Euroamerican ancestry, his undergraduate training at Hamilton College (1873; honorary Ph.D., 1894), his seminary studies at Andover Newton in preparation for the Congregational ministry, and the state of the historical profession at this time. In this era American historians, like their counterparts in other academic fields, created a professional organization, the American Historical Association (AHA, 1884). Initially, members of the AHA were "amateurs"[4] As a scholar, therefore, Love was typical. Although he was a minister and sometime businessman, he wrote *Samson Occom*, as well as a number of regional histories.[5]

---

[3] For further studies of Occom, see Harold Blodgett, *Samson Occom* (Hanover, N.H.: Dartmouth College Publications, 1935); Leon Burr Richardson, *An Indian Preacher in England* (1939; reprint, Hanover, N.H.: Dartmouth College Publications, 1933); Margaret Connell Szasz, *Indian Education in the American Colonies, 1607–1783* (Albuquerque: Univ. of New Mexico Press, 1988); David Murray, *Forked Tongues: Speech Writing and Representation in North American Indian Texts* (Bloomington: Indiana Univ. Press, 1991); Connell Szasz, "Samson Occom: Mohegan as Spiritual Intermediary."

[4] Peter Novick, *That Noble Dream, The Objectivity Question and the American Historical Profession* (New York: Cambridge Univ. Press, 1989), 49.

[5] Love was a member of the American Antiquarian Society, the Connecticut Society of the Sons of the American Revolution, the Society of the Colonial Wars, and the Connecticut Historical Society. For works by Love, see *The Colonial History of Hartford* (1935; reprint, Hartford: Author, 1914); *"The City of*

The quality of his research and writing also stamped Love as a member of this generation of scholars. Absorbing the nineteenth-century philosophy of positivism, Love and his colleagues researched assiduously, searching for "the facts." "The result," historian R. G. Collingwood once noted, "was a vast increase of detailed historical knowledge, based to an unprecedented degree on accurate and critical examination of evidence."[6] *Samson Occom* exemplifies this pattern. During his prodigious research trips, Love investigated manuscript collections ranging from the Occom Diaries and Wheelock Papers at Dartmouth College to the Letters and Journals of Samuel Kirkland, now located in the archives at Hamilton College. He also scoured town records in Connecticut and, returning to his childhood state of Wisconsin, visited Lake Winnebago, where the Brothertown and Stockbridge Indians settled in the 1820s and 1830s, several decades after their initial removal from New England to lands obtained from the Oneida in New York. Love described his meetings with the Brothertown Indians, recalling his "extended interviews with more than half a dozen aged people who were over sixteen years old when they left Brothertown, N.Y."[7] The understanding that he gained from speaking with these descendants of Samson and Mary Occom and other families was reinforced by the "many items [that] have been gathered in their homes." To this degree, Love had turned ethnologist, employing some of the methodology

Hartford," New England Magazine 27 (Feb. 1903), 643–72; *The Fast and Thanksgiving Day of New England* (Boston: Houghton, Mifflin & Co., 1895); *Half-Century History of Farmington Avenue Congregational Church ... 1851–1901* (n.p., 1901); "The Navigation of the Connecticut River." In American Antiquarian Society, Worcester, Massachusetts. *Proceedings* 15 (1904), 385–441; *Thomas Short, The First Printer of Connecticut* (Hartford: The Case, Lockwood and Brainard, 1901).

[6] R.G. Collingwood, *The Idea of History* (New York: Oxford Univ. Press, 1956), 127.

[7] Love to Professor North, Sept. 2, 1895. *Hamilton Literary Magazine* (Dec. 1895), 130. Hamilton College Library. The author would like to thank Frank K. Lorenz for obtaining this document.

adopted by Franz Boas and other early ethnologists, thereby incorporating field work into his archival research.[8]

Love's approach to the writing of history also placed him squarely in the middle of this generation of historians. In this era of scientific method, historians perceived themselves as scholars engaged in scientific inquiry.[9] They aimed for high standards of objectivity and sought to maintain their neutrality at all costs. Love exemplified this stance in his introduction to chapter IX, observing, "At all events, it is the office of the historian to set forth the facts without prejudice" (152).

Although the need to echo the contemporary fascination with science formed the central core of historians' goals in this era (especially for Love, who taught science and mathematics for a short time), such goals also reflected nineteenth-century mainstream America's celebration of the idea of Progress. Love's interpretation of American Indians and Samson Occom illustrates his overriding conviction in the inevitability of America's God-ordained Progress. Essential to this position are those characteristics that describe Love himself. As a minister, he viewed non-Christians as (in his words) "heathens" who had not yet become acquainted with the "true religion." As a Christian of Euroamerican ancestry, Love also perceived himself as "civilized." From this perspective, he interpreted "Progress" as the path that American Indians would follow, moving from "barbarism along the trail of civilization" (v). Love's description of the Fowlers, the Montauk family Occom married into during his dozen years of teaching on Long Island, typifies his perception of Euroamerican civilization. "[T]hrough the instruction of the Montauk schoolmaster," he

---

[8] In chapter XVII Love described his visits to Brothertown, Wisconsin, acknowledging the merits of ethnology: "The place is an interesting field for the ethnologist, for the types of the ancient tribes of New England are still to be observed among them" (330). In his 1893 search for Occom's grave, Love encountered Billy Paul, a descendant of Occom and his brother-in-law David Fowler, thereby enlarging on his field trip methodology (327).

[9] For an expansion of these characteristics, see Novick, *That Noble Dream*, 37.

wrote, "[t]hey [the Fowlers] became thoroughly civilized" (54). Translated, this meant that they became Christian, accepted farming, schooling, and removal to the Brothertown community that Occom later formed on Oneida lands.

Love's interpretation of Euroamerican civilization included a veneration for the sacred trilogy held in high esteem among the late-nineteenth-century reformers responsible for the passage of the Dawes Act in 1887 and other federal schooling measures that were aimed at remolding American Indians. The elements of this trilogy were Christianity, mainstream schooling, and individual land ownership intended to encourage farming. Farming had been an ancient tradition among many Native groups, but these Euroamericans believed their farming techniques to be superior. For Love's generation, the concept of farming as a traditional occupation merged with the contemporary elevation of science. Reflecting his times, Love incorporated this revisionism by dubbing mainstream farming "the science of agriculture" (62).

To his credit, Love recognized that the results of land leasing by the Brothertown Indians in the late eighteenth century were identical to Indian land allotment and leasing a century later: in both instances Indians generally lost their land. During the lifetime of the Dawes Act, Indians lost about two-thirds of their land base. Love points out that following Occom's death in 1792, the Brothertown Indians also lost extensive land holdings. Despite this recognition, Love maintained his faith in the core concepts of scientific agriculture, schooling, and Christianity. His convictions reflected nineteenth-century mainstream attitudes. Although the belief in Euroamerican cultural superiority would be eroded early in the twentieth century by the emerging concept of cultural pluralism and the denial of any absolute progress, introduced by anthropologists like Boas, the acknowledgement of the intrinsic worth of American Indian cultures by the general public and the federal policy makers lay several decades away. *Samson Occom* came at a transition point in American cross-cultural perception.

Given Love's acceptance of Euroamerican values, his admiration for Samson Occom is only natural. As an ordained Presbyterian minister, Occom had met Love's criteria for civilization. Nonetheless, Occom was an Indian, and consequently, he was subject to Love's stereotyping, which argued that the Indian could not "grow to the full stature of a civilized man without struggles against his hereditary weaknesses" (152). Since Love believed that Occom had faced greater hurdles than his eighteenth-century Euroamerican counterparts, Occom's accomplishments were more remarkable. In Love's view, Occom emerged as "a native Indian of no mean tribe, who had risen to the highest station of any Indian preacher in the century" (137).

Throughout the biography Love remained effusive in his praise for this Mohegan leader. For Love, the epitome of Occom's career was reached during the two-year tour of England and Scotland, between 1766 and 1768.[10] Since this experience is the subject of other writings, Love does not describe it in significant detail, but he does discuss it with considerable relish because it exemplifies for him Occom's successful adaptation to British society. During the trip, which was initially suggested by George Whitefield, the renowned evangelist and engineered by Occom and his former mentor, Eleazar Wheelock, Occom was accompanied by Nathaniel Whitaker, a Euroamerican minister.[11] Using Whitaker as a foil

[10] On Occom's fund-raising tour, see Richardson, *An Indian Preacher in England.*

[11] The earliest biography of Wheelock is David McClure and Elijah Parish, *Memoirs of the Rev. Eleazar Wheelock* (Newburyport, Maine: Edward Norris, 1811). Also see James Dow McCallum, *Eleazar Wheelock, Founder of Dartmouth College* (Hanover, N.H.: Dartmouth College Publications, 1939) and James Dow McCallum, ed., *The Letters of Eleazar Wheelock's Indians* (Hanover, N.H.: Dartmouth College Publications, 1932). For a more critical assessment, see James Axtell, "Dr. Wheelock's Little RedSchool." In James Axtell, *The European and the Indian, Essays in the Ethnohistory of Colonial North America* (New York: Oxford Univ. Press, 1981), 87–109; Connell Szasz, *Indian Education in the American Colonies,* 230–31, 256–57; Connell Szasz, "Samson Occom: Mohegan as Spiritual Intermediary."

to illustrate Occom's dominant position during the tour, Love suggested that "Mr. Whitaker very soon became a mere agent. . . . Occom on the other hand, won universal esteem" (147). Occom's initial strength lay in his ability to emulate the English. He had learned well during his six years of study with Wheelock and other local ministers. In London, "he conducted himself with the manner of the white man, as though he had never lived in a wigwam of bark" (141). Conversely, he retained certain qualities that Love attributed to his American Indian ancestry: "Calm, dignified and self-possessed, as many an Indian chief was wont to be, he exhibited those qualities which were esteemed in a minister of that day" (138). Occom's ability to adapt, combined with the strength of his spiritual conviction and his Indianness, persuaded the English and Scots to view him as a "novelty": "With true Indian sagacity he saw this, and made up his mind to use the sensation he caused to gather contributions for the Indian school" (140–141).

The fact that the English were fascinated with "Red Indians," and that the Scots also displayed keen interest, did not hurt Occom's cause. The Scots had long been acquainted with the Wheelock-Occom ventures in American Indian schooling through the Society in Scotland for the Propagation of Christian Knowledge (SSPCK), begun in 1709.[12] More recently, they had in their midst the well-known Peter Williamson, and Aberdonian-born Scotsman who had lived among the Iroquois as a captive and revelled in relating the saga of his adventures to the residents of Edinburgh.[13] Although Williamson's captivity narratives, which

[12] On the SSPCK and American Indians, see Donald E. Meek, "Scottish Highlanders, North American Indians and the SSPCK: Some Cultural Perspectives," *Records of the Scottish Church History Society* 23 (pt. 3, 1989), 378–96.

[13] Peter Williamson, *French and Indian Cruelty; exemplified in the life and vicissitudes of fortune, of Peter Williamson, a disbanded soldier* (Glasgow: Printed by J. Bryce and D. Patterson, for the benefit of the unfortunate author, 1758); Peter Williamson, *The Travels of Peter Williamson Among the Different Nations and Tribes of Savage Indians in America* (Edinburgh: Printed for the author, 1768).

appeared in the 1750s and 1760s, may not have sold as well in England as they did in Scotland, the English had also been made aware of American Indian schooling through the Anglican Society for the Propagation of the Gospel in Foreign Parts (SPG), founded in 1701,[14] and through occasional visits by "Red Indians" to the capital of the British Empire, such as the trip of the "Four Iroquois Kings" during Queen Anne's reign. These publicized tours whetted the English appetite for further exotica. Occom represented the fruition of evangelical missionary endeavours. He was the latest in a long line of American Indians who had converted to Christianity, including Pocahontas, or Lady Rebecca, whose London residence of 1616–1617 proved fatal to her health. Each of these Christianized Indians represented a "success story" for the SPG and SSPCK, thereby encouraging a flood of donations. Occom, therefore, was following a well-established tradition. Still, he incorporated a new twist by appearing both as an Indian preacher and as a spokesperson for Indian schooling, thus embodying the cause in his own person. Although his popularity could have been read on a number of different gauges, one of the most sensitive barometers was the London theater, where, as he noted in his Diary in 1766, "the Stage Players, had been Mimicking of me in their Plays, lately."[15]

On Occom's return from the adulation of Britain, where he had delivered hundreds of sermons and visited the most powerful figures in British society, including George VI, he stepped back into the reality of his role as an Indian preacher in the American colonies. The admiration and graciousness to which he had become accustomed were quickly replaced by what he perceived as an unwillingness by Wheelock and other regional ministers to ac-

---

[14] John Calam, *Parsons and Pedagogues: The SPG Adventures in American Education* (New York: Columbia Univ. Press, 1971); C. F. Pascoe, *Two Hundred Years of the S.P.G.: An Historical Account of the Society for the Propagation of the Gospel in Foreign Parts* (London: The Society, 1901).

[15] Transcript of Samson Occom's Journal [Diary], 3 vols., Dartmouth College Archives, Hanover (hereafter cited as DCA), Saturday, Feb. 22, 1766, 1:75.

knowledge his unique offerings to the spiritual and practical needs of the southern New England Algonquians.

Occom learned to his dismay that the impressive sum of over £12,000 that he and Whitaker had raised in Britain was not to be spent as he had hoped.[16] Most of the funds would be consumed by a college that would cater to English rather than Indian students. The carefully worded charter of Dartmouth College declared its purposes to be "for the education & instruction of Youth of the Indian Tribes in this Land in reading, writing & all parts of Learning which shall appear necessary and expedient for civilizing & christianizing Children of pagans as well as in all liberal Arts and Sciences; and also of English Youth and any others."[17] The words of the charter, however, were designed to please the British trustees, who had control over the purse strings. The reality for Occom was that "The Indian was converted into an English School & . . . the English had crowded out the Indian youth."[18]

In the years immediately following Occom's return from Britain, the experiments in Indian schooling that his scholarship had inspired collapsed. Moor's Indian Charity School had been transferred to Hanover. Established in 1754 by Wheelock, Moor's

[16] The total amount collected for Dartmouth College was £12,026, which included £9,497 in England and, during the short visit to Scotland, £2529. The expenses incurred by Occom and Whitaker were only £1,000. Net proceeds, therefore, were about £11,000. No other American institution soliciting funds "by a direct campaign" in Britain during the colonial era garnered this sum. Richardson, *An Indian Preacher in England*, 15.

[17] The Dartmouth College charter can be found in Jere R. Daniell, II, "Eleazar Wheelock and the Dartmouth College Charter," *Historical New Hampshire* 24 (Winter 1969), 3–44. On the history of the college, also see Frederick Chase, *A History of Dartmouth College and the Town of Hanover, New Hampshire (to 1815)* (Brattleboro, Vermont: Vermont Printing, 1928); Leon Burr Richardson, *History of Dartmouth College* (Hanover, N.H.: Dartmouth College Publications, 1932), 2 vols.

[18] This summary of Occom's position appeared in a letter written by David McClure, one of Occom's former Euroamerican students and coauthor of the first biography of Wheelock. David McClure to Wheelock, May 21, 1770, 770321 DCA.

School had provided the rudiments of Euroamerican knowledge and some vocational skills for over sixty Algonquian and Iroquois youth, sixteen of whom were girls.[19] In the 1760s Wheelock had sent about a dozen Indians, plus some Euroamerican students, from Moor's School to teach and serve as missionaries among several Iroquiois tribes. By the end of the decade all had abandoned the experiment, with the exception of Samuel Kirkland, a Euroamerican who remained among the Oneida and later founded Hamilton College, William DeLoss Love's alma mater.[20] The experiment in Iroquoia had failed because of strong opposition from Sir William Johnson, superintendent of Indian affairs for the northern colonies, and eventually opposition from the Iroquois themselves.

In the years after Occom's return the world that had supported him had fallen asunder. Wheelock was living at Dartmouth College, among the "English" students there, and Occom refused to visit him, despite invitations. The former Indian students from Moor's School had returned from the Iroquois villages full of tales about their failures in teaching Iroquois youth. For two years Occom had secured no employment, due to misunderstandings between Wheelock, Occom, and his supporters in Boston, who had opposed the British tour.[21] Moreover, Occom himself remained in ill health for some time.

[19] Margaret Connell Szasz, "Poor Richard" Meets the Native American: Young Indian Women at School in Eighteenth-Century Connecticut," *Pacific Historical Review* 49 (May 1980), 215–35.

[20] For background on Samuel Kirkland see Walter Pilkington, ed., *The Journals of Samuel Kirkland* (Clinton, N.Y.: Hamilton College, 1980); James Ronda, "Reverend Samuel Kirkland and the Oneida Indians." In *The Oneida Indian Experience, Two Perspectives* (Syracuse: Syracuse Univ. Press, 1972), ed. Jack Campisi and Lawrence M. Hauptman, 34–47; Colin Calloway, *The American Revolution in Indian Country* (New York: Cambridge, 1995), 14–15, 33, 103. On Moor's School students in Iroquoia, see Connell Szasz, *Indian Education in the American Colonies,* 232–57.

[21] On Occom's rupture with Wheelock, see Blodgett, *Samson Occom,* 132–137, and Richardson, *An Indian Preacher in England,* 349–57.

Describing this nadir of Occom's life, his biographer, Love, evinced considerable sympathy for Occom's disillusionment, concluding, "He had left every other employment to obey his patron, and having been used to his advantage, he was discharged" (156). Even the issue of Occom's self-confessed drinking during this time, a subject of considerable historical debate, did not deter Love from defending the Mohegan. Despite Love's generally critical position on the subject of American Indians and alcohol, encapsulated in his claim that "the curse of the race is rum" (166), in this instance Love assessed Occom's actions by placing him in historical context, writing, "The drinking customs of the time being what they were, it cannot be thought strange if an Indian took enough liquor in a few instances to feel the effect of it. If he had not taken any it would have been stranger" (163). Moreover, Love applauded Occom for having accused himself before the Presbytery of Suffolk at Easthampton (1769), carefully emphasizing that, having confessed, he was acquitted. This illustration of Love's approach to the Mohegan indicates that, in some instances, Love's intensive research led him to move beyond the stereotypes of Indians that occur elsewhere in the narrative. On occasion, this late-nineteenth-century biographer belied his times by demonstrating a degree of understanding about Occom's world view that moved beyond mainstream attitudes toward American Indians.

William DeLoss Love's admiration for Samson Occom is not matched by his appreciation for the Mohegan's fellow Algonquians. Love showed respect for the Algonquians only during the final years of Occom's life, the decade or so following the American War for Independence. In this post-revolutionary era, Occom and other southern New England Algonquian leaders gathered the remnants of their people, those who had survived Euroamerican encroachment, disease, and participation in warfare against the French and later the English, and led them to lands they had obtained from the Oneida. There they formed the community of Brothertown in the vicinity of contemporary Syracuse. From

Love's perspective, the establishment of Brothertown (which was linked with the adjacent community of Stockbridge, founded by Mahicans from western Massachusetts) marked the culmination of events occurring between the Great Awakening and the creation of the Young Republic.[22] Love saw this era as one of dramatic change for the Algonquians. In Love's depiction of these four decades, the Euroamerican influences cumulatively remolded the world views of Occom and his Algonquian neighbors and relatives. Love argued that by the end of this era Occom and his people had accepted sufficient Euroamerican values to form the new community of Brothertown, a town modeled to some degree on the Euroamerican communities among which the Algonquians had lived in Connecticut, Rhode Island, and Long Island. Love appeared to be so persuaded by this seeming metamorphosis that he devoted the last seven chapters of the biography to the Brothertown Indians and their consequent struggles to maintain their unique community, first among the Oneida in New York, and later in Wisconsin, following their "last remove." The Brothertown Indians earned his admiration in direct proportion to the degree of their departure from earlier customs and their adaptation of Euroamerican culture. When they became, in his view, similar to Euroamericans, they earned his accolades.[23]

---

[22] The groups represented at Brothertown included members from the communities of Mohegan, Montauk, Charlestown (Narragansett), Stonington (Pequot), Groton (Pequot), Farmington (Tunxis), and Niantic. Some Algonquians remained in their southern New England homelands, however, and these are discussed in Laura E. Conkey, Ethel Boissevain, and Ives Goddard, "Indians of Southern New England and Long Island: Late Period." *In Handbook of North American Indians, Northeast,* vol. 15, Bruce Trigger, ed.; William S. Simmons, *Spirit of the New England Tribes* (Hanover, N.H.: Univ. Press of New England, 1986); Lawrence M. Hauptman, *Pequots in Southern New England: The Fall and Rise of an American Indian Nation* (Norman: Univ. of Oklahoma Press, 1993).

[23] For a different interpretation of the motives that led these Algonquians to form Brothertown, see Richardson, *An Indian Preacher in England,* 349. Richardson claimed that Occom "had a mind of his own." Also see Connell Szasz, "Samson Occom: Mohegan as Spiritual Intermediary," 74–78.

Despite Love's empathy for the struggles of Occom and the Algonquians, he remained locked into the world view and language of his own people and his time. Nonetheless, his study retains commendable attributes. Love engaged in extensive research in archival sources, and he supplemented this primary research with his forays onto the Algonquian lands in southern New England, Oneida country, and near Lake Winnebago. This diverse terrain reflected the landscapes of his own life. After his childhood in Milwaukee, Love followed the path taken by his father by graduating from Hamilton College. He then settled in Hartford, Connecticut. In each phase of his own life he came to know a region familiar to Occom and his people. This sense of place anchors the biography to the land, but it cannot obviate the restrictions imposed by Love's own cultural views. These limitations of perspective restricted Love's ability to move beyond his personal cultural boundaries.

In the century that bridges Love's era of scholarship, one dominated by the amateur (but well-educated) historian, and our own, led by professional historians with a sprinkling of journalists, scholars have begun to move toward cross-cultural awareness. In the process, they have enriched our understanding of how different peoples bring the complexities of their world views and behavior patterns to the encounters of the cultural frontier. Let us take a brief look at these contemporary approaches to the cultural frontier, and speculate as to how their assessments of Samson Occom and the southern New England Algonquian might differ from those of W. DeLoss Love.

In the five decades or so since World War II, the primary academic means for understanding the interaction of cultures has emerged in the rise of ethnohistory, an interdisciplinary method/approach that draws on history, anthropology and other disciplines. Simultaneously, Native America has exerted a strong influence on professional scholarship through the increasing visibility of American Indians and Alaska Natives, along with the growing

movement among Native people to tell their own stories and re-
call their own past, whether as indigenous storytellers or as pro-
fessionally trained scholars. If *Samson Occom and the Christian
Indians of New England* were written today, it would still rely on
the high caliber of archival research, but it would be more sweep-
ing in the scope of that research and more inclusive in the breadth
of its subject matter. It would also introduce a balanced perspective on the cultures encompassed by Occom's eighteenth-century
world.[24]

The research for this contemporary *Samson Occom* would
begin with ethnology. By assessing ethnographic accounts of these
Algonquians, along with archaeological studies, a contemporary
biographer would evaluate Occom as an eighteenth-century Mohegan. The scholar would query Occom's role in Mohegan society,
and how that role changed as Occom interacted with the Great
Awakening, Eleazar Wheelock, Montauk society, the English and
the Scots, the colony of Connecticut, and his own people. Of particular interest to a modern ethnographer would be community
and individual assessments of Occom.

It is likely that the scholar of the contemporary version of
Love's biography would sense the divisiveness of opinion among
the Mohegans and their neighbors: some were Occom supporters;
others were critics. Those who stood behind him were often his
relatives, such as David Fowler, his brother-in-law, and others
who shared his goals for the people. They would probably be
those Algonquians who had accepted some Christianity, who were

---

[24] Some examples of this approach include Alfonso Ortiz, "Indian/White Re-
lations: A View from the Other Side of the 'Frontier.' " In *Indians in American
History* (Arlington Heights, Illinois: Harlan Davidson, 1988), ed. Frederick E.
Hoxie, 1–16; Douglas R. Parks, "The Importance of Language Study for the
Writing of Plains Indian History." In *New Directions in American Indian His-
tory* (Norman: Univ. of Oklahoma Press, 1988), ed. Colin G. Calloway, 153–97;
Daniel K. Richter, *The Ordeal of the Longhouse, The Peoples of the Iroquois
League in the Era of Colonization* (Chapel Hill: Univ. of North Carolina Press,
1992); Simmons, *Spirit of the New England Tribes.*

convinced that their children must learn English and be schooled, who believed that farming was the key to their economic survival, and who agreed that the people could not retain their identity unless they moved away from their homelands and up the Hudson and Mohawk rivers to lands among the Oneida. These supporters appreciated Occom for his advice and concern for the people. They believed he had their interests at heart.

The present-day biographer of Occom would also uncover the strength of Occom's opponents.[25] Occom's critics believed that he had become too much like the Euroamericans. After all, he had adopted their religion, their dress, even their two-story dwelling. Occom's wife, Mary, whom he had married during his dozen years of serving as teacher and minister among the Montauk on Long Island, and who bore seven children, was less swayed by the outside world. One of Wheelock's former Euroamerican students described her response to Euroamerican culture: "He [Occom] wished to live in English style; but his wife . . . retained a fondness for her indian customs. She declined, evening & morning setting at table. Her dress was mostly Indian, & when he spake to her in english, she answered in her native language, although she could speak good english." Even Occom's children clung to the older ways: "His children when they left him, adopted the wild & roving life of Savages" (153). In the eyes of his critics, Occom had stepped too far across the boundary dividing English from Mohegan. His zealous support for Christianity had angered the Oneida during his missionary work among them in the early 1760s. When he had suggested that they grow their hair long "as the English do" and that "they must not wear the Indian ornaments as wampum and the like: but put them off and burn them in the fire," they became resentful.[26] Occom's proselytizing among the Oneida set a precedent. When the Algonquian students began teaching in the Iro-

---

[25] I am grateful to William T. Hagan for his provocative commentary on how Occom was perceived by his own people.

[26] Samuel Hopkins to Wheelock, Sept. 30, 1761, 761530 DCA.

quois villages they harbored resentment against their hosts, criticizing Iroquois children and their families for their "uncivilized" ways. The young Delaware instructor Hezekiah Calvin wrote of his Mohawk hosts, "I should be very happy to see my Brethren become christians and live like Christians."[27]

Additional Algonquian opponents of Occom criticized him during the heated Mohegan land dispute with the colony of Connecticut. They accused him of arousing a level of Mohegan opposition to the colony that would lead to a dangerous level of independence. Native support and criticism of Occom, therefore, was not a simple matter: it was rooted in complex motivations that require a significant depth of understanding by the researcher.

The new biographer of Occom would also seek to understand Occom's influence and interaction with the non-Native communities of the region. In order to pursue this dimension of the story, the researcher would explore Algonquian and Euroamerican world views, ranging from spirituality to pragmatic economic concerns. What kinds of influence did Occom exert among the varied Euroamerican groups of the northeast colonies? What was his impact on the English and Scots? And finally, how did these experiences remold his world views, leading him to determine that his own people must move away in order to form their separate community?

For the contemporary scholar, these questions would seek to place Occom in the context of the southern New England Algonquian world that contested with the Euroamerican world on an everyday basis, absorbing, discarding, selecting, and attempting to retain some of that cultural continuity discussed by anthropologist William Simmons in *Spirit of the New England Tribes* (1986). Given the limitations of the 1890s, however, one could not expect Love to ask these questions, although one can sometimes find the answers by reading between the lines in his biography. The con-

[27] Calvin to Wheelock, Aug. 14, 1767. In McCallum, ed., *Letters of Eleazar Wheelock's Indians*, 58.

temporary scholar, therefore, would rely on *Samson Occom* as a dependable source, one that retained the flavor of those archives that Love probed, and a sense of the Algonquian lands that Love knew so well. Syracuse University Press is to be commended for making available a well-researched study of a renowned cultural broker who moved among the eighteenth-century colonial cultures but was, above all, a member of his own community, the Mohegan.

PREFACE

At the memorial services on the reinterment of Isaac Paris, Prof. Edward North, L. H. D., of Hamilton College, expressed the following sentiment: "After this day's memorial has been completed, an effort should be made to find the lost grave of Rev. Samson Occum, whose fame as a fervid Indian preacher lives in the early history and traditions of Oneida county." These words came to the author's notice as he was examining a portion of Occom's diary among the manuscripts of the Connecticut Historical Society. In this he found reasons to believe that an Indian cemetery was located on the farm of Occom's brother-in-law, David Fowler, where most naturally the famous Mohegan would rest. A class reunion shortly afterwards made it convenient to visit Deansville, N. Y., June 20, 1893, when the early burial-place of the Christian Indians was discovered. Out of the interest then kindled this volume has grown.

Samson Occom will always be regarded as the most famous Christian Indian of New England. Hitherto he has been but dimly known. Herein we have written the story of his life, woven as it is into Indian history, and particularly into the fortunes of that tribe which he created and named. We are able thus to follow these Indians in detail from barbarism along the trail of civilization for a century and three quarters, an opportunity which is afforded by no other North American Indians.

Our historical resources have been almost wholly unprinted manuscripts. These are widely scattered, and in some cases have been unexplored by historians. We name them that others may be spared our pains: Wheelock Papers, Occom's Diaries, Whitaker Papers and Sergeant's Journals—Dartmouth College Library; Indian Papers, including manuscripts of Samson Occom and Joseph Johnson, Mohegan and William Samuel Johnson Papers—Connecticut Historical Society; Records of the Society for Propagating the Gospel— N. E. Hist. and Gen. Society, Boston; Town, Court, and Superintendent's Records of the Brothertown Indians, Brothertown, Wis. ; Letters and Journals of Samuel Kirkland—Mr. Thornton K. Lothrop, Boston ; Stiles MSS.—Yale College Library ; Records of the Suffolk and Albany Presbyteries ; Connecticut Archives, Hartford ; Massachusetts Archives, Boston ; New York Archives, Albany ; Trumbull Papers—Massachusetts Historical Society and Connecticut Historical Society ; Solomon Williams' Letters—Mrs. B. E. Hooker, Hartford ; Town Records—Farmington, Montville, New London, Groton, Stonington, Conn., Charlestown, R. I., etc. ; Land Records, Utica, N. Y. ; and other sources less important. Such references have been given as may be most helpful, but the evidence on many facts in the narrative could not be cited. To all who have rendered their courteous assistance we make acknowledgment, and especially to the Brothertown Indians, in whose homes many items have been gathered.

It may seem to some that an Indian genealogy is more a curiosity than a contribution to history. Even so, it is not every tribe that can furnish such evidence that it is of the pure blood, which, in a study of Indian civilization, is essential. We have by means of it, however, condensed many facts of tribal and town history, identified families of Indians whose names the student will meet with in records, added notes which would have cumbered the text of our narrative, and perhaps rendered some service in establishing the property rights of many in the tribal inheritance. May we not also hope that such a record will quicken the conserving influences within the tribe and help them on into an honorable future?

W. D. L.

HARTFORD, CONN.,
October, 1899.

SAMSON OCCOM
AND THE CHRISTIAN INDIANS
OF NEW ENGLAND

SAMSON OCCOM

CHAPTER I

THE NEW ENGLAND FATHERS AND INDIAN CIVILIZATION

1620–1723

The civilization of the American Indians, to whom our land from sea to sea once belonged, is an endeavor nearly three centuries old. At no time since the forefathers came to New England have they or their descendants been wholly unmindful of this obligation. Heroic lives have been devoted to evangelizing the Indians, teachers have sought to educate them, laws have been enacted in their behalf, and a paternal government has expended vast sums in their maintenance. Although the results of all wisely ordered efforts have been better than is generally supposed, the ultimate issue is still undetermined. There seem, indeed, to be some reasons for believing that the race itself is gradually dying away toward the setting sun.

All the movements of this extended period have been due primarily to the spirit of Christian missions, to the histories of which we leave what more particularly exhibits the achievements of religion. We purpose rather to treat the subject as a problem of civilization. It has always been recognized as such. The main inquiry has been whether the Indian is capable of being permanently established in the ways of civilized life; and, if so, what conditions will best accomplish this end. He has been known in our literature chiefly as a savage. What may he become if he is Christianized, brought into church estate, educated in industrial pursuits, invested with rights in the land which supports him, and trusted with the responsibilities of government? Historical studies may throw some light upon this problem by tracing the experiences of a tribe which was collected from the Christian remnants in New England and has been seasoned in the beneficent influences of generations, traversing the distance from heathenism to American citizenship.

The Indian missions of New England during the first century furnish an interesting story which has been often told. We would call the reader's attention to the noble purpose of the fathers and the methods by which they hoped to accomplish the civilization of the Indian, as seen in the facts elsewhere stated by many historians.[1] An examination of the case seems to us to show more creditable aims, plans and results than we have been led by some writers to suppose. Especially is some review of this period desirable, because the work of the second century, in which Samson Occom was engaged, was the later harvest of this early seed-sowing.

One of the aims of the New England fathers in crossing the sea was the conversion of the natives to Christianity. Some writers have made much of this well-known fact, and have brought against them a charge of neglecting this labor throughout the early years of their settlement. The truth is, they deserve high praise for adopting such a philanthropic purpose when it was suggested to them. Those who have cited the language of their charters, as though they made pretensions which were soon forgotten, have misjudged the fact. This profession was not peculiar to them. All charters of the time contained it. The letters patent which King James gave to the Virginia Company, April 10, 1606, based the privileges

---

[1] See especially Dr. J. Hammond Trumbull's article on "The Origin and Early Progress of Indian Missions in New England."—*Am. Antiq. Soc. Proc.*, No. LXI, pp. 16 ff.

granted upon their undertaking "a work which may, by the Providence of Almighty God. hereafter tend to the glory of his Divine Majesty, in propagating of Christian religion to such people as yet live in darkness and miserable ignorance of the true knowledge and worship of God, and may in time bring the infidels and savages living in those parts to human civility and to a settled and quiet government."[2] In the Virginia charters of 1609 and 1611–12, the same design is announced.[3] A sermon was preached before these adventurers, April 25, 1609, by Rev. William Symondes of Southwarke, the Epistle Dedicatory of which is addressed to the "right noble and worthie Advancers of the Standard of Christ among the Gentiles." When a similar discourse was delivered by Rev. William Crashaw, February 21, 1609–10, on the departure of Lord De La Warre, the governor was admonished to remember that he was going to commend religion to the heathen. The Virginians subsequently undertook this work, but the desire was never sufficiently strong in their religious life to make it successful. The great patent of New England, dated November 3, 1620, has been repeatedly quoted as though it contained unusual missionary pretensions. In that the king declared that "the principall effect which we can desire or expect of this action, is the conversion and reduction of the people in those parts into the true worship of God and Christian religion." This precise language, however, is found in the Virginia charter of 1609, from which we may suppose it was taken. The Massachusetts Bay charter, dated March 4, 1628–29, directed that the people "maie be soe religiously, peaceablie and civilly governed as their good life and orderlie conversacon maie wynn and incite the natives of the country to the knowledg and obedience of the onlie true God and Savior of mankinde and the Christian fayth, which, in our

---

[2] *Charters and Constitutions*, II, 1888.
[3] *Ibid.*, II, 1902.

royall intencon and the adventurers free profession, is the
principall ende of this plantacon." But this language should
be interpreted in the light of the fact that several other nearly
contemporary patents contain like expressions. This was, then,
a common article in the emigrant's creed. It meant more or
less according to his character. The late Dr. J. Hammond
Trumbull, to whom every writer on the Indian must be
indebted, has called attention to Thomas Thorowgood's statement in his tract on the "Jewes in America," which sum-
marizes the facts thus: "The mutuall and interchangeable
fact and covenant of donor and receiver is, in all those charters and patents, the conversion of the heathen." The distinguishing characteristic, therefore, of the New England colonists was not in unusual pretensions made in their charters.
We shall see that it was rather in the sincerity of this profession and their earnestness in endeavoring to fulfil it.

The missionary purpose was grafted into the life of the
Pilgrims. The works of their leader, John Robinson, exhibit
only the remotest interest in the evangelization of the heathen.
Ecclesiastical freedom was his uppermost thought. But so
early as 1617, when they were contemplating emigration under
the auspices of the Virginia Company, and very likely because
they had noted the above clauses in the charter, the Pilgrims
declared their intention of crossing the sea "that they might
be means of replanting the Gospel amongst the heathen." [4]
One of their enemies had suggested in ridicule that they
"remove to Virginia and make a plantation there in hope to
convert infidels to Christianity," but they had adopted this
purpose in earnest. Thus they made fast to what had been
only a stereotyped expression in the ventures of those Puritan
times. As they thereafter pondered over the matter, the idea
was strengthened within them. It is frequently referred to in
their writings. Bradford mentions it among their reasons for

[4] Hanbury's *Historical Memorials*, I, 368.

removal, thus: "Lastly (and which was not least), a great hope & inward zeall they had of laying some good foundation, or at least to make some way therunto, for ye propagating & advancing ye gospell of ye kingdom of Christ in those remote parts of ye world; yea, though they should be but even as stepping-stones unto others for ye performing of so great a work." [5]

The Puritans of the Massachusetts Bay Colony adopted the same design. They put life into a formal profession. As their governor was pledged by his oath to this work, he reminded the colonists of their obligation in his instructions. "That these pledges might be had in perpetual remembrance," says Dr. Trumbull, "on the seal provided in England for the colony, an Indian with extended hands raised the Macedonian cry, 'Come over and help us.'" These New England colonists should be credited, therefore, with an extraordinary reception of the missionary impulse. They committed themselves to an enterprise which had so engaged no other emigrants of the time. The utterances of earlier charters were taken into their hearts and lives with all the solemnity of a creed.

It has been asserted also that the forefathers wholly neglected this work for a score of years. Here again they have been misjudged. The error arises from an ignorance of the particular method by which they hoped to civilize the Indian. The plan adopted was the one then current, and just what we should expect the Puritan life to depend upon— that of winning the heathen by the exhibition of their civilization and Christian institutions. Robert Cushman put it thus: "To displaie the efficacie & power of the Gospell both in zealous preaching, professing, and wise walking vnder it, before the faces of these poore blinde Infidels." The

---

[5] Bradford's *Hist.*, p. 24. See also Young's *Chronicles of the Pilgrims*, pp. 243, 257, 258, 271, 274, 328, 329, 339 n., 383.

opinion then prevailed that it was necessary to reduce the natives to some measure of "civility" ere they could be Christianized. The later method of evangelization was not contemplated. It was not in discussion until about 1640. The forefathers had prominently in mind the giving up of a wandering life in the forest, the acquisition of the English language, and an education in the customs of civilized society. Hence, the main feature of their plan was the training of Indian youth in the Puritan household.

In 1618 the Virginians, with similar opinions, had undertaken this method of bringing native children to "true religion, moral virtue, and civility." Their first legislative assembly the year following ordered that every plantation should procure such youth by just means for this purpose. This plan was explicitly approved in England. No one there had thought of any better, not even those who afterwards charged New England with neglect. It was, indeed, a very sensible procedure, which has never since been outgrown, and the only method possible in the early years of the colonies. The Pilgrims began with Squanto and Hobomok, both of whom died "leaving some good hopes." Winslow declared that they had special interest in providing tutors for the Indian children of both sexes. So early as 1621, when Cushman was at Plymouth, they were entertaining great expectations in this direction, as we may infer from these words concerning the "younger sort" : "If we had means to apparel them, and wholly to retain them with us, as their desire is, they would doubtless in time prove serviceable to God and man, and if ever God send us means, we will bring up hundreds of their children, both to labor and learning."[6] Among the Puritans of the Bay Colony this same plan was in mind as most feasible. Governor Cradock, in his letter to Endicott, Feb. 19, 1628-29, when he reminded him of this end of their

---

[6] Young's *Chron. of the Pilgrims*, p. 260.

plantation, wrote thus : " Endeavour to get some of their children to train up to reading and consequently to religion whilst they are young." This was done, so far as it was possible, in both colonies and more generally than has been supposed. Winthrop informs us that this disposition was made of the captives in the Pequot war : "Ye women & maid children are disposed aboute in ye towns." At a later time the youth were apprenticed by law to the English. Many who were able had Indian servants in their households, where daily, painstaking religious instruction was given after the Puritan custom. The results of all this early labor are dwelt upon with satisfaction in the record made in 1542 of "New England's First Fruits." A better summary cannot be presented than is there given : " Divers of the Indians Children, Boyes and Girles, we have received into our houses, who are long since civilized, and in subjection to us, painfull and handy in their businesse, and can speak our language familiarly ; divers of whom can read English, and begin to understand in their measure, the grounds of Christian Religion ; some of them are able to give us account of the Sermons they heare, and of the word read and expounded in our Families." This, then, was the early scheme for Christianizing the natives. For twenty years, whilst the colonists were engaged in the trials incident to their settlement, they could not hope for more than this plan promised. The results in many known instances were salutary. It was, moreover, the very best preparation for the later work. Many Indians became well acquainted with the religion and life of their neighbors. A general desire was awakened among them to know the God of the English and imitate their government and institutions. Those who knew most about the later plan of evangelization affirmed that this familiar intercourse in the English home was one reason for their subsequent success.

This early work furthermore promoted an interest in the acquisition of the Indian language. Out of this fact the later movement arose. The fathers had entertained this hope from the first, but they had not imagined its outcome. Francis Higginson had written in 1629, " We purpose to learn their language as soon as we can, which will be a means to do them good." [7] Roger Williams within a few years went to lodge in their wigwams that he might " gain their tongue." Some discussion soon arose as to whether more could not be accomplished by a new plan involving the use of the native language. Henry Dunster, the president of the college at Cambridge, was urgent in advocating this novel proposition. In 1641 Thomas Lechford wrote of him, " He hath the platforme and way of conversion of the Natives indifferent right. . . . . He will make it good that the way to instruct the Indians, must be in their owne language, not English, and that their language may be perfected." [8] This idea, notwithstanding some opposition, gained in favor. John Eliot and Thomas Mayhew adopted it with enthusiasm. It was a long step forward and opened the way to a new type of Indian civilization. The evangelizing method then became possible. Instead of bringing the natives into the colonists' homes to be Anglicized, it sent the English out into the Indian villages to teach, and there Christianity could work out a civilization in the natural environment where it was compelled to subsist. The study of their language and its reduction to form could not but result, as it did, in the translation of sundry tracts and the Bible itself as necessary agencies in this evangelization. Thus the work which Eliot is generally thought to have originated was developed out of a previous design and endeavor. It does not detract from his honors as the " Apostle to the Indians " to say that he was himself a product of the New England people. The Puritan in heathendom was bound to be a missionary. In him was that spirit, that love for education, out of

[7] Young's *Chron. of the Pilgrims*, p. 258.
[8] Lechford's *Plain Dealing*, p. 53.

which civilization was certain to arise. Others were affected as Eliot was by the condition of the savage tribes about them ; but he was *facile princeps* because he excelled them all in comprehending the problem, in creating adequate agencies, and in missionary zeal. The movement was general and except for the results of the earlier work it would not have been so successful.

The story of Eliot's missionary labors is familiar to all readers. We call particular attention to his plan and its development. He began about 1643, it is supposed, to study the Indian language. His tutor was a certain Long Island Indian, a captive in the Pequot war, who had been made a servant in the family of Mr. Richard Calicott of Dorchester.[9] The aforementioned tract, "New England's First Fruits", was published in England that same year, and Roger Williams' "Key unto the Language of America" appeared a few months after it. This revived interest manifested itself in 1644, by the action of the General Court, ordering that the Indians in the several counties be " instructed in the knowledge and worship of God." The year following the reverend elders were explicitly requested to consider means to this end. Thus the problem was thrust upon them, and Eliot, with others, had it under consideration some months before he began his mission.[10] On the 28th of October, 1646, he went to Nonantum with several others, and there preached his first Indian sermon in Waubun's wigwam. His success probably influenced the decision of the ministers in favor of the new plan. At that visit the Indians expressed a desire to have land given them near at hand that they might " build a town together," at which the Englishmen were greatly pleased and promised to speak for them to the General Court. That body assembled in a few days and probably upon a report

---

[9] See *Cockenoe-de-Long Island*, by W. W. Tooker.
[10] Winthrop's *Hist.*, II, 326; *The Day-Breaking*, etc., p. 3.

from the reverend elders, supplemented by a second visit, took important action in the matter. "Considering yt interpretation of tongues is an appointment of God for propagating the truth," it was ordered that two ministers be chosen annually "to make knowne ye heavenly counsell of God among ye Indians." A law was passed prohibiting their powwows, which the elders had judged to be great obstacles to their conversion. But the most far-reaching action was the appointment of a committee to purchase lands for the prospective Indian town, where Shepard, Allen and Eliot should advise, and make rules for improving and enjoying the same. The Indians of Waubun's company were much interested in this project. They at once adopted ten laws for their moral improvement. The lands at Watertown Mill were bought and there at Nonantum the first experiment was made in this novel plan of Indian civilization.

The ultimate design of John Eliot was to raise up native missionaries. He recognized from the first the fact that "God is wont ordinarily to convert nations and peoples by some of their own countrymen who are nearest to them, and can best speak and most of all pity their brethren." In order to this, however, he thought it necessary not only to evangelize them but also to establish them in the ways of civilized life. Hence he conceived the idea of a community, formed wholly of Christian Indians, and in a measure self-governing, where educational, industrial and religious privileges might hope to accomplish most in a favorable environment. This was precisely the idea upon which Samson Occom built, more than a century afterwards. Eliot found the natives anxious to imitate the civilization of the whites. The plan was favorable to his hopes of giving them a Christian literature. So he wisely fostered every suggestion the natives made in this direction, and the General Court endorsed his measures. In 1647 the magistrates were empowered to hold quarterly courts

among them, and their sachems were authorized "to keep a
court of themselves every month if they see occasion, to
determine small causes of a civil nature, and such smaller
criminal causes as the said magistrates shall refer to them."[11]
Such powers would have been dangerous except under Eliot's
leadership. They enabled him to put the Indian government
in the hands of his trusted converts. Schools were soon
established. The children were regularly catechized. All
their industrial ambitions were furthered. The men began to
fence their fields and cultivate them after the English manner.
The women took up spinning. Trade between them and the
whites was encouraged. All these measures wrought together
to assist Eliot in evangelizing them. He correctly judged that
the results of such a colonizing scheme would be more permanent.

The experiment at Nonantum had not been two years under
way before Eliot discovered that an enlargement of his plan
was necessary. The grant of land was not large enough, and
it was too near the English. Moreover, it was not a suitable
place to gather his converts from other native villages and
tribes into the Indian town which had come to be his ideal.
This latter fact was important. So early as 1649 his original
design had grown to a hope of founding a community where
all the Christian Indians should be governed after the theocratic ideal of the Scriptures. He seems to have been
impressed with the notion, then entertained by many, that the
American Indians were the lost tribes of Israel. He even
thought that such an assembling of dry bones might be a ful-
filment of prophecy.[12] At all events, with this problem in view,
he sought to ascertain what form of government was approved
in the Bible. The result was the writing soon afterwards of

---

[11] *Mass. Col. Rec.*, II, 188; *The Clear Sunshine*, etc., pp. 15, 16, 28.
[12] *The Light Appearing*, etc., pp. 23, 24; *Glorious Progress*, etc., Appendix;
Strength out of Weakness, p. 1c

that condemned book entitled " The Christian Commonwealth," and some application of his theory among the Indians.[18]   In his letters he declared his purpose in this language : " The present work of God among them is to gather them together to bring them to political life, both in ecclesiastical society and in civil, for which they earnestly long and enquire."   " Touching the way of their government . . . I intend to direct them according as the Lord shall please to help and assist, to set up the kingdom of Jesus Christ fully, so that Christ shall reign both in church and commonwealth, both in civil and spiritual matters ; we will, through his grace, fly to the 'Scriptures for every law, rule, direction, form, or whatever we do." [14] His project, however, was delayed.   The corporation entitled " The President and Society for [the] Propagation of the Gospel in New England " was constituted by act of Parliament July 27, 1649,[15] but no funds were then at hand for its work.

[13] See preface to *The Christian Commonwealth*, John Eliot.

[14] *The Light Appearing*, etc., pp. 23, 28.

[15] The following societies, all of which were engaged in Indian missions, have been frequently confounded : (1) The corporation entitled " The President and Society for [the] Propagation of the Gospel in New England " was constituted by an act of the Long Parliament in 1649.   The commissioners of the United Colonies were its agents in New England.   It died at the Restoration, May 29, 1660.   (2) " The Company for [the] Propagation of [Propagating] the Gospel [amongst the Heathen Natives of] in New England and the Parts Adjacent in America " was incorporated by Charles II, February 7, 1661-2, and was the successor of the former.   The commissioners of the United Colonies were its agents until 1685, after which a Board of Commissioners at Boston was constituted.   They called themselves " Commissioners of the Society for Propagating the Gospel in New England."   This was also called the " London Society."   It cut off remittances to New England May 31, 1779, excepting arrearages and the Daniel Williams legacy, which was paid to the President and Fellows of Harvard College to 1787.   This society is still in existence as " The New England Company" of London, and conducts Indian missions largely in Canada.   (3) The " Society for Promoting Christian Knowledge " was formed in England in 1698.   It sent over some books for use in Indian missions.   (4) " The Society for the Propagation of the Gospel in Foreign Parts " was chartered by William III, June 16, 1701.   This was a sectarian society of the Church of England. It conducted some Indian missions in early days among the Oneidas.   See David Humphreys' *Historical Account*, etc., and a series of anniversary sermons.   (5) The

Eliot consulted the ministers, who advised him to proceed. A tract of about six thousand acres was decided on and secured. In the spring of 1651, the town was laid out and the Indians with great zeal began the work of construction. They named the place Natick. On the 6th of August, the Indians met and after Eliot had expounded the eighteenth chapter of Exodus, upon which his theocratic government was based, they elected their rulers—one over a hundred, two over fifties, and ten "tithing men." Each Indian chose which "ruler of ten" he would be under. The 24th of the following month was observed by fasting and prayer, and toward its close they entered, not into a church estate, as some have supposed, but into a civil covenant to be the Lord's people.[16] Eliot saw thus his desire realized as to their government. He found, however, that the form of it was impracticable. It was not adapted to Indian life. A ruler in civil affairs, which their tribal instincts approved and the General Court had authorized, was all that the Indian town needed. To that the scheme finally came under Eliot's wise guidance. When he was permitted in 1660, after years of patient preparation and some opposition, to form a church among them, the ruler and the religious teacher or pastor became the two sources of authority in their Christianized communities. Meanwhile the movement had spread.

"Society in Scotland for Propagating Christian Knowledge" was formed in 1709. It is usually called the "Scotch Society." A Board of Correspondents at Boston was appointed in 1730, but was suspended in 1737. In 1756 it was revived and continued operations thereafter for many years. Another Board of Correspondents was constituted at New York in 1741, which in 1769 gave place to a board composed of the trustees of the College of New Jersey at Princeton. The Connecticut Board of Correspondents was formed at Lebanon July 4, 1764 and continued in existence about five years. (6) A "Society for Propagating Christian Knowledge" was incorporated Feb. 11, 1762, by the Massachusetts government, but its charter was not ratified in England [*Acts and Resolves of Mass.*, iv : 520-523]. (7) "The Society for Propagating the Gospel among the Indians and others in North America" was incorporated by the General Court of Massachusetts, November 19, 1787. It has conducted various Indian missions in New England, New York, and the West.

[16] *Strength out of Weakness*, pp. 9-13.

The plan of Indian town government had been adopted by Thomas Mayhew and others. Eliot gave up the idea of gathering all the Christian Indians at Natick. After that model other towns were formed. Industry and education advanced. The results began to appear, particularly in the work of the converts he had raised up. His earlier problems were lost to view in the greater religious success, which was always his main purpose and which won for him the merited title, "Apostle of the Indians."

As we have already suggested, the educational work of John Eliot was a prominent feature. A Puritan could not do otherwise than make it such, and the sequel proved his wisdom. At the beginning of his mission, the Indians expressed a desire that their children might be taught. Some of them were given over to English families for instruction after the older custom. Schools were established under white masters. It soon became evident, however, that an education in English was not best adapted to his purpose, nor easiest for the Indian children to acquire. He was preaching to them in the Indian language, and he felt that he must give them the Bible in their native tongue and they must be taught to read it. This he had determined upon so early as 1649, and his catechism was printed in 1653 or 1654. Parts of the Scriptures followed, and the famous " Mamusse Wunneetupanatamwee Up-Biblum God " appeared in 1663. The results of this work were visible from the first. Eliot found that the children and adults were very quick to learn in Indian. Even three years before the whole Bible was printed about one hundred of his Christian Indians had been taught to read. His helpers were greatly multiplied and some from the older towns went out in a humble way to teach other tribes. A careful examination of the progress shows that this Indian literature gave a new impetus to the work. The greatest success came during the ten years following. Eliot was moved by it, furthermore, to see the necessity of the educated Indian teacher. The well-fitted native accomplished more than the inexperienced Englishman. In 1670 he wrote, " And . seeing they must have Teachers amongst themselves, they must also be taught to be Teachers ; for which cause I have begun to teach them the Art of Teaching, and I find some of them very capable."[17]

The claim has been made that the Indian Bible was of no service to the natives because it was not intelligible.[18] One of Eliot's biographers says, " It failed to answer the pious purpose for which the translator labored in preparing it."[19] Dr. Trumbull, than whom no one was more competent to judge, in answering these claims has given this opinion : " There is abundant evidence that many of the praying Indians *did* acquire the art of reading with facility books printed in their language."[20] We emphasize further in reply this fact: it was because of Eliot's discovery that the Indians made easy progress in their own tongue that he was led to do the greater part of his work as a translator. He witnessed the good results even before he had finished his Bible. The volume was not only intelligible to the Indians, it was a valuable means of spreading his work. Whatever permanent quality that had was largely due to this native literature. We do not doubt that more good would have been accomplished by this agency had it not been for King Philip's War, which was an overwhelming disaster to the Indian missions of New England.

Most writers on the work of John Eliot have seemed to think that its results sank away like water in desert sands. Such was not really the case. The stream has been flowing onward in the shadows since those early times. Indians are now living whose enlightened estate may be attributed re-

[17] Brief Narrative, etc., p. 5.
[18] *North American Rev.*, Oct., 1860.
[19] Francis' *Life of Eliot*, pp. 237, 238.
[20] *Am. Antiq. Soc. Proc.*, No. LXI, pp. 37 ff.

motely to that good man who has been more than two centuries in his grave. As his settlements of praying Indians in the Massachusetts Bay Colony began to die out, the seed, scattered abroad, sprang up in other places where it was nourished.

The Christian influences of Nonantum in 1647 spread in three directions, northward, westward and southward, and can be followed from town to town.[21] Eliot's first convert, Waubun, was, says Thomas Shephard, " the most active Indian for stirring up other Indians to seek after the knowledg of God." He is known to have carried the news in advance of Eliot to several distant Indian settlements. Indeed, the work so wisely conducted by the Mayhews on Martha's Vineyard, although it may have had an independent origin, was very closely associated with Eliot's by visitation and correspondence; and the success in the Plymouth Colony and on Cape Cod was due to the latter rather than the former. To the northward there arose Nashobah (Littleton) and Wamesit (Lowell), into which those at the upper falls of the Pawtucket were afterwards gathered. The latter lived until the uncivilized Indians joined the St. Francis tribe and the Christians retreated to Natick. Thither also those of Concord and Sudbury finally came. To the westward Christian Indians went from Natick and established a town at Hassanamesit (Grafton), where a church was formed in 1671. This was the center of all the preaching stations in that vicinity—Okommakamesit (Marlboro), Pakachoag (Worcester), and Waeuntug (Uxbridge)—until in King Philip's War they were all swept away and the Christian remnants were absorbed at Natick and Dudley. The work at the latter place, Chabanakongkomun, was begun in 1672, by Indians of the

[21] See Series of " Eliot Tracts;" Daniel Gookin's *Historical Account*, etc., *Archæologia Americana*, II, 423 ff; Articles on "Early Indian Missions," by Dr. H. M. Dexter, in *The Sabbath at Home*, 1868; *Mass. Hist. Soc. Coll.*, I, vol. x, p. 129; Mather's *Magnalia*, 1853, II, 422 ff; and *MS. Rec. Soc. for Prop. Gos.*, with N. E. Hist. and Gen. Soc.

Grafton church. It survived the war, took in that at Manchaug (Oxford), and other abandoned towns westward, and lived under the labors of Revs. Perley How, Charles Gleason and others for three quarters of a century. Some of the survivors at last moved southward into Connecticut and Rhode Island. The several settlements in Woodstock, Conn., Maanesit, Quinnatesset and Wabquisset, where Eliot visited in 1674, were absorbed by Connecticut tribes along the Thames river. To the southward Punkapoag (Stoughton) continued for many years under the patronage of the whites. A grandson of their first Indian ruler was ministering to them in 1729, and a few remained even until after the Revolution. At Titicut (Middleborough), whither Waubun carried the gospel in 1648, religious privileges were maintained for nearly a century. They had a succession of native ministers and English lecturers. Thither Indians from surrounding settlements gathered, until the reduced remnant joined the southward movement which ended at Marshpee. So early as 1647 Eliot made a journey to Yarmouth and visited the Indians on Cape Cod. He afterwards sent some of his converts in that direction. Within a few years Christian settlements became numerous thereabouts. Richard Bourne labored to the south and east of Sandwich from 1666 to his death in 1685. "He was a man of that discernment," said Rev. Gideon Hawley, "that he considered it as vain to propagate Christian knowledge among any people without a territory where they might remain in place from generation to generation." This idea resulted in the Marshpee reservation, where in time the surviving Indians of the Plymouth Colony were gathered. After him Simon Popmonet, an Indian minister, labored in the same field for nearly forty years. He was followed in turn by Joseph Bourne, Solomon Briant, an Indian, Gideon Hawley, Phinehas Fish, and William Apes, the well-known native author of Marshpee. Here was, therefore, a continuation of the work down to recent times. To the north and west of Sandwich Captain Thomas Tupper began missionary labors about 1654, which he carried on until he was incapacitated by old age. A small meeting-house was built at the expense of Samuel Sewall on the hill east of Herring River (Bournedale), and there a church was formed. In after years his grandson, Eldad Tupper, and his great-grandson, Elisha Tupper, were ministers to the Indians there and throughout that region. Further to the eastward in Eastham, Samuel Treat began his work in 1672, which was in a flourishing condition twenty years later, and was maintained largely by native ministers until about the middle of the next century. Here were, therefore, some centers in which the missions of the fathers survived for generations. At the end of the first century there were in the old fields, not including Martha's Vineyard, " twenty or thirty congregations of Christianized Indians, whereto there belong some thousand souls. These had ten English preachers who gave them instructions and assistance, and between twenty and thirty Indian teachers by whom the exercises of the Lord's Day are mostly maintained." [22] The history of Natick, which is so familiar, is too frequently taken as illustrating the permanent value of that early work. Greater success attended that in the Plymouth Colony. It did not suffer so much during King Philip's War, and it was more directly under the supervision of white ministers. The proximity of Mayhew's mission on the islands resulted in frequent visitations of zealous Indian ministers. Their lands, too, were not so generally coveted by the English, and they were out of the emigration current of the time. This made greater permanency possible. The Indians of Massachusetts slowly moved toward the south. Some who had been born at Natick left descendants at Marshpee. The mother church in its early years was constantly giving out Indian teachers who settled

[22] *India Christiana*, p. 37; Mather's *Early History*, p. xxxiii.

permanently elsewhere, and it therefore deserves an honor which its later history would not suggest.

It is difficult to measure the results of this first century movement toward civilization. Still, it has always been misjudged because the accounts of it after King Philip's War are not so detailed or familiar as those of earlier times. Thousands, however, became nominal adherents to Christianity. The census of 1674 numbers these as about four thousand in Massachusetts and Plymouth colonies, including those under Mayhew on Martha's Vineyard and Nantucket. At that time many of the early converts had died. The ingathering afterwards in missions at the southward was considerable. A careful estimate, based upon the history of individual congregations and churches, makes the number of Christian Indians in New England during this period about seven thousand. Comparatively few of these became church-members, and the type of Christian living was at no time very high; but they were reduced to law and order and dwelt together in peace. Many, of course, lapsed into intemperance, but we have good evidence that a characteristic of the Christian Indian was that he sought to recover himself. On the other hand, some families maintained their respectable character for generations. As the years went by, their numbers decreased at an extraordinary death-rate, or, in the words of Cotton Mather, "by a strange Blast from Heaven confusing them." During the first half of the eighteenth century they melted away like snow in the springtime.

The methods adopted by the fathers for civilizing the Indian were all that we could fairly expect. They had no experience to guide them. Such missions were in their infancy. On the whole their efforts met with a success which is an honor to their piety, wisdom and zeal. In the endeavors of this first century we have in the germ nearly all the ideas which have since been developed and are now in use. The fathers considered the Christian training of Indian youth as of the greatest importance. They exalted the necessity of education. In this work they tried both the separation of the native from his heathen environment and the instruction of the tribal schoolhouse. One of their fundamental problems was whether the Indian should remain such or be Anglicized. They employed both the English and the Indian languages. The white teacher and the native helper were both known to them. They recognized the value of industrial pursuits as adapted to bring the savage into the ways of civilized life. By the action of their General Court the reservation was brought into existence. There Eliot set up the first experiment in Indian self-government after the customs of civilization. They contended with the difficulties attending the holding of lands, and experienced the evils of government aid. The Indian agent was one of their creations. All which could be accomplished by the missionary in evangelization they attempted. The native churches which they founded were not unlike many that have since existed. Although the fathers were by no means above reproach in their treatment of the Indians, they did much in the ways that were open to them to fulfil the obligation which their religion prompted and their royal charters had imposed.

CHAPTER II

A MOHEGAN YOUTH

1723–1749

On some unknown day in the latter part of the seventeenth century, an Indian of the Mohegan tribe, who had dwelt in the region between the Shetucket and Quinebaug rivers, moved southward and set up his wigwam west of the river Thames in the vicinity of Uncas Hill, the ancient home of his sachem. The name of this Indian, as given in a document of 1738, was "Tomockham alias Ashneon," and he was the grandfather of Samson Occom.[1] At this time the tribe had not gathered to any extent in villages. In 1725 they were said to number 351, and Jonathan Barber stated in 1738 that there were then only 19 males above 16 years of age who lived at Mohegan, and only 30 who had a permanent location on the Mohegan lands. Their territory, by the survey of 1705, had for its corner bounds Lyme, Stonington, Pomfret and Bolton.[2] Throughout this region or beyond it they wandered in the avocations of the forest and their canoes crossed the waters to the fishing-grounds of Montauk. It may have been some fortune of war which led to this removal of Tomockham.

---

[1] The earliest written form of this Indian's name is "Tomockham" which is also spelled "Tomockam," "Tomocham," and "Tomocum." The name of Occom's father is written "Joshua x Ockham," "Joshua x Aucum" and "Joshua x Mawcum." Although the manuscripts show many spellings of the son's name, such as Ockam, Alcom, Aukum, Aucum, Occum, and Aucom, he himself wrote it Samson Occom. As the name "Tomockham" was sometimes written "Tom x Maucam," and one of the family wrote his own name "Thomas Occcm," we conjecture that the original Indian name was "Ockham" (Aukum, etc.) meaning "on the other side," and that he adopted the prefix "Tom," which had possibly been given him by the English.

[2] *Mass. Hist. Soc. Coll.*, I, vol. IX, p. 80; *Conn. Hist. Soc. Coll.*, V, 6.

Zachary Johnson, an aged councilor of the Mohegans, afterwards testified in enmity that Occom's grandfather was originally from a town at or near Union, that he came and fought
the Mohegans at Massapeak, and later lived at Niantic. There
is no doubt that Tomockham was a Mohegan, as much so as
any who were gathered by Uncas in the formation of that
clan of Connecticut Indians. Of his family little is known.
He was an aged man in 1738 when he and two sons, " Tomocham Junr " and " John Tomocham," signed a document declaring their loyalty to Sachem Ben Uncas, and probably he died
soon thereafter. Joshua Ockham, another and doubtless
older son, was then living about a mile north of Uncas Hill,
near the place where his famous son, Samson, afterwards built
his house, and by the latter's testimony his "father was the
first that ever lived there." Here in the course of time an
Indian village sprang up, which in the wider fame of the place
was called Mohegan. In the tribal quarrel between Ben and
John Uncas, rivals for the sachemship, this village became
known as " Ben's town" in distinction from " John's town," which
was situated about one-half mile south of it, both being east
of the road from Norwich to New London. In the wigwam of
Joshua Ockham the son Samson was born in the year 1723, on
a certain day which our hero never knew. His mother's name
was Sarah and she is said to have been a descendant of the
famous Mohegan chief, Uncas.[3] This may have been true, notwithstanding the statement of her son that she was a Groton
Indian, and on account of her marriage had been adopted
into the Mohegan tribe. Uncas himself was a Pequot, as were
the Indians of Groton, and he had descendants whose names
do not appear in the royal genealogy. Occom's references to
the Wauby family as his kindred and particularly to Roger
Wauby lead us to conjecture that these were relatives on his
mother's side, and that her maiden name was either Wauby or

[3] *Life and Times of Selina, Countess of Huntingdon*, I, 411

Sampson. At all events she was above the average as an Indian mother in intelligence, industry and affection. When in due time she became a convert to the Christian faith and a member of the church, she exercised a powerful influence over the life and character of her son. There were at least four children in the family, though Joshua, the eldest, may have been a son of Ockham by a former marriage. Sarah had Samson, Jonathan, who outlived the experiences of the French War and the Revolution in which he was a soldier, and Lucy, who became a woman of pious character, married John Tantaquidgeon, and died in 1830 at the age of ninety-eight.[4] The father of this family was a "mighty hunter," wandering abroad during the season of the chase and returning to Mohegan when the winter snows began to fall. On the 1st of July, 1742, the sachem, Ben Uncas, made choice of twelve councilors and among them were Joshua Ockham and his son Samson, then only nineteen years of age. This is the last trace we have of the father, and in a memorial to the General Assembly, May 17, 1743, it is stated that all these councilors were living "except onely Joshua Aucom who is lately dead."[5] Thus the home which had only been a humble hunter's wigwam at Mohegan was broken up and the care of the family fell to "Widow Sarah Occom." Twenty-five years later, when Samson Occom was thinking of preparing an autobiography, he wrote a few pages concerning his early life which have been preserved.[6] In this manuscript he speaks thus of his heathen home:

> I was Born a Heathen and Brought up in Heathenism till I was between 16 and 17 years of age, at a Place Called Mohegan, in New London, Connecticut in New England. My Parents lived a wandering life as

---

[4] Her daughter Lucy married Peter Teecomwas, and she and her daughter, Cynthia Hoscott, gave the land on which the Mohegan chapel is built. *Bostonian*, March, 1895, p. 679.

[5] *Conn. Archives, Indians,* I, 248, 249.

[6] *Wheelock Papers,* Dartmouth College, MS., Sept. 17, 1768.

did all the Indians at Mohegan. They Chiefly Depended upon Hunting, Fishing and Fowling for their Living and had no connection with the English, excepting to Traffic with them in their small trifles and they strictly maintained and followed their Heathenish ways, customs and Religion. Neither did we cultivate our Land nor keep any Sort of Creatures, except Dogs which we used in Hunting, and we Dwelt in Wigwams. These are a sort of Tent, covered with Matts made of Flags. And to this Time we were unacquainted with the English Tongue in general, though there were a few who understood a little of it.

There is no doubt that at the time of Occom's birth the Mohegans were heathen. Rev. James Fitch of Norwich had, indeed, long before endeavored to Christianize some of them.[7] This was in 1671, when he gathered a few in his own house once a fortnight and delivered to them a lecture on Christian doctrines. At first he was encouraged by Uncas and his son Oweneco; but as they became familiar with the demands which the new religion made upon their lives they resisted his efforts. The General Court moved the commissioners of the United Colonies as agents of the missionary society to assist him, which they did. It also announced its purpose to favor those who would listen to their teacher. Fitch had a company of about thirty in 1674, which was increased to forty the year following. In the hope of getting them to live together in one place he is said to have given them three hundred acres of land. All his efforts, however, came to little, though we cannot say what might have been but for King Philip's War. He died in 1702. Nothing further was attempted until 1713, when Rev. Experience Mayhew of Martha's Vineyard, at the desire of the commissioners, set out from Chilmark on the 12th of October to make a tour among the Indians of southern New England. On the 21st of September, 1714, he started on a second tour. The journals of both are in print.[8]

[7] DeForest's *Indians of Connecticut*, pp. 274-279; *Conn. Col. Rec.*, II, 157, 158; *Mass. Hist. Soc. Coll.*, I, vol. i, pp. 191, 192, 208, 209; *Mass. Hist. Soc. Proc.*, Nov., 1879; *New England Company*, p. 44; and *Conn. Archives, Indians*, I, 33.

[8] *New England Company*, London, 1896, pp. 97-127.

He was accompanied in the former as far as the Narragansett country by William Simons, an Indian minister of Dartmouth, who had been ordained by Japhet of Martha's Vineyard.[9] After a short stay at Ninegret's settlement he passed on to Stonington, whence he was conducted by Rev. James Noyes and others to the Pequot reservation. Here he had a meeting a few days later with all he could gather of the tribe. Thence he went to New London, thinking to arrange a meeting with the Mohegans. In this he failed, the Indians being off hunting, but he wrote an address "to the Mohegin and Nahantick Indians" informing them of the object of his visit, which Governor Saltonstall communicated to them later. On his second tour he visited the Pequots at North Stonington and Groton, being assisted by their overseer, Captain James Avery, who could act as his interpreter. At this time he went to Mohegan, where the Indians were gathered in a large double wigwam in the presence of Major Ben Uncas, uncle of the sachem, Cæsar, and, in an address an hour and a half long, Mayhew commended unto them the Christian religion. He received their thanks for the interest of the English; but as for their religion the Indians denied the necessity of it, pleaded that they had their own way of worship, declared that in Fitch's time their fathers had found it too hard, and asserted that the English were no better for it, as they would cheat the Indians of their land just the same. So he left them, having some hopes in further efforts to be made by Governor Saltonstall and Rev. Eliphalet Adams. It was doubtless to this occasion that Cotton Mather referred when he wrote in 1715 : "There

[9] Japhet was born at Chilmark about 1638, and was ordained by Hiacoomes in 1683, as teacher of the first Indian church of Martha's Vineyard, and the successor of Tackanash, the associate of Hiacoomes. He ordained William Simons in 1695. Both of them had preached some to Wamsuttan's company of Rhode Island Indians. Japhet died July 29, 1712, and Simons continued the work at intervals. See Report of 1698, *Mass. Hist. Soc. Coll.*, I, vol. x, p. 129; Mayhew's *Indian Converts*, pp. 10, 15, 44.

has been Something done to Christianize the Mohegins, and other Indians in the Colony of Connecticut; but, Lord, who has believed! They have been obstinate in their Paganism; however their obstinacy has not put an End unto our Endeavours." [10] One incident of these tours is worthy of note, namely, Mayhew's acquaintance with Joseph and Benjamin Garret, the sons of Catapezet (Kottupesit), and grandsons of the famous Hermon Garret or Wequash Cook (Wequashcuk). The former was his interpreter, his assistant in translating the Lord's Prayer into the Pequot tongue and the ally of his efforts—"of very good quality among the Indians," who "gave him [me] some hopes that he would become a Christian himself." Joseph Garret had been chosen by the Niantics of Lyme as their sachem, and his daughter was the wife of Cæsar, sachem of the Mohegans.   Mayhew also met his brother Benjamin, who understood some English and had a son then seven years old whom he was "willing to devote to learning that so he may be a minister." That boy became the Benjamin Garret of later times, the father of Hannah Fowler, who kept the cabin of Samuel Kirkland in Oneida.   The earliest known grand sachem of the Niantics had been Momojoshuck, and here we see the flow of his royal blood through his son Hermon Garret, Catapezet, Benjamin Garret, Benjamin, Jr., Hannah, the wife of David Fowler, who was Samson Occom's brother-in-law and companion in the first westward mission from Connecticut, James Fowler, a judge in the Indian Peacemaker's Court, David Fowler, the honored deacon of their church, to Lathrop Fowler, the intelligent American citizen.   But we anticipate our story.

The greatest good which resulted from Mayhew's tours was the new interest he awakened in Indian missions in southern New England.   Governor Saltonstall and his pastor, Rev. Eliphalet Adams, were especially aroused to their duties.   His

[10] Mather's *Just Commemorations*, p. 53.

Excellency gave himself to a careful examination of the conditions, and communicated his interest to the General Assembly
of Connecticut. That body, in May, 1717, recorded its belief
that something should be done toward "gospelizing the
Indians," and referred the matter to the governor and council.
At the next session the governor proposed certain measures to
that end, the most important of which was that the Indians
should be gathered in villages "where they might have distinct properties and these secured to the use of their respective families," and might receive instruction from a schoolmaster.[11] These measures were duly enacted, and village life
among the Mohegans and the Connecticut tribes generally
dates from that time.

The very year of Occom's birth Captain John Mason, the
guardian of the Mohegans, who had some acquaintance with
their language, received permission from the General Assembly to live among them, and it was recommended that he set
up a school and acquaint the Indians with the Christian
religion.[12] This he attempted with the assistance of the
assembly, under the patronage of the "Society for Propagating the Gospel," which thereafter maintained such privileges
as they had. Probably at first he taught a few children in his
own hut; but in 1727 a schoolhouse was occupied and he was
established as schoolmaster. This building was an unpretentious one, only twenty-two feet by sixteen, and had been
erected by the colony at a cost of £60.[13] The following year
his pupils were examined by two neighboring ministers,
Eliphalet Adams of New London and Benjamin Lord of
Norwich. It was found that they could "spell very prettily,"
and some could read "pretty tolerably without spelling" from
their primers and psalters. "They could say the Lord's

---

[11] *Conn. Archives, Indians,* I, 86; *Conn. Col. Rec.,* VI, 15, 31, 32.

[12] *Conn. Col. Rec.,* VI, 429.

[13] *Conn. Col. Rec.,* VII, 75 ; *Conn. Hist. Soc. Coll.,* IV, 82, 83, 389, 390.

Prayer, the Ten commandments and a pretty deal in Mr. Cotton's Catechism Milk for Babes."[14] This was not very advanced education, but under the circumstances it was encouraging. Captain Mason kept this school for about seven years, when a revival of the Mohegan land troubles turned the Indians against him and the school was discontinued. During this time also Rev. Eliphalet Adams was employed by the missionary society to deliver occasional lectures among them, following the Puritan example of John Eliot. As a means of religious instruction these may not have been very fruitful, but they made the Indians acquainted with one of the foremost ministers of the region—one whom they loved and trusted, and who ever remained their firm friend. To him more than any other individual the maintenance of educational and Christianizing privileges at Mohegan was due. He was always consulted by the missionary society, and his judgment was received without question.

One of Mason's pupils was the young Ben Uncas, the third of the name, only son of the sachem. He proved to be so proficient that in 1729 he was taken into Mr. Adams's home, and for five years he remained under his care, being in 1731 about to be " put upon grammar learning " to qualify him for a preacher, which he and his family wished.[15] In the summer of 1734 he was brought by Rev. Oliver Peabody to his home in Natick, and on the 14th of November was apprenticed to Thomas Russell of Sherburn, cardwainer. He did not remain throughout his full term, however, but was sent for in 1737 in pursuance of a political purpose, and married to Ann, daughter of the late Sachem Cæsar.[16]

Here we may see how those lingering influences of John Eliot at Natick were propagated at Mohegan. At Mason's

[14] *Conn. Archives, College and Schools*, I, 69; *Conn. Hist. Soc. Coll.*, IV, 107-112.
[15] *MS. Rec. Soc. for Prop. Gos.*
[16] *Ibid.*; *Conn. Archives, Indians*, I, 236; *Conn. Hist. Soc. Coll.*, V, 204; *Mohegan Case*, p. 210.

request a Christian Indian of that town, Thomas Pegun by name, was sent to the Mohegans in 1732 "to introduce among them family worship and the observation of the Lord's Day," and the Natick missionary, Rev. Oliver Peabody, visited them a few weeks later, bringing back such a report to the commissioners of the missionary society that it was decided to send a minister to labor there. After some search for a proper person, Mr. Jonathan Barber of Springfield was appointed at a salary of £100 a year, and about the middle of August, 1733, he commenced his work.[17] He was a licensed preacher, and began at once to gather the Indians for religious instruction. When Mr. Peabody in 1734 took the young Uncas to his home, he had been at Mohegan to encourage this mission. He made a favorable report, and everything seemed promising. Mr. Adams continued his lectures, and supervised the work in behalf of the society. In 1736 an attempt was made to revive the school under one Samuel Avery as master, but after one year he was displaced for neglect, and the school was put under the charge of Mr. Barber. Meanwhile, however, the controversy between the Indians and Captain Mason had been increasing animosities. Unfortunately their teacher seemed to the Indians to side with Mason against them, and his early influence waned. The children would not attend school, and their parents refused to hear their enemy preach. So the mission failed, and Barber was dismissed by the society June 22, 1738.

[17]Jonathan Barber was born in West Springfield, Mass., Jan. 31, 1712-13, being the son of Thomas and Sarah (Ball) Barber. He graduated at Yale College in 1730, studied theology, and was licensed to preach by the Hampshire County Association. He labored a short time among the Indians at Agawam, Mass., before he went to Mohegan. After his dismissal in 1738, he preached at Oyster Ponds, L. I., and was in 1740 made superintendent of Whitefield's Orphan House in Georgia. He returned to Long Island in 1747, and was ordained at Oyster Ponds, Nov. 9, 1757, by the Suffolk Presbytery, Rev. Ebenezer Prime preaching the sermon, which is in print. On Nov. 3, 1758, he was installed pastor of the Congregational Church in Groton, Conn., where he labored until 1765, when he became insane. His princi-

These attempts to civilize the Mohegans did not make any impression upon the youth, Samson Occom. In the manuscript already referred to, he gives the following pithy account of them :

> Once a Fortnight in ye Summer Season a Minister from New London [Rev. Eliphalet Adams] used to come up and the Indians to attend; not that they regarded the Christian Religion, but they had Blankets given to them every Fall of the year and for these things they would attend. And there was a Sort of a School Kept, when I was quite young, but I believe there never was one that ever Learnt to read anything. And when I was about ten years of age there was a man [Jonathan Barber] who went about among the Indian Wigwams, and wherever he could find the Indian Children would make them read, but the Children used to take Care to keep out of his Way : and he used to Catch me some times and make me Say over my Letters and I believe I learnt some of them. But this was Soon over too, and all this Time there was not one amongst us that made a Profession of Christianity.

The most prominent friend of the Christian religion during this period was the sachem, Ben Uncas, 2d. Whatever his motive may have been, and however much his subsequent conversion may be questioned, he was certainly favorable to the introduction of Christianity into his tribe. So early as 1729, when he sent his son to live with Rev. Eliphalet Adams, he expressed the desire to have his children instructed in the Christian religion. His interest increased. At his request the missionary had been sent to Mohegan, and the testimony at that time was that he had been " of late greatly reformed," and both he and his wife had begun to learn to read. In 1736 he made a declaration of his acceptance of Christianity, at which the General Assembly expressed their satisfaction, and presented him with a hat and greatcoat—on more than one

pal delusion was that he was a leper. In 1768 his pastorate was dissolved, but he lived on at Groton, dying Oct. 8, 1783. He married Nov. 2, 1740, Sarah Noyes, daughter of Rev. James Noyes of Westerly, and granddaughter of the Stonington minister. She was born Nov. 17, 1714, and died May 30, 1761. They had nine children.—Dexter's *Yale Biographies*, I, 410, 411.

occasion the attire in which the fathers arrayed their Indian converts for the heavenly course.[18] This event more than any other gave occasion for the action of the General Assembly in May, 1736, noting the revival of Indian missions, and ordering a general collection therefor in the churches on the next Thanksgiving Day.

Mr. Adams seems to have had confidence in the sachem's sincerity, and on the 31st of October, 1742, upon their making "profession of the Christian faith," he baptized "Benjamin Uncas, sachem of the Mohegan Indians, and his son Benjamin with his wife Ann also Lucy Uncas," whose names were duly entered in the records of the First Church of New London.[19] Probably they did not thus become communicants, for it had long been customary to baptize Indians who professed Christianity. So far as we know, however, this sachem lived a reformed and creditable life. He died in 1749, and his will, like that of the white man, recommended his soul to God, "trusting in Christ for the free and full pardon of all his sins."[20] The son who succeeded him was Adams' pupil. In 1739, after an examination in which his proficiency had been proven, he had been placed in the schoolmaster's chair at Mohegan. We know nothing about the school he kept, but he was no doubt successful, as he remained in charge for nearly ten years and his salary was increased by the missionary society to £80 a year. Now the time had come for him to surrender the school for the sachemship. Thus the chief

[18] *Conn. Col. Rec.*, VIII, 72, 73 ; *Conn. Hist. Soc. Coll.*, IV, 354; and *The Church Review*, Hartford, November, 1898.

[19] Lucy Uncas married, Oct. 23, 1744, Samuel Pye. Two younger children of the sachem, Esther and Mary, and a son of Ben. Uncas, Jr., Benjamin, were baptized at the same time. Other children of the sachem's son were baptized as follows : May 1, 1743, " Benjamin Uncas Jr. child Ann and his wife her child Mary ;" Aug. 13, 1744, Josiah ; April 10, 1748, Esther ; April 23, 1750, "Isaiah—Mercy child Mercy." The first wife Ann died before 1750, and Ben. Uncas, Jr., married Mercy, who survived him.

[20] DeForest's *Indians of Connecticut*, pp. 447, 448.

of the Mohegans, during the next quarter-century, was both a nominal adherent to Christianity and a missionary school-master.

Another important factor in Mohegan affairs was the North Church of New London, now in the town of Montville. Here, in 1739, Rev. David Jewett was settled as minister.[21] He interested himself from the first in the condition of his Indian neighbors. An attempt had been made before his coming to remove the meeting-house one mile to the eastward, nearer the Indian settlement, and unite them in one parish with the English, the " Society for Propagating the Gospel " to contribute the share of the Indians. This plan was favored by the commissioners, but it failed, for the location of a meeting-house was always a troublesome question and much more so under these conditions. However, the young minister felt a responsibility in the matter and had a sincere desire to do what he could for the heathen at his door.

When Mr. Jewett had been settled about a year, the great religious awakening of the time began. It is unnecessary to give here an account of this movement. The Mohegan Indians were located in the midst of a region where its impressions were most positive. It was the day of Rev. George Whitefield, who felt so keenly the power of a missionary motive and imbued his followers with the same spirit. Some ministers of eastern Connecticut had already met him. In the spring of 1741 Rev. Gilbert Tennent visited New London and preached there and at Lyme. Soon after him there came Rev. James Davenport, the enthusiast, who labored earnestly in the

[21] David Jewett was born in Rowley, Mass.. June 10, 1714, being the son of Stephen Jewett. He had a twin brother Daniel. After his graduation at Harvard College in 1736, he studied theology and was ordained pastor of the North Church in New London (Montville), Oct. 3, 1739. In 1756 he was chaplain of a Connecticut regiment raised for the expedition to Crown Point. He married (1) Patience Philips of Boston, who died Nov. 14, 1773, aged 66, and (2) Mary, widow of William Prince, who survived him. He died in office June 5, 1783.

neighborhood and stirred up the ministers, particularly concerning their obligations to the Indians, many of whom went
to hear him preach. The desire of Mr. Jewett was kindled to
a flame. Davenport's brother-in-law, Rev. Eleazar Wheelock
of Lebanon Crank, the Second or North Parish of the town,
now Columbia, Rev. Jonathan Parsons of Lyme, Rev. Benjamin Pomeroy of Hebron, and other ministers thereabouts
were deeply moved. Thus it happened that the way was prepared for the subsequent missionary enterprise of Dr. Wheelock. His neighbors were born into the same interest. As
friends of Whitefield they made him a friend to their Indians.
He afterwards visited the locality more than once, and in 1745
he held a great meeting of Indians at Mohegan.[22] The result-
ing evangelistic efforts were not confined to that tribe. Ministers labored among the Pequots at Groton and Stonington,
the Western Niantics in Lyme, and the Eastern Niantics or
Narragansetts in Charlestown, Rhode Island. Of these we
shall speak more particularly later; we now note that the foundations of this work were laid in the "Great Awakening."

The people of Mr. Jewett's parish shared in this new interest in the Indians. The movement for a union was revived,
but again nothing was effected. In 1742 an effort was made
to settle a minister at Mohegan over the Indians, but this also
failed. The result was that the Indians came under Mr. Jewett's pastoral care, for which he was paid by the missionary
society. Bibles, psalters, primers and catechisms were
secured and distributed among them. Such as were interested attended worship at his church. In the course of time
some who gave good evidence of fitness were admitted to
fellowship with his people, and among them was the Widow
Sarah Occom.[23]

[22] Caulkins' *History of Norwich*, p. 321.

[23] These members were as follows : Cyrus Junco and his wife; Sarah Junco and
Lucy Junco, sisters to Cyrus ; Widow Shokket ; Peggy ——; Henry Cocquid ; Joshua
Nonesuch and Hannah Nonesuch ; Andrew Tantapah ; Joseph Tanner ; Widow

Samson Occom was converted, according to the testimony of Doctor Wheelock, "by the blessing of God on the labors of Rev. Mr. Davenport." The account of his experience can be best given in his own words :

When I was 16 years of age, we heard a strange Rumor among the English that there were extraordinary Ministers Preaching from Place to Place and a Strange Concern among the White People. This was in the Spring of the Year. But we saw nothing of these things till Some Time in the Summer, when Some ministers began to visit us and Preach the Word of God; and the Common People also came frequently and exhorted us to the things of God which it pleased the Lord, as I humbly hope, to Bless and accompany with Divine Influences to the Conviction and Saving Conversion of a Number of us, amongst whom I was one that was Impresst with the things we had heard. These Preachers did not only come to us, but we frequently went to their meetings and Churches. After I was convicted I went to al lthe meetings I could come at, & continued under Trouble of Mind about 6 months, at which time I began to Learn the English Letters, got me a Primer and used to go to my English Neighbours frequently for Assistance in Reading, but went to no School. And when I was 17 years of age I had, as I trust, a Discovery of the way of Salvation through Jesus Christ and was enabled to put my trust in him alone for Life & Salvation. From this Time the Distress and Burden of my mind was removed, and I found Serenity and Pleasure of Soul in Serving God. By this time I just began to Read in the New Testament without Spelling, and I had a Stronger Desire Still to Learn to read the Word of God, and at the Same Time had an uncommon Pity & Compassion to my Poor Brethren According to the Flesh. I used to wish I was Capable of Instructing my poor Kindred. I used to think if I could once Learn to Read I would Instruct the poor Children in Reading and used frequently to talk with our Indians Concerning Religion. Thus I continued till I was in my 19th year, and by this Time I could Read a little in the Bible.

It was at such a crisis in the life of this Mohegan youth that he came under the influence of Rev. Eleazar Wheelock of Lebanon, who became his instructor and friend—a relationship

Bette Occom ; Lizze Nimrod; Lucy Cochegan; Widow Anna Uncas ; John Nannipoon and Hannah Nannipoon ; Sarah Occom ; Anna Uncas, wife of the sachem ; Widow Hannah Cooper, and Samuel Ashpo.—*Manual of the First Congregational Church, Montville, Conn.*, 1875, p. 19.

which was no less important in the career of the teacher than
in that of the Indian pupil. The biography of this minister
has been fully written and must be sought elsewhere.[24] A few
facts will tell his story to this date. He was born in Windham, Conn., April 22, 1711, being the son of Deacon Ralph'
Wheelock, a farmer in that town, and Ruth, daughter of Mr.
Christopher Huntington of Norwich. Having become a Christian at the age of sixteen, he entered Yale College with the
design of preparing himself for the ministry. After his graduation in 1733, he studied theology, was licensed to preach in
1734, and on the 4th of June, 1735, was ordained as pastor of
the Second Congregational Church of Lebanon. The same
year he married Sarah, daughter of Rev. John Davenport of
Stamford, Conn., and widow of Captain William Maltby, after
whose death, in 1746, he married Mary Erinsmead of Milford,
Conn. By his first wife he had six children, among them his
son Ralph, and by his second wife, five, among whom were Mary
and Abigail, whose husbands, Prof. Bezaleel Woodward and
Prof. Silvanus Ripley, became assistants in his work, and his
son John, who followed him in the presidency of Dartmouth
College. We are thus introduced evidently to the home of a
Connecticut minister, where learning, piety and culture were
bred. The father was a superior scholar. He had also the
teacher's gift, which inspired the youth about him with zeal
in their studies. In addition to his pastoral duties and occasional labors in revivals, he had found time to instruct a few
pupils gathered in his family. Of his personal appearance, his
biographer has said: "He was of a middle stature and size,
well proportioned, erect and dignified. His features were
prominent, his eyes a light blue and animated. His complex-
ion was fair, and the general expression of his countenance
pleasing and handsome. His voice was remarkably full, har-

[24] McClure's *Memoirs of Wheelock;* Chase's *Hist. of Dartmouth College;* Dexter's
Yale Biographies, I, 493-499; and Sprague's *Annals,* I, 397-403.

monious, and commanding."[25] This description, however, does
not make mention of that personal magnetism which was characteristic of him as a teacher. The Indians especially felt the
power of this gift and remarked upon it. His winsome presence impressed them. Savage natures sometimes came easily
under his control. A desire for a new life was awakened
within them by his tender words. Thus they became attached
to him, and in this friendship between teacher and pupil is to
be found in large measure the secret of his success. Surely in
the home of this minister an ambitious young Indian could
hope to find his opportunity.

It has been generally supposed that Doctor Wheelock dug
Samson Occom as a rough diamond from the earth. Evidently
this was not the case. It was already glittering before he met
with it. We have Occom's own account of the way their
acquaintance came about. In his manuscript he says:

> At this time my Poor Mother was going to Lebanon, and having had
> some knowledge of Mr. Wheelock and Learning that he had a number of
> English Youth under his Tuition I had a great Inclination to go to him and
> to be with him a week or a Fortnight, and Desired my Mother to Ask Mr.
> Wheelock whether he would take me a little while to Instruct me in Read-
> ing. Mother did so, and when she came Back, she said Mr. Wheelock
> wanted to see me as soon as possible. So I went up thinking I should be
> back again in a few Days. When I got up there, he received me with kind-
> ness & compassion, & instead of staying a Fortnight or 3 weeks, I spent 4
> years with him.

It should be said to the honor of Doctor Wheelock, the
father of Indian missionaries, that he thus, without hope of
remuneration or other aim than to do good, took this young
Mohegan into his care and home. It proved to be an event
in the history of Indian missions. In listening with compassion to the plea of this mother who stood at his door, he was
hearing a cry from Macedonia. A man less benevolent or
sympathetic or appreciative of the value of education would

[25] McClure's *Memoirs of Wheelock*, p. 131.

have hesitated. Wheelock opened the door and a youth who was to become the foremost of his race entered with a new hope. So it was Occom who sought out Wheelock and not Wheelock who sought out Occom.

The teacher recognized at once the slumbering talents of his pupil. He began with patience and wisdom to develop them. The youth's progress was encouraging. He had his reading lessons from the Bible and thus advanced at the same time in Christian knowledge. In writing he copied passages set for him by his teacher. One specimen of that early time has been preserved among the Wheelock Papers at Dartmouth College, and is reproduced underneath his portrait in our frontispiece. On the sheet, the pupil had written the Lord's Prayer in Latin, Greek and French, and then, as school-boys are wont to do, he inscribed on the reverse in his best penmanship " Samson Occom, The Indian of Mohegan, Ejus Manus." It was customary at that time to begin early with the study of the classics. The young Indian was soon engaged in Latin, attempting to compose sentences in that language. So the days went by. Occom became acquainted with family life in the Wheelock home and its refining influences were a great blessing to him. As he was associated with other pupils he noted the deficiencies of his heathen training and was quick to profit by the examples set before him. It is known that he soon became a member of Doctor Wheelock's church, but the church rolls are lost which recorded the date of his profession of faith, as that of other Indian pupils in later years. A few names have been recovered from the minister's manuscripts.

It was the 6th of December, 1743, when Samson Occom went thus to live with Doctor Wheelock. He was then twenty years of age. On that day he began to keep a diary, which he wrote in an easy and distinct hand—a practice which he continued throughout his life, though parts of it are not

known to be extant[26] which would be of great interest. He
seems to have had in mind at first mainly his own pleasure
and profit; but later when he became a beneficiary of the
" Society for Propagating the Gospel " it was necessary for him
to keep some account of his life upon which to make report.
In his subsequent missionary labors this was insisted on, and
to this fact we owe much information concerning his career.
He naturally chronicles more particularly his journeys to and
fro, the meetings he attended, his sermon texts and the like.
We have to thank him for the omission of the tedious medita-
tions so commonly found in ministers' diaries of that time;
but we should have been grateful for more details of his observations among the various Indian tribes he visited, the condition of frontier settlements and withal for an opportunity of
studying more closely this most remarkable Indian character.
However, we are able thus to follow him through many critical periods of his life.

As we have stated, Doctor Wheelock took Occom into his
home without any expectation of receiving assistance in his
support. The widowed mother could not contribute anything
except possibly her own labor. She may have attempted to
do this, as Indian women frequently did in English families,
for the son made this entry in his diary under February 23,
1744-45 : " Mater mea et Duo Libri Ejus Venierunt ad Domi-
num Wheelock manere ibi Tempori." There is a tradition at
Columbia that Occom lived some of the time in a hut which
he built in the woods some distance from the minister's home.
This is not unlikely. Soon the teacher acquainted some of

[26] The following parts are at Dartmouth College: Dec. 6, 1743–Nov. 29, 1748;
June 21, 1750–Feb. 9, 1751; June 28, 1757–Sept. 7, 1760; May 30, 1761–July 7,
1761; Nov. 21, 1765–July 23, 1766; July 8, 1774–Aug. 14, 1774; May 8, 1784–April
26, 1785; May 1, 1785–Oct. 2, 1785; Oct. 4, 1785–Dec. 4, 1785; Dec. 5, 1785–Jan.
22, 1786; June 26, 1786–Nov. 13, 1786; Dec. 11, 1786–April 7, 1787; April 7, 1787–
July 3, 1787; Sept. 20, 1787–Dec. 4, 1787; Dec. 10, 1787–Aug. 9, 1788; May 11,
1789–Sept. 18, 1789. The Connecticut Historical Society has one part, July 5, 1787
to Sept. 16, 1787.

his friends with the case and his benevolent purpose, which resulted in some contributions, mostly of clothes—"Some old and some new clothes," in the language of the recipient. Finally the " Society for Propagating the Gospel" became interested, and in 1745 the commissioners granted an allowance of £60 old tenor per annum for his maintenance. This they continued while he was pursuing his studies. During one year, 1744-45, on account of circumstances in Mr. Wheelock's home, the school was kept at Hebron by Alexander Phelps, who had just graduated from Yale College. His course was also interrupted from time to time by journeys to visit the Indians at Longmeadow, Windham, Niantic, Groton and Long Island, among whom he held meetings with an evangelistic purpose. One reason for this was doubtless the necessity for relief from constant study, to which he had not been accustomed. Indeed he at length so overstrained his eyes by his earnest application to his books that he was unable to take the course which had been designed in preparation for the ministry. On the 10th of November, 1747, after nearly four years of instruction, he left Lebanon to take charge of a school in some part of New London. This he taught during the winter. In the following spring, by the advice of the neighboring ministers with whom he was a protégé, and with the encouragement of the missionary society, he came under the care of Rev. Benjamin Pomeroy of Hebron, that he might be further instructed, particularly in Hebrew. How much of this language he actually acquired we do not know. It is said, however, that he was able to translate passages with ease, and his Hebrew Bible, which has survived, bears some evidences of use.[27] After nearly a year of such study it became evident

[27] Benedict Theological Library, First Church, Plainfield, Conn. The Bible is in two volumes, printed at Amsterdam in 1705. The covers of deerskin were doubtless Occom's own work. At some time, and probably after the owner's death, the volumes came into the hands of Rev. Joel Benedict, D. D., of Plainfield, by whom they were given with his library to the church. They were deposited in the library

that his eyes would not permit him to take a college course. Still it was hoped that he might study theology under some minister, and Rev. Solomon Williams, of Lebanon, was solicited by the missionary society to undertake this service. He would have done so, being always a faithful friend, but unfortunately just at this time, in the winter of 1748-49, Occom was compelled by his health to give up all study for a time. This proved to be the last of his education except such as he acquired by himself. He had foreseen for some time that such would be the result, and though it somewhat depressed his spirits, he was not without hope that he might find some field in which to labor for his degraded people. His restless ambition had not been quenched. A missionary zeal was still aflame in his soul. Probably it received an additional impulse when, in November, 1748, he visited the Christian Indians at Natick, and heard from Deacon Ephraim, with whom he lodged, the story of John Eliot's labors. He must then have learned about that famous Indian town, its founding and earlier usefulness, and have seen but too clearly the evidences of its decay. We may wonder whether that visit was not the means of suggesting to him the Indian town which he established years afterwards. It must at least have set him to thinking upon the problem of civilizing his people in New England, who were being hemmed in on all sides by the whites.

As to the education which Samson Occom had thus acquired it is not possible to speak as one might now, after the completion of a course of study in our schools. He certainly had an ample preparation for Yale College, whither it was proposed to send him. Rev. Samuel Buell says of him: He made such "Progress in Learning that he was so well fitted for Admittance into College (which was designed) that he doubt-

of the Connecticut Historical Society for safe keeping in 1851, and were reclaimed in 1890. Occom's Hebrew Grammar is in Dartmouth College Library—the work by Judah Moņis, Boston, N. E., printed by Jonas Green in 1735. It was evidently used by Occom in 1748.

less would have entered upon his Second year at his first admission." [28] His knowledge of the languages and mathematics was probably limited to what he learned in Doctor Wheelock's family school. He is known also to have studied music, which was a daily exercise in the minister's home. In his letters and sermons he shows a familiarity with English grammar and composition which it was difficult for an Indian to acquire. Yet it must not be supposed that Occom was a scholar judged by present standards, or even by the English youth of his day. His main attainment was a knowledge of the Scriptures, which he had studied with a living interest. He had not gathered any treasures of theology with which to fill his discourses; but he understood and held with intellectual vigor and clearness the principal doctrines of the Christian faith. In these it had been his teacher's aim to establish him. This was the education which was demanded in his life's mission. With his native aptitude at illustrating these truths he was fitted to become a useful teacher among his brethren.

[28] Buell's *Sermon at the Ordination of Occom* ; Letter, p. vii.

CHAPTER III

1749–1761

The eastern extremity of Long Island, known as Montauk, has been from time immemorial a favorite resort of Indians. Its famous fishing and hunting grounds made subsistence easy, and in the season attracted the natives from a distance. Here the Montauk tribe, well known in the early history of the New England Indians, made their home. It was their privilege, about the middle of the eighteenth century, to live at large on the lands anciently possessed by the tribe, but they seemed to have a particular title to a tract west of the Great Pond, called "North Neck," and to another east of the same called "Indian Field," which now is only peopled with lonely graves. In 1741 a census was taken of these Indians, and they were reported to comprise thirty-two families and one hundred and sixty-two souls, which is about the same as a statement made by Rev. Solomon Williams to Secretary Willard ten years later.[1] The prominent families had then assumed surnames such as Pharaoh, Fowler, Peter and Charles. Except in a few cases they were unable to speak the English language, and lived according to their heathen customs. Since 1741 some missionary service had been done among them at intervals by Rev. Azariah Horton, who was principally engaged with the Shinnecock Indians under the patronage of the New York correspondents of the " Society in

---

[1] *Mass. Hist. Soc. Coll.*, I, vol. x, p. 110. *MS. Lett.*, July 24, 1751, in possession of Mrs. B. E. Hooker, Hartford.

Scotland for Propagating Christian Knowledge."[2] He had followed in the wake of Rev. James Davenport, already mentioned, who as minister at Southold had occasionally preached among the Indians. Mr. Horton's work declined as the years passed, notwithstanding his faithfulness, and in 1750 he was ready to surrender his field to another.

In the month of November, 1749, Samson Occom, then in his twenty-seventh year, began a work at Montauk as schoolmaster, preacher and judge, which continued for nearly twelve years. His service was greatly blessed to the permanent elevation of some in that tribe who have a prominent place in our story. He had previously sought for employment as a teacher at Niantic and Narragansett; but at the former place they had a schoolmaster and at the latter they were quite indifferent in the matter. Occom had visited Montauk while he was yet a pupil at Doctor Wheelock's school. He had some acquaintance with the Indians there and their language was his own. It chanced, however, that he went thither in the summer of 1749, with some of his tribe on a fishing excursion. He was something of a fisherman himself; but he was more interested in men just then than in the denizens of the briny deep. So he left his companions at their employment and went among the wigwams to hold meetings. He was kindly received and continued some weeks in this service. Ere the time came for the party to return, the Indians had invited him to come and set up a school among them. The only support offered him was such as they could contribute themselves, and they were very poor. He immediately com-

[2] Azariah Horton was the son of Jonathan and Mary (Tuthill) Horton, and was born in the "Old Castle," at Southold, L. I., March 20, 1715. He graduated at Yale College in 1735, studied theology, and for a time preached at New Providence, N. J. In 1741 he was ordained by the Presbytery of New York with a view to his mission which he began in August of that year. He continued in this work until 1751, and the year following was installed as pastor of the Presbyterian Church in South Hanover (Bottle Hill), N. J., where he labored to his death, March 27, 1777.— Dexter's *Yale Biographies*, I, 536, 537; Prime's *Hist. of L. I.*, pp. 104-110; and Whitaker's *Hist. of Southold*, pp. 265-269.

municated with Doctor Wheelock, expressing his fear that the commissioners, being displeased at his leaving his studies, would not favor his engagement or grant him their assistance. On the 10th of July, as appears from their records, they had " voted that inasmuch as Samson Occom is taken off from his studies by a pain in his eyes, Mr. Williams of Lebanon be asked to advise in the affair as to his keeping school or engaging in manual labor and on his recovery they would be willing to help him and in the meantime allow what is necessary toward effecting a cure." In view of this action Doctor Wheelock replied to Occom on the 6th of September advising him to take the school for six months pending his restoration and on the same sheet Mr. Williams wrote to the same effect.[3] Thereupon Occom agreed with the Indians to return soon and teach a school for six months as an experiment. We are thus particular because there was a misunderstanding in the matter. Occom and his advisers thought the missionary society would grant him an allowance in this work, but the commissioners were not intending to do so. During the first two years he received nothing from them towards his support. Then at the earnest solicitation of friends, among them Messrs. Williams of Lebanon and Buell of Easthampton, L. I., and upon the testimony of Mr. Horton as to the value of his labors, they made him a beneficiary of the society. Occom afterwards wrote that during his years at Montauk they granted him in all £180. This will explain the trials of his early experiences. His circumstances were those of poverty. During the first term of six months the Indians gave him besides his board £10 York money, to which some English friends added about forty shillings. His annual salary from the missionary society was only £20. The young Uncas at Mohegan had received three times that sum. We shall not wonder, therefore, at finding that he became involved in debt, in which the missionary

[3] *Wheelock Papers*, Lett., Sept. 6, 1749.

society at the entreaty of his friends generously aided him. More especially, however, do we refer to this matter because Occom always felt that he did not receive an adequate support. It seems to have been a sore point with this sensitive Indian that white missionaries doing the same service were given larger salaries. He thought he ought to receive at least half as much as his white brother and expressed himself as "willing to leave it with the world as wicked as it is, to decide." The saints, however, never came to his view of the matter. They gave him such remuneration as they had other native teachers. Thus his feelings were wounded by the suspicion that a distinction was made against him because of his race. He was compelled to toil on, as he did throughout all his days, in poverty. Sometimes, he says, he was in actual need of the necessaries of life. He had a large measure of Indian pride which would not permit him to beg. In consequence he was at times diverted from his service to engage in manual labor. At the same time it should be said that Occom was not an economical manager of his affairs. The Indian instinct was strong in him to eat while he had the means and leave the future to provide for itself. He profited much by his experience in all these respects as he grew in years and became settled in the ways of civilized life.

Yet this inadequate provision for his support at Montauk did not discourage him. He took up his work with zeal and wisdom. The first winter he gathered about thirty scholars into his school, and instructed in the evening such as could not attend during the day. As a teacher he was always successful. He had a kindergarten method of his own in teaching the alphabet. Finding that the children could distinguish the letters by ear, but could not so well by sight, he cut letters out of paper, pasted them on cedar chips, and at his word the one named would be brought to him out of the pile. Such ingenuity was characteristic of him in his teaching. By these means he soon aroused an interest in learning among his pupils, and under his native patience they progressed rapidly, advancing from the primer to the reading of the Bible.

In addition to his labors as schoolmaster, he began religious ministrations among the Indians, in which he shortly succeeded Mr. Horton. On the Sabbath he conducted three services for worship, and a wigwam meeting was also held every Wednesday evening. In these assemblies he prayed, expounded the Scriptures in his native tongue, and led in the singing of Christian hymns, which he taught old and young. This work was a means of educating him for his missionary life. It concentrated his interest in the study of the Bible, which was about the only book he then owned. Even in 1756, Wheelock wrote Whitefield that Occom had " scarce any books but what he borrowed," and asked for a copy of Poole's Annotations. This was given him, and the same year he received from the missionary society a " Commonplace book to the Bible," and Cruden's Concordance. As was natural, the natives soon came to regard him as their minister. He visited their sick and attended their funerals. As they had letters to write or legal documents to draw up they went to him. So great was their confidence in his character that they frequently made him a judge over them to settle matters in dispute. This was a similar office to that which Eliot had established among his Christian Indians, and possibly Occom imitated this custom. Thus he soon attained a great influence among all the natives in those parts of Long Island.

Occom lived while at Montauk in the same simple manner as the Indians thereabouts. His' home was a wigwam. In the summer season it was near the planting-grounds, and in the winter he removed with the tribe so as to be near the woodland. His household effects were no great embarrassment to a sudden and easy migration—the simple utensils of Indian cookery, a few clothes, well worn, except the suit which he reserved for appearances among the whites, the dozen books, more or less, which he could easily carry in his saddle-bags, and the odds and ends of an Indian's wigwam life. All these, to which he doubtless added as he came to have a family, he lost at sea afterwards when he removed to Mohegan. Many times in his life he had occasion to remark upon the "adverse providences" which depleted his store of worldly possessions. We read, with some amusement, the serious narration of his experiences. He bought a mare with which to travel to and fro among his Montauk parishioners, but she fell into a quicksand. He purchased another, but some rogue stole her from him. The third died of the distemper. The fourth had a colt and then broke her leg, and "presently after the colt died also," whereupon he gave up the attempt to maintain such luxury, and traveled afoot. The understanding when he began his work was that the Indians would take turns in providing him with food. Doubtless this plan left him to keep too many unappointed fast days, for he tells us he was compelled to resort to hunting and fishing to supply the necessary food to his family. In both of these occupations he was expert, and it was well for him on many an occasion of his life that he was. He also worked in wood, making spoons, ladles, gun-stocks, pails, piggins and churns. A tract of land was assigned to him, and this he also tilled, sometimes with the assistance of his pupils. In 1755, he tells us, he had "four acres of good corn." His most novel employment, however, was that of binding old books for the English people at Easthampton and other settlements. If any of the books of Rev. Samuel Buell have survived, there is doubtless among them a specimen of his work, the value of which would be enhanced if it could be identified as from this wigwam bookbindery. So he labored, many a time at night by the light of a smoking torch, that he might keep the wolf from the door.

After Occom had been at Montauk nearly six months, the question arose as to the continuance of his mission there. He wrote Doctor Wheelock on the matter, and received the following reply :

[My Dear] Samson
    Yours by the Bearer [came] to my Hand the night before last. I 've wrote to Mr. Horton what I know & can say in y^r case of your continuance in y^r school 6 months longer. I perceive the Hon^{le} Com^s are very unwilling to give up the purpose of your being fitted for the ministry if it may be & so is Mr. Wi.liams—& my own disposition you have known has al along been so. If you are well to persue your studies I cant but think it advisable to return to them, if otherwise you may safely continue in the school. Dr Child, watch against pride & self esteem. Pray much. Accept Love from me & all my family. I am
                                    Yours affectionately
    Leb^n Apr 3, A. D. 1750.   ELEAZ^r WHEELOCK.[4]

So it happened that Occom continued another six months at Montauk, and at the expiration of that time he engaged himself again. When he had been there a year and a half Rev. Aaron Burr, acting in behalf of the New York correspondents of the " Society in Scotland for Propagating Christian Knowledge," invited him to come to New Jersey and labor in the mission then under the care of Rev. John Brainerd and go on a journey to Susquehanna. The consent of the commissioners at Boston was secured, with their pledge of support, but hostilities among the Indians in those parts made it necessary to abandon the plan. By this time the success of his work had become known. The missionary society came to his assistance. President Burr became so interested in him that he secured a pledge from a merchant of Philadelphia, Mr. Grant, " a dear, honest Christian," to do very considerable towards his support if he would qualify himself to become a licensed preacher to the Indians.[5] Occom would gladly have accepted

    [4] *Conn. Hist. Soc. Indian Papers.*
    [5] *Conn. Hist. Soc. Indian Papers,* Jonathan Badger to Samson Occom, April 19 1755.

the offer had he thought his health sufficient for the study. He had come to see that he must have more out-of-door service. This he had at Montauk. He was also unwilling to leave a work so promising. The Indians there had measurably advanced in civilization. They had begun to want houses, to clothe themselves like the whites, to live orderly and sober lives. A revival of religion brought some to avow Christianity. Mr. Horton testified that Occom's sensible view of the nature of true religion was the means of quenching the wild notions of some foolish exhorters, holding the opinions then so prevalent in southern New England.[6] The Christian Indians of Occom's day were strongly inclined to Separatism, as we shall have occasion to notice. Throughout his life, as well as thus early at Montauk, Samson Occom was never the victim of any idiosyncrasies of religion.

On the 12th of November, 1756, the commissioners of the "Society for Propagating the Gospel" having before them Occom's case, passed the following vote : " Inasmuch as said Sampson is represented to be a person of virtuous life and useful as a preacher to the Indians, the commissioners would recommend to Rev. Mr. Wheelock, Mr. Pomeroy, and other ministers of the same Association to consider of the expediency of his being ordained to the pastoral office and to proceed to do it as they shall think best."[7] This step was suggested on many accounts. It had been all along Occom's desire. He was then doing the service of a minister, and his ordination would bring him into fellowship with his brethren and friends for his profit. Moreover, it was foreseen that a larger field than the Montauk village would soon claim him and to that end his ordination was considered preparatory. The Windham Association considered the matter as requested. On the 13th of July, 1757, they met at the house of Rev. Solomon Williams in

---

[6] McClure's *Mem. of Wheelock*, p. 17 ; *Wheelock's Narrative*, 1763, p. 29.
[7] *MS Rec. Soc. for Prop. Gos.*

Lebanon. Their records contain no notice of this meeting, but Wheelock referred to it and in his diary Occom makes the following entry concerning it :

They came together about one o'c P. M.—and there I Passed an Examination Before the Revd Messrs Solomon Williams, Eleazar Wheelock, Benjamin Pomroy, Nathan Strong, and Stephen White,—and they were so far satisfied as to Conclude to proceed to an ordination hereafter.

This was equivalent to a license to preach if not actually such, and with this encouragement Occom resumed his work at Montauk. The winter following was one of great awakening among the Indians. It spread from the Montauks to other neighboring tribes.[8] This led Rev. Samuel Davies of Virginia, afterwards president of the College of New Jersey, to urge his ordination with a view to his undertaking a mission among the Cherokee Indians, under the patronage of the New York correspondents of the Scotch Society, which had also been contemplated by the London Society. The former board also considered the ordination question and referred it to the Presbytery of Long Island, two of whose members, Rev. Messrs. Buell and Brown, had warmly commended Occom to them. Hence there were cross-purposes and delays, the candidate wondering meanwhile that there should be so much discussion over the ordination of one poor Indian. The Boston commissioners rather wished to make a Congregationalist of him, and so referred the matter to the Windham Association. They subsequently agreed, however, to release Occom for the Cherokee mission or they would increase his salary to £30 if he remained at Montauk. The Association had no hesitation as to ordaining Occom, as one might infer from their records, but they thought it best for him to unite with the Presbytery if he was to engage under Presbyterians in the Cherokee mission. The Indian was willing to be ordained by either body and

8 *Wheelock Papers*, Lett. July 22, 1758.

labor under any board ; but he felt his obligations to his friends in the Windham Association, and would not proceed without their approval. Finally that body met at Lebanon on the 15th of May, 1759, and Occom was present to hear their decision. Of this meeting their records contain the following minute :

> The Association being by Mr. Wheelock requested to ordain Mr. Samson Occum, Indian, a Minister at large for the Indians, thought it inexpedient for them, but recommended the doing of it to the Long Island Presbytery if they think best.

They also wrote a letter to that body which Occom carried to his friend, Rev. Samuel Buell. Thus it came to pass that this Indian minister became a Presbyterian, which has been thought strange. It was in fact merely incidental to his expectation of going on a mission to the Cherokees under the Scotch Society.

The Presbytery appointed the 29th of August as the time for his ordination, and Easthampton as the place. A few days before that time news came of warlike disturbances among the Cherokees, which overturned the contemplated scheme. Had those Indians only dug up the tomahawk a few months earlier, Occom would have been without doubt a Congregationalist and a member of the Windham Association. However, the Presbyterian fathers had another plan of sending him to the Mohawks, which seemed thus providentially brought forward, and so the ordination went on according to program. The following account of the occasion is given in their records :

> Suffolk Presbytery, East Hampton, August 29, 1759.
> Sampson Occum candidate for the indian Mission having had a Text given him to compose a Trial Sermon upon, and a Subject for an Exegesis, now offered himself upon Examination with a view to ordination. The Presbytery entred upon the Preliminaries of his Ordination and having examined him in the learned languages, enterd upon Theology, and heard his Trial Sermon from Psalm 72. 9.

August 30th 8 o'clock Resum'd the Examination of Mr. Occum—And having attended his Exegesis, and finish'd his Trials in Divinity, with other Things relative thereto, Inquir'd into his Acquaintance with experimental Religion together with his Ends and Views in desiring to be introduced into the Work of the evangelical Ministry by Ordination &c—And then upon an Interloquitur, the Question being put by the Moderator—Whether this Presbytery approves of Mr. Occum as one in any good Measure qualified for the Work of the Gospel Ministry, especially among the aboriginal Natives of this Land or not? Resolved in the Affirmative. Then proceeded to the Ordination of Mr. Sampson Occum in the Meeting-House, a numerous assembly, upon Notification given, attending.

Mr. Buell began the publick Worship with Prayer—and preach'd the Ordination Sermon from Gal. 1. 16—Mr. Browne introduc'd the Solemnity of the Ordination and made the Ordination Prayer during the Imposition of Hands—Mr. Barker gave the Right-hand of Fellowship—Mr. Prime gave the charge and made the concluding Prayer—Mr. Occum, the candidate ordain'd, pointed out the Psalm and pronounced the Blessing.

This ordination was certainly at that day an interesting occasion. It was remembered years afterwards by many who were present as most impressive. There had never been thereabouts such a vivid portrayal of the missionary idea as the people beheld when the ministers present laid hands on the head of the young Mohegan teacher. Some of his Indian converts were conspicuous in the audience—a solemn justification of the act. Many of his English friends were there, with whom he was decidedly popular. The ministers themselves looked upon it as a new departure in the history of Indian missions. In after years, when Occom had attained some fame, he was welcomed many times in the meeting-house at Easthampton and those friends of his early ministry were ever dear to him.

It should here be noted that the examination to which Occom was subjected was no mere formality. He must have had some creditable knowledge of the " learned languages " to have passed any sort of an examination before the assembled divines. The text of his " Trial Sermon " was most fitting, " They that dwell in the wilderness shall bow before him ; and

his enemies shall lick the dust." It was trial enough for an
Indian to preach at all before a Presbytery, yet he is said to
have acquitted himself well. What he said on the text that
day we do not know ; but he afterwards chose it on more than
one occasion in discoursing to large audiences in England and
America. He was probably relieved when the occasion was
over, for in noting the facts in his diary he adds, " Thus the
solemnity ended, *Laus te Deum.*"

The ordination sermon, preached by Mr. Buell, was printed
in 1761, as a means to excite interest in the Oneida mission,
which Occom was then about to undertake.[9] A letter is added
to the sermon giving some account of his early life. All the
references to him are creditable. His talents seem at that
time to have been recognized by all who knew him. " In
short," says Mr. Buell, " he is an ornament to the Christian
Religion and the glory of the Indian nation."

Ere we end our review of this period of Samson Occom's
life we must make the acquaintance of some of his Indian
friends. One of the most influential Indians at Montauk
when Occom went there to begin his work was James Fowler.
His father or grandfather had doubtless taken the English
name of some white family, as the custom was even before the
year 1700. The census of 1741 mentions James Fowler as
the head of a family of eight. At least half of these were
children, and others were afterwards born to him and his wife
Elizabeth. Some of his descendants continued to live at

[9] The Excellence and Importance of the saving knowledge | of the Lord Jesus
Christ in the Gospel-Preacher, | plainly and seriously represented and enforced :
And | Christ preached to the Gentiles in Obedience to the Call of God. | A |
Sermon, | preached at | East-Hampton, August 29, 1759 ; | at the | Ordination | of |
Mr. Samson Occum, | A Missionary among the Indians. | By Samuel Buell, M. A. |
Pastor of the Church of Christ, at East-Hampton, | Long-Island. | To which is
Prefixed, | A Letter to the Rev. Mr. David Bostwick, Minister | of the Presbyterian
Church, in New York, giving | some Account of Mr. Occum's Education, Character,
&c. | .... | New York : | Printed by James Parker, and Company, | M. DCC. LXI. |
8° pp. xvi, viii, 38.

Montauk down to quite recent times. One of them was doubtless William Fowler, who was well known at the ancient home of his tribe by all visitors, and whose house stood as a landmark for many years and was only lately destroyed. In this family of James Fowler, then a heathen, living in an Indian wigwam, Occom found a welcome in 1749. The children attended his school, and he took unusual interest in them, for they were ambitious to learn. As there was a daughter in the family, Mary by name, intelligent, virtuous and comely, it was natural that a friendship should spring up between her and the young schoolmaster. His diary shows that his attention in the spring of 1751 was somewhat divided between the Epistles to the Thessalonians and this Indian maiden. When he visited Rev. Solomon Williams that summer, he mentioned the affair, but was advised "to be cautious in choosing a wife lest he should put himself in such circumstances as might render him less able to answer the design of his education, being uncertain where the commissioners would employ him." Occom answered, however, that "his marrying there would not prevent his readiness to go where the commissioners should please to send him either on the Island or on the main." [10] Soon after his return to Montauk, in the autumn of 1751, he was married, and Mary Fowler was thereafter a partner in the trials and toils of his missionary life.

The family of James Fowler received a lifelong impression through the instruction of the Montauk schoolmaster. They became thoroughly civilized. The parents accepted the Christian faith, lived to age, and died in it—the father at Montauk and the mother in the home of her son David on the Oneida hillside. Another daughter, Phœbe, married Ephraim Pharaoh—of a second family at Montauk who owed much to Occom—and they were staunch supporters of the missionary's subsequent plans for the Christian Indians. But the most

[10] *MS. Lett.* Solomon Williams, Oct. 7, 1751, in poss. of Mrs. Hooker.

conspicuous of the Montauk pupils were the two sons of James Fowler, David and Jacob, who henceforth become actors in our story. David was born in 1735, and was therefore fourteen years of age when the schoolmaster began his work. Jacob was born in 1750—a babe whom Occom often carried in his arms. These two lads, whom he taught to read in the Bible, his brothers-in-law, became the dearest friends of his life, and their services are interwoven with his to the end.

CHAPTER IV

The success of Samson Occom in acquiring an education, and the prospect of his usefulness, first suggested to the Rev. Eleazar Wheelock the introduction of Indians into his family school. A missionary zeal all aflame in one so recently a savage was an awakening fact. Missionary motives were kindled in the teacher's mind. As his pupil seemed to prosper in the school at Montauk and advance steadily toward the life of an Indian missionary, supported by existing societies, and gathering to the cause friends among the whites, the question naturally arose, why could not others be brought to follow his example? Thus Doctor Wheelock was led to devise a plan for propagating the gospel among the Indians which he thought with good reason was most feasible. In its prominent feature it was different from all other schemes which had been attempted in New England. His ideal, like that of John Eliot, was the native missionary. He recognized the many advantages arising from the Christianized Indian, who understood the temper, customs and language of his people, would disarm their prejudices, and could live anywhere with little expense. The great "Apostle to the Indians" had builded his work on this corner-stone. The distinguishing feature of Doctor Wheelock's plan was that he proposed to cultivate this Indian teacher in the nursery of the Christian family, and establish under his own personal instruction a school for the special training of missionaries. In his opinion, which had doubtless been formed in his experience with Occom, there was also an advantage in having these Indians trained with whites who were interested in the same work. So he wished to gather the most promising youth of all tribes out of their heathen environment, under a master who would instruct them in civilized life, where they would have mutual acquaintance, and after years of seasoning in Christian truth be fitted to return as examples and leaders to their own people. Girls as well as boys were to be brought into this school and instructed in domestic concerns. Thus he hoped by natural means to introduce among distant tribes a native Christian family. In early New England history many Puritan homes had done such a service with some success, as we have seen; but Doctor Wheelock's plan, based on the same principle as to the value of a civilized environment, was of larger extent and added other features. Eliot had placed great emphasis on community life. Hence he had sought to further civilization by self-government in his Indian towns and the organization of churches. Wheelock depended rather upon the high ideal which he hoped to produce in the individual. Hence he sought to gather the fittest apart where they might after years attain it. There was wisdom in both principles, and they are essential to each other. Both are to some extent illustrated in the methods of the present day. Indian civilization will never flourish unless the educated individual is placed in a favorable environment. That was precisely what Samson Occom afterwards sought to secure by his scheme of gathering the Christian Indians of New England in a town away from demoralizing influences. Doctor Wheelock did not sufficiently consider the corresponding perils attending the young native teacher when returned to his heathen surroundings. Others have made the same mistake since his day. The strongest could with difficulty stand against such temptations. Apostasies have always arisen thus in the history of Indian missions. He entrusted the faith to mere youth, gave them a measure of authority, sent them far away from the protection of his school, and then was easily discouraged if they failed to stand the test. His plan was nevertheless a good one. If it did not accomplish all he anticipated for the Indians the reason was rather in the circumstances which he could not control. Still we shall hope to show the reader that the influences of his "Indian Charity School" were more salutary and permanent than any have thought or than he himself lived to see.[1]

Having, therefore, after careful deliberation, resolved upon his experiment, Doctor Wheelock wrote in May, 1754, to Rev. John Brainerd, then employed among the Delaware Indians under the New York correspondents of the Scotch Society, requesting him to send to Lebanon two promising Indian boys. Before they arrived, he had awakened the interest of his ministerial friends in the Windham Association. He had, moreover, unfolded his purpose to Rev. George Whitefield, as we learn from later references, and had received his encouragement. We doubt not that this was a prominent topic of conversation when they met at Wheelock's house, even as the boys were on the way. Thus he made Whitefield an adviser and supporter in his work at the very outset. On the 18th of December, 1754, there arrived at Lebanon John Pumshire, aged fourteen, and Jacob Woolley, aged eleven, both of the Delaware tribe. The former continued there to November 14, 1756, when he was sent home on account of his failing health, and died, January 26, 1757. The latter, being a good scholar, advanced so rapidly in his studies that he could "read Virgil and Tully and the Greek Testament very handsomely" in 1758. He entered the college of New Jersey in May, 1759, but during his last year, in 1762, was returned in disgrace to Lebanon, where he studied for some time the Mohawk tongue. Later, he went back to college, but ran away, and so he drops

[1] On Wheelock's plan see his *Narratives*, 1763, pp. 10-29, 34; 1771, pp. 18-22.

out of our story. These two Delawares were Wheelock's only Indian pupils until February 8, 1757. He could not take others until he had ascertained what assistance he might expect in their support. At this time, there were two missionary societies engaged in such work, namely, the "Society for Propagating the Gospel," having commissioners at Boston, and the "Society in Scotland for Propagating Christian Knowledge," having boards of correspondents at New York and at Boston.[2] Both of these societies assisted him during the twelve years before the "Trust Fund" was raised. He also had help from the Sir Peter Warren legacy, through the General Assembly of Massachusetts, from the General Assembly of the Province of New Hampshire, and from donations and legacies of individuals at home and abroad. In the later years of this period he was forced to depend mainly on collections made in the churches, for which legislative authority was obtained in Connecticut. The "Society for Promoting Christian Knowledge" made him several grants of books. These were the sources of the school's income outside of the country parish in which it was located.

When the two Indian pupils appeared at Lebanon, the minister's family school assumed at once the character of an institution. Subscriptions were made for its maintenance, contingent upon its incorporation, to the extent of £500, each subscriber agreeing, meanwhile, to pay the interest on his pledge. Amid this aroused interest, Doctor Wheelock visited Mr. Joshua More, a farmer of Mansfield, Conn., who was pleased to purchase for the school, at a cost of £500, old tenor, a place contiguous to the minister's mansion, containing about two acres, and having upon it a "small dwelling-house and a shop or schoolhouse." This property he deeded, July 17, 1755, to Colonel Elisha Williams, Esq., "late rector of Yale College"—whose service ended with his death on that

[2] See Chapter I, note 15.

very day—to Rev. Samuel Mosely of Windham, and Rev. Benjamin Pomeroy of Hebron, who, with Doctor Wheelock, were to hold it in trust "for the Educating such of the Indian Natives of any or all the Indian Tribes in North America or other poor Persons." The institution was to bear the donor's name, which he spelled " More," but the usual title became " Moor's Indian Charity School." It happened, however, that Mr. More died, October 2, 1756, without making further provision for the school, as was expected ; that the deed was held to be defective ; that Wheelock failed to secure incorporation from the crown, and so the property was eventually held by Doctor Wheelock himself by a new conveyance from the widow, Dorothy More, dated May 10, 1763. This deed thus describes the property :

One certain Messuage or Tenement situate in s^d North Society in s^d Lebanon, bounded & Described as follows (viz) beginning at a stump on the west side of Hartford Road & which is the Eastwardly corner of Land belonging to the Heirs of Philip Judd Deceased, thence running by s^d Land Southwardly about 22 Rods to an heap of stones in the Dam-Brook adjoining to Jehiel Rose's Land, thence running down the brook in the Line of s^d Rose's Land 12 & an half Rods to a stake with stones about it on the East side of s^d Brook, thence running North easterly with a Stone wall 20 Rods to Hartford Road, thence North westerly by Hartford Road 17 & ½ Rods to the first mentioned Bounds, being in quantity about Two Acres of Land.

While the institution remained at Lebanon, it was usually styled " Wheelock's Indian Charity School," but the earlier title was afterwards restored. Mr. Frederick Chase, in his " History of Dartmouth College," has pointed out the fact that this property was bought from Moses Barrett, " late schoolmaster in Lebanon," and conjectures that the new school supplanted an earlier one. The first " master" of Doctor Wheelock's school was a young man of that name, whose position may have had some place in the transfer. If this is true, the schoolhouse was already prepared for use, and the " mantion house " was suitable for a dormitory. Evidently this gift gave the enterprise a substantial character, which was essential in its plea for pecuniary assistance.

Here, then, was a little group of buildings—the center of a country parish—in which Doctor Wheelock could conveniently carry on his work. The meeting-house stood on the green where the two main roads crossed, one leading from Hartford to Norwich and the other from Middletown to Windham and Providence. It was a simple structure, forty-six feet by sixty-four, built in 1748, and at this time it was covered with a coat of sky-blue paint. As an encouragement to the school, the parish voted in 1755 to set apart for the boys "the pew in the gallery over the west stairs," and in 1761 it gave the "Indian girls liberty to sit in the hind seat on the woman's side below." At times these pews must have been filled to overflowing. Some of the pupils, both boys and girls, became members of this church. On several occasions the congregation gathered here on the Sabbath was honored with the presence of Indian chiefs from distant tribes bedecked in royal attire. Thither missionaries returned with stories of adventurous experience—Samson Occom from his pioneer visit to the Oneidas, and Samuel Kirkland, the first white charity pupil of the school, from his hazardous attempt to carry the Gospel to the Senecas. Surely that little sky-blue meeting-house was the place of many an interesting service !

Southward from the church was the Barrett dwelling-house, transformed to serve as a home for the charity pupils. Here successive masters presided in turn after Moses Barrett: Chandler Robbins, Ralph Pomeroy, Benjamin Trumbull, Edmund Davis, John Huntington, John Leslie, John Lothrop, Aaron Kinne, Ralph Wheelock, Bezaleel Woodward, Samuel Wales, and David McClure. In that house the newly-arrived and half-clad Indian boy spent his first homesick night in civilization. "We reposed on Straw Beds in Bunks," wrote

David McClure in his diary, "and generally dined on a boiled dish & an Indian pudding." The two acres round about offered the Indian his first lesson in the science of agriculture. The schoolhouse was near at hand. It was such a building as the reader has many times seen at the crossroads in the country, and its frame is said to survive to this day in the district schoolhouse of the place. Here or in the hall of the minister's house the pupils were gathered with their instructors for morning and evening prayers—for a time by the sound of a bell " decently hung " thereon, which had been presented by Rev. George Whitefield.[3] Later their signal was the blowing of a shell. In this schoolhouse they attended upon their studies during the day. Northward from the sky-blue meeting-house, facing the green, was the minister's home, a very respectable mansion for that day, having ample room in its twenty-acre lot. A gigantic pine-tree, which the minister may have planted in front of his house, now marks the place, and is all that remains of those early days except the sacred dust in the graveyard. In this home many distinguished divines lodged on their journeys to and fro. In its study meetings were held, from time to time, of the Windham Association and later of the board of correspondents which stood as trustees toward the humble missionary school. One can scarcely imagine, without a perusal of Doctor Wheelock's voluminous correspondence, how many letters were written there and how many important messages were dispatched thence to all quarters. The country round about was wholly devoted to

---

[3] Wheelock wrote Mr. Dennys DeBerdt of London, " The Schoolmasters Complain of the want of a Bell that May be well heard about a mile. Indian children are inclined to ramble in play time & it is difficult to get them together."— *Wheelock Papers*, Lett. Nov. 16, 1761. He wrote Whitefield later, " I have received the Bell which you sent and it is decently hung on the House which I have devoted to the Service."— *Wheelock Papers*, Lett. Sept. 16, 1762. This bell, which weighed eighty pounds, was broken within two years, and having been sent to Elizabethtown, N. J., to be recast was returned broken as it went.—Chase's *Hist. of Dart. Coll.*, p. 27.

farming. There was no village—only this group of buildings where two highways of travel crossed. Yet here was a school which had a purpose and a name, honored in its day through-out New England, to the southward, and beyond the sea.

We are not intending to repeat the story—so well told in the "History of Dartmouth College"—of Doctor Wheelock's hopes, trials and labors in connection with his "Indian Charity School." Our desire is rather to make the acquaintance of the Indian pupils instructed there, whose names have been all but lost to notice, but whose lives are associated with the career of Samson Occom. Who, then, were those pupils, and what became of them?

The third Indian to attend this school, and the first of the New England tribes, was Samson Wauby, whose name is also spelled Wobby, Wobi and Woyboy. He was a Pequot of Groton, a relative and probably a cousin of Samson Occom through his mother. Of his early life we only know that he had been brought up in an English family. He had sufficient education to enable him to teach the Indian school at Mushantuxet in Groton for a time; but was finally forced to give it up because they needed one who could "write and cipher" better than he. On the 3d of February, 1757, Rev. Jacob Johnson of Groton wrote Doctor Wheelock that Wauby had done well in the school, but he should have further instruction. So he became a pupil at Lebanon on the eighth of that month. He remained only nineteen weeks, having some "bodily infirmities of long standing" which unfitted him to pursue an extended course of study. The commissioners at Boston again appointed him teacher of the Mushantuxet school October 8, 1759, and in the following year he had charge of the Stonington school. Soon afterwards he became a soldier, serving in 1762 in the company of Captain John Wheatley. He died within a few years, possibly while still in military service. His brief attendance at the Lebanon school did not profit him much; but his friendly relations with Doctor Wheelock continued, and his kinsman, Roger Wauby, became associated with the later life of Samson Occom.

The fourth and fifth pupils were Delawares, Joseph Woolley and Hezekiah Calvin, who arrived April 9, 1757. The former is described as "of middling capacity, naturally modest and something bashful," and the latter as "a smart little fellow, who loves play, and will have his hat in one place and his mittens in another." They remained at the Indian school for eight years, and were among those examined, March 12, 1765, by the Connecticut correspondents of the Scotch Society and approved as schoolmasters. Joseph Woolley had gone to the Six Nations with Samuel Kirkland in the autumn of 1764, and during the following winter he taught an Indian school at Onohoquaga on the Susquehanna river. He returned thither in 1765. His service did not continue long, but he was faithful unto the end and died of consumption in his mission, November 27, 1765, greatly mourned by the Indians. Hezekiah Calvin taught among the Mohawks at Fort Hunter and was so engaged for two years. He eventually disgraced his name, however, and in 1769 Doctor Wheelock wrote of him, "he is turned drunkard and apostate." He is said to have reformed, but his later life is unknown.

The next five pupils were New England Indians, who entered as follows: Joseph Johnson, December 7, 1758; David Fowler, April 12, 1759; Aaron Occom, April 28, 1760; Isaiah Uncas, November 26, 1760; and Amy Johnson, June 2, 1761. Fowler was Occom's pupil at Montauk and the others were Mohegans. Isaiah Uncas was that babe who had been baptized by Rev. Eliphalet Adams in 1750, the son of Sachem Ben Uncas, 3d, once the Mohegan schoolmaster. He was supported by the "Society for Propagating the Gospel" for about two years. Being the chief's son great hopes of his usefulness were at first entertained; but he proved to be "a youth of feeble health and dull intellect." He left the school, though he was afterwards "taken back to work on the farm." As his father died in 1769, he was heir to the sachemship, and received some friendly attentions from the colony. When he married Mary Sowop at North Stonington, November 30, 1769, he was recorded as the "Mohegan Chief," but he did not live to be recognized generally as such, dying in 1770, the last male of the Ben Uncas line. Aaron Occom was another disappointment. His parents brought him to Lebanon in great hope, and his father thus recorded his entrance in his diary; "Delivered up my little son Aaron to Rev. Mr. Eleazar Wheelock to be Brought up by him." He remained there until October, 1761, entered a second time December 8, 1765, and a third time November 9, 1766; but he had no taste for learning, and his life was something of a trial to his father, as related elsewhere.

Joseph Johnson and Amy, his sister, were of a prominent Mohegan family. Their parents were Captain Joseph and Betty Johnson, and the well-known councilor, Zachary Johnson, was their uncle. The father had been a captain of Indian scouts in the French war, and he is doubtless the soldier in Captain Nathan Whiting's company who died September 4, 1758, as his death occurred about that time.[4] Thus being left

---

[4] The following commission is among the *Wheelock Papers, Dart. Coll.*—By Lieutenant Colonel John Young at the Royal-American Regiment: Whereas, Daniel Webb Esquire, Major-General of his Majesty's Forces, hath authorized me to send a Detachment of our faithfull Indians, And being well assured of the Fidelity and Courage of Joseph Johnson, I hereby authorize him to chuse out of the Indians now in our Camp, to the Number of Six and Twenty; whom he is to command, and who are to obey him, not only upon the present Scout, but upon any other he may be employed [on] during the Course of this Campaign (if so long a Time is necessary) But that the said Joseph Johnson and his said Party, shall be at full Liberty to return to their respective Companies and Habitations, either after the present expedition, or when the Time of their present Engagement is expired.

Given under my Hand, at the Camp by Fort Edward, this Second Day of August 1757.

JOHN YOUNG,

Mr. JOSEPH JOHNSON.   Lt Col Royal American Regt

fatherless in his seventh year, Joseph entered the Indian Charity School. He continued there until, "in the third month of his fifteenth year," he was sent out as a schoolmaster to the Oneidas, and his life thereafter is a part of our story. While at school he was a bright, mischievous boy, quick to learn but not very fond of study. His sister Amy left the school early in 1766. She lived in various families, and was employed at Captain Bull's tavern, the "Bunch of Grapes," in Hartford, when David Fowler contemplated making her his wife. Later she returned to Mohegan, and is lost to us.

David Fowler had two advantages when he entered the school—he was older than the other pupils had been, being then in his twenty-fourth year, and he had been trained at Montauk by his brother-in-law, Samson Occom. He was not an exceptional scholar, but he was practical and faithful in every form of service. Doctor Wheelock wrote of him to Mr. William Hyslop, treasurer of the Boston correspondents of the Scotch Society, under date January 29, 1761: "I have one now with me from Montauk whom Mr. Occom taught to read and who is zealously pursuing his studies with a single view to a distant mission if God pleases; who, I apprehend is as promising and every way tempered and turned for that business and as likely to be useful as any I have seen or heard of." The sequel proved the truth of this opinion. Many a time David Fowler was called into important service. He was very skilful in the use of tools and had some knowledge of farming. Hence he became very useful to Doctor Wheelock, as he acknowledged, overseeing the work in the fields which sometimes engaged the Indians. This labor was beneficial also to Fowler. It furnished him an experience in agricultural matters and mechanics which was greatly needed in his after life. It is part of our purpose to follow him to his grave.

On the 1st of August, 1761, three Mohawk boys were

received at the school, Joseph, Negyes and Center. The first was well-clad in Indian fashion and could speak a little English, but the other two were nearly naked. Center became ill and Negyes was sent home with him in the autumn. The former died soon afterwards. The latter did not return to the school, but married and is heard of no more. Joseph's career needs not to be recorded here, for he was the celebrated Mohawk chief Joseph Brant, Thayendanegea, brother of Mary Brant, the Indian companion of Sir William Johnson, and his biography has been fully written.[5] He remained at the school until July 4, 1763, during which time he made commendable progress in his studies and is said to have been converted to Christianity. He was the guide of Samuel Kirkland in his journey westward in the autumn of 1761, became his instructor in the Mohawk language, and was ever his powerful friend. His former schoolmates were many times entertained at his home and he assisted them in their missions. When he left the school he had set out as the interpreter of Rev. Charles J. Smith on a mission which an Indian war interrupted, and Joseph remained among his people. After the lapse of nearly forty years, when his home was in Canada, two of his sons, Jacob and Joseph, were sent to Hanover to school in affectionate remembrance of his own school-days.

During the years while the Indian school was at Lebanon, fifteen other Mohawks became pupils. Moses and Johannes entered November 27, 1761 ; Abraham Primus or Major, Abraham Secundus or Minor, and Peter, July 18, 1762 ; William Primus, William Secundus, and Elias, November 30, 1764 ; Susannah, Katharine, and Mary, June 12, 1765 ; John Green, January 11, 1766 ; Paulus and Margaret, September 28, 1766 ; and Seth, December 8, 1766. The first five of these were examined at Lebanon by the Connecticut correspondents of the Scotch Society, March 12, 1765, and were approved as

<hr/>

[5] *Life of Joseph Brant*, Wm. L. Stone, 2 vols., N. Y., 1838.

"well accomplished for schoolmasters," but on account of
their youth they were appointed to serve as "ushers" in the
mission schools.   There was less dignity in this office, but
they did the same service as their superiors.   Moses taught at
Lake Utsage [Otsego] at the head of the Susquehanna river;
and Abraham Primus and Abraham Secundus among the
Mohawks, where also Peter was established, but did not long
continue on account of illness.   In 1766 "Little Abraham"
was invited to teach a school at "a new settlement of Indians
about eight or ten miles below Fort Stanwix" called Willheske.[6]
Johannes went out as an interpreter for Theophilus Chamberlain, in which capacity he afterwards served Aaron Kinne and
other white missionaries.   The rest of these Mohawks were
not at the school long enough to receive much education.
William Primus was the natural son of Sir William Johnson.
Of him Doctor Wheelock wrote, "William is a very good
Genius and capable of making a very likely man, but his Pride
and the Violence of his Temper have sometimes rendered him
troublesome and obliged me to be severe with him."   He was
sent home December 10, 1766.   Afterwards he was engaged
against the Americans in the Revolution and lost his life in
the struggle.   All the girls returned January 9, 1767, excepting Susannah, who remained some months longer.   Paulus also
returned with the girls.   "Little Elias" was hurt and unable
to continue.   John Green was probably the Mohawk chief's
son taken home by his father February 16, 1767.   At the
same time Doctor Wheelock sent home Seth, who was "so fired
with having been to the wars and killed some Indians that the
house was scarcely good enough for him to live in."

    We have a record of eight or more Oneidas who attended
the school.   Dawet entered June 12, 1765; Mundius and

    [6] This settlement was Oriskany, which is said by Belknap to have been a corrup-
tion of Ol hiskè, a place of nettles.   Gridley, in his History of the town of Kirkland,
spells the Indian word Ockrisk or Orisca.   Samuel Kirkland spelled it Oriske.

Jacob, October 5, 1765 and William, one of David Fowler's pupils, June 27, 1766. When Ralph Wheelock returned from his tour among the missions, October 25, 1767, he brought " Little Peter," son of the deceased Oneida chief, Gawke, a girl and two boys whose names are unknown, and Jacob, who had been kept at home since the spring by his "bad aunts." In his tour the following spring he received five children, three Oneidas, a Tuscarora, and one of the "Uriskee" Indians, besides the son of the Seneca chief, Tekananda, the "Black General," who visited New England with Samuel Kirkland.[7] These were to be sent after him by Thomas, the pious Oneida deacon, who arrived about the first of July, 1768, and probably brought them. His own daughter, Hannah, became then or earlier a pupil. Mundius, having been very ill, was returned by him, and another died at Lebanon. Thus the number decreased so that when Thomas came, January 20, 1769, to remove all the Oneida children, there were only six and none of them had been three years in the school.

There were, therefore, not less than twenty-six, and possibly thirty-two, pupils at the school from the Western tribes. Excepting the eight who came before 1763, they were not there long enough to become civilized. Many of them learned to read, but that was all. We do not know what manner of lives they afterwards lived; Dr. Wheelock did not. They certainly should not be counted as failures of the school. Of the schoolmasters, some, at least, continued faithful.

Who were the remainder of the pupils at this Indian Charity school? Miriam Stores was a Delaware, who entered in September, 1761. She remained until 1764, but her subsequent career is unknown. Enoch Closs and Samuel Tallman were also Delawares who came July 22, 1762, intending to learn trades. The former ran away in 1765. Samuel Tall-

man became a carpenter, lived among the New England
Indians, being at one time at Stockbridge, and was eventually
associated with them in the westward emigration. All the
others were New England Indians, numbering twenty-five,
who are known by name. It is said that seventy Indians
attended the school while it was at Lebanon. This division
accounts for the entire number—thirty-one from New England, thirty-two from the Western tribes, and seven Delawares.
By this detailed study, it is shown that the school accomplished greater results among the Indians in its immediate
neighborhood. When its removal was contemplated, Samuel
Kirkland and Samson Occom both advocated its location
among the Six Nations for this very reason. This, too, was
one consideration which moved Kirkland afterwards to found
Hamilton Oneida Academy. At Hanover the school had to
depend upon remote tribes, which was one cause of its decline.
The Western pupils entered the Lebanon school as savages,
and returned to their native environment. The New England
Indians went from their reservation schools, and even though
some of them did not remain long, they had the encouragement of a civilized element on returning home. They were
lost to Doctor Wheelock, but the influence of the school
remained as a potent factor in their after lives. Samson
Occom perpetuated it and gathered up the fruits.

Of the twenty-five New England Indians who entered the
school after those already mentioned, most are well known to
us. Daniel Mossuck entered July 18, 1762. He was of the
Tunxis tribe at Farmington, and his father, Solomon Mossuck, was one of the prominent Christian Indians in that town,
of whom more is related elsewhere. He only remained a few
months at the school, but he afterwards led a worthy life,
became a soldier in the Revolution, and engaged himself in
Occom's emigration movement. Jacob Fowler, the younger
brother of David, who was born in 1750, entered the school

November 20, 1762. He was, of course, one of Occom's pupils at Montauk, and continued at the school until he went forth on a mission, as the reader will presently learn. He was more of a scholar than his brother and made excellent progress in his studies. Some of these pupils were girls. Sarah Wyoge, who entered April 20, 1762, and Patience Johnson, who entered August 24, 1762, were Mohegans, and both were dismissed in 1764. Hannah Nonesuch, who came March 11, 1768, was also of that tribe, and her parents, Joshua and Hannah, were members of Rev. David Jewett's church. She is said to have Christian descendants now living. Hannah Poquiantup, who entered in September, 1763, was of Niantic, and a relative of Occom. The Narragansett tribe furnished the remainder, excepting Nathan Clap, a Cape Cod Indian, who was possibly at the school a short time and turned out badly.[8] Five of these were children of one family, having a pious mother, Sarah Simons, a widow. Emanuel entered April 10, 1763; Sarah, December 13, 1765; James, in 1767, and Abraham and Daniel in 1768 or 1769. This mother wrote Doctor Wheelock thus when she sent up James: "I have sent my Lettel Son up to you, take him to your self and keep him in subjection. Keep him as Long as you ples til you think that he shall be capabel of bisness."[9] All these children were converted at the school. Sarah is known to have joined Doctor Wheelock's church in November, 1767. Emanuel became a soldier in the Revolution and a settler later at Brothertown. Abraham and Daniel were the only two pupils who removed with the school to Hanover, and we shall meet them both again. Mary Secutor, who entered December 17, 1763, and John, her brother, who entered in 1757, were children of John Secutor, a prominent man in the tribe, and both were enlisted in Occom's emigration plan. James Niles, who was a pupil

---

[8] Chase's *Hist. of Dart. Coll.*, p. 83 ; *Wheelock's Narrative*, 1769, p. 45.
[9] *Wheelock Papers*, Lett. Oct. 12, 1767.

in 1768, was doubtless a nephew of Rev. Samuel Niles, the Indian minister of the Narragansetts, and Samuel Niles, a pupil in 1767, was his son. James became a soldier in the Revolution and removed westward with the Christian Indians. John Matthews was a pupil in 1768 and 1769. He became a member of Wheelock's church, went among the Oneidas with Levi Frisbie in 1769, learned the language under Samuel Kirkland, and in 1772 went on a mission thither with his cousin, Abraham Simons.[10] Hannah Garret entered the school December 17, 1763. She married David Fowler and her descendants have kept the faith for five generations. Of Charles Daniel, who entered December 14, 1765, we know nothing except that he was the son of John Daniel, a prominent Indian at Charlestown, R. I. Abigail and Martha came April 3, 1767, but as we have not their family names, we are unable to follow them.

Two of these Narragansett young men became conspicuous in their tribal affairs, and have an interesting story. John and Tobias Shattock were brothers, and their father was John Shattock or Shaddock, who opposed the sachem Ninegret in selling their lands. They entered the school December 16, 1766. "Toby" was at that time married, and his wife and child also came to Lebanon soon afterwards. They had been pupils of Edward Deake in the Narragansett school where they had already acquired a fair education. Doubtless their purpose was to fit themselves for some mission, as both are known to have been earnest and consistent Christian Indians. It was, however, interrupted by their participation in the land controversy.[11] One or both of them made several trips to Sir William Johnson in the interest of the tribe, bearing Doctor Wheelock's hearty recommendation. Finally the Indian

---

[10] *Wheelock's Narrative*, 1773, pp. 7, 8.
[11] See *A Statement of the Case of the Narragansett Tribe of Indians*, by James N. Arnold, Newport, 1896.

council, despairing of relief from the Colonial government, determined to appeal to the king, and to send John and Tobias Shattock to England in their behalf. They therefore wrote Doctor Wheelock a letter expressing their thanks for his efforts, and their regrets at being compelled to take the young men from the school.[12] This was on the 8th of December, 1767, and they had been pupils about a year. In this letter they say, "we have none so capable of doing business as they are." Having been offered a free passage in the ship of Captain William Chase, they sailed from New York early in January, 1768, and arrived safely at Greenock, Scotland. They bore a letter from Rev. Doctor Clark to Mr. Alexander Moubray, a merchant of Edinburgh, commending them to his care as "some fruits" of Doctor Wheelock's school. On the 15th of April they arrived at Edinburgh, and arrangements were made to forward them on a ship sailing the 18th to London. Mr. Moubray lodged them next door to his home, and they ate at his table. A storm delayed the ship, and on the 21st, as they were at Leith about to sail, John showed symptoms of the smallpox. They were taken back to Mr. Moubray's home, where both were soon at the height of the disease. The best physicians in the city attended them. Nurses were provided, and the merchant's wife "laid aside all concern in her family in order to attend them." The news awakened the compassion of many godly people, who were anxious to do something for the Indian strangers. Rev. Charles Beatty of Philadelphia chanced to be in the city, and with Doctor Erskine ministered to them. On the 6th of May, at about 4 o'clock in the morning, Tobias died. He had been four days blind, but knew the voices of his friends to the last. When he was dying his brother, who was less zealous in the Christian life, was told of his condition. The sad announcement had such an effect upon John that Tobias was com-

[12] McClure's *Mem. of Wheelock*, p. 277.

forted. On hearing it he exclaimed, "Good news! good news!" and fell asleep. Those Good Samaritans of Edinburgh dressed the dead Indian in "a Suitt of fine Mournings," and at 6 o'clock the next evening they bore him to his burial in Grayfriars churchyard, Mr. Moubray carrying his head, Mr. Beatty his right shoulder, Doctor Erskine his left, and a number of ministers and gentlemen following round about the pall. "The best people in town," it is said, "were invited and attended the funeral." Thus says Mr. Moubray, in his letter to Doctor Wheelock detailing this event, "in our Churchyard was Interred the first Christian Indian that ever we heard of, very near the place where is Interred the bodys of those who suffered for the word of Christ's patience in Scotland against Oppressing powers."[13] One Christian Indian of New England at least received a proper burial far away from the graves of his fathers! His mound has, however, long since been leveled by time, and we bring out his forgotten story from the wasting yellow sheet. This was indeed the first Christian Indian who had died in Edinburgh, which is doubtless the meaning; but they knew of another, Samson Occom, who had aroused the interest of Christians throughout England, and who had preached in their churches the year before.

The sequel of this journey is soon told. Tobias, when it was certain that he could not live, made over his right to represent the tribe to his brother, and the assignment received the seal of the mayor of Edinburgh. John went on to London with Mr. Beatty, where his mission was a failure, as so many others were in those days. He returned to America in the September following, and became one of the head men of the Narragansetts.

Samuel Ashbow, the last in our catalogue, was connected with the school only about six months, but he deserves more extended notice, as he became a prominent Indian preacher. He

[13] *Wheelock Papers*, Lett., May 14, 1768.

was born at Mohegan in the year 1718, and his epitaph records
the fact that he was " one of the royal family." What his title
to this honor was we do not know. The Mohegan councilor,
Zachary Johnson, testified before William Williams that the
grandfather of Samuel came from Springfield and fought in
the war with the Pequots; but it was acknowledged that " his
right in the tribe was as good as that of Ben Uncas." His
father was probably the Indian Ashobapow, named in a list of
1692, abbreviated afterwards to Ashpo or Ashbow. Samuel
was one of the pupils of Jonathan Barber in the Mohegan
school, and was converted about the time Samson Occom was.
He seems to have known Doctor Wheelock before the Indian
school was established, for he first united with his church. In
1753 he was teaching the Indian school at Mushantuxet, under
the patronage of the commissioners at Boston, in whose records
he is erroneously called *John* Ashpo. This school he taught
until 1757, when he went into the government service as interpreter. At that time he fell into intemperance. Doctor
Wheelock says : " He behaved very well several years till he
got into a bad company of sailors at New London and got
drunk. He soon after came and with tears informed me of his
fall and seemed much affected, and desired to make a public
confession, and has never tasted since."[14] In 1759 he returned
to Mushantuxet, where he taught the school and exercised his
gifts as an Indian preacher. Soon after his conversion he had
come under the influence of certain lay exhorters of the Separatist school by whom he had been examined and ordained in
their way. "He was not," says Doctor Wheelock, "one of the
most bitter, sensorious, furious and uncharitable sort, but he
has imbibed such independent and Brownistic principles as I
find many good sort of people zealous to defend."[15] Rev. Jacob
Johnson says he taught the school very well, but like Samson

14 *Wheelock Papers*, Lett. to Rev. Gideon Hawley, June, 1761.
15 *Ibid.*

Wauby, who succeeded him in 1757, he could not write and cipher well enough, from which testimony we may judge of his education.[16] He made his home among these Groton Indians for many years until he returned to Mohegan. In a census of 1762 he is called their minister, and was living in a house, having a wife and six children. We conjecture that he had married Hannah Mamnack of the Wangunk tribe, for in 1765 they seem to be among those who had rights in the Mattabesett lands. Most of his children were sons, of whom four, Samuel, Simeon, James and John, died as soldiers in the Revolution. It was in the year 1760 that he first entered the missionary service, going to Onohoquaga. On his return he lodged at Doctor Wheelock's house. He brought news of " a great concern " among the Indians at Jeningo, to whom he was ready to go as a missionary. At that time Doctor Wheelock was projecting such a venture ; but he hesitated in sending out one of Separatist notions. Ashbow, therefore, first made his peace with the orthodox fold by returning to his " Duty and Privilege " in the North church of New London, to which he had taken a letter from Lebanon, agreeing to " desist from preaching until approved by those who may be appointed to examine his qualifications."[17] Meanwhile he had been to Jeningo, and the Indians had invited him to become their minister. On the 29th of July, 1762, a small council met at Mohegan, consisting· of Rev. Messrs. Wheelock, Jewett, Whitaker and Powers. They examined him " concerning his principles and knowledge in Christianity, and enquired into his moral character, and were so far satisfied as to advise that he be devoted to the study of divinity under the care and tuition of some divine for some convenient space of time, and then submit to another examination." In writing Rev. George Whitefield of this council, Wheelock said, " they advised to his

[16] *Ibid.*, Lett. to Wheelock, Feb. 3, 1757.
[17] *Wheelock Papers*, Lett., Jewett to Wheelock, Nov. 1, 1761.

being fitted as fast as may be for a mission, and accordingly I expect him to this school."[18]　He entered on the 25th of September following, and studied under Doctor Wheelock during the autumn and winter, retaining his residence at Mushantuxet, and ministering to the Indians. At the annual "Convention of Ministers," held at the house of Rev. Elnathan Whitman in Hartford, May 12, 1763, a committee was appointed to examine him with reference to a mission at Jeningo. He was approved and received this testimonial that he was a " Man of good Understanding in the most important Doctrines and Principles of Christianity, considering the great Disadvantages he has been brought up under, and he appears to have a truly religious Turn of Mind and to be inspired with a well tempered zeal to introduce and spread the Knowledge of the true God and Saviour among his Savage Brethren in the Wilds of America." The committee accordingly approved of his " Preaching the Gospel among the Indians where the Providence of God shall open the Door for it."[19]　Doctor Wheelock had meanwhile fitted him out for his mission, and he immediately set forth. He was, however, only away six weeks, being obliged to retreat on account of a rupture among the Indians in that region. In the spring of 1764, preparations were made to send him to the Onondagas. He went to Jeningo in the summer of 1766, and remained there during the winter. It is said that he again fell into intemperance, but he reformed, and for years, upon the discontinuance of Wheelock's missions, he labored among the New England Indians, especially at Niantic　His later affiliations were with the Baptists, and he never got rid of his Separatist opinions.[20]　In his latter days he visited Occom's settlement at Brothertown, but he did not remove thither. So far as we know his life in his

[18] *Wheelock Papers*, Lett. Sept. 12, 1762.
[19] *Wheelock Papers*, May 12, 1763.
[20] *Diary of David McClure*, pp. 189, 190.

age was above reproach. Many of the whites knew and respected him. Sometimes he preached in their rural communities. He died at Mohegan, and in the neglected burial-place,
west of the Norwich and New London highway, about half a
mile from the Mohegan church, his grave is marked by a
stone bearing this epitaph : " In memory of Revd Samuel
Ashbow one of the Royal Family who died Novr 7th 1795 in
the 77th year of his age." Mrs. Hannah Ashbow, his wife,
died July 10, 1801. This Mohegan minister was no doubt as
useful as his education and circumstances would permit. He
certainly had some talent as an exhorter and exercised considerable influence among the Indians whose religion was of the
erratic and emotional type.

This introduction we give to the pupils of Wheelock's
Indian Charity School. It has always been said that this
institution was a failure. The immediate results were not, in
some cases, encouraging. Doctor Wheelock, who had depended on charity for their support, felt this most keenly.
He surrendered, in consequence, his early purpose, and turned
to the whites. Yet he himself, in his first Narrative, had said :
" If the one half of the Indian Boys thus educated shall prove
good and useful men, there will be no reason to regret our toil
and expense for the whole." Of those who remained a sufficient time at the school to receive its impressions, the larger
proportion led useful lives, and some of his disappointments
afterwards brought him joy. The New England Indians, at
least, justified his efforts in their behalf. The history of the
Brothertown tribe is the sequel to his Indian Charity School.
It must be remembered, moreover, that the foremost white
missionaries of the time were among his pupils. The heroic
life of Samuel Kirkland and some other ministers received an
impulse in that school at the country crossroads.[21] He never

---

[21] We have not seen any list of the white pupils at Wheelock's school while it was at
Lebanon. In 1762, he had three, in 1765, five, and others later. Those who are

professed to establish a school for Indians alone. Coeducation with the whites was a feature of his plan. This he endeavored to perpetuate, when, in 1770, the school removed to Hanover, N. H., and was incorporated with Dartmouth College.

Some account should be given, in conclusion, of the manner in which this Indian school was conducted. Two descriptions have survived. One is Doctor Wheelock's own, as given in his first Narrative. Of the scholars, he says :

They are obliged to be clean, and decently dressed, and be ready to attend Prayers before Sun-rise in the Fall and Winter, and at 6 o'clock in the Summer. A Portion of Scripture is read by several of the Seniors of them : And those who are able answer a Question in the Assembly's Catechism, and have some Questions asked them upon it, and an Answer expounded to them. After Prayers, and a short Time for their Diversion, the School begins with Prayer about 9, and ends at 12, and again at 2 and ends at 5 o'clock with Prayer. Evening Prayer is attended before the Daylight is gone &c. They attend the publick Worship, and have a Pew devoted to their Use in the House of God. On Lord's-Day Morning, between and after the Meetings, the Master, or some one whom they will submit to, is with them, inspects their Behaviour, hears them read, catechises them, discourses to them &c. And once or twice a Week they hear a Discourse calculated to their Capacities upon the most important and interesting Subjects. And in general they are orderly and governable : They appear to be as perfectly easy and contented with their Situation and Employment as any at a Father's House. I scarcely hear a Word of their going Home, so much as for a visit, for years together, except it be when they first come.[22]

The other account is found in a letter from Mr. John Smith, a Boston merchant, who was interested in the school, and

known to have been pupils there are : Samuel Kirkland, Samuel Gray, David Avery, Phineas Dodge, Eleazar Sweet and, David McClure, Levi Frisbie, Augustine Hibbard, Allyn Mather, John McClaren Breed, Josiah Dunham, John Hall, and Josiah Pomeroy. We conjecture that Sylvanus Ripley and Ebenezer Gurley may also have studied there. Gray, Frisbie, and Ripley graduated at Dartmouth College in 1771, Gurley and Hibbard in 1772, and Sweetland in 1774. [Chapman's *Alumni of Dart. Coll.*] McClure, Avery, and Hall graduated at Yale College in 1769, Breed in 1768, Pomeroy in 1770, and Dunham died while in college.

[22] *Wheelock's Narrative,* 1763, p. 36 ; Cf., *Diary of David McClure,* p. 8.

visited it in 1764. He found, before reaching the place, that
Mr. Wheelock had the reverence of a man of God, and that his
school was held in high esteem. His description is as follows :

I reached his house a little before the evening sacrifice, and was movingly
touched on giving out the psalm to hear an Indian youth set the time, and
the others following him and singing the tenor and bass with remarkable
gravity and seriousness; and though Mr. Wheelock, the schoolmaster and
a minister from our Province (called, as I was, by curiosity) joined in Praise,
yet they, unmoved, seemed to have nothing to do but to sing to the Glory of
God. I omit Mr. Wheelock's prayer, and pass to the Indians; in the
morning when on ringing the schoolhouse bell they assemble at Mr.
Wheelock's house about five o'clock with their master, who named the
chapter in course for the day, and called upon the near Indian, who read
three or four verses, till the master said " Proximus," and then the next
Indian read some verses, and so on till all the Indians had read the whole
chapter. After this, Mr. Wheelock prays, and then each Indian parses a
verse or two of the chapter they had read. After this they entered successively on Prosodia, and then on Disputations on some questions pro-
pounded by themselves in some of the arts and sciences. And it is really
charming to see Indian youths of different tribes and languages in pure
English reading the word of God and speaking with exactness and accu-
racy on points (either chosen by themselves or given out to them) in the
several arts and sciences; and especially to see this done with at least a
seeming mixture of obedience to God, a filial love and reverence to Mr.
Wheelock, and yet with great ambition to excel each other. And indeed in
this morning's exercises I saw a youth degraded one lower in the class who
before the exercises were finished not only recovered his own place, but
was advanced two higher. I learnt that my surprise was common to ministers and other persons of literature who before me had been to visit this
school, or rather College, for I doubt whether in colleges in general a
better education is to be expected; and in mentioning this to a gentlemen
in this town who had visited this Seminary, he acquainted me that he
intended at his own charge to send his son to obtain his education in mixture with these Indians. There were 4 or 5 of these Indians, from 21 to 24
years of age, who did not mix with the youth in these exercises; these I
learnt were perfected in their literature, and stand ready to be sent among
the Indians to keep schools and occasionally to preach as doors open. On
my return, Mr. Wheelock accompanied me a few miles; and on passing by
one house, he said, here lives one of my Indian girls, who was, I hope con-

verted last week; and calling to the farmer, he, unperceived, brought the young girl into our sight; and the pleasure was exquisite to see the savageness of an Indian moulded into the sweetness of a follower of the Lamb.[23]

Such was the school which these Indian pupils attended—unpretentious in its buildings, without charter or other trustees than its friends, dependent wholly upon the charity of a few, and the meager assistance of burdened societies—a school created, maintained and governed by a country minister of Connecticut, who had an idea and a will to carry it out.

[23] *Wheelock Papers,* Lett. May 18, 1764.

CHAPTER V

OCCOM'S MISSIONS TO THE ONEIDA INDIANS

1761–1764

The most attractive field for the missionary enterprise of New England about the middle of the eighteenth century, was among the Six Nations of New York. The influence of this alliance of savages had long been recognized, and their conversion to Christianity had been years before the fond dream of the Jesuits. Among them, too, the Episcopal church had labored through "The Society for the Propagation of the Gospel in Foreign Parts."[1] But interest in these tribes had been revived in consequence of the French and Indian War. On the 2d of June, 1747, the commissioners of the "Society for Propagating the Gospel," meeting at Boston, appointed a committee to look up a suitable person to go among the Six Nations, the same to be supported by the benefaction of Rev. Dr. Williams. Rev. Elihu Spencer was finally secured, and in the autumn of 1748 he was established on the Susquehanna river. He returned the next year and was released.[2] In 1753

[1] Humphreys's *Historical Account ;* Hawkins' *Historical Notices of the Missions of the Church of England ;* Anderson's *Colonial Church,* III, 286 ff ; and Prof. A. G. Hopkins in *Trans. Oneida Hist. Soc.,* 1886.

[2] Elihu Spencer, the son of Isaac and Mary (Selden) Spencer, was born Feb. 12, 1721, at East Haddam, Conn., being a second cousin of David and John Brainerd. He graduated at Yale College in 1746, studied theology, was with John Brainerd among the Indians in the winter of 1747, and with Jonathan Edwards the following summer, and was ordained with a mission in view, Sept. 12, 1748, at Boston. After leaving the mission he was in the Presbyterian ministry at Elizabeth, N. J., Jamaica. L. I., and Trenton, N. J. He died Dec. 27, 1784.—Dexter's *Yale Biographies,* II, 89 : Sprague's *Annals,* III, 165 ; Hopkins's *Hist. Mem. of the Housatunnuk Indians :* and *MS. Rec. Soc. for Prop. Gos.*

the same society sent out Rev. Gideon Hawley, who labored at Onohoquaga until 1756. He then became the Indian missionary at Marshpee, though he visited his old field in 1761 and 1765. Mr. Hawley was the most successful missionary who had hitherto labored in that region.[8] He hid the good seed at least in a few hearts where it germinated. One of his converts was Gwedelhes Agwerondongwas, or "Good Peter," who grew in strength like an oak, and in whom the charter of the faith was safely kept for many a day.[4] To him and his fellow laborer, Isaac Dakayenensere, a reference is made in Kirkpatrick's letter which we shall presently quote.

[3] Gideon Hawley, the son of Gideon and Hannah Hawley, was born in Stratfield, Conn., Nov. 5, 1727. He graduated at Yale College in 1749, and was licensed to preach by the Fairfield East Association, May 1, 1750. In February, 1752, he became instructor in the Mohawk School at Stockbridge, Mass. At the suggestion of Jonathan Edwards, he went in May, 1753, on a mission to Susquehanna, having Mr. and Mrs. Benjamin Ashly as interpreters. Having engaged in this service for a year, he was ordained as the missionary there under the Society for Propagating the Gospel, July 31, 1754, at the Old South Church in Boston. He continued in this field until 1756, served as chaplain of Col. Richard Gridley's regiment in the expedition against Crown Point, and in 1757 was engaged as missionary among the Indians at Marshpee, where he was installed April 8, 1758, and labored until his death, Oct. 3, 1807.— Dexter's *Yale Biographies*, II, 205 ; Sprague's *Annals*, I, 497 ; *Doc. Hist. of N. Y.*, 8°, III, 1031 ; and *MS. Rec. Soc for Prop. Gos.*

[4] Gwedelhes Agwerondongwas [Agwelentongwas] as Wheelock spelled the name, or " Good Peter " [Domine Peter, Peter the Priest, Petrus the Minister] was a chief of the Oneida tribe and belonged to the Eel Clan. He was born early in the century on the Susquehanna River, and was one of the prominent friends of Hawley's missions there. After his conversion he acquired some education and could read and write fairly well. His greatest gift was in Indian oratory, in which he had no equal among the Six Nations. After Hawley left the field he carried on the work alone, preaching and making missionary tours among his people ; and throughout his life he was foremost in all such efforts. The universal testimony is that he was judicious, sober, faithful and consistent as a Christian, and did much to enlighten his people. Rev. Eli Forbes testified that he was as eminent a Christian as any among the English. Rev. Samuel Kirkland, in a letter of Dec. 26, 1792, records his death at Buffalo Creek while attending the Grand Council there, and adds this tribute : " The Oneidas have sustained an almost irreparable loss in the death of Good Peter. His equal is nowhere to be found in all the five nations." He had been one of Kirkland's deacons. A portrait of him is said to have been once exhibited in Mr. Steward's museum in Hartford, and John Trumbull's miniature painted in 1792 is in the Yale Art School.

The attention of the New York correspondents of the Scotch Society having been turned toward Samson Occom as a suitable person to undertake a mission to some distant tribe, they were only awaiting a favorable opportunity to send him forth. This Indian minister, though continuing at Montauk after his ordination, was uneasy there, having hopes of larger usefulness than that small tribe offered him. A call to service soon came by a letter which he received in the last days of 1760. It is given in full from the manuscript in the Connecticut Historical Society :—

New York, Novr 25th 1760

Revd Sir.

Having been called, in this last Summers Campaign, to act in the Capacity of Chaplain to the N. Jersey Regim^t. commanded by Col. Peter Schuyler, I think it my Duty to inform you—That, in our March from Fort Stanwix to the Oneida Lake, we happend to meet with a Number of the Oneida Indians, who seemed to pay a great Respect to that sacred Character, which, from my Apparrel, they easily imagined I sustained—and upon entring into Conversation with them, they agreably surpriz'd me by discovering an earnest Desire of having a Minister setled among them—They informed me that they had collected together (I think) 300 Dollars for erecting an House of Worship, which would be applied to that Purpose as soon as They cou'd get a Minister—They likewise informed me that they had their Children baptized by Ministers in their occasional Visits—and desired me to marry a Couple which I complied with—They appear to have considerable Notions of a Supreme Being, and of Revealed Religion—and there are two Indians of their Nation who attempt something like Preaching on the Sabbath Days. I was further informed by them that not only their own Nation of the Oneidas, But also their Cousins, the Tuscaroras were willing to join in this Affair—and they pressed it upon me to endeavor to send them a Minister, and promised, if I did, they would be Kind to him.

I came under Obligations to use my Influence to have their Desires in this Respect fulfilled. In consequence therefore of my Promise I now write to you—As I have been informed, Sir, you have lately enter'd into the Doors of the Sanctuary, and stand waiting for Employment in any Part of God's House where he shall providentially call you, therefore I hope you will be easily induced to engage in this important Mission—I hope, Sir, your own zeal and forwardness in the Cause of God and for the Salvation of the Heathen supersedes the Necessity of using any Argum.^{ts} I sho'd however add a few were it not that I write in the greatest Hurry, and principally as a Historian of these undoubted facts—for other Argum.^{ts} and Encourag.^{ts} in this Affair I refer you to Mr Bostw.ck's Letter, and in the greatest Hurry subscribe myself. Rev^d and dear Sir.

Your Bro^r and Fellow Labourer in the

Work of the Gospel Ministry

W. KIRKPATRICK.

[To REV. SAMSON OCCOM]

The hurried visit which Rev. William Kirkpatrick had paid to the Oneidas led him to write in too sanguine a strain of their condition. It appears that, on his return to New York, he had mentioned the affair to Rev. David Bostwick, president of the correspondents of the Scotch Society, who had inspired the above letter and who also soon wrote Occom, giving some encouragement of the necessary support if he would go on this mission. Rev. Samuel Buell was greatly interested. It was such a field as he had hoped his Indian friend would find. The time had come for him to print his sermon, preached at Occom's ordination. This he did and he added his own letter to Mr. Bostwick. He referred to Mr. Kirkpatrick's letter when he wrote: "We receive the information as well authenticated that the Oneida Indians (to whom Mr. Occom is going) make the first motion themselves and earnestly request that a gospel minister may be sent among them." He also wrote to Doctor Wheelock, January 13, 1761, saying "Several letters have come to hand (I mean to Mr. Occum and myself) from gentlemen westward . . . a glorious door seems opening for their [Six Nations] being evangelized and for promoting your important school."[5] This letter arrived at Lebanon on the 29th instant with one from Occom on the same subject. Doctor Wheelock was thus led to add a postscript to the letter which, on that day, he had written to Mr. William Hyslop of Boston so warmly commending David Fowler. In this he

---

[5] McClure's *Mem. of Wheelock*, p. 226.

said, "I am informed y^t in consequence of the Invitation of a number of ministers at the westward (I suppose the Correspondent Commissioners in N. Jersie) Mr. Occom has determined to go early next spring on a Mission to the Oneida Indians. He has wrote me desiring that David Fowler, his Brother in Law, the Indian of whom I wrote in ye foregoing Letter may go with him a few months."[6] Moved, therefore, by the desire to send Fowler with Occom to secure some Mohawk youth for his school, Doctor Wheelock visited Boston and met the correspondents of the Scotch Society. Upon his representation they voted, May 7th, " That the Reverend Mr. Wheelock of Lebanon be desired to fit out David Fowler, an Indian Youth, to accompany Mr. Sampson Occom, going on a Mission to the Oneidas, that said David be supported on said Mission for a Term not exceeding 4 Months, and that he endeavour on his Return to bring with him a Number of Indian Boys, not exceeding three, to be put under Mr. Wheelock's Care and Instruction."[7] Thus encouraged, David Fowler was made ready. Occom was intending to start about the middle of May, but he was delayed at Montauk by illness. Fowler was sent to Mohegan to see if they had news of him.[8] Everything was ready and delay at that season might be disastrous. On the 30th of May Occom left his home at Montauk, went to Easthampton to bid his friend Mr. Buell farewell, tarried a day at Mohegan with his mother and on the 8th of June arrived at Lebanon.

On the 10th of June, at three o'clock in the afternoon, an interesting group was gathered before Doctor Wheelock's house opposite the Lebanon sky-blue church. It was one of those historic scenes which might inspire the artist—the dignified Connecticut minister, the comforting presence of his

[6] *Wheelock Papers*, Lett. Jan. 29, 1761.
[7] *Wheelock's Narrative*, 1763, p. 39.
[8] *Conn. Hist. Soc.*, Lett. Wheelock to Occom, May 27, 1761.

matronly companion, a few Indian boys and the young man from a neighboring minister's household, known by name as Samuel Kirkland, but then unknown to fame. Two horses are led out and two Indians leap to their backs, the one a Mohegan in his prime, the other an athletic young Montauk—and thus they set forth to carry the gospel and civilization to the Oneida Indians. These were the first missionaries sent out under the auspices of Connecticut people. The day had come of which Wheelock had often dreamed—that country parson whom an Oneida chief once called "The Great Minister that takes the care of Indians."

Samson Occom shall give his own account of his journey:

Wednesday June yᶜ 10 about 3 P. M. Brother David and I took Leave of Mʳ Wheelock and his Family and Sot out on our Journey for Onoyda by way of New York—Reach'd Heartford about 9 at Night, Lodg'd [at] Capᵗ Daniel Bulls, and were very kindly Treated—the Man seems to be Truely Religious, keep very good order in his House.

Thirdsday June yᵉ 11 about 9 in the Morning we Sot out on our Journey, and got about 6 miles Westward of N. Haven and Lodg'd at one Woodroffs—

Fryday June yᶜ 12. Sot [out] Early in the Morning, got to Stanford at Night Lodgd at a Certain Tavern—

Saturday June yᶜ 13. Went on our way, got within 5 miles of the City of New York, and turn'd in to one Mʳ Goldsmiths.

Sabbath June yᵉ 14 taried at Goldsmiths, we did not go to the City to Publick Worship for fear of the Small Pox, being Informed very Brief [rife ?] there—But I never Saw a Sabbath Spent so by any Christian People in my Life as some Spent it here. Some were Riding in Chairs, some upon Horse Back orthers traveling foot, Passing and Repassing all Day long, and all Sorts of Evil Noises Caried on by our [door] Drunkards were Realing and Stagaring in the Streets, others tumbling off their Horses, there were others at work in their farms, and [if] ever any People under the Heavens Spoke Hells Language, these People did, for their Mouths were full of Cursings, Prophaning Gods Holy Name—I greatly Mistake if these are not the sons and Daughters of Belial.

O thou God of Heaven, thou yᵗ Hast all the Hearts of the Children of men in thine Hands, Leave me not to Practice the Works of these People, but help me, O Lord to take warning and to take heed to my self according to thy Holy Word, and have mercy upon the Wicked, Convince and Convert them to thy Self, for thine own glory.

I have thought there was no Heathen but the wild Indians, but I think now there is some English Heathen, where they Enjoy the Gospel of Jesus Christ too, Yea, I believe they are worse than y^c Savage Heathens of the wilderness,—I have thought that I had rather go with the meanest and most Dispis'd creature on Earth to Heaven, than to Go with the greatest Monarch Down to Hell, after a Short Enjoyment of Sinful Pleasures with them in this World—I am glad there is one defect in the Indian Language, and I believe in all their Languages they Can't Curse or sware or take god's Name in Vain in their own Tongue.

Monday June y^c 15, to the City, and were Conducted to Mr Well's at fresh waters and were Very Kindly receiv'd by him and by all his Family. I believe the Fear of God [is] in their House and this was our Home as long as we Stay'd in the place. The People of the City were Extremely kind to us there was not a Day Scarsly, but that I was invited to Dine with one Gentleman or other. The Ministers of all Sects and Denominations were uncommonly kind to me—my Friends Increased Daily while at New York.

Thirdsday June y^c 25 we left New York and went on our Journey, Reach'd Peekskills at Night—

Fryday June 26 Sot out very Early in the Morning and we made it Night at Rynbeck.

Saturday June ye 27 Sot out very Early, and made it Night between Claverack and Kinderhook—

Sabbath June ye 28. Went to Kinderhook about five Miles, and there Stopt all Day,—but did not go to Publick Worship, Because the People were Barbarians to us and we to them, in our Toungs, they were Dutch.

Monday June y^c 29 left the Place very Early, and got to Albany about 12 o'c and were Conducted to one Mr Hants Vn Santvoord & taried there and the People in Albany were very kind to us, I went to wait upon his Excellency, Gen.^{ll} Amherst the After Noon after we got to Albany, but he was busy and I Coud not see him, one of his waiters Came out to me, and told me I should have the Generals Assistance and I should make my Appearance about 10 in the Morning.

Tuesday June y^c 30. I made my Appearance before his Excellency at the Time Apointed according to orders, his Excellence Met me at the Door and told me he had wrote a Pass for me, and he unfolded it and Read it to me, and when he had Read it, he Delivered it to me, and gave me good Advice and Counsel and wish'd me success in my undertaking & I return^d unfeigned Thanks to him and then took my leave of him &c—The Pass which he gave me was very good one indeed, which I will coppy Down here

By his Excellency Jeffery Amherst & Esq⁵ Major General, and Commander in Chief of all His Majestys Forces in North America &c &c &c— To All Whom it may Concern

Whereas the Corresponderts of the Society in Scotland for Propagating Christian Knowledge, have Acquainted me that the Bearer hereof, the Revd Mʳ Occom, is sent by them, as a Missionary to Reside amongst the Indians about the Onoyda Lake, These are to order and direct the officers Commanding at the Several Posts, to give him any Aid or Assistance he may Stand in need of to forward him on his Journey, and on his Arival at yᵉ Onoyda Lake, the officer Commanding there will grant him all the Protection and Countenance he may want, in the Execution of his Duty &c

Given under my Hand & Seal at Head Quarters in Albany, this 29ᵗʰ Day of June 1761

By his Excellencys
Command   JEFF. AMHERST
ARTHUR MUIR

Wednesday July yᵉ 1 left Albany about 10 in the Morning, got to Scenectady about 3 in the after Noon. Stayed there one Night.

Thirdsday July 2 Went from Senectady In Company with Colo¹ Whiting and Dʳ Rodman, they Seemed to be Quite Friendly gentlemen to us, we got about Seven miles westward of Sir William Johnsons.

Fryday July yᵉ 3 went to See Sir William at His Farm Seven Miles out off the Road, in the Wilderness, got there about 9 in the Morning, and were very Kindly Entertained by his Honor. I Showed him my Recommendatory Letters, and a Pass from Gen¹ Amherst, he Promised me his Assistance as Need Should Require, he was exceeding free with me in conversation—But we stayd there but about two Hours, for he was geting in Readines to go on our way on the Next Day towards Detroit with five Battows Laden with Presents for the Indians, he said he wou'd overtake us on the Morrow before Night—We took Leave of his Honor and went our way, after we had got to the Main Road, we Call'd in at Certain House, and there we were Detained one Night by a Storm.

Saturday July yᵉ 4. Went on our Journey and Reach'd the German flats at Night, and we Turn'd in at one Mʳ Frank's, a Tavern Keeper—

Sabbath July yᵉ 5 we stayᵈ at Mʳ Franks. but did not go to Publick Worship with the People, because they Spoke unknown Toungue to us, But it did Seem like Sabbath by the appearance of the People—

July the 6—Sir William came to us at Mʳ Franks

Tuesday July yᵉ 7. Sir William and the Chiefs of the Onoyda Indians Met at this Place, to make up a Breach, which one of the Indians made lately, by Killing a Dutchman, they talked about an Hour at this Time, and then Brok up. Towards Night they Met together again, and talk'd together about 3 quarters of an Hour, then finaly Brock up without being fully Satisfied on both sides for, the Indians Insisted upon an old agreement that was Settled between them and the English formerly, that if any Such Acident Should ever happen between them in Peaceable Times, they Shou'd make it up in an Amicable manner without sheding of Blood. But Sir William told them it was the Comand of General Amherst, that the murderer Shoᵈ be delivered up to Justice—but the Indians said that [the] murderer was gone off no body knows where &c.[9]

What further transpired during Samson Occom's first mission to the Oneida Indians must be gathered from other sources, as the diary suddenly breaks off. It appears that the correspondents at New York, though they had urged Occom to undertake this service, had not made ready to support him. His own account is given in a letter to Doctor Wheelock:

NEW YORK, June ye 24, 1761.

Revᵈ Sir.

We reached New York yᵉ 15 Inst and to my Surprize, the Gentlemen had concluded not [to] send me at all, and all the Reason that they can give is, they are affraid the Indians will kill me. I told them, they cou'd not kill me but once, and told them I intended to Proceed on my Journey and if I Perish for want of Support I perish. But I intended to use your Money Sir that David has with him, and when they Perceived my Resolution, they Emediately Consulted the Matter and Concluded that I should go, and a Collection should be made for me, and Recommendations shou'd be sent by me to Genˡ Amherst and to Sir William.

And the whole Matter is Acomplished to my Surprize beyond all my expectations. The Last Sabbath after the afternoon Service was over at Mʳ Bostwick's Congregation, they made a Collection for me and my Family's support, and it mounted to £60, s. 15, d. 7, and Monday Evening the Baptists made a Collection for me at their Meeting House and it mounted to £13. And my Recommendations are done by the Most Noted Gentlemen of this Place, not only to the generals, but to other genⁿ of their Acquaintance, from this City to the furthermost English Settlements. The People are uncommonly kind to us in this great City. But we live in yᵉ suburbs with one Obediah Wells an old Disciple. I am Invited to the City every Day to Dine with Some gentleman or other. Some times Two or three Invitations at once. Especially the Ministers of all Sects and

---

⁹ *Occom's MS. Diary*, Dartmouth College.

Denominations are Extreamly kind to me—Yesterday 3 o'c P. M. I was Intr[oduced] to wait upon his [Excellency] Colden, President and Commander in Chief in the Province of N. York, and [he] wished me good Success and Gave me good advice and Counsil—I believe tomorrow Morning we Shall [set] out from here on our Way to Onoyda.

Please to remember us in your Fatherly Pray' Continually. Except Duty and Sutable Regards to the Family from

Your Most Obedient Indian Son

SAMSON OCCOM.[10]

To Revd Mr. WHEELOCK

The recommendations to which reference is made were signed by Hon. William Smith, Rev. David Bostwick, Mr. P. V. B. Livingston, Mr. David Vanhorne, and William Livingston, Esq. These, with the passport of General Amherst and letters which he bore from Doctor Wheelock and others to Sir William Johnson, were a guarantee of favor and protection.

In response to Doctor Wheelock's request, Sir William Johnson sent on from German Flats, where he then was on his way to Detroit, the three Indian boys, who arrived on the 1st of August.[11] One of these was Joseph Brant. Fowler was going on farther, partly to accompany Occom, but also in the hope of conducting other boys whom Sir William Johnson intended to secure farther west. He had even been authorized to go as far as the Senecas, but he tarried with Occom among the Oneidas. From German Flats they went on with Sir William Johnson to Oneida Old Castle, where they arrived on the 16th of July. We have in Johnson's diary the following entry as to that day:

Thursday 16th.—Sent off the baggage boat, and went up in a whale boat toward the Oneida Old Castle, in order to meet with the chiefs of that place, who were sent for the night before; but they not being at home, I delivered what I had to say to one of their chiefs in the presence of several of their women, and the Reverend Mr. Oaum, whom I very strongly recommended to them, as I did, also, a friendly behavior toward all their

---

[10] *Wheelock Papers.*

[11] McClure's *Mem. of Wheelock*, p. 228.

brethren, that I might hear no more complaints against them on my return, nor from them against the officers, soldiers or others as usual.[12]

This was a very auspicious introduction which Occom and Fowler thus had to the Oneidas. The best account we have of their labors is in a letter which Doctor Wheelock wrote to Rev. George Whitefield.[13] It is as follows:

My black Son Mr Occom has lately returned from his Mission to the Onoyadas, and the last week I had the Pleasure to see him with one of that nation (who designs to winter with him and learn the English Language & teach Mr Occom Mohawke) and I was agreeably entertained with Mr Occom's Journal. I can only suggest to you a few things most material in it. And to begin where I left off in my Last. When he first came among them they seemed shy of him thro' a Jealosie that something was designed by the English against them, but when Genl Johnson had read his Letters Recommendatory, they appeared well satisfied & much pleased, and as a Testimony of it the Kings of the Onoydas and Tuscaroras, & many others of their Chiefs came & shook hands with him and bid him wellcome among them. Their Chiefs then held a Council to fix upon the best methods to accomodate him with that which was necessary for his comfortable subsistance among them, and you would not wonder that their Chiefs held a councel upon this Head if you knew how extreamly poor they are, having scarce anything that may be called Bread or anything else except what they get by hunting to subsist upon. They proposed to Mr Occom to Chuse where to Live, and whether to live in a house already Built. He chose the Place and let them know y^t he chose to live with David (my Indian Schollar) and to live by themselves. They immediately built him a House the structure of which, could the Form & Workmanship thereof be truly represented, might gratify not a little the curiosity of a Brittain, though there was nothing in it y^t resembled the Temple of old save that there was not the noise of axes or Hammers in the Building of it. The Materials were the simple Product of nature, the Remains of the Oakes & chestnuts fell many years ago by the violence of wind. Many of them attended his Ministry & appeared attentive. Numbers from distant Nations came to hear him, and some seemed really desirous to understand and know the truths which most nearly concerned them. And when he was about to leave them their chiefs held another council. The consequence of which was that Old Connoquies (who had been King among the Onoyadas but had now resigned by Reason of Age) the King of the Tuscaroras and other Chiefs, presented

[12] Stone's *Life and Times of Sir William Johnson*, II, 432.
[13] *Wheelock Papers*, Lett. Nov. 25, 1761.

him a Belt of Wampum to these Instructions which he received from old Connoquies, viz.

1—We are glad from the inside of our Hearts that you are come hear to teach the right way of God. We are also thankful to those who sent you, and above all to God

2—We intend by the help of God to repent of all our sins and all our heathenish ways & customs. We will put them all behind our Backs, and will never look on them again but will look strait forward and run after Christianity.

3—If we shall try to set up a School we beg the Assistance of the English if they see fit.

4—We desire that strong Drink may be prohibited, that it may not be brought among us for we find it kills our Bodies and Souls; and we will try to hinder it here.

5—We desire to be protected on our Lands, that none may molest or encroach upon us.

6—This Belt of Wampum shall bind us fast together in perpetual Love and Friendship.

Mr. Occom delivered it to those Gentlemen to whom it was directed, but obtained their Leave to bring it hither to gratify my Curiosity, and a curious Girdle it is. Mr Occom says it could not be made for less than £15 sterling.[14]

This address was delivered to Occom in the council-house after an hour's deliberation, and in the presence of "a great number of Indians." He regarded the occasion as significant —the Oneidas' formal welcome to Christianity.[15] As this meeting was on the 18th of September, the night before he

[14] The whereabouts of this famous wampum belt is now unknown to us. Two years afterwards the Indians wished it returned, thinking themselves neglected. [*Narrative*, 1767, p. 28.] Doctor Wheelock had sent it back to New York. When Occom went to England, Doctor Whitaker wrote for it, as follows: "Mr. Occom says y^t w^n he was in N. York last fall he saw the religious belt of Wampom sent by him to New York when he returned from his Mission among the Oneidas, which belt was to be sent to Scotland. He says it was then in Judge Wm Smiths. . . . This would be of great use to us as Mr. Occom remembers the Speach. Pray procure it and send it to us in all haste" [*Wheelock Papers*, Lett. December 3, 1765]. They received it either before they sailed or after reaching London, and it was used in presenting the cause to the General Assembly and churches in Scotland [Communication in the *New London Gazette*, Sept. 25, 1767, dated at Edinburgh, July 8, 1767].

[15] *Wheelock's Narrative*, 1767, pp. 27, 28. The date here should be the 18th instead of the 8th, as we learn from other sources.

left them, he had been there about nine weeks. A part of
the time Edward Johnson had been his interpreter; but such a
method of communication was unsatisfactory. Therefore, he
took a young Oneida Indian home with him as his tutor in the
language during the winter. He and Fowler soon learned to
speak in the Oneida tongue with fluency, and to some extent
they acquired the languages of other tribes.

While Occom was at Oneida, he wrote a letter, it seems, to
Mr. Bostwick, giving some account of his experiences. Thereupon the president of the correspondents addressed a communication to the directors of the society in Scotland, September
23d, which was printed in connection with the anniversary
sermon of Thomas Randall in 1763.[16] From this we quote Mr.
Bostwick's opinion of the mission and the missionary :

He has met with a very favourable reception; perhaps the more so, on
account of his being an Indian. He writes, That there are four considerable towns on the Oneyda lake : That they have already built a house for
religious worship, where he preaches every Lord's day : That he has baptized five or six persons this summer; and that there are many adjacent
tribes among whom he intends to make excursions. He has retained his
mother-tongue, and can speak the language of his own tribe (which is the
Mohegon) something better than he can the English. But the Oneyda language differs so much from the Mohegan, that he is obliged to use an interpreter for the present, tho' doubtless he would learn their language well in
a little time, could he reside among them. He is married to an Indian
woman, who is also esteemed truly pious, and has six children, with whom
he would gladly dwell in the wilderness if he could be supported as a Missionary, and very easily might his children be educated in that language—
He well understands the bissiness of farming, having chiefly supported his
family by it, while he preached to the handful of Indians upon Long Island ;
and therefore, could instruct the Indians in cultivating their lands, which
are very good. He has acquired a tolerable acquaintance with Latin,
Greek and Hebrew, with the sciences &c. and is really a good Divine. His

16 Supplement to Randall's sermon on "Christian Benevolence," preached Jan. 3,
1763, with the title "An Account of some late Attempts by the Correspondents of the
Society for Propagating Christian Knowledge to Christianize the North American
Indians. Edinburgh. Printed in the Year M.DCC.LXIII." 8° pp. 12.

piety is unquestionable, having been manifested by a more than ten years exemplary conduct. His temper is very amiable and Christian like, full of humility and meekness. His heart is much set on preaching the gospel to the Indians, and he seems willing to spend and be spent, to do or suffer any-thing for their conversion and salvation. In short, nothing is wanting to fix him there, but a support. He purposes to come down this autumn and spend the winter with his family (yet on Long Island), and 'tis likely he will try to remove his family to the Oneyda lake in the spring. We shall endeavour to support him by contribution till some surer method can be found or assistance be obtained from some charitable Society in Scotland or England. I therefore humbly request, as this event has opened so agreeable a prospect for spreading the gospel among the Heathen, that the Society would receive Mr. Occom as their Missionary with proper instruc-tions, and liberty to draw upon them for such salary as they shall fix; and would commit the management of said mission to those of the Correspond-ents who reside in this city, as we are most convenient to write to, or receive intelligence from that part of the wilderness.

His journey homeward was begun on the 19th of September from Kanawarohare via Tuscarora and Old Oneida. At the latter place he preached on the following Sabbath to a large assembly of Indians. On the 25th they were at Fort Herki-mer, and Occom was compelled to remain there several days because his horse strayed. He was then somewhat broken in health. The life in the wilderness had so affected his eyes that he had been unable to read or write for some weeks. During his mission he had received no word from Doctor Wheelock, though several letters had been sent. Fowler probably left him there, going directly to Lebanon, and Occom returned by the way of New York to Montauk, where he arrived on the 22d of October. Thus ended his first mis-sion to those Oneida villages where Samuel Kirkland after-wards spent his life.

He set out on his second mission in the month of June, 1762. That season he did not have the companionship of David Fowler. This Mercury of the Indian missions made a trip to Johnson Hall in behalf of the school, and returned the

18th of July with three Indian youth.[17]   The best account we have of the Oneida mission that season is in a letter from Doctor Wheelock to Rev. George Whitefield :

Lebanon 16 Sep[r] 1762

My very dear and Hon[d] Sir.

David, my Indian Scholar returned July 18 from the Mohawk Country, where I informed you in my last I sent him, and bro[t] with him 4 Indian Boys, three Mohawks and one of the Farmington Tribe.   The Boys and Girls which I expected from Onoyada were detained by their Parents on acco[t] of a Rumour, & Suspicion of a War just comencing between them and the Nations back of them and in such a case they s[d] they did not chuse to have their Children at such a distance from them, but perhaps they were Suspicious y[t] they should be obliged to Joyn those Nations against the English.   The English youth of which I informed you, who has been a Captive with the Senecas till he is Master of their Language, and which I sent for with a view to fit him for the Interpreter to that Nation, was under such ingagements to a Trader at Block Fort as that he could not get released for the present.   I have again wrote to Gen[l] Johnson who was not at Home when David was there till the Night before David came away, to procure and send y[e] youth if he esteems him likely to answer the Design.

M[r] Occom writes me a very meloncholly Letter, viz, that by an untimely Frost last fall their Indian Corn was all cut off—y[t] the Onoyadas are almost starved hav[g] nothing to live upon but what they get by Hunting— that they had then just come in from their Pigeon Hunt—and were going a fishing—as soon as they return from that they will go after Deer—that he followed them, but found it very Difficult to get a number of them together to preach to them—that by hard living (tho' they were as kind as they could be) and especially lying upon the wet ground his old Disorder, (viz Rhumatic) returnd, and he was apprehensive he must return before the Time appointed—that he lived in fear of being killd, tho' the Indians had promised him in case a war should break out, they would send him under a Sufficient Guard, down as far as the English Settlements.   But there was Something good in his Letter, viz. that there were visible good Effects of his Labours among them last year & especially a Reformation among them as to their Drinking. . . .

ELEAZAR WHEELOCK.[18]

---

[17] *Wheelock Papers*, Letts. July 6, 1762, and Aug. 20, 1762. *Doc. Hist. of N. Y.*, IV, 313.   The date of Fowler's return, in Doctor Wheelock's letter, is the 18th, though he enters the pupils in his list on the 28th.

[18] *Wheelock Papers*, Lett. Sept. 16, 1762.

Occom returned earlier that autumn than was intended "on account of the present ruffle which ye Oneidas are in, being engaged in a war with some of the natives back of them." This condition of affairs also affected the Indian mission at Onohoquaga.[19]   On his way home he preached in the white settlements along the Hudson river wherever he could gather a congregation.   His ministry was very acceptable, particularly in the region about seventy miles above New York, where there was considerable religious interest.   This fact was made known to the Suffolk Presbytery, meeting at Huntington on the twenty-eighth of October, whereupon they passed the following minute : " A great Number of People adjoining or near to the North River, being Destitute of a preached gospel as Represented to the Presbytery by Mr. Sacket, together with a prospect of Mr. Occum being greatly serviceable among them, the Presbytery doth Recommend it to Mr. Occum to go & Labour among sd People in the work of the gospel Ministry as much of the Ensueing Winter as his Circumstances may

[19] The mission at Onohoquaga (Colesville, Broome Co., N. Y.) had been resumed in 1761 by the Boston commissioners of the London Society. They voted July 13th to send Hawley thither with Amos Toppan on a visit. They went and returned in October. In 1762 Rev. Eli Forbes and Asaph Rice [Sprague's *Annals* I. 493] were sent out, some say by the London commissioners and others by the Boston correspondents of the Scotch Society. The fact is, this was a union mission, entered into by the commissioners, correspondents and authorities of Harvard College, in view of the incorporation, Feb 11, 1762, of the "Society for Propagating Christian Knowledge among the Indians of North America" by Massachusetts, which was intended to combine these agencies, and whose charter failed. The Scotch Society took the lead and was assisted by the others, hence the confusion. Messrs. Forbes and Rice started June 1st and arrived at Onohoquaga about the middle of the month [*Conn. Hist. Soc.*, Lett. Forbes to Occom, July 26, 1762.]. They established schools and formed a church. Mr. Forbes returned in September, and his place was to be filled by Rev. Joseph Bowman, ordained Aug. 31, 1762 (ordination sermon by Dr. Chauncey in print), who was delayed by illness. The wars then interrupted this mission. In 1765 it was resumed under the Boston commissioners, who sent out Rev. Ebenezer Moseley (son of Rev. Samuel Moseley of Windham [Hampton], Conn.), with James Dean as interpreter and Rev. Gideon Hawley to introduce them. Mr. Moseley remained in this mission until Feb., 1772, when he was succeeded by Rev. Aaron Crosby, who continued there until August, 1777.

admit." Undoubtedly he went. It was his first experience as an itinerant preacher in the region where he was afterwards a frequent and welcome visitor.

Again, in the season of 1763, Occom made a visit to the Oneida country. He was, however, soon compelled to return on account of the Pontiac War. The same calamity befell the mission that year undertaken by Rev. Charles Jeffry Smith, with Joseph Brant as guide and interpreter, upon which they set out on the fourth of July. Mr. Smith had been a tutor at the school and was ordained at Lebanon on the thirtieth of June, Doctor Wheelock preaching the sermon, which was printed in London in 1767.[20] That season, also, Rev. Samuel Ashbow was turned back from Jeningo, whither he had gone on the 6th of August. In consequence of the war all missionary operations were suspended.

Meanwhile Doctor Wheelock, at the suggestion of the Ministers' Association which met in Hartford, May 12, 1763, had memorialized the General Assembly of Connecticut, requesting that a brief be issued for collections in the churches. This request was granted. The brief contained the following statement of the case: " And seriously considering the present new and extraordinary Prospect (by the Blessing of Heaven on his Majesty's Arms) Doth greatly encourage an Attempt to promote Christian Knowledge and Civility of Manners among the Indian Nations of this Land."[21] This public approval seemed

---

[20] Charles Jeffry Smith, the son of Henry and Ruth (Smith) Smith, was born in Brookhaven, L. I., in 1740, and graduated at Yale College in 1757. After studying theology for some years at New Haven, he assisted Doctor Wheelock in his school during the winter of 1762 and further prepared himself for an Indian mission. Upon the failure of his mission in 1763, he returned to Long Island where he had a considerable estate. Subsequently he preached about in Virginia and the south, whither he purposed to remove in 1770, but on the 10th of August he was killed by the discharge of his gun, either by accident or intent while temporarily insane. Rev. Samuel Buell preached a sermon on the death of his friend which is in print.— Dexter's *Yale Biographies*, II, 495-497.

[21] *Wheelock Papers*, MS. and Broadside, which was printed at New London by T. Green. The Conn. Hist. Soc. has the broadsides of 1763 and 1766. See *Conn. Col. Rec.* XII, 151, 152. *Conn. Archives, Coll. and Schools*, II, 1, 2.

encouraging. Governor Fitch even promised to mention the matter in his Thanksgiving proclamation. But before the brief had been published in all the churches, the Indian War had caused a reaction in popular sentiment unfavorable to such ventures. The General Assembly, therefore, in the October session, at the suggestion of some who had not contributed, ordered the discontinuance of the publication.[22] Three years afterwards, that body at its May session, upon Doctor Wheelock's memorial, ordered a second brief.[23] He received from the first about £40, and from the second about £155, which proved of great assistance in his accounts.

The failure of Doctor Wheelock hitherto to secure a charter for the Indian school had led him to look for some organized board in which to vest the responsibility. His enterprise needed the confidence of the public, which no private management could long retain. He had enemies at Boston among the correspondents of the Scotch Society. It was also evident that the commissioners of the "Society for Propagating the Gospel" would aid him only to a limited extent. He saw that the appropriation from the Sir Peter Warren legacy would soon cease, as it did in 1765. In his perplexity he turned to his friends abroad, and made application to the "Society in Scotland for Propagating Christian Knowledge" for the establishment of a Board of Correspondents of that society in Connecticut similar to those in New York and Boston.[24] This request was granted and such a board was constituted by a vote of the parent society, March 13, 1764.[25] The following men, nominated by Doctor Wheelock, were appointed to comprise it: Jonathan Huntington, Esq., of Windham, Elisha Sheldon,

---

[22] *Conn. Col. Rec.*, XII, 193; McClure's *Mem. of Wheelock*, pp. 236, 237.

[23] *Conn. Col. Rec.*, XII, 490, 491.

[24] Wheelock seems to have made an application March 24, 1762, which was not received, and to have renewed it September 21, 1763.—Chase's *Hist. of Dart. Coll.*, p. 35. Cf. McClure's *Mem. of Wheelock*, p. 242.

[25] See the commission in McClure's *Mem. of Wheelock*, pp. 34–36.

Esq., of Litchfield, Mr. Samuel Huntington of Norwich, Rev. Messrs. Solomon Williams of Lebanon, Joseph Fisk of Stonington, William Gaylord of Norwalk, Samuel Moseley of Windham, Eleazar Wheelock of Lebanon, Benjamin Pomeroy of Hebron, Richard Salter of Mansfield, Nathaniel Whitaker of Norwich, and David Jewett of New London.   These names are given to make evident the fact that most of them were his personal friends and in fact members of the Windham Association, which had long fathered his school. The purpose of this board, as expressed in its commission, was "to receive donations from well-disposed persons, and to employ the same for promoting Christian knowledge, in such manner as shall be directed by the donors, and failing such direction, to devise schemes for propagating our holy religion among the Indians, and to carry them into execution."   This commission was forwarded March 15, 1764, by Doctor Wheelock's friend, Rev. John Erskine, of Edinburgh, was received in June, and on the fourth of July the correspondents met for organization.   Rev. Solomon Williams was chosen president, Mr. Jonathan Huntington, treasurer, and Doctor Wheelock, secretary.   By this board the standing of the school was greatly improved.   The secretary wrote Doctor Erskine, "I feel my hands strengthened, and heart encouraged thereby; and account it a great token of God's favour towards the general design."

After the discouragements of 1763, Samson Occom, seeing no prospect of doing service among the Six Nations, turned to his friends, the commissioners at Boston, who had hitherto supported him.   On the twenty-third of February, 1764, they voted to employ him as missionary to the Niantics, "apprehending that he might serve them as also the Mohegans and other Indians in that neighborhood," fixing his salary at £30 per annum, as they had proposed in 1759.   This was a service much to Occom's desires.   He knew these tribes and was respected among them.   Doctor Wheelock wrote Whitefield say-

ing, " He is zealous, preaches to good acceptance, ye Indians
at Mohegan and Nihantic are all to a man attached to him, his
assemblies much crowded with English as well as Indians & I
think a good prospect of his usefulness."[26]   He accepted this
ministry on the third of April, and at once set about removing
his family from Montauk to Mohegan.   It was then that he
" lost by distress of weather a considerable part of what he
had."   This was partly made up to him by his friends.

At Mohegan was his tribal inheritance.   His mother, his
brother Jonathan and his sister Lucy were then living there.
He held, according to the customs of his tribe, a tract of land
containing several acres.   Probably it was the very place in
" Ben's town " where his father had lived.   Here he set about
building a house for the accommodation of his large family.
It stood on the hillside about half a mile north of the present
Mohegan chapel and east of the Norwich and New London
highway.   He has left us no record of its dimensions, but it
was well built and clapboarded with cedar.   The cost was
something over £100 and the account shows that much of the
labor on it was performed by his fellow Indians.   This house
survived until quite recent times.   It became a famous landmark and was frequently visited by those who were interested
in the tribe or knew the story of the Mohegan minister.

In 1772 Messrs. McClure and Frisbie tarried there over
night, and the former wrote in his diary : " His house was a
decent two-story building.   We lodged in a good feather bed
in a chamber papered & painted ; adjoining was his Library of
a handsome collection, brought by him, principally from Great
Britain."

The well-known sketch of this house, here reproduced, was
made by John W. Barber when on his tour in that region and
was published in his volume of Connecticut Historical Collec-

---

[26] *Wheelock Papers*, Lett. May 18, 1764.

tions.[27]   Doctor Wheelock wrote Whitefield about it, "Mr. Occoms house is covered and likely to be made comfortable for his Family this winter. The expense of which is much more than I expected."[28]   Occom intended to do much of the work himself, but he was called away by Wheelock, as we shall presently see, and the house was not completed that season. Moreover, the bills were not paid as Wheelock had agreed when Occom went into his service. As matters turned out for the Indian, the building of this house was a providential circumstance. It gave him a home in the midst of his acres at a time when he had not much beside to depend on. He was thus established in the midst of the Indian settlements of Connecticut where he afterwards labored. Thither many of them went to seek his counsel. Even the white man, as he traveled along the turnpike road from the north or the south, turned aside to greet the Indian preacher. We have the words of one who met him there in the May of that very year: "In passing . . . through the Mohegan country, I saw an Indian man on horseback whom I challenged as Mr. Occom, and found it so. There was something in his mien and deportment both amiable & venerable; and though I had never before seen him, I must have been sure it was he."[29]

It will be noted that Occom had only been at Mohegan a few weeks before the commission constituting the Connecticut correspondents of the Scotch Society was received. At their first meeting they voted to take him into their service if the commissioners at Boston would release him. This they did on the twenty-fifth of July, on condition that the correspondents would employ him in a mission westward. The release was received on the third of August and three days afterwards the

[27] *Conn. Hist. Coll.*, p. 340; De Forest's *Indians of Conn.*, p. 463; *Bostonian* March, 1895, p. 677.
[28] *Wheelock Papers*, Lett. Oct. 10, 1764.
[29] *Wheelock Papers*, Lett. John Smith, May 18, 1764.

THE MOHEGAN CHAPEL, 1831

SAMSON OCCOM'S HOUSE AT MOHEGAN

correspondents met. They agreed to send him to the Mohawk country as soon as possible, to teach and preach as he had opportunity, and to go on the way to Lake Ontario until he met Sir William Johnson, then returning from Detroit, with a view to offering missionaries to the Western Indians who were in his company. He was also to prepare the way for the schoolmasters whom Wheelock was intending to send to the Six Nations the following season. David Fowler was to be again his companion and they were to bring back fifteen or twenty Indian youth.

This move was a mistake and in some respects a serious one. It was, however, the means of strange developments, which altered the course of Occom's life and eventually affected the future of the Indian school. The Connecticut correspondents had no means to forward this mission. Doctor Wheelock was already in debt for the maintenance of his pupils. He presumed to depend upon the efforts of Rev. George Whitefield, then in New York, through whom he had only shortly before received £120, York money. On the seventh of August he wrote Whitefield a letter in which he said, "We have done this without money on the credit of the great Redeemer." His patron did not look at the matter in that light. Occom and Fowler did not. Armed with letters to General Gage and Sir William Johnson, they set out August 27th by boat from Norwich to wait on Whitefield at New York, "by whom or some other means" they had been led to expect their mission would be supported. Occom doubtless summed up his thoughts on the voyage when he wrote, "It looks like Presumption for us to go on a long Journey thro' Christians without Money, if it was altogether among Indian Heathen we might do well enough"—a characteristic remark which he did not intend to be humorous. They reached New York safely and met Whitefield. He was greatly displeased at the plan, not a little offended at Wheelock's course, and declined to aid in forwarding the mission.   Thus the scheme of reaching the Indians of the far West was crushed.   Occom was returned home to Mohegan, and Fowler resumed his place in the school. This ended Occom's connection with the Oneida missions. He only made a hasty journey the next season to Sir William Johnson to obtain testimonials which he might take to England.   He had done a worthy service in the early dawn of a brighter day for Kanawarohare.

CHAPTER VI

SAMUEL KIRKLAND AND HIS INDIAN FRIENDS

1765–1768

Among all the English youth who devoted their lives to Indian missions, and went out from New England to the Six Nations, Samuel Kirkland was the foremost.[1] His name will always be honored in that region of New York where once the Oneidas roamed through the primeval forest, and where now he sleeps under the protection of Hamilton College with the Christian chief Skenandoa by his side. His ancestors were among the original settlers at Saybrook when that romantic colony was planted in 1635, and thence his father, Daniel Kirtland, went to Yale College to prepare for his ministry of thirty years over the Newent Society in Norwich, now the First church of Lisbon, Connecticut. Here the son, Samuel, was born December 1, 1741, being the fourth in a family of eleven children. He seems to have had his thoughts turned in his youth toward a missionary life, and possibly through an acquaintance with Samson Occom, who was known in every minister's household of the region. Having at least this purpose distinctly in view he entered the Indian Charity School, October 31, 1760. He there formed those friendships with the Indian pupils which were of great service to him and to them throughout his life. Prominent among these was Joseph Brant, of

[1] See on the life of Samuel Kirkland, *Life of Kirkland*, Sparks' *Am. Biog.*, Vol. XXV ; McClure's *Mem. of Wheelock* ; Gridley's *Hist. of Kirkland* ; Jones' *Annals of Oneida County* ; Chase's *Hist. of Dartmouth College* ; Sprague's *Annals*, I, 623 ; *Ded. of Monument to Samuel Kirkland*, Utica, 1873 ; MSS. *Wheelock Papers*, Dart. Coll.; *New York Arch.*, Albany ; *Conn. Hist. Soc. Indian Papers* ; and *Papers of Mr. Thornton K. Lothrop.*

whom he began to learn the Mohawk language, and with whom
he set out November 4, 1761, on a journey to Sir William Johnson, returning on the twenty-seventh of the same month.   On
the third of November the year following he entered the sopho-
more class of Princeton College, on that day opening what he
called his "Accompt with the Christian World."   Here he
was largely supported by charity.   The reason why he left
college before his graduation, which has never been fully
stated, was twofold—the difficulty of obtaining the funds to
continue him there, and the need Doctor Wheelock had of
sending just such a man into active missionary work.   So the
young college student, who had taken the fancy of spelling
his name Kirkland, was despatched November 20, 1764, to
the savage Senecas, having the Delaware, Joseph Wooley, as a
companion part of the way.   The Indian then began his work
at Onohoquaga, whence he shortly passed to his reward.   Samuel Kirkland went on to the Senecas, where he was engaged
for a year and a half in the most adventurous mission of the
time.   It raised him at once to the front rank as a missionary
to the Indians.   Doctor Wheelock wrote of this service to the
Countess of Huntingdon thus: "This bold adventure of his,
which considered in all the circumstances of it, is the most
extraordinary of the kind I have ever known, has been
attended with abundant evidence of a Divine blessing."[2]

The season of 1765 was the most eventful in the history of
Doctor Wheelock's Indian missions.   It seemed to him that
the time had come to prove that his pupils were fitted for
usefulness.   On the twelfth of March the Connecticut Board of
Correspondents met at Lebanon to examine his candidates.
It was a memorable day.   At the very hour of their meeting
there arrived from Onohoquaga "Good Peter" after a journey
of three hundred miles through the deep snow—the envoy of
the Oneidas to ask for a minister.   Within half an hour Elisha

[2] McClure's *Mem. of Wheelock*, p. 264.

Gunn knocked at the minister's door. He was an interpreter of ten years' experience by whom they were enabled to understand the message of Good Peter. Doctor Wheelock was impressed with this coincidence, that the Indian, the interpreter and the minister designed for that very place should thus meet "without any previous appointment or the least knowledge of each other's design." Messrs. Titus Smith and Theophilus Chamberlain were examined, and on the 24th of April ordained.[3] David Fowler, Joseph Wooley and Hezekiah Calvin were approved as schoolmasters. Jacob Fowler, Moses, Johannes, the Abrahams and Peter were thought fit to be ushers. Our story has to do mainly with the Fowlers and Joseph Johnson — subsequently approved as an usher—though others were employed in the Western missions during the next four years.[4]

[3] Titus Smith was born in Granby, Mass., June 4, 1734, and graduated at Yale College in 1764. After his brief missionary service he lived at South Hadley, Mass., and New Haven and Danby, Conn. He became a Sandemanian and a Tory, and took refuge after the war in Nova Scotia, where he died in 1807. [Chase's *Hist. of Dart. Coll.*, p. 43 n. 1.] He started with Chamberlain June 19, 1765, having Elisha Gunn as interpreter, and was destined for Onohoquaga; but famine scattered the Indians there and Smith with Moses went to Lake Utsage (Otsego), where they remained some weeks. In August he went to Onohoquaga, but his purpose failed through the jealousy of the commissioners who had sent Moseley thither and he returned home.—Chase's *Hist. of Dartmouth College*, p. 43; *Narrative*, 1767, p. 44.

Theophilus Chamberlain, son of Ephraim Chamberlain, was born in Northfield, Mass., Oct. 20, 1737. He was in Capt. John Burke's company at Fort William Henry in 1757, and was taken prisoner by the Indians. On his release he entered Yale College and graduated in 1765. Doctor Wheelock put him in charge of the Mohawk schools, where he continued in service until he was released, July 1, 1767. He is said to have lived afterwards at New Haven and Danby, Conn.

[4] David McClure, the son of John and Rachel (McClintock) McClure of Boston, was born in Newport, R. I., Nov. 18, 1748, and entered Wheelock's school in June, 1764. In 1765 he went to Yale College, where he graduated in 1769. He was absent on a mission to Oneida from July 7, 1766, to Dec. 8, 1766, teaching in the place of David Fowler. After his graduation he became the master in the Indian school, removing with it to Hanover, and was ordained there May 20, 1772, with Levi Frisbie. They started June 19th on a mission to the Delaware Indians at Muskingum, and returned Oct. 2, 1773. [*Narr.*, 1773, pp. 44-68.] McClure was subsequently settled at North Hampton, N. H., from 1776 to 1785, and at East

David Fowler was appointed to teach a school at Kanawarohare. His testimonial from Doctor Wheelock spoke of him
as "a youth of good abilities, whose activity and prudence,
fortitude and honesty have much recommended him. . . .
He goes to settle down among the Oneidas as school master,
and has a design to set them an example of agriculture for
support, and do what he can to recommend that manner of
living to the Indians." This industrial feature of the mission
seems to have originated with Fowler. He, at least, was its
warmest advocate. His experience in superintending such
affairs at Lebanon had disposed him to consider it as important. It certainly was a feature favorably received by the Indians, as their letters show.[5] He set out on the twenty-ninth
of April, carrying a letter to Sir William Johnson informing him

Windsor, Conn., from 1786, to his death there, June 25, 1820.—Sprague's *Annals* II,
7-9; *Diary of David McClure.*

Aaron Kinne was born in 1744, in Newent (Lisbon), Conn., and graduated at
Yale College in 1765. He went out July 7, 1766, to teach the school at Old Oneida
and returned in October. Again he was sent to supply Kirkland's place in May,
1768, and returned August 16th. He was ordained in 1770 at Groton, Conn., and
settled there until 1798. His death occurred at Talmadge, Ohio, July 9, 1824.
—Allen's *Biog. Dict.*

David Avery was born at Norwich Farms (Franklin), Conn., April 5, 1746, being
the son of John and Lydia (Smith) Avery. He entered Wheelock's school Jan. 2,
1764, and afterwards Yale College where he graduated in 1769. The summer of
1768 was spent in teaching the school at Canajoharie. In 1770 he began preaching
at Smithtown, L. I., and thereabouts, and was ordained at Hanover, N. H., Aug. 29,
1771, to be sent out as an assistant to Kirkland; but he left the service the year following on account of his health. He was a well-known chaplain in the Revolution,
and had settlements at Gageborough (Windsor), Mass., and Bennington, Vt. He
died Feb. 16, 1818.—Chase's *Hist. of Dart. Coll.*; Sprague's *Annals* I, 697; and
Jennings' *Mem. of Bennington.* His manuscript diaries are in the possession of his
descendant, George A. Clark, Esq., of Utica, N. Y.

Phineas Dodge was sent out in the autumn of 1767 to assist Kirkland and teach
Fowler's school. He returned with Kirkland the following spring. Allyn Mather
went with Ralph Wheelock in his journey in the spring of 1768. Augustine Hibbard
went on a similar journey in 1767. [*Narr.*, 1769, p. 138; Chapman's *Alumni of
Dart. Coll.*] Samuel Johnson, of Yale College in the class of 1769, was also employed
in these missions.

[5] *Wheelock's Narrative*, 1767, pp. 46–48.

of the design, money and letters for Samuel Kirkland, and an address from Doctor Wheelock to the Indian sachems.[6] He reached Johnson Hall on the eleventh of May, met there with Kirkland, and they journeyed westward together. To secure Indian youths, he went to Onohoquaga, but in this he failed. He then began his school at Kanawarohare, where he had been with Samson Occom in 1761. We will let him tell his own story in two of his letters :[7]

Onoyda, May 29th 1765

Rev^d & Hon^d Sir

After much Fatigue and Discouragement by the Way I reach'd here last Sabbath Day in the Morning. I got up to Johnson Hall 11th instant. deliver'd all what you sent by me both money and Letters to Mr Kirtland, —His Honour Sir William Johnson was in such great Business that we could not speak to him under five Days.—I have been down to Onohoquawge to get those Boys Joseph appointed to go down to School, but I could get none of them. Some said, they had too much Work to do and others said that I came away too soon, and some said they will let their Children go [to] School there [a] little while and they 'll send them. I suppose they would send their Children if I waited two or three weeks, but I was unwilling to tarry so long for the Gentlemen's motion.

I have settled Joseph Wooley with his Help, as School Master at Onoho-quawge, he is greatly belov'd there, it will be best for him to return as soon as possible. He has done nothing there worth mentioning besides learning their Language.—We heard how he was settled last Fall. I understood when I was down that there was no such thing mentioned.—Mr. Kirtland is gone up to Seneke Country again : he sot out from this Place 24th instant and with a heavy Heart : things go on contrary to his Mind.—I am greatly concernd about him.—He took my Horse up with him, he told me that he would bear all the Blame, for he should kill himself if he carried all what he wanted upon his Back.—I believe he will send the little Creature very soon by those men whom Sir William sent to fetch down the English Pris-oners from that Place. I understood so much about our Ministers when I was down to Onohoquawge I think it will not do for them to go together, they must be separate, one of them must come up here, and the other to Onohoquawge. If they should go together from Place to Place their com-ing will be to none affect : Because they expect the Ministers will settle &

[6] *Doc. Hist. of N. Y.*, IV, 356 ; McClure's *Mem. of Wheelock*, pp. 259-263.

[7] *Wheelock Papers.* Another letter, of June 15th, is in print, *Narrative*, 1767, pp. 38, 39. Chase's *Hist. of Dart. Coll.*, p. 44.

tarry with them.—They are suspicious People. They'll soon get something another against them if they don't tarry in one Place that will strike off all their Affections from them.   If they lose the Affections of these People it is over with them.—I can't express myself by writing as I could by talking.—I live like a Dog here, my Folks are poor and nasty. I eat with Dogs, for they eat & drink out of the same as I do.—I shall need ten Dollars more. It would best for Calvin to come here, here is one pretty Town just by me and good many Children. I must go down to German Flats to get Provision, after that I shall set down to my School. Here are great Number of Children, but I cant tell how many Scholars I shall have. I believe my singing School will exceed the other in Number. I cant get but one Boy here.—You will know why I could get no more by the Speach I send you. Joseph Wooley is almost nacked. I am oblig'd to let him have one of my Shirts.

I shall be glad [if] you would send me another   Sir, I hope you won't let this Letter be seen. I have no Table to write upon, besides I have not writ so long my Hand is out of order.—Please to give my kind Respects to Madam, Master and Ministers.   Please to accept much Love & Duty from Your affectionate

though unworthy Pupil

DAVID FOWLER

Hon^d and Revd Sir.   Oneida, June 24. 1765

I now write you a few Lines just to inform you that I am well at present, and have been so ever since I left your House. Blessed be God for his Goodness to me. I am well contented here as long as I am in such great Business. My Scholars learn very well. I have put eleven into a, b, ab, &c. I have three more that will advance to that place this Week, & some have got to the sixth page. It is ten thousand pities they can't keep together. They are often going about to get their Provision. One of the Chiefs in whose House I keep told me he believed some of the Indians would starve to Death this Summer. Some of them have almost consumed all their Corn already.

I came too late this Spring. I could not put any Thing into the Ground. I hope I shall next year. I believe I shall persuade all the Men in this Castle, at least the most of them to labour next Year. They begin to see now that they would live better if they cultivated their Lands than they do now by Hunting & Fishing. These Men are the laziest Crew I ever saw in all my Days. Their Women will get up early in the Morning, and be pounding Corn for Breakfast, and they (the men) be sleeping till the Vicuals is almost ready, and as soon as the Breakfast is over, the Women take up their axes & Hoes & away to the Fields, and leave their Children with

the Men to tend. You may see half a dozen walking about with Children
upon their Backs—lazy and sordid Wretches—but they are to be pitied.

I have been miserably off for an Interpreter—I can say but very little to
them. I hope by next spring I shall be my own Interpreter.

It is very hard to live here without the other Bone. I must be obliged to
wash & mend my Clothes & cook all my Victuals, & wash all the Things I
use, which is exceeding hard. I shan't be able to employ my Vacant hours
in improving their Lands as I should do if I had a Cook here.

I received a Letter from Mr Kirtland last Sabbath wherein he informs me
that the Indians who accompanied him left him with all his heavy pack.
He had the most fatiguing Journey this Time he ever had. He designs to
come down to get Provision, and if he don't he will eat no Bread till Indian
Harvest, and his Meat is merely rotten having no Salt.

> May the Blessing of Heaven rest on you
> Your affectionate tho unworthy Pupil
> DAVID FOWLER

The fears to which Fowler refers were realized. A famine
reduced the Indians that summer to great distress. In consequence they left their villages, and scattered in search of food.
Fowler, therefore, went to New England, and returned again
as the harvest drew near. We again produce his letters :[8]

Onoyda September 23, 1765

Honoured Sir.

I arriv'd here on the fourth instant and immediately began my School;
but it is very small at present, occasion'd by gathering Corn and building
Houses. I believe I shall have thirty after the hurry is over—My Scholars
learn very fast, some have got to the eighth Page. I am yet teaching both
Old and Young to sing, they can carry three Parts of several Tunes neatly.

I made it a long time before I got up here because I had such [a] heavy
Pack.—I bought me Plow Irons and several other Things which I could not
do without very well. I have got the little Horse : the Man ask'd a Dollar
for keeping him and half a Dollar for going with me ten Miles before he
would deliver the Horse to me.—My coming up so slow, buying so many
things, giving Money to those Women and bringing two Horses almost
took all my Money before I got up; I think I was very prudent with my
Money.—I shall want twenty Dollars more, also I shall be exceeding glad
[if] you would send me a Compleat Letter Writer and Guide to Prayer.

---

[8] *Wheelock Papers.* Another letter, of Jan. 21, 1766, is in print, Chase's *Hist. of
Dart. Coll.*, p. 45.

I design to come down next year after I have planted Corn and my Garden things come up, so that I may be able to tell my Children how they must manage the Garden in my Absence.

Give my kind Regards to Madame and Master. I could not write to him this Time.—And accept much Love and Duty from

your affectionate

though unworthy Pupil

DAVID FOWLER

Canawarohare Feb^{ry} 17, 1766

Revd Sir.

I receiv'd yours [of the] 25th of January which offer'd me much Pleasure and also warn'd me against those things which I am so much addicted to : I hope your Admonition will not be entirely lost, I will try to mind what you wrote to me.

I wrote you a large Letter in the month past which exhausted all the Matter that was in my Head. I now write you but a few Lines.—I am pursuing my Business with all Courage and Resolution that lies in my Power or Capacity. Revd Mr Chamberlain can enform you what Progress my Scholars have made in learning to read as well as I can.

Sir, I am almost nacked, my Cloaths are coming all to pieces : I shall be very glad all the Cloth that is intended for me be in readiness against my coming. I design to come down latter End of May or beginning [of] June. I have nothing new to acquaint you [with]. I am well and harty also contented.

I am

Revd Sir

your affectionate Indian Son

DAVID FOWLER

P. S. Regards to Madam, Sir Wheelock and to all the rest.

Canowarohare May 13, 1766

Reverend Sir

I am very sorry I can't write you a Letter which can be seen abroad, because Mr Kirtland is so much hurried to get down : but he can give you a proper Idea of my School and my own Affairs.—I believe I may venter to write my secrets to you as I wont to do, since I have so often seen and felt your tender Care and Affections. I have wrote a large Letter to Hannah Pyamphcouh which will either spur her up or knock her in [the] Head.—I therefore ask a Favour as a Child from [a] kind Father or Benefactor, that this Letter may be sent to the Supperscrib'd Place as soon as you get it into your Hands. For I shall be down the 13 or 14 of June and in very great Hast. I must tarry at your House a Week or ten Days the longest to shed my skin, for I am almost nacked now. I want all my Cloaths to be blue and that which is good: The Reason why I want this Letter to get down so soon is that she may have some time to think and dress herself up, & another which is the greatest that I may clear myself from those strong Bonds wherewith I bound myself to her and which could not let me rest Night and Day from the time I left her till I return'd to her again, what I mean about clearing myself is if she denies. If she won't let her Bones be join'd with mine I shall pick out my Rib from your House.

Sir, Dont be angry with me for write[ing] so bold and foolish. I hope you will not expose me—Give my Kind Regards [to] Mrs Wheelock and Sir Wheelock and to all the Family. accept much Love and Duty from
Your unworthy Pupil
DAVID FOWLER

It will be noted that David Fowler had some longings for a certain missing rib to which he several times refers. At first it was uncertain who would officiate in that capacity. In one letter he wrote Doctor Wheelock, " I have determined to have Amy Johnson for my companion. Shall marry as soon as I return from Oneida. I have given her a gold ring which cost me two dollars." Amy was then living at Bull's Tavern, in Hartford. We conclude that she was otherwise minded, for in the above letter he seems to have made a proposal to Hannah Poquiantup, which he judged would "either spur her up or knock her in the head." It did the latter ; but he kept his promise of patronizing the female department of Wheelock's school, for when he returned, June 27, 1766, he speedily consummated an engagement with Hannah Garret. She was a Pequot maiden, a daughter of Benjamin and Hannah Garret, and a descendant of the well-known Sachem Hermon Garret or Wequash Cook, as already stated. Her parents seem to have cast in their lot with the Narragansetts, as some others of the Stonington Pequots did. On the twenty-sixth of July they set out to visit her parents at Charlestown, R. I., where the nuptials were soon after celebrated. " I have clothed them well," says Wheelock, "and furnished her in part for housekeeping, have also supplied them with two Horses and Furniture, and must likewise let him have some Husbandry Tools, besides one or two Cows and a Swine : and hereby I hope they will soon be able to live with little Expence to the Public." All they had, however, they carried in a " Horse-Cart " drawn by "a good Pair of Horses," when, September eighth, they started for Oneida.

The favorable opportunity at this time among the Oneida Indians had led Doctor Wheelock to withdraw Samuel Kirkland from the Seneca mission and establish him at Kanawarohare. Thither he had gone early in July ; and in his company were Tekananda, the Seneca chief, clad in the scarlet regimentals given him by the Connecticut Assembly ;[9] Aaron Kinne, destined for Old Oneida ; David McClure, going to abide with Kirkland and learn the language ; Joseph Johnson, to keep Fowler's school until his return and then to serve under him as usher, and others for the Mohawk schools. Jacob Fowler was the companion of Samuel Johnson, going to Canajoharie, and it was his first experience. Then began the more intimate acquaintance between Samuel Kirkland and David Fowler, which continued for many years. The first task which engaged them was the building of a house, concerning which some information is given in the following letters :

Oneida, 15 Nov. 1766

Rev. and ever Honoured Sir,

Your kind affectionate Letter by David Fowler came safe to Hand, since which have had no Opportunity of Conveyance ; gladly embrace the present though amidst the greatest Hurry and Crowd of Business. I have found myself under a necessity of Building this Fall, to live with the least possible Conveniency and Comfort. Am now sorry I did not follow your Advice in season, though David's Delay put me much back. Constant and very hard Labour abroad for upwards of seventy Days, with many other Troubles, bring me down very much. I fear I have seen my best Days for Hardships and an Indian Life ; a little over-straining brings an old Pain in my Breast. Am not able to carry a Pack of a moderate Size (30 or 40 Weight) without spitting Blood. Yet in the main I have enjoyed usual

[9] See chapter IV, note 7.

Health through many Fatigues. Blessed be God, I am not discouraged ; I am willing to wear out sooner or later, if only it may be in the Cause of my Divine Master. The School here grows, the Scholars have made good Proficiency under Mr. McCluer. Johnson will tarry as Usher to David till next Spring, when I think best for Moses to take his Place, if he will answer for an Interpreter. I have had Provisions to get for the whole Company, &c. shall want Money, &c. The Building my House cost £20, besides the Work we have done. I cut and drawed all the Timber, dug the Cellar 12 Feet square and six deep with my own Hands, before David came. Mr. McCluer has afforded me much Help as well as Comfort; he bids fair for Usefulness. I do not expect to get my Provisions without much Difficulty, the Roads are so very bad. I design a Journey to New-England in the Spring, &c.

I am, Rev. Sir, Yours, &c

SAMUEL KIRKLAND [10]

Oneida, Decemb^r 2, 1766.

Dear Sister,

I take this opportunity to write you a few lines just to let you know that I and my wife are well at pre[sent]. I was very sorry I could not come down & see you before I came away from Lebanon. I was [in very great confusion. I hope you wont take it hard no longer. I suppose you did. I did not get up here till 28th Day of September, but we got up very well. Mr Kirtland and [I] have built us a comfortable House with Rooms and two Chimnies. We have [a] hard task to go through this Winter. We [are] oblig'd to fetch all our Provisions seventeen Miles on our Backs. I tarried too long down Country, it put us Back vastly

I have no strange thing to tell you. I and my [wife] are contented here. No more.

I am your loving Brother

D. FOWLER

P. S. Give my [love] to all your children & all your Relations.

[Address].

To. Mrs MARY OCCOM
Mohegan
New-London [11]

In this cabin, then, at Kanawarohare, Kirkland was established with David and Hannah as his housekeepers. His health, as appears from his letter, was even then impaired, and yet there

---

[10] *Wheelock Papers*, Lett. Nov. 15, 1766; *Narrative*, 1769, pp. 3, 4.
[11] Conn. Hist. Soc., *Indian Papers*.

were sore hardships ahead of him. The winter was cold and the snow was deep. Provisions grew scarce at the forts. What they could get had to be carried in their packs as they tramped over the seventeen miles on snowshoes. In the spring Kirkland was obliged to go to Lebanon for money and supplies; but he at once returned to his post. Soon it became evident that there was to be a famine in the land, more severe even than those of previous summers.[12] Kirkland anticipated the emergency, and, to diminish the force needing maintenance and to advise Doctor Wheelock, he sent Jacob Fowler and Joseph Johnson home to Lebanon. The treasury there was empty and Wheelock went on a tour eastward to secure funds. Meanwhile Kirkland and David Fowler came into great distress. They were obliged to give up all other work and go eeling in Oneida Lake. While David was away on one of these expeditions for food, " a stately boy " was born to him in Kirkland's cabin. This was the young David, in after years a trusted messenger through the wilderness on more than one occasion. Still the food failed. In some wigwams the corn was reduced to a single measure. Their only hope was to hold out until the squashes came on. "I have eat no Flesh in my own House for nigh eight Weeks," says Kirkland. "Flour and Milk, with a few Eels, has been my Living—Such Diet with my hard Labour abroad doth not satisfy Nature—My poor People are almost starved to Death. . . . I would myself be glad of the Opportunity to fall upon my knees for such a Bone as I have often seen cast to the Dogs." Had Sir William Johnson then seen him he would have had as good reason as when he returned from the Senecas to exclaim, "Good God! Mr. Kirkland, you look like a whipping-post." And yet those savages, who had begun to love him, would creep out of their

<hr/>

[12] These famines were common among the Indians, but there had not been a good crop in the Oneida country for several years. In 1765 frosts cut off the Indian corn, vermin destroyed it in 1766, and some kind of worm in 1767. The latter year they had no pigeons. See the account of a pigeon-hunt in Cooper's *Pioneers.*

hovels, as skeletons might out of their graves, to help him hoe his little patch of corn. Finally, on the fourteenth of July, exhausted, sleepless and hungry, he penned these words: "David is going down for Relief, without which I shall perish soon. My Nature is almost broke."

Then it was that David Fowler distinguished himself as an Indian athlete. In ten days, on foot and alone, he covered the distance, "above four hundred miles," going first to Lebanon, then to Springfield and back, and on to Boston, seeking "the Great Minister that takes the care of Indians," to whom he came at last one evening. After two days he set out to return with relief by the shortest route, and in less than ten days he arrived at Kanawarohare with food for the starving missionary.

These relations between Kirkland and Fowler, however, were soon to end. It was inexpedient to keep up the schools during the summer. Jacob Fowler and Joseph Johnson were detained at Lebanon until the autumn, when they came again. Johnson taught at Old Oneida until 1758, when he fell into immorality and was disgraced. He was then, be it noted, only a youth eighteen years old. Jacob Fowler remained faithful so long as there was work for Indians in the Oneida mission. The main reason for David Fowler's withdrawal was that he was needed at Montauk "to take the care of his aged and suffering parents". His life with Kirkland had been on the whole pleasant, though perhaps the white man had been too much inclined to treat the Indian as his servant. Fowler taught his school successfully, and his pupils made "laudable proficiency;" but he found no opportunity to instruct them in agriculture, which, he wrote, "*is the only thing that will keep them together and will make them multiply and thrive in the world.*" [18] It must be said, however, that there was some dissatisfaction with Doctor Wheelock's management of his missions, in which Kirkland, Occom and Fowler shared. This was increased to

[18] *Wheelock Papers*, Lett. Dec. 2, 1766.

serious proportions by the ill-advised visits of his son, Ralph Wheelock.   It led eventually to the withdrawal of Kirkland and the alienation of the Indians.   One fact at least is evident, the good man who took the care of Indians had assumed a burden which he had not the means to support.

So David Fowler, of whom Wheelock says at this time, " He is the best accomplished of any Indian I know "—severed his connection with his friends at Kanawarohare, and Kirkland, with a shade of sadness, wrote on the 8th of September, 1767, " David and Hannah set out for New England tomorrow morning."

CHAPTER VII

1764–1769

The failure of Doctor Wheelock's proposed mission in 1764, through the disapproval of Mr. Whitefield, returned Samson Occom to Mohegan. He had good reason to be disappointed, if not disaffected, because of the way his friends were using him. They had tempted him from Montauk by a mission westward which had received meager support. Then, after he had reengaged himself, under the commissioners of the "Society for Propagating the Gospel," to be a missionary among the Mohegans, Niantics, and neighboring tribes, they had secured his release to serve under them—the Connecticut correspondents of the Scotch Society. The "imprudent scheme" they had devised came to nothing through no fault of his; but he was thrown out of employment and sent home. The friendship between Whitefield and Wheelock barely withstood the strain, and doubtless there would have been a rupture had not the celebrated English evangelist already suggested a plan for assisting the Indian Charity School, as we shall relate in the next chapter.

Occom's reappearance at Mohegan, however, was an important circumstance. Interest in the famous Mohegan Land Case, or Mason Controversy, as it was sometimes called, had been lately revived by the approaching final decision on the matter in England. This dispute between the Mohegan Indians and the Connecticut Colony as to the ownership of certain lands, which the tribe claimed, had been going on since the beginning of the century. It had been bred in the bone of the Indians of Occom's generation. The whites also, in

that region particularly, had arrayed themselves on one side
or the other—mostly on the other.   Many manuscripts on the
subject survive.   The proceedings of the royal commissioners
in print fill a volume and any adequate explanation of the
issues involved would fill another.[1]

The case for the Colony was, in brief, that the famous Sachem
Uncas, in a deed, dated September 28, 1640, had conveyed to
the English his right in all the lands which he had occupied
as tributary to the Pequots, excepting those he was accustomed
to plant, and had confirmed the same by a conveyance, dated
August 15, 1659, to Major John Mason, which, in turn, the
latter had surrendered to the General Court of the Colony as
its agent March 14, 1660.   It was also claimed that Uncas, in
1681, had renewed this covenant with the English, and had
empowered the General Court to dispose of the Mohegan
lands for plantations, farms and villages.   The Indians, on
the other hand, maintained that the instrument of 1640, for
which Uncas had received " five and a half yards of trucking
cloth, with stockings and other things as a gratuity," had only
conveyed a right of preemption to settlers of the Connecticut
Colony made in consequence of protection against the Pequots,
and that this " jurisdiction power " was all that had been confirmed to the Colony by Mason in 1660 and by Uncas in 1681.
They also asserted that the conveyance to Major John Mason
and his heirs merely constituted a trusteeship, made for their
protection against foolish sales to the English.   He was then
acting as their guardian and continued to do so after the professed surrender of their lands to the Colony.   In 1671, being

[1] The manuscript volume containing the proceedings of the Court of Review in
1743 is in the collections of the Connecticut Historical Society.   The State Library
and Conn. Hist. Soc. have the same in print with the following title: " Governor
and Company of Connecticut, and Mohegan Indians, by their Guardians.   Certified
Copy of Book of Proceedings before Commissioners of Review, MDCCXLIII,
London: Printed by W. and J. Richardson, MDCCLXIX," 4°, pp. 283.   See also,
William Samuel Johnson Papers and *Indian Papers* in Conn. Hist. Soc.; and State
Archives, *Indian Papers.*

then aged and fearing that the Indians might be wronged after his death, he entailed to the tribe a tract, thereafter called the "Sequestered Lands." This view of the case, however, was greatly prejudiced by this act, for if he was a trustee he should have restored all the lands, and if they belonged to the Colony he had no right to entail any part of them to the Indians. The Mason heirs contended for the rights of this trusteeship, which Owenaco, the son of the sachem, confirmed to Samuel and Daniel Mason, sons of the guardian. Upon a petition of the Indians, drawn by their advocate, Nicholas Hallam, Esq., and presented to Queen Anne, a commission was issued July 19, 1704, for the trial of the case. Governor Joseph Dudley of Massachusetts presided over the court, and, though the agents of Connecticut protested against the commission as an infringement of their charter, a decree was given in favor of the Indians. The Colony appealed to the crown, and a commission of review was granted in 1706; but this was never used. A committee was finally appointed by the General Court in 1718, to examine all claims within the sequestered lands; but after three years they decided to set apart and entail to the tribe about five thousand acres and allow the white claimants to keep the rest. The Mason party were not satisfied, and, failing to obtain satisfaction from the General Court, an appeal was made to the crown. The case was reopened, and a new commission of review was granted June 3, 1737, which, failing in its duty, was succeeded by another ordered January 8, 1741-42. This latter commission was composed of Cadwallader Colden, Philip Cortland, John Rodman, Daniel Horsmanden, and Robert H. Morris. After reviewing the case at length the majority decided in favor of the Colony, Horsmanden and Morris dissenting, and so the decree, which had stood in support of the Mohegan claim for thirty-eight years, was reversed, except as to the aforementioned five thousand acres.

Meanwhile the Indians had become divided on the matter. The action of the General Court in supporting the claim of Major Ben Uncas for the sachemship against Mamohet in 1723, had naturally created a party favorable to the Colony, who were willing to accept the settlement of 1721. On the other hand, the tribal attachment to the Masons and the hopes of redress won many to their cause. Thus, in view of a final decision on the Mason appeal to the king, the Indians and the whites round about were in a turmoil when Samson Occom returned, in 1764, to Mohegan. As to the case itself, which, notwithstanding the attempts of sixty years, had never received a fair and full trial, the decision was against the Indians. It was said that a desire to conciliate the Colony in a distracted time had much to do with this result. Occom wrote, "It is a pure favour."

This long-standing contest, or the revival of it in his time, had a great influence over the subsequent opinions of Samson Occom, as to the Indian's relation to his land. It educated him in such matters. He saw the necessity of a compact tribal organization; recognized the weakness of his people in foolishly selling their lands; realized the dangers of allowing the whites to settle among them; and concluded that the Indians would never advance greatly in civilization until they were forced to cultivate the soil for support. We shall see how he used his knowledge and experience for the benefit of the New England Indians. Most of all, this dispute led Occom to see and to assert, as he did many times, that his people would never accept the Christian religion until they were treated with more justice by their neighbors. One of the New England fathers, the best known judge of the Massachusetts Bay courts, once wrote: "It will be a vain attempt for us to offer heaven to them, if they take up prejudices against us, as if we did grudge them a living upon their own earth." This was an opinion which Samson Occom formed in consequence of his acquaintance with the Mohegan Land Case and which he expressed in almost the same words. He believed that his tribe had been cheated, and doubtless he said so. His family had long been loyal to the Ben Uncas claim to the sachemship. Yet he was one of that party, among which were the most intelligent of the tribe, who thought that the overseers, as agents of the Colony, were using the sachem as a tool for their own ends. He refused to surrender his opinion or compromise by any agreement with the overseers. This brought him at least under suspicion of antagonism to the Colony. He seems never to have expected redress. At the same time he entertained no animosity toward the Colony or the whites. He knew well that they had done much for his people. When the final decision came at last, he wrote as follows: " The grand controversy which has subsisted between the Colony of Connecticut and the Mohegan Indians above seventy years, is finally decided in favor of the Colony. I am afraid the poor Indians will never stand a good chance with the English in their land controversies, because they are very poor, they have no money. Money is almighty now-a-days, and the Indians have no learning, no wit, no cunning: the English have all." [2]

There was a sequel to this controversy in the life of Samson Occom, to which we now turn. The school at Mohegan had been kept since 1752 by a Scotchman named Robert Clelland, under the patronage of the Boston commissioners. His salary was not large—only £20 a year—but, in his own words, his " Scots spirite was bigger than his salary." He had lived in a tenement attached to the schoolhouse or near it,[3] and by means of his noonday distributions of bread, paid for by the Colony, he had succeeded in maintaining the cause

[2] Caulkins' *Hist. of Norwich*, p. 269.

[3] This was the schoolhouse of former years, and stood, we think, where the one does at present. It had been repaired in 1742 and 1752. In 1757 the teacher's house was repaired.—*Conn. Archives, Coll. and Schools*, I, 109, 125.

of education. Rev. David Jewett, as minister of the Indians in the town, was lecturing to them at £15 per annum, and overseeing the school. Messrs. Jewett and Clelland were friendly to the colony in the land case. The former would lose all his acres if the Indians should win—so it was reported. Remember now that Ben Uncas was considered to be a tool of the Colonial party, in consequence of which the majority of the tribe were alienated from him, and we have a situation out of which trouble was sure to arise. It began when Occom expressed an unfavorable opinion of the schoolmaster, and cast some blame on Mr. Jewett for keeping him in the place. The fact was that the commissioners themselves were not fully satisfied, and had questioned him in the matter. He did make the following charges against Clelland: that he took so many English youth that the Indians were crowded out, that he had no government and did not teach carefully, that he did not pray in his school nor teach the Indians English manners, that he neglected the school and did not furnish the dinners according to agreement, and that he used the Indians' horses without their leave.[4] These seemed to him to be good grounds for dismissing the schoolmaster; but his action awakened great opposition. When later he went to Boston, Ben Uncas wrote, "Samson is an uneasy, restless man, he is gone to Boston to get the commissioners to dismiss our school-master."[5] This was not true. Clelland had already been dismissed by their vote of September 19, 1764. He did not seem to understand this or he did not receive their notice, and was again dismissed the 5th of July, 1765, having served for thirteen years.[6] Mr. Jewett had some feel-

---

[4] *Conn. Hist. Soc., Indian Papers*, Doc., April 26, 1764.

[5] *Conn. Archives, Indian Papers*, II, 258.

[6] Clelland continued to live at Mohegan some years. The society aided him in his "old age" in 1770, and he petitioned again in 1775. He was succeeded by Willard Hubbard, who taught until operations were suspended by the Revolution.—*MS. Rec. Soc. for Prop. Gos.*

ing toward Occom on account of this affair. He considered that he was the authorized supervisor of the school, and that Occom had interfered. On the other hand, the Indian resented the meddlesomeness of the whites, and the English minister in particular, in their tribal affairs. He was a councilor. His influence was great. He openly expressed his views on the land case and advised his people. Probably also he had something to say about Mr. Jewett's own land interests. Yet all this was not so great a cause for trouble as the success which Occom met with as a preacher when he removed to Mohegan. The Indians had long been considered as belonging to Mr. Jewett's parish. Some of them, it will be remembered, were members of his church. Occom began to hold services in the schoolhouse, and at once all the Indians of his party and some of the whites gathered to his standard. He was not at fault in this,—it was the work he had been commissioned to do for the Indians, and he made no effort to influence the English. However, the white minister quite naturally became jealous. Doctor Wheelock wrote thus to Whitefield :

The Breach between Mr Jewett & Mr Occom grows wider—Mr Jewett's People and a great Number from other neighbouring Parishes flock to hear M^r. Occom on Lord's Days at Mohegan &c the Effect of which you may easily guess. And Mr Jewett is like to lose all his Land in his Parish, if the Indians there should gain their point in their Suit against the Government in an old affair called Mason's Case lately revived. And Mr Occom can't avoid being considered as a Party while he continues there. The affair is too long (if I were enough acquainted with it) to give you such a particular acco^t as perhaps will be best you should have if you should take Mr Occom to England with you. This together with their Controversy with their School Master has made a great Ferment among them, and Mr Occom is blamed by some that he will advise the Indians, that he will suffer the English to flock to hear him &c [7]

This was an affront which a minister could hardly bear in those days of his autocratic power. Here was a prophet, and

[7] *Wheelock Papers*, Lett. Oct. 10, 1764.

he an Indian, who had some honor in his own country. But
Doctor Wheelock did not tell the whole story. Those who
flocked to hear Occom were mostly such as sympathized with
the Indians in their contest against the Colony. The consequence was that a storm of popular feeling was raised against
Occom. It grew to such proportions that "one scarcely dared
to mention his name." He was called an enemy of the Colony,
a "bad, mischievous and designing man," and other names
which a pious person of that time could consistently use against
an Indian. Mr. Jewett also wrote the commissioners at Boston,
making charges against him. We do not doubt that Occom
resented this treatment. He may have used some expressions
which were not altogether to his credit.

When the excitement had somewhat subsided, the newly-
organized Connecticut Board of Correspondents, meeting at
Lebanon on that eventful day when "Good Peter" unex-
pectedly arrived, took up the matter with the design of sifting
the charges and effecting a reconciliation. Occom and Jewett
were present. We give the result in the words of Doctor
Wheelock, the secretary :

At a Meeting of the Board of Correspondents in the Colony of Connecticut on the 12th day of March, A. D. 1765 at the Revᵈ Mʳ Wheelock's House
in Lebanon—Upon a public and loud Clamour of the Revᵈ Mʳ Samson
Occom's Misconduct in a Number of Instances relative to the Separations
in and about Mohegan, and ill Conduct towards the Overseers in the Affair
of leasing the Indian Lands, and some proud and haughty Threatenings to
turn Episcopalian and Unsettledness respecting the Constitution of our
Churches and Infant Baptism, and disrespectful Treatment of the Revᵈ
Mʳ Jewet and illegal proceedings against the School Master at Mohegan,
and engaging in the *Mason Controversy* (so called) against the Government :
And, the Glory of God, Mʳ Occom's Character and Usefulness and particularly the Reputation of Indian Affairs, requiring that these Reports should
be publicly looked into, that his Innocence or Guilt therein might thereby
publickly appear : Wherefore, the Revᵈ Mʳ Jewet, at the Desire of some
of this Board, exhibited a Charge consisting of a Number of Articles
against the said Mʳ Occom which were deliberately heard with Evidences
and Pleas on both Sides. And upon most carefully weighing the whole

Controversy, Mr Occom was not found guilty of any of the charges laid against him, excepting that of the *Mason Controversy* in which he was blamed only agreeable to the Tenor of what follows—

" Although, as a Member of the Mohegan Tribe and, for many years, one of their Council, I thought I had not only a natural & civil Right but that it was my Duty to acquaint myself with their temporal affairs; Yet I am, upon serious and close Reflexion, convinced, that as there was no absolute Necessity for it, it was very imprudent in me, and offensive to the *Public* that I should so far engage as of late I have done, in the *Mason Controversy:* which has injured my Ministerial Character, hurt my Usefulness, and brought Dishonor upon Mr Wheelock's School and the Correspondents. For this imprudent, rash and offensive Conduct of mine, I am heartily sorry, and beg Forgiveness of God—of this honorable Board of Correspondents, of whom I ought to have asked farther Advice—and of the Public; determining that I will not for the future act in that affair, unless called thereto and obliged by lawful Authority."

This Submission, being offered to this Board, by the Revd Mr Occom, was accepted. Moreover Mr Occom desired that a copy of the Letter which the Revd Mr Jewet wrote to the Commissioners at Boston some time last Fall, in which he thinks there are several Things injurious to his Character, might be laid before the Board. Which being read and considered the Board are of Opinion that it is Mr Jewet's Duty, in Justice to Mr Occom's Character, to write said Commissioners of the Satisfaction which he now professes to have received from Mr Occom's defence; and that a copy of said Writing should be laid before this Board at their next Meeting for their Approbation, which Mr Jewet agreed to do [8]

Occom's conduct at this meeting was very creditable. It won him new esteem from his old friends. Doctor Wheelock reported that "he made a bold and truly manly and Christian defence in a spirit of meekness, and vindicated his conduct to have been judicious, prudent and becoming a Minister of the Gospel." The reverend company must have been a little amused at the outcome of some of the charges. Occom admitted frankly that he had proceeded against the schoolmaster. He urged that Clelland's usefulness was evidently at an end when none of the Indians would send their children to his school. On examination, it appeared that Mr. Jewett entertained the same opinion. Occom denied that he had spoken

[8] *Wheelock Papers*, Doc., March 12, 1765.

disrespectfully of Mr. Jewett; he had only written the schoolmaster that because Mr. Jewett called him bad names it was
no reason he should do so. He had, in fact, used these
words: "If Mr. Jewet has called me a Serpent I dont See
that you have any Business to call me so." As to his "proud
and haughty threatenings to turn Episcopalian," he admitted
that he had, in jest, said he would turn Churchman, because
some of his meddling ministerial neighbors were a nuisance.
After this manner all the charges melted away except one.
That was a serious matter. The company, as loyal ministers
of the colony, frowned upon this Mohegan councilor who said
he had advised his ignorant brethren in their affairs. They
argued that he had thus injured his ministerial character, and
brought dishonor upon Indian missions! He had done that
which was "offensive to the public!" So Samson Occom,
who was morbidly sensitive, loaded this sin upon this honest
soul, and humbly asked forgiveness. We have no doubt that
the Almighty granted him a full pardon. The correspondents
did, and so did the Colony of Connecticut when the case was
decided in its favor. There was, professedly, a reconciliation
between Jewett and Occom. The former said he was satisfied,
and they shook hands. In the ample fireplace of the minister's study they burned up so many valuable papers on the
case that the doctor was afraid they would set his house afire.
Nevertheless, Doctor Wheelock wrote, "I fear the injury done
Mr. Occom's character will not soon nor readily be wholly
undone."

Mr. Jewett went home. Weeks grew into months, and still
he did not write the commissioners at Boston the letter he
had promised. Occom very justly felt aggrieved. "I wonder,"
he afterwards wrote, "what ails that good, bad man." Finally,
on the twentieth of June, Doctor Wheelock wrote his white
brother a "sharp letter," in which he said: "If you have nothing against Mr. Occom more than you said to us, I advise you

to settle according to your agreement." This brought out from Mr. Jewett the promised letter to the commissioners, dated June 26th, which was laid before the correspondents on the second of July, and accepted. So the trouble ended. It was not much, after all—a conflagration kindled by a little fire. At the time, however, it created a widespread feeling against Samson Occom and his Christian Indians. The consequences in his life might have been serious, had he not soon been called to make the Indian's plea in England. When he returned, it was with honor. The people forgot that he had ever been an enemy of their Colony, and his old neighbors were proud to own him.

CHAPTER VIII

THE INDIAN PREACHER IN ENGLAND

1765–1768

The idea of sending Samson Occom to England in behalf of the Indian Charity School was first suggested by Rev. George Whitefield. He knew the times and the cause, and was well acquainted with the temper of the English people. So early as 1760, he wrote: "Had I a converted Indian scholar that could preach and pray in English, something might be done to purpose."[1] At that time, however, nothing in a missionary way had been accomplished. The early Oneida missions gave Occom a story to tell, and when the plan was actually in operation several of Wheelock's pupils were engaged in the work. Moreover, the wars of the time, in which the Indians were so important a factor, made the cause somewhat unpopular. So matters stood until 1764, when Whitefield visited New England. He then had a better opportunity of making the acquaintance of Occom, who attended him on his journey through part of Connecticut, riding one of the horses of his chariot.[2] A new interest also was kindled in the mind of the great evangelist by his meeting with the Indians here and there, and by his long and earnest conversations with Doctor Wheelock concerning the Indian school. Whitefield was then so certain of the success of the plan that he proposed to take Occom to England with him on his return. His later consideration of the matter led him to determine otherwise, and doubtless his conclusion was in the interest of a larger success. It was thought better to send

[1] McClure's *Mem. of Wheelock*, p. 223.
[2] Larned's *Hist. of Windham County*, II, 39.

Occom in the care of some white minister who had been associated with the school or Indian missions. Here difficulties
and delays arose. An application was made to the New York
correspondents of the Scotch Society, endorsed by the Connecticut board, March 12, 1765, for the assistance of Rev.
John Brainerd in this capacity. It was denied. He could
not be spared. At another meeting, held at John Ledyard's,
in Hartford, on the 10th of May, it was voted to send Rev.
Charles Jeffrey Smith. He would have been a good man,
but for various reasons he declined. Meanwhile, Doctor
Wheelock, with Occom and Rev. Nathaniel Whitaker, pastor
of the church at Chelsea in Norwich,[3] went eastward on a
soliciting tour. They visited Boston, Salem, Ipswich, Rowley,
Newbury, Exeter, Portsmouth and other places. They also
appeared before the New Hampshire legislature. About
£300 sterling were collected. Mr. Whitaker had been on a
similar journey the year before, and had met with some success. It then became more than ever evident to Doctor
Wheelock that the presence of the Indian preacher was calculated to convince an audience of the usefulness of his enterprise. He determined to send Occom to England, at once,
with some one. He would like to have gone himself, but he
could not leave in a year so critical. Finally the Connecticut
correspondents, at a meeting held July third, voted to commit
the mission to Mr. Whitaker.

Preparations were immediately begun for their departure.
"A Continuation of the Narrative" was prepared and printed

[3] Nathaniel Whitaker was born Feb. 22, 1732, on Long Island. After his graduation from Princeton College in 1752, he studied theology, and until 1759 was pastor
of the Presbyterian church at Woodbridge, N. J. He was installed at Norwich,
Feb. 25, 1761, and on account of some difficulties attending his ministry there he was
dismissed in 1769, shortly after his return from England From 1769 to 1784, he was
pastor of the Tabernacle church in Salem, Mass., from 1784 to 1790, he ministered at
Skowhegan, Maine, and he was subsequently at Taunton, Mass. He died, Jan. 21,
1795, in Virginia.—Chase's *Hist. of Dart. Coll.*, p. 60 ; Caulkins' *Hist. of Norwich*,
pp. 460–465.

at Boston.   Occom was sent to Sir William Johnson to secure
his written endorsement. Mr. Whitaker went to Smithtown, L. I.,
where the Suffolk Presbytery met on the twenty-first of August,
to obtain from them a recommendation for Occom.   Apparently they did not approve of the plan.   It doubtless seemed
absurd, as it did to many.   They could not see their way clear
to give him a recommendation, as he was to be sent under the
auspices of another body ; but they agreed to give him a dis-
mission and testimonials if he wished to sever his connection
with them.   This Occom did not care to do.   At a later
meeting, October 30, 1765, they voted to recommend him " as
one they ordained with special relation to the Indians and certify that he is of good moral life and of good standing."   At
the same time they gave their consent to his employment
under the Connecticut Board of Correspondents.   This cleared
the way so far as Occom was concerned.

Mr. Whittaker also went southward as far as Philadelphia
and later to the eastward to secure testimonials.   To a letter,
which had been prepared by Doctor Wheelock, he obtained the
signatures of sixty-nine gentlemen prominent in Church and
State in New York, New Jersey, Pennsylvania and New Hampshire.   Three ministers of the Church of England signed this
testimonial—Samuel Seabury, afterwards the first bishop of
Connecticut, Thomas B. Chandler, and Jacob Duché.   There
was only one Massachusetts name in the list, though probably
some would have signed had they been asked.   The reason
will presently appear.   Governor Fitch of Connecticut also
granted his endorsement, warmly commending the purpose of
the Indian Charity School.

The ministers of eastern Connecticut added their testimony,
among them being Rev. Matthew Graves, missionary of the
Episcopal Church at New London.   This minister was especially
interested in Samson Occom, and they were on most friendly
terms.   In a letter of commendation which he then gave he

speaks thus of his Indian brother : " He has shewed himself a
Pattern of good Works, of blameless Conversation, a Lover of
good Men, sober, just, holy, temperate, gentle to all, commending himself to every Man's Conscience in the Sight of God.
    .   .   .   He is of a most catholic Spirit, prudent and exem-
plary in his Behaviour.   The Dissenting Ministers, to my
Knowledge, allow him in his Clerical Capacity to be a Person
justly deserving their greatest Esteem.   And I faithfully believe there are few of greater Credit to their Function."   This
was the clergyman in whose presence the Indian had in jest
said he would turn Episcopalian.   He really seems to have had
some hope of Occom, as he wrote him after he had reached
England expressing the wish that his Indian friend would
" come home with Episcopal ordination."   We conjecture also
that he wrote to some church dignitary in a similar strain,
which gave rise to the overtures Occom received from that
quarter.

Evidently Whitaker and Occom had testimonials enough to
command the attention of all England.   Robert Keen afterwards
wrote that " Whitaker's recommendation looked like Ezekiel's
scroll, full on both sides from one end to the other."   They
were all published in " A Brief Narrative of the Indian Charity
School," issued after their arrival in England, and printed in
London in 1766, of which a second edition, with an Appendix,
was printed the year following.   Whitefield is believed to have
written the introduction to this narrative, and Whitaker to have
edited it.   Copies were distributed throughout the kingdom,
and thus a complete and interesting statement of the work
was made.   Doctor Wheelock's " Memorial to the People of
God in England, Scotland and Ireland," which it contained, was
itself a most winsome plea.

The commissioners of the " Society for Propagating the
Gospel " at Boston were earnestly opposed to this venture.
Among them were some who had long been unfriendly to Doc-

tor Wheelock's plan of conducting missions. His education
of Indian youth was one thing, which they had to a limited
extent approved; but the sending out of missionaries on his
personal responsibility was quite another. Even the formation of the Connecticut Board of Correspondents had not
wholly satisfied their objections. Probably they thought also
that such a mission to England would throw their substantial
work into the shadow and injure their prestige in the mother
country. It would be likely to divert contributions of which they
were in need. How general such a sentiment was we do not
know. This, however, was the reason why no effort was made
to secure testimonials in Massachusetts. Indeed, the scheme
was well under way before the commissioners were aware of it.
As it finally came to them, Occom was to be sent over as an
Indian who had been converted from heathenism and particularly as the fruit of Dr. Wheelock's work. To this they very
properly objected, for they had long supported a school at
Mohegan and had maintained Occom while he was being educated. Some credit, they thought, was due to their society.
This Indian preacher is often spoken of at the present time as
one who was educated at the Indian Charity School, whereas
he was the means of its establishment. At all events the commissioners wrote a letter to Jasper Mauduit, governor of the company in England, dated October 2, 1765, which was decidedly
prejudicial to Occom's mission. They asserted that the Indian
preacher had been brought up in the midst of Christian influences in their school, and that he had not been converted from
heathenism at all. The inference from this statement was
untrue. They had indeed supported a school at Mohegan;
but Occom's conversion and education were in no way due to
it. Doctor Wheelock was greatly distressed over this letter
when he heard of it. The commissioners' records show that it
was read to him and he replied to it, but this was after his
emissaries had departed and their success was assured. The

commissioners, moreover, made their disapproval known round about. It came thus to the ears of the Connecticut correspondents, so that Whitaker and Occom went to England forewarned in the matter. On their arrival in Boston, as they were about to sail, they met the commissioners and endeavored to adjust the trouble, but they failed. We are indebted to this attack on Occom for a statement of facts concerning his early life which he drew up at Boston on the 28th of November. He intended later to amplify this into an autobiography—a purpose which he unfortunately never carried out. He wrote thus to Doctor Wheelock, December 6th: "The Honorable Commissioners here are still very strong in their opposition to your Scheme. They think it is nothing but a Shame to send me over the great Water. They say it is to impose upon the good People. They further affirm I was bro't up Regularly and a Christian all my Days. Some say I cant Talk Indian. Others say I cant read. In short I believe the old Devil is in Boston to oppose our Design, but I am in hopes he is almost superannuated, or in a Delireum. . . . I have a struggle in my mind at times, knowing not where I am going. I dont know but I am looking for a spot of ground where my bones must be buried and never see my poor Family again, but I verily believe I am called of God by [a] strange Providence and that is enough."[4] This opposition increased the discouragement of the good man at Lebanon who carried the burdens. He was not very sanguine of success himself, and the unkind words, amounting even to ridicule, which were heaped upon him still further depressed him. In a letter to Whitefield, he wrote: " I am concerned for Mr. Occom. He has done well and been useful as a missionary among his Savage Brethren, but what a figure he will make in London I cant tell."[5] Some of his friends were more confident. Rev. Charles Jeffrey Smith said :

[4] *Wheelock Papers*, Lett. Dec. 6, 1765.
[5] *Ibid.*, Lett. Nov. 11, 1765.

"An Indian minister in England might get a Bushel of money for the School." The doctor would have been satisfied with a few handfuls. Mr. John Smith, the Boston merchant and old friend of the school, was then in London. He heard there of an attempt by another society to anticipate Occom with a converted Indian, who is said to have been sent over and to have been ordained in the Episcopal order at Bristol. Thereupon he wrote urging haste in the following words: "He must not stay to put on his wigg but come in his night cap. All that's wanted is to have Mr. Occom here. He is expected & waited for by many. I know an influential nobleman that expects him and has asked me after him."[6] So the plan was finally to be put to a test.

On the 21st of November, 1765, Occom set out from Mohegan for Boston, having reverently committed his family to the care of Almighty God. He reached there on the twenty-third, and on the twenty-seventh Mr. Whitaker returned from a journey to Portsmouth, having collected almost enough money to pay their expenses. After a delay of several weeks waiting for a ship, they finally embarked on the packet *Boston*, John Marshall, master, on the twenty-third of December. The price of their ocean passage was twenty guineas, and among the many good works of that worthy patriot, John Hancock, who was part owner in the ship, was his contribution of his share, being one fourth.[7]

The Indian preacher who had thus gone to storm the Christian people of England, was no ordinary man for such a work. It is confessed that he had some attainments as a preacher. President Dwight, who heard him twice, says: "His discourses, though not proofs of superior talents, were decent, and his utterance in some degree eloquent." It would be a mistake to infer from this opinion that Occom was quite like

[6] *Wheelock Papers*, Lett. Sept. 11, 1765.
[7] *Ibid.*, John Marshall's Receipt, Feb. 25, 1766.

the average English minister of his day. He was neither a logician nor a theologian. His sermons were always simple. They had, however, the indescribable scent of the forest in them. He could of course speak best in his native tongue, not only because he could better command the language, but also because of his familiarity with the figures of speech so popular in all Indian oratory. One who knew him well said he was "vastly more natural and free, clear and eloquent" when addressing the Indians. But this habit of figurative expression passed over into his English speech. He had many apt illustrations of his points, some of which have survived and are sometimes heard in this distant day. One can easily imagine how this characteristic would charm an English audience. He made thus a clear and close application of the truth which impressed his hearers. His mission also afforded him an opportunity of extemporaneous preaching, in which he appeared to the best advantage. The few surviving manuscripts of his sermons are those of his early life. Later he rarely wrote and never read from his notes. He had no need of the variety of a settled ministry, and, going from place to place, he doubtless often repeated the substance of his sermons. So it was in England. He had substantially the same story to tell everywhere. This he had soon mastered and could deliver with interest and effect. He seems also to have come under the influence of Whitefield's fervor. After his return from England this impression remained. It contributed largely to his success as an evangelist, which indeed he was. In truth, this Indian preacher was no novice. He had been already before large audiences in Boston and New York. Yet, of course, the secret of his power was in the fact that he was himself the embodiment of his cause—a native Indian of no mean tribe, who had risen to the highest station of any Indian preacher in the century. He was in earnest, and never once did he forget the main object of his long journey. Withal, his manners were such as intercourse with some of the best New England families could cultivate, for he had been often a welcome guest in their homes. Calm, dignified and self-possessed, as many an Indian chief was wont to be, he exhibited those qualities which were esteemed in a minister of that day. Surely he was as well equipped for his mission as any Indian could hope to be.

The voyagers sighted land on the second of February and the next day they were taken ashore in a fishing boat at Brixham, about two hundred miles from London. On horseback they went to Exeter, thence by night coach to Salisbury, and on the sixth instant they arrived safely at the house of Mr. Dennys DeBerdt in London, where they lodged. Their host had been for years a warm friend of their cause, and he was a gentleman of some means and influence. Mr. John Smith of Boston was also awaiting them. He had written that " Occom on coming should shut himself up in a coach and come directly to Mr. Whitefield's in London." In accordance with this plan, shrewdly devised by Whitefield himself, that they might be properly launched in their mission, the visitors were conducted the next morning by Mr. Smith to the minister's home. There they remained two weeks. After a few days in retirement, during which we may be sure their host was quietly preparing the way for their introduction to London society, they were carried by Whitefield to be presented to the Earl of Dartmouth, whom Whitefield called the " Daniel of his age." So well is this nobleman known in history that we need give no account of him. He was without a doubt the main pillar of the enterprise, and his honored name deserves to be kept in remembrance in the American college which bears it. Surely if he had then opposed we should have heard little more of the Indian Charity School. Occom only says of the visit to him in his diary : " He appeared like a worthy Lord indeed." We learn from other sources that he was the nobleman who had anticipated Occom's coming and that he gave him a cordial reception. Then they were taken to pay their respects to the aged and noble Lady Hotham, the wife of Sir Charles Hotham, who became a trustee of the fund and died before Occom's return. After several days they had met most of the "religious nobility" and many of the distinguished ministers of London.

The time had now come for the Indian preacher's début. It was on the sixteenth of February, in Whitefield's tabernacle. At the appointed hour of service the edifice was thronged. Many of the nobility were present, and indeed out of a genuine interest in the occasion. England had heard a great deal about the North American Indians, especially during the recent wars; but one had never been heard before in the pulpit. We can imagine the interest and stillness of the congregation as the stalwart figure of the Mohegan appeared before them. He was then forty-three years of age. His face, while distinctly that of an Indian, had a nobility of expression which some must have remarked on then, as many do who now gaze upon his picture. His flowing locks reached almost to his shoulders. In attire he was becomingly clad in ministerial black, with vest of colonial cut and knee breeches. Alas! we do not know where his text was, or if he had one. He himself only noted the "great multitude." Whitefield wrote that he preached with "acceptance." The indications are, however, that he made a decided and very favorable impression. From that time, at least, his success was assured, and so his friends wrote to Doctor Wheelock, awaiting the result with anxiety in his home on a Connecticut hilltop.

Whitefield saw that a movement, which he hoped would appeal to all denominations and sects, would do better if it preserved an attitude of independence. He arranged therefore that Occom should " go round the other denominations in a proper rotation." He also engaged for Whitaker and

Occom private lodgings, at the end of two weeks, where they were accessible to all. A servant was hired for them, whose name may have been Mary Joyner, and soon they were established in comfort. It was necessary that Occom should be inoculated as a protection against the smallpox, before he traveled much abroad. This was done at the hands of his companion, Mr. Whitaker, on the 11th of March, on which day the Indian wrote to his wife of the fact and said, "You will soon hear whether I am well of it or dead of it." He got well of it, and probably did not find it a very unpleasant experience, as he was attended by servants, had two of the best physicians in London to treat him, and was visited daily by gentlemen and ladies whose acquaintance he had made. Those days of convalescence had many pleasures to which he had not been accustomed. He became popular from the first—a center of religious interest. While he was thus entertained, his companion was about seeing the sights of the metropolis and preparing the way for Occom's appearance in the churches. He saw the king when he went to the Houses of Parliament, "amid shouts and acclamations of a joyful people," in order to sign the bill for repealing the Stamp Act. He interested further the Earl of Dartmouth, through whom "the way to the throne" he wrote "is very short." He arranged to have Occom meet His Majesty as soon as he recovered. This he did, and the king contributed £200 to the cause. It is said also that he preached later before the king in one of his chapels, and we think he did, though the date and place are unknown to us.

It is unnecessary to follow the Indian preacher, on his recovery, from church to church. As he became accustomed to the situation he improved. Large congregations were gathered, and generous collections were taken up. As a novelty he had an advantage. With true Indian sagacity he saw this, and made up his mind to use the sensation he caused to gather contributions for the Indian school. He was lionized everywhere, but we have testimony to his modesty in enduring it. In a short time he had become such a conspicuous and distinguished character in London that the players in the theaters made him an object of their mimicry. This was much to his advantage, no doubt, in advertising him. It did not trouble him in the least; he only wrote, "I little thought I should ever come to that honor." Soon they were flooded with invitations. They dined with the Earl of Dartmouth, where others of the nobility were present as guests, with Sir Charles Hotham and with many of the most celebrated divines in the city. No doubt the Indian enjoyed this. He had many a time had the hard fare of the wilderness or gone hungry. Still, his attention was not diverted from the main purpose of his visit. In this society of ladies and gentlemen who were accustomed to sit before kings, he conducted himself with the manners of the white man, as though he had never lived in a wigwam of bark. The soft tones of his voice were said to be remarkably pleasing in conversation. At that time there was unusual interest in the study of Indian life. The Earl of Dartmouth was a student of such matters. At his desire Doctor Wheelock sent him some Indian curiosities which David Fowler gathered among the Indians—"a stone pipe covered with porcupine quills, a burden band to bind loads to the back, a thong of elm bark with which captives were tied, a tobacco pouch, a knife case, and shoes and garters." No one could better entertain a company at dinner with conversation on Indian customs and stories of adventure in the wilderness than Occom. If he spoke as he sometimes wrote there was a dry humor in his sayings, at which he never laughed himself, but which must have amused his listeners. One of the most remarkable things we know of his conduct was that, having such an opportunity, with his tribal land-controversy on hand and Mason then in London in its interests, he held strictly to his pledge and did not meddle in the matter. This was certainly an indication of a strong character. His companion wrote home in triumph that Occom had not said a word on the Mason case. "I can assure the folks of Connecticut," he said, "that Mr. Occom is full as peaceable as any of them."

It was necessary, of course, that the Indian preacher should see the historic places in London. He was attended hither and thither by friends, and was greatly interested in the Houses of Parliament, Westminster Bridge, the Abbey and the Tower. Yet these sights only brought more vividly before him the contrast between such magnificence and his poor, ignorant people across the sea. He was not carried away by the most gorgeous spectacle. They took him to the royal robing-room, and he saw the king, George III, arrayed for Parliament, and watched him as he put on a diamond-studded crown ; but the sight only led him to make in his diary some disparaging comparisons between the earthly robe and crown and the heavenly. He witnessed the festival of the queen's birthday, but when he saw the attire of the nobles and thought of his naked brethren he said it reminded him of Dives and Lazarus. In fact, it appears that some who had been inclined to regard him as a visiting savage from abroad, found out, after a little, that he was not so verdant as they had thought. As religious people came to know him, they valued more and more the real spiritual earnestness of his character.

Among the notable personages of the time whom Occom met were some who had a great influence over him. One of these was Selina, the Countess of Huntingdon, to whom he was presented by Whitefield. He wrote of her in his diary, "She is the most Heavenly woman I believe in the world." Her heart had long been engaged in the Indian school. The two had frequent meetings. She hospitably entertained him at her country-seat and is said to have regarded him as "one of the most interesting and extraordinary characters of her time."[8] He made a firm friend in John Thornton, Esq., of Clapham, a most religious and benevolent gentleman.[9] To this man, who in large measure maintained Occom afterwards in his missionary labors, his later usefulness was due. Another noted person with whom the Indian formed an acquaintance was Rev. John Newton of Olney, who invited him to his home. He also met and preached for the following ministers: Martin Madan, John Conder, Samuel Stennett, Andrew Gifford, Thomas Gibbons, Samuel Brewer, William Romaine and Samuel Chandler. Indeed, there was scarcely a distinguished divine in England whom he did not meet during his stay.

As might have been expected from his friendship with Whitefield, the conservative wing of the Church of England did not grant their hearty support to the movement. At first they seemed to do so. Whitaker and Occom waited on the Archbishop of Canterbury, who "appeared quite agreeable and friendly" to the Indian, and to Whitaker expressed his approval of the plan.[10] The Archbishop of York also declared his interest in the cause. Soon, however, these churchmen altered their minds, and finally they opposed the mission. It is said that the established churches were publicly advised not to contribute. Whitaker attributed this to misrepresenta-

[8] *Life and Times of Selina, Countess of Huntingdon*, London, 1840, I, 411.

[9] John Thornton was the son of Robert Thornton, a London merchant, and was born at Clapham, April 1, 1720. He also became a merchant and acquired large wealth, which he so generously devoted to benevolence that he was esteemed as one of the philanthropists of his time. His religious affiliations were with the "Clapham Sect," but he maintained friendly relations with all Christians. He died at Bath, Nov. 7, 1790.—Chase's *Hist. of Dart. Coll.*

[10] "We waited on his Grace of Canterbury some days since, introduced by Dr. Chandler (who died last Thursday). His Lordship told us that they had tried to procure Indian youth to educate & never could—that [it was] his opinion that their Society should send some youth to your [School] & support them, if you would take them, who, when fitted should [be in] their imploy & that he would lay it before the Bishops. He says he greatly approves the Scheme & so says his Grace of York (on whom we waited the next day).'—*Whitaker Papers. Dart. Coll.*, Lett. to Wheelock, May 14, 1766.

tions from America, and it might have been in part due to the
letter of the Boston commissioners. It was during the earlier
period that William Warburton, Bishop of Gloucester, expressed to Occom the hope that he would see his way to
" Holier Orders "; but the Indian blandly answered, " I had
no such view when I came from home." This noted divine is
said to have taunted Mr. Whitaker unmercifully for being a
Presbyterian. Probably he was the one who made the overtures of Episcopal ordination and dignities to Occom.[11] Notwithstanding this opposition among ruling authorities, many of
the Episcopal churches did contribute to the cause, as well as
ministers and laymen among them. Occom did not suffer himself to be disturbed by his treatment. He had honestly no
desire for honors ; he wanted money for the education of Indians. Liberality of views in ecclesiastical matters was always
characteristic of him. He expressed a willingness to fellowship
all Christian sects, and he uniformly did so throughout his life.
This sentiment augmented his success in England. He knew
the differences between the denominations, but he never
uttered a word which made a personal enemy of Independent
or Episcopalian, Baptist, Quaker or Methodist. This was no
easy task, for he was warned by each against the other. Even
Dr. Chandler advised him "not to own Mr. Whitefield as a
friend either to Dissenters or to the old standards of the
Church of England." Such words did not seem to prejudice
him. Still, he never forgot the treatment he received from
some of the bishops in England. When he was safely at
home among the hills of Mohegan he uttered his mind after
this fashion :

[11] " We are informed that the Rev. Mr. Occum, during his residence in England,
had the offer of a Gown and with some considerable lucrative offer, which he refused." [*New London Gazette*, June 3, 1768.] Occom wrote Mr. Green, the pub-
lisher of this newspaper, April 17, 1769, that he received an offer of Episcopal ordination soon after he reached London and that his refusal highly displeased the
bishops. This was probably the sequel of Rev. Matthew Graves' sanguine hopes.

Now I am in my own country, I may freely inform you of what I honestly and soberly think of the Bishops, Lord Bishops, and Archbishops of England. In my view, they dor't look like Gospel Bishops or ministers of Christ. I can't find them in the Bible. I think they a good deal resemble the Anti-christian Popes. I find the Gospel Bishops resemble, in some good measure their good Master; and they follow him in the example he has left them. They discover meekness and humility; are gentle and kind unto all men—ready to do good unto all—they are compassionate and merciful unto the miserable, and charitable to the poor. But I did not find the Bishops of England so. Upon my word, if I never spoke the truth before I do now. I waited on a number of Bishops, and represented to them the miserable and wretched situation of the poor Indians, who are perishing for lack of spiritual knowledge, and begged their assistance in evangelizing these poor heathen. But if you can believe me, they never gave us one single brass farthing. It seems to me that they are very indifferent whether the poor Indians go to Heaven or Hell. I can't help my thoughts: and I am apt to think they don't want the Indians to go to Heaven with them.[12]

Whitaker and Occom were occupied in the canvass of London and vicinity until the last of July. Then they made a tour through the west of England, which engaged them about four months. After this they were in and about London and in the eastern counties for a time. The contributions increased. Everywhere it was a new story. Immense audiences were gathered. On one occasion the service was held in the churchyard, and the congregation was estimated at three thousand. In the spring of 1767 they set out for Scotland by the way of Liverpool,[13] preaching as they went. They arrived in May, and were present at the session of the General Assembly. It was known here, as it had not been at first in England, that they were acting under the authority of a board of correspondents of the Scotch Society. Here their work, therefore, received the official endorsement of the society which all Scotchmen revered, through its president, the Mar-

---

[12] Sprague's *Annals*, III, 193, 194 ; Prime's *Hist. of Long Island*, p. 111.

[13] " Liverpool is a pool of errors & wickedness. The ministers here are Socinians, one Arminian & a Baptist the same, and another Baptist sound, who is alone in a town containing 30,000 souls & his congregation is a handful. Fifty years ago the Gospel flourished here."—*Occom's Diary*, May 2, 1767.

quis of Lothian. In the presence of the Assembly Occom brought out the address of the Oneida Indians and the wampum belt, for which they had sent in haste as they were leaving America. He also carried it about among their churches.[14] It was a telling note to sound in Scotland. Their religious fervor was aroused as the Highland clans were wont to be by the flaming torch. The funds collected were to be paid to the Scotch Society, and to be held by them " towards building and endowing an Indian academy for clothing, boarding, maintaining and educating such Indians as are designed for missionaries and schoolmasters, and for maintaining those who are, or hereafter shall be employed on this glorious errand." Their stay in Scotland was not long, but they collected there for the above purpose £2,529.[15] On the fifteenth of July they went to Ireland, expecting to meet the synod. They were too late, and " finding there a Mr. Edwards collecting for a Baptist college to be established in Rhode Island," they wisely returned to England to finish the work there.

The friends of the cause in London had early determined to appoint an English board of trustees to receive and care for the funds raised in England. This had not been at first contemplated. A charter had always been Doctor Wheelock's desire ; but it was opposed by some of his influential friends. The trustees having been selected, Mr. Whitaker, in whose name the contributions had been received as the agent for Doctor Wheelock, transferred his authority to the board, November 28, 1766. On the twenty-sixth of January following, the trustees met and organized with the choice of the Earl of Dartmouth as president, John Thornton, Esq., as treasurer, and

---

[14] See chapter V, note 14.

[15] The Scotch Society still holds this fund. In 1803 it amounted to £2,626, and it is now said to be over £6,000. The interest only can be expended, and it can neither be added to the principal nor draw interest. Our American schools have many promising Indian students, and it would seem as if this honorable society could devise some acceptable plan for assisting them.

Robert Keen, a merchant of London, as secretary. The public were duly advised of this action in the appendix to the narrative of 1767, and in a continuation of the same issued two years later a complete statement was made of the funds collected. With what was received later, the amount raised in England was about £9,500, or more than £12,000 in all. Whitaker and Occom were engaged in this work two years and one month, at an expense of about £500. From the fund, also, their families were supported, and they each received as a gratuity £100. Occom delivered more than four hundred sermons or addresses. Such a charity toward a missionary cause in the colonies had never before been known. It did not pass without recognition. The General Association of Connecticut, at its meeting, June 21, 1768, passed an appropriate vote of thanks to the churches of the mother country.

No one can read the scattered correspondence relating to this mission without being convinced that its success was due almost solely to Samson Occom. Mr. Whitaker very soon became a mere agent. He seems not to have conducted himself with discretion at all times, expressing his opinion too freely on political matters. He even brought upon himself the severe censure of the trustees for his mismanagement of certain remittances. It should be remembered, however, that his position was a difficult one, as that of the fifth wheel to a coach always is. He went to England to care for the Indian, but, as it turned out, his services were hardly needed in that capacity. Occom, on the other hand, won universal esteem. Robert Keen wrote of him, he is a "plain, honest-hearted man, who is well received wherever he goes." John Thornton and George Whitefield, who saw much of him, gave him their unqualified commendation. After his return he received a letter from Dr. Andrew Gifford, in which the writer said, "Your very decent and proper behaviour charmèd most, if not all, who had the pleasure of conversing with you; and your hu-

mility and piety I doubt not contributed much to the success
of your application for the Indian school."[16] Such, in substance, was the opinion of all. McClure says in his diary that
'Occom's reputation was such in Scotland that some Gentlemen there offered to obtain for him a Doctorate in Divinity from the University of Edinburgh, but he modestly declined the honour." He received from friends here and
there some tokens of this regard, mostly in the way of
books which he brought back to his home at Mohegan. The
king presented him with a number of volumes. When, years
afterwards, Occom removed to the Oneida country, most of
these remained behind and became scattered. A few have survived to this day and are cherished by their owners as memen-
toes of the great Indian preacher.[17]

We are indebted to this mission to England for the pictures
of Samson Occom which have come down to us. Something
should be said concerning these. It is known that two portraits of him were made in oil, from which all that have since
been reproduced here and there originated. One was painted
by Mason Chamberlain, a well-known artist of the time, somewhat famous for the remarkable fidelity of his likenesses.
This was done at the motion of the Earl of Dartmouth, and
probably at his expense. He also had a portrait of Doctor Whitaker, painted by the same artist, which was presented to him,
and now hangs in the gallery at Dartmouth College. We think

---

[16] *Conn. Hist. Soc., Indian Papers*, Lett. May 22, 1769.

[17] Rev. James Houghton, Bryn Mawr, Pa., has a Bible which belonged to Occom—
a "Breeches Bible" of 1561. It has within the book-plate of " Henry Williams "
and below it the words "Shepton Mallet, Somersetshire to the Rev^d Mr. Occom, pres-
ent." The Conn. Hist. Soc. has a psalter in Latin and Syriac [Liber Psalmorum
Davidis Regis & Prophetæ] which was presented in 1880 by Mrs. L. F. S. Foster of
Norwich, Conn. In the possession of the Ripley family at Norwich there is also a
"Paraphrase of the New Testament," which is said to have been given Occom by
George III. It is inscribed "Samuel Warren's Book, which he bought from Samson
Occum, which he brought from England 1766." [Caulkins' *Hist. of Norwich*, p.
465.] We have also heard of other volumes from his library.

that both these portraits were made in the winter of 1766, while they were in London. Occom's was retained in England, and although some search has been made, its owner and place are unknown to us. Another portrait of the Indian preacher was painted, we think later and by another artist, though it may have been at the same time and by Chamberlain for aught we can prove to the contrary. This picture was presented to him, and brought home to Mohegan. We infer from the action of the Earl of Dartmouth in Doctor Whitaker's case that he also had this second portrait made, and possibly Occom had his choice. It remained at Mohegan hanging in his old home, under the care of his kindred, until 1830, when it was secured by Miss Sarah L. Huntington. She placed it in the hands of John Trumbull, the Connecticut painter, for restoration, since which it has been lost to view.[18] Happily both these pictures were reproduced; the Chamberlain portrait being chiefly known through the excessively rare mezzotint published in 1768, and the Mohegan portrait through the lithographs, two hundred and fifty of which were struck off shortly after its recovery, and sold for the benefit of the Indians.[19] The difference between them and all copies made since can

[18] DeForest's *Indians of Connecticut*, Preface, p. x.

[19] The following pictures of Occom are noted. After the Chamberlain portrait: (1) "Mezzotint by [John] Spilsbury after Chamberlain." Inscribed "The first Indian Minister that ever was in Europe, and who accompanied the Rev. N. Whitaker in an application to Great Britain for Charities to support ye Rev. Dr. Wheelock's Indian Academy, and Missionaries among ye Native Savages of N. America. Published according to Act of Parliament, Sept. 20, 1768, by Henry Parker at No. 82. in Cornhill, London." Inscriptions have verbal differences. Early impressions have none, as the author's, from which the frontispiece was made. After one of these, belonging to Samuel G. Drake, several photographs were made by Kimball, Concord, N. H. [Ex-Gov. B. F. Prescott: Columbia Town Library] and thus came the painting by U. D. Tenney, presented by Governor Prescott to Dartmouth College. This mezzotint is a folio, and has been sold as high as two guineas. (2) Engraving, "Ridley & Blood Sc — Revd Samson Occom, Indian Preacher. Pub by Williams & Smith Stationers Court 1st Octr 1808." [*London Evangelical Magazine*, October, 1808.] Sometimes sold with Occom's sermon. After the Mohegan portrait: (1) Lithograph. Inscription: "The Reverend Samson Occom The First Indian Minister that ever was in

be readily detected.   In the Chamberlain portrait the subject
faces to his right, the uplifted hand is pointing to an open
folio Bible upright on a table, and there are implements of
Indian warfare on the wall.   In the Mohegan portrait the subject faces to his left, the hand rests on an open Bible flat on
a table before him, and on the wall there is a bookcase, with
books.   The former has the hair flowing back from the fore-
head, the latter has it parted in the middle.

It was near the close of the year 1767 when Doctor Whitaker
and the Indian preacher returned to London.   They made
thereafter some short tours round about.   In the spring they
prepared for the homeward voyage.   It has been said that
there was a disagreement between them, in consequence of
which they did not return together.[20]   We have found no evidence of any personal differences, though Occom probably
sided with the trustees in their criticism of Doctor Whitaker
already noted.   The latter was doubtless detained by the business.   He did not sail until April and then came in a ship to
New York, reaching Norwich on or about the second of June.
Occom was ready to depart in March and sailed for Boston
the latter part of the month in Captain Robert Calef's ship,
London Packet, which arrived on the twentieth of May.[21]   He
had a stormy passage of eight weeks.   Soon after they sailed
he was taken very ill and for some time he was in a delirium.

Europe who went to Britain to obtain charities for the support of the Rev^d Dr
Wheelocks Indian Accademy & Missionaries among the savages of North America in
1768." Other copies have " Sampson Occom " and " Academy." The Conn. Hist.
Soc. has both.   From this lithograph De Forest's cut was made [p. 459] by " N. Orr
Sc." [See De Forest's *Ind. of Conn.*, Pref., p. x ; *Mem. of Mrs. Sarah L. Huntington Smith*, p. 123.]   This is a folio, two hundred and fifty copies being made at the
expense of Miss Murray of New York about 1831, and perhaps more later.   They
are now scarce.   (2) *Schoolcraft's Indian Tribes*, large edn., vol. V, p. 518.   Engraving by Illman & Sons. • (3) Picture in India ink, by Edward G. Kunkely, Utica,
N. Y., in Hamilton College gallery.

20 Caulkins' *Hist. of Norwich*, edn. 1845, p. 296.

21 *New London Gazette*, May 27, 1768 ; McClure's *Mem. of Wheelock*, p. 175 ;
Narrative, 1769, p. 144.

At the end of a month he began to amend and before the voyage ended he had quite recovered his strength. So with gladness at last he greeted once more his native land, reflecting on the joy of a safe arrival "at the haven of the New Jerusalem." There were then hearty congratulations for him in Boston. These he hardly waited to receive. He started on horseback the next morning and soon he was again among the hills of Mohegan—at home.

CHAPTER IX

The portrait which an artist puts upon the canvas owes its likeness oftentimes to the shadows. It is hardly possible that an Indian, with all the defects of his race, could grow to the full stature of a civilized man without struggles against his hereditary weaknesses. At all events it is the office of the historian to set forth the facts without prejudice. Thus we are brought to consider the darkest period in Samson Occom's life.

The Indian preacher, whose mission to England had been discouraged by most and its full success anticipated by none, came back to Mohegan a distinguished character. He had won a fame among the whites. Many pulpits, into which he would never have been admitted before, were now open to him. His own people were brought more than ever under his influence. Some of the baser sort were jealous of him; but most of them regarded him with respect and many with affection. He was surely the foremost man of their race in the colonies. In this situation Occom may have developed some pride. His friends had feared he would. Still we fail to detect any evidences of it in his extant writings. So far as they give us light, the reaction came to him from his personal discouragements and his sore disappointment at the sequel of his mission to England in behalf of the Indian school.

The agreement under which Occom had left his family provided that they were to be cared for and supported by Doctor Wheelock in his absence. The expenses of the missions were large, the resources were small. There was, indeed, no stated income which could be applied to this purpose. This Indian family were by no means forgotten ; but amid his many cares Doctor Wheelock was undoubtedly remiss in supplying, promptly, their necessities. Mary Occom had to remind him of her wants in such words as these : " I am out of Corn and have no Money to buy any with and am affraid we shall suffer for want." Of this apparent neglect Occom heard on returning home. His feelings were wounded. The father at Lebanon had not dealt kindly by his Indian son. For some time he did not go thither to see him.

Occom also found his family in a distracted state. His wife was in poor health ; his children showed the need of paternal government. McClure has the following paragraph on this family in his diary : " He appeared to preside in his family with dignity & to have his children in subjection. In these, however, & in his wife, he was not happy. He wished to live in English style ; but his Wife who was of the Montauk Tribe retained a fondness for her indian customs. She declined, evening & morning setting at table. Her dress was mostly indian, & when he spake to her in english, she answered in her native language, although she could speak good english. His children when they left him, adopted the wild & roving life of Savages." There is much truth in this statement, though the wife was certainly an estimable Christian woman, and all his children did not turn out as indicated.

Occom had then seven children, ranging from sixteen to three years of age, as follows : Mary, Aaron, Tabitha, Olive, Christiana, Talitha and Benoni. Three others, at least, were afterwards born to him : Theodosia, Lemuel Fowler and Andrew Gifford. As a father he was always affectionate, and anxious that his children should rise above the Indian's estate and enter useful lives. Some of them did so, but others brought him, as he afterwards wrote, " sorrow on sorrow." We have an instance of his playfulness—the only one we have met with—in a letter which he wrote from England. As such it is worth recording :

My dear Mary and Esther—

Perhaps you may query whether I am well : I came from home well, was by the way well, got over well, am received at London well, and am treated extremely well,—yea, I am caress'd too well. And do you pray that I may be well; and that I may do well, and in Time return Home well. And I hope you are well, and wish you well, and as I think you begun well, so keep on well, that you may end well and then all will be well.

And So Farewell,
SAMSON OCCOM.[1]

The eldest son, Aaron, had been a second time put under Doctor Wheelock's care in the father's absence. He had, however, no particular interest in obtaining an education and was inclined to be wild. He did not behave well in the school, and the minister was compelled to write the father about him. The reply betrays Occom's disappointment : " If he Inclines to Book Learning, give him a good English Education, but if not, let him go to some good master to Learn [the] Joiners Trade if he Inclines to that, and if that Won't do Send him over to me and I will give him away to some gentlemen here."[2] In this same letter he expressed the fear that his peregrinations had compelled him to neglect his children. Their training had been left to his wife and they needed a father's restraint. This son continued to be somewhat wayward. He married at eighteen Ann Robin, a daughter of Samuel, an adopted Indian from Middletown, and died in February, 1771, leaving a posthumous son named Aaron. The conduct of this son was a trial Occom had to meet when he returned from England. Yet he had been a faithful father. His letters con-

[1] Caulkins' *Hist. of Norwich*, p. 465. Miss Caulkins says this was written to his two daughters. We know no daughter Esther, and think she was a cousin or friend of Mary.

[2] *Wheelock Papers*, Lett. Feb. 12, 1767 ; see also Mary Occom to Wheelock, Nov. 8, 1766.

tain such tender words as these to his children : " Remember wherever you are, you are in the presence of that God that made you and to him you must give an account of your conduct and remember the Day of your Death is hastening."

There were also many perplexities and cares awaiting him at. Mohegan. His house had never been thoroughly completed. It was necessary that he should at once bring his acres under proper cultivation for the support of his family. Indeed, the main question was what he should do for a living. He was again out of employment. The work which he desired to undertake was that of a general missionary to the New England tribes. For this he was preeminently fitted. He had relatives or friends in most of the Indian settlements thereabouts. This was the work, it will be remembered, which he had begun under the commissioners when he was called off to serve under the Connecticut correspondents. But he could not now return to this, for the commissioners had been offended by his going to England, as we have related. The correspondents had been superseded by the English trustees. They took up no new work and in 1769 ceased to meet. Moreover, Doctor Wheelock refused to support him in such a work, because missions among the seacoast tribes were under the jurisdiction of the commissioners at Boston.[3] The only service which was offered him was a mission westward to the Onondagas, which Doctor Wheelock repeatedly urged upon him. This would take him away from his family. He felt that it was his duty to remain with them more than he had ; they needed his care and training. Still, there were other reasons for declining this mission, as will presently appear. These Doctor Wheelock did not then understand and hence he misjudged Occom. He wrote of him thus to Whitefield : " He is averse to seek any settlement more convenient for future usefulness y^n at Mohegan—He consents to take a tour into

[3] *Wheelock Papers*, Letts. Jan. 8, 1770, and June 20, 1771.

ye wilderness y^t season.   What he will do for future support I
cant tell—There is no probability y^t ye Boston Commissioners
will do anything for him—I suspect his principal dependence
is upon ye tillage of his lands.   I am fully convinced y^t God
does not design y^t Indians shall have ye lead in y^s affair at
present."[4]   The sum of the matter was, therefore, that Samson
Occom, at a time when he had most reason to expect some
consideration on account of his services, was stranded at
Mohegan.   He had left every other employment to obey his
patron, and having been used to his advantage, he was discharged.   So the Indian viewed the situation.   Whitefield
had told him, he said, that "they had made him a tool to collect monies for them in England, but when he got to America
they would set him adrift."   It is unnecessary to say that
Doctor Wheelock had no such intention.   He thought for
some time that Occom had an annual pension from England.
This was not the fact.   He had only received several private
gifts from Mr. Thornton, who, after the Trust had ceased,
wrote Occom that he might draw on him for £50, if he was at
any time in distress.   When the trustees in England learned
how matters stood, they openly declared that Occom had been
ill-treated.   In 1772 they wrote him to draw for £50 at once,
and for £25 every six months or for £50 annually during
their pleasure.[5]   The Scotch Society also made him a grant.
At this time Doctor Wheelock had begun to see the other
side of the case.   His trusted pupil, David McClure, visited
Occom, learned the situation, and wrote thus to his patron :
" Before he went to England, he was under the pay of the
Boston board, and since his return has been rejected by them
and by the School too.   And considering what Indian Genius
& temper are, has there not, Sir, been too much occasion for

---

[4] *Wheelock Papers*, Lett. April 24, 1769.
[5] *Conn. Hist. Soc., Indian Papers*, Lett. Thornton to Occom, May 12, 1772 ;
Chase's *Hist. of Dart. Coll*, p. 243.

him to complain of neglect?"[6] Thus, after four years, this cause for ill-feeling was in a measure removed.

This, however, was not the only reason why the friendly relations of many years between Wheelock and Occom were disturbed. When the Indian returned from England he found his patron wholly engaged in his scheme for the removal of the Indian Charity School. Of this movement the historian of Dartmouth College has given an admirable account.[7] So early as 1761, Doctor Wheelock had conceived the idea of locating nearer the Indian tribes westward. He wrote Sir William Johnson in 1762, as follows: " If way could be made for setting up this school in some convenient place and the settlement of three or four Towns round about it, I would remove with it and bring several Ministers with me of the best character and take care to people the place with Inhabitants of known honesty, Integrity and such as love Indians and will seek their Interest." Here in the germ was his plan, designated the year following, in his plea to the Privy Council for a charter, as " A Proposal for Introducing Religion, Learning, Agriculture and Manufacture among the Pagans in America." The place then in view was on the Susquehanna river. Sir William Johnson was even then opposed to a removal among the Six Nations. He would have been intensely hostile to it later, and this was reason enough why a location, favored by both Kirkland and Occom, was impracticable. Various propositions were made to Doctor Wheelock, from Albany, Stockbridge, Hebron and other places ; but the most advantageous was of a tract of land in the western part of the Province of New Hampshire. The formation of the Board of Trust in England to hold the funds there collected, was a fatal blow to all hopes of a royal charter, for the trustees were opposed, but they finally consented to the removal, and, on the 3d of April, 1769, approved the

" *Wheelock Papers*, Lett. June 30, 1772.
[7] Chase's *Hist. of Dart. Coll.*, pp. 32-35, 46, 90 ff, 217 ff.

location. This was not Occom's affair. He had, however,
while in England, declared his judgment in favor of remaining
at Lebanon, where the school was near the New England Indians. On his return he expressed the opinion that, if the
school removed, it should be to a location in the midst of the
Indians of the Oneida country. He feared, long before the
result was apparent, that a college in "the woods of Coos"
would be no advantage to the Indians for whom all the money
had been collected. Still, it was not so much the removal that
he opposed as the alteration in Dr. Wheelock's plan, to educate
more white missionaries and fewer Indians. To this change
Occom was never reconciled. It seems that when he had left
England, the trustees, who had great confidence in him, " engaged him to write particularly of the school and the disposal
of the moneys collected in England."[8] He did not wish to do
so, but they insisted. Yet it was some time before he wrote
at all, which his patron attributed to neglect. In 1770 David
McClure visited Mohegan and found out the reason, which he
stated as follows : "If he wrote he must not be silent concerning the state of the school as friends there w'd expect that
from him if he wrote, and as the school is at present constituted he imagined an account of it would not be agreeable to
gentlemen at home nor answer their expectations. He complained, but in a friendly manner, that the Indian was converted into an English School and that the English had
crowded out the Indian youth. He instanced one Symons a
likely Indian who came to get admittance but could not be admitted because the school was full. He supposed that the
gentlemen in England thought the School at present was made
up chiefly of Indian youth, and that should he write and inform them to the contrary, as he must if he wrote, it would give
them a disgust and jealousy that the charities were not applied in a way agreeable to the intention of the donors and

[8] Chase's *Hist. of Dart. Coll.*, p. 63 n.

benefactors, which was to educate Indians chiefly."[9] Some correspondence ensued between Wheelock and Occom on this point. The latter wrote thus: "In my apprehension your present plan is not calculated to benefit the poor Indians, it is no ways winning to them and unless there is an alterative suitable to the minds of the Indians you will never do much more good among the Indians : your First Plan was much better than the last. you did much good in it and if you rightly managed the Indians your Institution would have flourished by this Time."[10] When Doctor Wheelock expressed to him the hope that he would see many of his "tawny" brethren nourished in that Alma Mater, the Indian replied : "I am very jealous that instead of your institution becoming Alma Mater to my brethren, she will be too Alba Mater to nourish the tawnies."[11] He was besought by his patron "if he did not favor the institution, not to harm it, as he well knew no one could do it so much harm as he should he attempt it." For some time Occom did maintain a friendly silence. He was compelled at length to disclose his feelings to friends in England. The charge that the funds had been perverted was to such an extent current in 1771, that Doctor Wheelock was forced to make answer in his narrative.[12] He certainly did not intend to divert funds contributed for the Indians ; but he thought they would be profited most by the education of white missionaries. Such was his reply. Still, Occom was never persuaded to alter his opinion. Several years after Doctor Wheelock's death, he wrote thus : "Doc[r] Wheelock's Indian Academy or Schools are become altogether unprofitable to the poor Indians. In short, he has done little or no good to the Indians with all that money we collected in England since we

[9] *Wheelock Papers*, Lett. McClure to Wheelock, May 21, 1770.

[10] *Ibid.*, Lett. June 1, 1773.

[11] *Conn. Hist. Soc., Indian Papers* and "Havermeyer Letter," Occom to Wheelock, July 24, 1771, Dartmouth College.

[12] *Wheelock's Narrative*, 1771, p. 18.

got home.   That money never educated but one Indian and
one Mollatoe—that is part Negro and part Indian—and there
has not been one Indian in that Institution this some time."[13]
This was not exactly the truth.   Such, however, was Occom's
opinion—the funds had been perverted.

Why had this teacher, who had once considered the Christianizing of Indians by Indians so important, now come to
place his hope in white missionaries ?   He had lost confidence
in his Christian Indians.   Some of his pupils had apostatized
or lapsed into the evil habits of their race.   At the same time
it came to pass that they lost confidence in him.   His influence over the tribes he had befriended was impaired.   When
they came to suspect that he had cast them off, his chances
of prosecuting missions among them or gathering their children in his school, were gone.   He had held his scholars by
his personal, fatherly interest in them ; but the bond was
broken between the father and his children.   It was never restored.   The decline of the Indian Charity School was not
caused by its removal.   It had received its death-blow the
year before that matter was finally decided.   Its founder was
right in thinking that a good foundation, with lands and
friendly whites round about, were favorable conditions.   He
might have recovered what he had lost by locating among the
Six Nations ; but that is uncertain.   The enlargement of the
school into a college, and the broadening of its purpose to educate more white youth, were not necessarily fatal departures.
It had always professed to exist in part for such pupils.   This
institution, which had attained an honorable fame, lost within
a year its *esprit de corps* as an Indian school.   It was the mis-
fortune rather than the fault of its noble founder.

Samson Occom had been at home only a few weeks when
he received a visit from a company of Oneida Indians.   He
had then from Deacon Thomas, their leader, a true account of

[13] *Conn. Hist. Soc., Indian Papers.*

the Western missions. Troubles had arisen which he then saw would lead to their utter collapse. This was the reason, already hinted at, why he would not accept the offer of a mission to the Onondagas. The Indians told him about the behavior of Doctor Wheelock's eldest son, Ralph, who had only lately returned from his third and most fatal journey westward in behalf of his father.[14] It was a mistake to send this "imprudent, domineering and irascible" young man on business so important. His conduct toward Kirkland had been very offensive. When the missionary that spring had broken down in health and retired for a time from his work, Ralph Wheelock had accused him to the Indians of running away. They had nobly defended him. He was their beloved father. This was the reply they received from his lordship: "Who do you think your father is? Do you think his power and authority are equal to mine? He is no more than my father's servant, and so are all those ministers and schoolmasters he sends here." Was it likely that the Indians would be favorably disposed toward this young Rehoboam who announced that he was to be his father's successor? He went on to Onondaga, and there had a high-voiced quarrel in their council-house. Can any one wonder that Occom did not wish to carry the gospel under the patronage of Doctor Wheelock to this mortally offended tribe? The son made garbled reports of his journeys to his father, so the real state of affairs was not known for some time. Another mistake was made when Doctor Wheelock sent back with these

[14] Ralph Wheelock, born in 1746, graduated at Yale College in 1765, and became for nearly two years the master of the Indian school. He made three journeys westward in behalf of the missions, the first July 11, 1766, with Rev. Benjamin Pomeroy; the second with Augustine Hibbard, about Sept. 1, 1767 [*Narr.*, 1769, pp. 29-36], and the third with Allyn Mather, from March 7, 1768, to April 29, 1768 [*Narr.*, 1769, pp. 44-54]. In 1770 he was a tutor at Dartmouth College. His health was impaired by epilepsy, and he was thought to be irresponsible in part for the trouble he caused. Subsequent attempts to heal the disaffection of the Indians failed. [See Avery's MS. Reports, Dart. Coll., Oct. 1, 1771, and May 31, 1772.] Ralph Wheelock died at Hanover, Feb. 7, 1817.

Oneidas as his envoy to the Indian congress about to meet at
Canajoharie, Rev. Jacob W. Johnson, of Groton. He had no
experience, and was not qualified for a diplomatist. In the
course of his negotiations he made a breach between Doctor
Wheelock and Sir William Johnson, who was all but an Indian
emperor.[15] What favor could the Indian Charity School expect
thereafter ? So in the storm of a season its hopes were swept
away. The Oneidas came again in a few months to Lebanon
and took home their children. Several remaining Mohawks
were sent for. The New England Indians seem to have been
no longer wanted. The springs had dried up.

All these discouraging circumstances prepared the way for
the so-called fall of Samson Occom. He was disheartened.
The dreams of many an hour abroad had vanished. In the
autumn of 1768 he was taken sick, and for a long time was in
poor health. As he could, he went hither and thither among
the New England Indians without commission or support.
Some time in the month of February following he was overcome
on an occasion with strong drink. The circumstances of this
fall are unknown to us. It happened shortly after a second
visit of the Oneida chiefs, when they came to take home their
children. Our earliest information is derived from the letters
of Doctor Wheelock, who wrote of the fact to Occom's friends.
In a letter to Whitefield, on the 24th of April, he said : " God
has left him to fall into Intemperance (I hope in Great Mercy
to him) he appears considerably humble." [16] Much to Doctor
Wheelock's regret, it seems from the same letter, he was not
humble enough to accept a mission to the Onondagas, for
which he still thought him fit. Most writers who have noticed
the career of Occom have made much of this matter. Some

---

[15] Rev. Jacob W. Johnson was then the minister at Groton [Ledyard], where he
had ministered some to the Mushantuxet Pequots. See on his life Dexter's *Yale
Biographies*, I, 649-651 ; Chase's *Hist. Dart. Coll.*, pp. 79-84 ; and *Doc. Hist. of N. Y.*,
IV, 244-250.

[16] *Wheelock Papers*, Lett. April 24, 1769. See also letter of March 9, 1769.

have thought it an important argument against attempts to civilize the Indian that this man, "the glory of his race," suffered a fall.[17] The drinking customs of the time being what they were, it cannot be thought strange if an Indian took enough liquor in a few instances to feel the effect of it. If he had not taken any it would have been stranger. He would doubtless have been the sole clerical representative of a total abstinence party in Connecticut. Occom was in truth greatly humbled. He made known his fault at once to his friends, and was far more concerned about himself than they were. The most remarkable feature of the case was, that he accused himself before the Suffolk Presbytery. A copy of his confession is extant, in which he says: "I have been shamefully overtaken with strong drink, by which I have greatly wounded the cause of God, blemished the pure religion of Jesus Christ, blackened my own character and hurt my own soul."[18] This is how it came to pass that "his intemperance drew upon him the discipline of the Church." Let us see what this ecclesiastical body thought of this terrible fall:

In the Presbytery of Suffolk at Easthampton, April 12, 1769. . . . The Presbytery received a Letter from Mr. Occom in which he accuses himself of having been guilty of intemperate drinking, for which he very highly condemns himself; and at the same Time understood that a Report had become Publick. The Presbytery entered upon Consideration of the Matter, and from the best Light they can now obtain are of the Opinion that said Accusation arises from a very gloomy and desponding Frame of Mind, under which they are informed that Mr. Occom has, for some time Past laboured; and do therefore refer the further Consideration of this Matter

[17] " There has never been a more idle scheme of philanthropy, than that of converting a savage into a civilized man. No one attempt, it is believed, has ever been successful. Even Sampson Occum, before his death relapsed into some of the worst habits of his tribe; and no North American Indian of unmixed blood, whatever pains may have been taken with his education, has been known to adopt the manners of civilized men, or to pass his life among them."—Spark's *Life of John Ledyard*, Am. Biog., XXIV, 91. See also, Prime's *Hist. of Long Island*, p. 110, and Sprague's *Annals*, III, 194. Sprague follows Prime in erroneously giving the date as 1764.

[18] *Conn. Hist. Soc., Indian Papers;* Sprague's *Annals*, III, 194.

to our next session of Presbytery, desiring Mr. Buell in the Mean Time to obtain all possible Intelligence with respect to s^d. Affair, & make report thereof at our next Session.

In the Presbytery of Suffolk at Bridge Hampton, November 1, 1769. . . The Presbytery next entered upon the Consideration of Mr. Occom's Affair, which on reading the Minutes of last session of Presbytery, we find refered to this. Mr. Occom being now present was very particularly examined by the Presbytery with respect to all the Circumstances of s^d. Affair, and Mr. Buell having reported to the Presbytery the Intelligence he had obtained relating thereto. The Presbytery are fully of Opinion that all the Sensations of Intoxication, which he condemned himself for arose, not from any Degree of intemperate drinking, but from having Drank a small Quantity of Spirituous Liquor after having been all day without food.[19]

This record is very remarkable ; first, in that a minister confessed at all, and second, in that, having confessed, he was acquitted. The reader who has looked over the ministerial rum-accounts of those days, will wonder whether the other members of the Suffolk Presbytery would have dared to take such a risk. Had the Rev. Eleazar Wheelock, D. D., never had any such "sensations"? He paid for a considerable quantity of spirituous liquor. What a unique case! Occom accused himself, was examined, and pronounced not guilty! These interesting points are brought out,—he had been for some time in "a very gloomy and desponding frame of mind," he had been on the occasion "all day without food," and he had not indulged in "intemperate drinking." If this were all, the case would be closed. Doctor Wheelock, however, in his letters, says that again, in the summer of 1770, Occom had a "Second grievious fall into the sin of intemperance," and in a "public and agravated manner," the report of which "spread far and wide."[20] The report went to England in one of these letters to John Thornton, Esq., the Indian's true friend. This benevolent gentleman made a reply, which could not have been

[19] *MS. Rec. Suffolk Presbytery.*
[20] *Wheelock Papers*, Letts. Nov. 9, 1770, and June 20, 1771.

altogether agreeable to Doctor Wheelock. " I was grieved," he wrote, " at what I heard of Mr. Occom. Indeed, I fear he had hard usage and that drove him into the horrid sin of drinking. Pray my dear Sir, use him tenderly, for I am much mistaken if his heart is not right with God." [21] David McClure made a somewhat similar remark, when he suggested to Doctor Wheelock that Occom had been neglected. " The Crimes of intemperance," he wrote, " with which he has been charged are very much extenuated by the temptations he was under." [22] The Lebanon minister has left no evidence, unfortunately, that he did deal tenderly with the Indian in this matter. He wrote him reproachful letters, he magnified his fault, and himself spread the report of it. This was his excuse—he had, the year before, lost faith in some of his boy schoolmasters for the same reason, and was easily persuaded that there was no good in them. Occom's fall was his final reason for turning to the whites.

We do not know that this Indian minister was ever again guilty of taking too much spirituous liquor, though he often went all day without food. He certainly was never in the habit of drinking. He says " he was too poor to provide for his family anything but the plainest food and they drank only cold water with occasionally a little beer." He did not " relapse into some of the worst habits of his tribe," as has been charged. The suspicion, however, followed him to the close of his life. It is known that his enemies kept it alive. Years afterwards, when he was ministering to his Indian church in New Stockbridge, this report seems to have come to the notice of the Presbytery of Albany, of which he was then a member. " March 1st 1791 a letter was sent to Mr. Occom requiring him to state his reasons for not attending Presbytery and he was warned that in case of failure his name would be striken

---

[21] *Wheelock Papers*, Lett. April 26, 1771.
[22] *Ibid.*, Lett. June 30, 1772.

from the roll." [23]   His reason was that he was too poor to make the long journey.   But this action probably concealed an inquiry into rumors which had reached them concerning his intemperance.   We find in the manuscript diary of Samuel Kirkland, under date August 10, 1791, the following entry: "Visited by Rev^d Mr. Lindley member of the Presbytery of Albany, who was sent by that body to enquire into some instances of misconduct reported concerning Mr. Occom: particularly the sin which most easily besets poor Indians." [24]   A thorough inquiry was made into this matter by Mr. Lindley on the ground, but he found nothing to report at all detrimental to Mr. Occom; and on the eighth of September the Presbytery gave assurances of their confidence in him, by directing his ministrations in his little church among the Indians.   We have some light on this case in this characteristic of the man—he was given to humiliations by his temperament.   If on any occasion his conscience smote him for misconduct, which others less sensitive would have passed by, he thought it mete to shrive his soul in confession.   In " despondencies, discomforts and almost desperations," he says, he thus found some peace and resignation to the will of God.   Thus in the discipline of humility he strove to subdue that Indian nature which he was always conscious of possessing.   There are abundant evidences of his victory, and testimonials of his subsequent good character.   "In his latter years his life is said to have been entirely exemplary." [25]

Here is the lesson which the history of Indian civilization so clearly teaches.   The curse of the race is rum.   In those days of old, when drinking was a universal custom, the Indian was unintentionally tempted by his friends.   He could not be a moderate drinker—it was a constitutional impossibility.

[23] *MS. Records of Pres. of Albany.*
[24] *MS. Diary of Kirkland*, in possession of Mr. Thornton K. Lothrop.
[25] *Sprague's Annals*, III, 194, 195.

The white man could take his dram three times a day and be sober; when the Indian took it once his blood was set on fire. We shall see how this experience of Samson Occom prepared him to preach the greatest temperance sermon ever delivered to the Indian race.

The dark days at Mohegan passed away. The Indian minister's friends across the sea still had confidence in him. Their letters greatly cheered him. When they learned of his straits they generously came to his assistance. The faith of his old patron was restored. Doctor Wheelock saw afterwards that he had been so depressed over the young prodigal, Joseph Johnson, that he had quite forgotten the elder son, David Fowler, and his brother Jacob, too, who had stood amid all discouragements. One of the fruits of Occom's labors at Mohegan in those dark days was a revival among the Indians thereabouts in which this prodigal came home. As Occom ministered there, possibly to a church he had formed,[26] there was an awakening of new life. Meetings were held in other Indian settlements. Rev. Samuel Ashbow, himself, we suspect, restored to a sober life, was a prominent exhorter in them— preaching with vigor on "The voice in the wilderness," and "inviting all to set their minds heavenward." Some of the converts were old pupils in the Lebanon school. Joseph Johnson, since his desertion of the cause in the autumn of 1768, had led an abandoned life. In the winter following he was at Providence.[27] Then he went on a whaling voyage— "wandering up and down in this delusive world." He visited the West Indies and other distant parts. At last he returned to Mohegan, being then only twenty-one years of age. Here he worked for a year on the lands of his uncle, Zachary John-

[26] Occom makes references to certain Indians as church-members, who were not connected with the North Church of New London. Henry Quaquaquid is called a "deacon." We find no records of such a church. It probably did not survive long.

[27] Dartmouth College Library has his Prayer-Book [Lawrence Classe, 1715] inscribed with his name and the address "Providence Dec. 28, 1768."

son, with whom his sister also lived. He was one of the first to be awakened in this religious interest. On the thirteenth of November, 1771, he tells us, he turned anew to the Scriptures and began to call on the name of the Lord.[28] So he returned to the life he had been taught to live in the Indian Charity School. His spiritual father, who was so distressed by his fall, lived to see him approved as a missionary to the Indians and to mourn his early death.

The sorrowful experience which Doctor Wheelock had with his Indian pupils was nothing new. John Eliot had similar discouragements. Wherever since Indian missions have been attempted, some who have been well-instructed and have promised allegiance to the Christian religion, have been swept away by the temptations of Indian life. The subsequent environment of the educated Indian has never been enough considered. At the same time it is true that the good seed has not utterly perished, even though it has seemed to fail. After the flood has passed, the shoots have become green again and they have grown to a harvest.

[28] *Wheelock Papers.* Fragmentary account of his life. See Allen's *Biog. Dict.*

CHAPTER X

1772–1774

An unusual congregation was gathered on the second of September, 1772, in the brick meeting-house of the First Church in New Haven. The occasion was the preaching of a sermon by Rev. Samson Occom at the request of Moses Paul, an Indian, who on that day was to be executed for murder. Although the weather was very stormy, the place was crowded to its utmost capacity. As there had not been a hanging in that town for twenty-three years, the event was somewhat novel; but many had come expecting to hear from the distinguished Indian preacher a sermon to his race appropriate to such a solemn day. Lawyers and judges were present, having more than a professional interest in the case. Ministers had gathered from all the region round about. But most conspicuous in the assembly were the Indians, who had come from great distances and all quarters. It was, in fact, the cause of a general meeting of representatives from the decaying tribes of southern New England, and the last, as though they had come to attend the funeral of their race. Surely the event was appropriate for such a service—the execution of an Indian who had committed murder in his drunkenness—for rum more than war or pestilence had wasted them to pitiful numbers.

Moses Paul was born at Barnstable, Mass., in 1742, whither his parents had come from Martha's Vineyard. His father died in 1745, at the siege of Louisburg, and the widowed mother had been one of the Christian Indians who attended the Barnstable church. When Moses was five years old he

was bound out as an apprentice to Mr. John Manning of
Windham, Conn., who gave him good instruction in religion.
In due time he enlisted and served in Israel Putnam's company in the French and Indian war. Afterwards he was a
sailor on a man-of-war ship and in the merchant service for
several years. At last, wearying of this employment, he
returned to Connecticut and led an idle, vagabond life. The
crime for which he was to be hanged was committed December 7, 1771, at Clark's tavern in Bethany. A contemporary
newspaper gives the following account:

New Haven, Dec. 9.—Last Saturday evening Mr. Moses Cook, of
Waterbury, being at Mr. Clark's tavern in Bethany, where there was an
Indian named Moses Paul, who had behaved so disorderly (on Mrs. Clark's
refusing to let him have a dram) that he was turned out of doors, when he
swore to be revenged on some one person in the house; and Mr. Cook
going out soon after, received from the Indian (who 't is supposed lay in
wait near the house, in order to put his threat in execution) a violent blow
on his head, with some weapon, that broke his scull in so terrible a manner,
that he died of the wound last night. The Indian was apprehended and
committed to the gaol in this town last Sunday. [1]

The Indian was tried in the Superior Court at New Haven,
found guilty and sentenced to be hanged. During his impris-
onment he received faithful ministrations from the ministers
of the town; but he naturally turned to the man of his own
race upon whom the Indians generally had come to look as
their friend in trouble. Some time before the execution day
it was known that Occom would preach the sermon according
to an ancient custom. So the throng had gathered out of curiosity or to hear him—a solemn congregation within the meeting-house and a crowd without. The condemned man, surrounded by his guards, was brought into his presence and the
service began. Occom took for his text the words " For the
wages of sin is death; but the gift of God is eternal life

---

[1] *New London Gazette*, Dec. 20, 1771. Moses Cook was the eldest son of Samuel
Cook of Wallingford, and a man much respected. *Hist. Waterbury* I. App. p. 40.

through Jesus Christ our Lord" [Rom. 6:23]. After developing the two propositions, "that sin is the cause of all the miseries that befall the children of men, both as to their bodies and souls for time and eternity," and "that eternal life and happiness is the free gift of God, through Jesus Christ our Lord," he addressed in turn the criminal, the ministers and the assembled Indians. His words to his own people are pertinent to our study. For that reason and because they furnish us a good example of his composition they are given in full.

My poor kindred,

You see the woful conseqnences of sin, by seeing this our poor miserable country-man now before us, who is to die this day for his sins and great wickedness. And it was the sin of drunkenness that has brought this destruction and untimely death upon him. There is a dreadful woe denounced from the Almighty against drunkards: and it is this sin, this abominable, this beastly and accursed sin of drunkenness, that has stript us of every desirable comfort in this life; by this we are poor, miserable and wretched; by this sin we have no name nor credit in the world among polite nations; for this sin we are despised in the world, and it is all right and just, for we despise ourselves more, and if we do not regard ourselves, who will regard us? And it is for our sins, and especially for that accursed, that most hateful sin of drunkenness that we suffer every day. For the love of strong drink we spend all that we have, and every thing we can get. By this sin we cannot have comfortable houses, nor any thing comfortable in our houses; neither food nor raiment, nor decent utensils. We are obliged to put up any sort of shelter just to screen us from the severity of the weather; and we go about with very mean, ragged and dirty clothes, almost naked. And we are half starved, for most of the time obliged to pick up any thing to eat. And our poor children are suffering every day for want of the necessaries of life; they are very often crying for want of food, and we have nothing to give them; and in the cold weather they are shivering and crying, being pinched with the cold—All this is for the love of strong drink. And this is not all the misery and evil we bring on ourselves in this world; but when we are intoxicated with strong drink, we drown our rational powers, by which we are distinguished from the brutal creation; we unman ourselves, and bring ourselves not only level with the beasts of the field, but seven degrees beneath them; yea, we bring ourselves level with the devils; I do not know but we make ourselves worse than the devils, for I never heard of drunken devils

My poor kindred, do consider what a dreadful abominable sin drunkenness is. God made us men, and we chuse to be beasts and devils; God made us rational creatures, and we chuse to be fools. Do consider further, and behold a drunkard, and see how he looks, when he has drowned his reason; how deformed and shameful does he appear? He disfigures every part of him, both soul and body, which was made after the image of God. He appears with awful deformity, and his whole visage is disfigured; if he attempts to speak he cannot bring out his words distinct, so as to be understood; if he walks he reels and staggers to and fro, and tumbles down. And see how he behaves, he is now laughing, and then he is crying; he is singing, and the next minute he is mourning; and is all love to every one, and anon he is raging, and for fighting, and killing all before him, even the nearest and the dearest relations and friends: Yea nothing is too bad for a drunken man to do. He will do that which he would not do for the world, in his right mind.

Further, when a person is drunk, he is just good for nothing in the world; he is of no service to himself, to his family, to his neighbours, or his country; and how much more unfit is he to serve God: yet he is just as fit for the service of the devil.

Again, a man in drunkenness is in all manner of dangers, he may be killed by his fellow-men, by wild beasts, and tame beasts; he may fall into the fire, into the water, or into a ditch; or he may fall down as he walks along, and break his bones or his neck; he may cut himself with edge tools. Further if he has any money or any thing valuable, he may lose it all, or may be robbed, or he may make a foolish bargain, and be cheated out of all he has.

I believe you know the truth of what I have just now said, many of you, by sad experience; yet you will go on still in your drunkenness. Though you have been cheated over and over again, and you have lost your substance by drunkenness, yet you will venture to go on in this most destructive sin. O fools when will ye be wise? We all know the truth of what I have been saying, by what we have seen and heard of drunken deaths. How many have been drowned in our rivers, and how many have been frozen to death in the winter seasons! yet drunkards go on without fear and consideration: alas, alas! What will become of all such drunkards? Without doubt they must all go to hell, except they truly repent and turn to God. Drunkenness is so common amongst us, that even our young men and young women are not ashamed to get drunk. Our young men will get drunk as soon as they will eat when they are hungry. It is generally esteemed amongst men, more abominable for a woman to be drunk than a man; and yet there is nothing more common amongst us than female drunkards. Women ought to be more modest than men; the holy scriptures recommend modesty to women in particular: but drunken women have no modesty at all. It is more intolerable for a woman to get drunk, if, we consider further, that she is in great danger of falling into the hands of the sons of Belial, or wicked men, and being shamefully treated by them.

And here I cannot but observe, we find in sacred writ, a woe denounced against men, who put their bottles to their neighbours mouth to make them drunk, that they may see their nakedness: and no doubt there are such devilish men now in our day, as there were in the days of old.

And to conclude, consider my poor kindred, you that are drunkards, into what a miserable condition you have brought yourselves. There is a dreadful woe thundering against you every day, and the Lord says, that drunkards shall not inherit the kingdom of God.

And now let me exhort you all to break off from your drunkenness, by a gospel repentance, and believe on the Lord Jesus and you shall be saved. Take warning by this doleful sight before us, and by all the dreadful judgments that have befallen poor drunkards. O let us all reform our lives, and live as becomes dying creatures, in time to come. Let us be persuaded that we are accountable creatures to God, and we must be called to an account in a few days. You that have been careless all your days, now awake to righteousness, and be concerned for your poor and never dying souls. Fight against all sins, and especially the sin that easily besets you, and behave in time to come as becomes rational creatures; and above all things, receive and believe on the Lord Jesus Christ, and you shall have eternal life; and when you come to die, your souls will be received into heaven, there to be with the Lord Jesus in eternal happiness, and with all the saints in glory; which God of his infinite mercy grant, through Jesus Christ our Lord. Amen.

After the service Occom accompanied the condemned man to his execution. The following is the newspaper account of the affair :

New Haven, September 4. Last Wednesday, Moses Paul was executed agreeable to his Sentence, about a Mile from this Town. The Rev. Mr. Occom, preached a Sermon, previous to the Execution, in the Brick Meeting House, from Rom. vi. 23, and attended the Criminal to the Place of Execution, where he made a short but well adapted Prayer to the Occasion. The Criminal behaved with Decency and Steadiness, and appeared to be in the Exercise of fervent Prayer all the Way from the Gaol to the Gallows. A little while before he was turn'd off he took a most affectionate Leave of his Countrymen the Indians, (many of whom were present) and exhorted them to shun those Vices to which they are so much addicted, viz. Drunkenness, Revenge &c. He acknowledged that he kill'd Mr. Cook, though not with a Flat Iron, as was supposed, but with a Club. Notwithstanding the Day was very stormy, there was a very great Concourse of People, whose Curiosity was as much excited to hear Mr. Occom preach, as to see the Execution, altho' there has not been one in this Town since the Year 1749.[2]

As to the sermon, it was exceedingly well received and made a deep impression. Temperance sermons were scarce in those days and in some quarters wholly unknown. In this respect it had a unique interest, especially as applicable to the Indians. The *Connecticut Courant* commended its "honest simplicity and Gospel sincerity" and of the conclusion said : " The Plainness of Speech to his Brother Indians against the Sin of Drunkenness is striking, and his address to the Indian that was then to be executed very affecting." [3]   There was at once a demand for the publication of the sermon, to which Occom reluctantly yielded. The first edition was issued October 31, 1772, from the press of Thomas and Samuel Green at New Haven.[4]   This was soon exhausted. So general was the demand that a second edition was issued before November thirteenth by Timothy Green of New London, who also advertised "the third edition," December fourth, and "the fourth edition," January twenty-second following, in the *New London Gazette*. Many other editions were afterwards printed, at Hartford, Boston, Salem, Bennington, Vt., Exeter, N. H., Springfield, Northampton, and London, England.   Thirty-five years after Samson Occom's death it was translated into the Welsh language and an edition issued at Caernarson, Wales. There may have been others which we have not met with or seen noted by bibliographers. Surely a sermon which went through at least nineteen editions has some claim to fame.[5]   Of

---

[2] *New London Gazette*, Sept. 11, 1772.

[3] *Conn. Courant*, Feb. 9 and 16, 1773.

[4] Advertisement in *Conn. Courant*, Oct. 20 and Nov. 3, 1772.

[5] We note the following editions; (1) New Haven ; T. & S. Green, n. d. [Oct., 1772] 8° pp. 32. [Has unabridged preface, and without the " Dialogue " or sketch of Paul.]   (2) New London ; T. Green, n. d. [Nov., 1772] 8° pp. 23 (1). [Has

course, its Indian authorship and the occasion had more to do with its popularity than its homiletic merits. Occom had an extensive acquaintance among the English, who were interested to procure the only sermon which he had published. So far as we know this is the only printed sermon of that time preached by an Indian. This is, however, in its simplicity and directness, a good illustration of Occom's manner of discoursing. He never builded any great sermons. In his ordinary treatment of religious themes, especially in his later years, he made use of more similes and stories, interrupting his discourse by such illustrations. To this his popularity was largely due, and many people admired these features in him who would have disapproved the same in their own ministers.

This tragic incident in the Indian minister's life had a decided influence upon him. It quickened his zeal in behalf of the degenerate of his race. He labored more industriously to suppress the traffic in intoxicating liquors among the Indians, in which he was in advance of his times. More than

unabridged preface, and without the "Dialogue," but has sketch of Paul.] (3) New London; T. Green, 1772 [Dec.], 8° pp. 23 (1). (4) New London; T. Green, 1772, 8° pp. 23 (1). [Printed in January, 1773, though the date on title-page was unchanged.] (5) Hartford; Reprinted and sold by Ebenezer Watson, n. d. [Feb., 1773] 4° pp. 22 (2). (6) Boston: Printed for and Sold by Seth Adams, Hartford Post, 1773, 8° pp. 31 (1). (7) Boston; J. Boyles, 1773, 8° pp. 32. (8) Boston; 1773, 8° pp. 22 (2) [Sabin] (9) Salem; 1773. 8° pp. 31. (10) Boston; Eldad Hunter, 1774, 8° pp. 24 [Sabin]. (11) Springfield; Henry Brewer, n. d. 8° pp. 26 [Sabin]. (12) London; Reprinted, 1788, 8° pp. 24. [With Edwards's "Observations on the Language of the Muhhekaneew Indians." Has "Advertisement" by I. Rippon, preface abridged, "Dialogue" and appendix on Samuel Kirkland.] (13) London; Reprinted 1789, 8° pp. 24. [Like preceding, except that the error in date of Occom's visit to England, given as 1776 and 1777, is corrected.] (14) Bennington; William Watson, n. d. 8° pp. 14 (1). [Sabin.] (15) N. P. 178-, 8° pp. 24. [Sabin.] (16) Northampton; 1801, 8°. [Brinley Coll. No. 5478.] (17) Exeter; Printed for Josiah Richardson, the Lord's Messenger to the People, 1819, 12° pp. 22. (18) "Indian Eloquence, A Sermon, etc.," n. p. Reprinted July 17, 1820, 8° pp. 24. (19) Caernarson; Argraphwyd gan L. E. Jones, Dros Evan Evans, 1827, sm. 8° pp. 44. [Reprinted from London edition of 1788. A copy was presented to the Conn. Hist. Soc. in 1896, by B. F. Lewis, Utica, N. Y. See *Utica Herald*, Jan. 14, 1896.]

ever before he felt his own responsibility as their representative, and realized that nothing remained in New England for his people except to decline under the terrible sway of vice and finally die amid the graves of their fathers.

We may as well just here make record of this Indian's opinion as to slavery. At that time most wealthy families in New England held slaves. The ministers very commonly had one or more blacks as servants in their households, and the servant class being then small they could hardly do without them. Doctor Wheelock himself, in 1757, paid £50 for a negro, "Ishmael" by name, whom he bought from William Clark of Plymouth, Mass. The Indian of the full blood generally despised the negro and such of his own race as would marry among them. It was Occom's opinion that such marriages wrought degeneracy in both races. At the same time he had a warm sympathy for the slave, whose estate was not always pleasant or respectable, even in New England. Who would think to find in Samson Occom an abolitionist? Such, however, he was. He lifted up his voice boldly for emancipation seventy years before Uncle Tom's Cabin was written. In one of his discourses he made the following pointed application on the subject referring to slaveholders :

I will tell who they are, they are the Preachers or ministers of the Gospel of Jesus Christ. It has been very fashionable for them to keep Negroe Slaves, which I think is inconsistent with their character and function. If I understand the Gospel aright, I think it is a Dispensation of Freedom and Liberty, both Temporal and Spiritual, and [if] the Preachers of the Holy Gospel of Jesus do preach it according to the mind of God, they Preach True Liberty and how can such keep Negroes in Slavery? And if Ministers are True Liberty men, let them preach Liberty for the poor Negroes fervently and with great zeal, and those Ministers who have Negroes set an Example before their People by freeing their Negroes, let them show their Faith by their Works." [6]

The success of the publication of Occom's execution sermon may have encouraged him to undertake another venture

[6] MS. in *Conn. Hist. Soc., Indian Papers.*

—the printing of a "Collection of Hymns and Spiritual Songs." This introduces a subject of much interest, for Occom is himself included among the hymn-writers of New England. Indeed he has been known chiefly as the author of a familiar hymn, found in many modern collections but now going out of use—"Awaked by Sinai's awful sound."

Several facts should preface a consideration of this subject. The Indians of New England were in a way a poetic and musical people. They delighted in figures of speech and commonly used them. As to their music, without discussing it, we can at least say they were fond of it, for Winslow relates how "they vse to sing themselves asleepe" with "barbarous singing." [7] There was a tradition among the Narragansett Indians that a certain tune "was heard in the air by them, and other tribes bordering on the Atlantic coast, many years before the arrival of the whites in America; and that on their first visiting a church in Plymouth Colony, after the settlement of that place by the whites, the same tune was sung while performing divine service, and the Indians knew it as well as the whites." Thomas Commuck, himself a Narragansett Indian, who records this tradition, has preserved the tune in his collection of "Indian Melodies," under the name "Old Indian Hymn," with the words to which the Brothertown Indians were accustomed to sing it. However incredible this tradition may seem, it illustrates the fact that the Christian Indians were influenced by the psalm-singing of the English. John Eliot's converts adopted the practice and delighted in it. The Psalms in meter were printed with his Indian Bible in 1663 for such use. Afterwards the missionary society distributed many copies of psalm-books among the natives of southern New England. At Mohegan and other Indian settlements thereabouts this exercise had a prominent place in their religious services. We have already referred to

[7] *Mourt's Relation,* edn. 1865, p. 109.

13

the singing of the pupils at the Indian Charity School, and
from other sources we learn that some advance had been
made among some there in the study of music. It was but
natural, therefore, that Samson Occom, who is said to have
been a good singer himself, and acquainted with music, being
persuaded that his people would find greater pleasure in the
spiritual songs which were then coming into general use,
should conclude to prepare a collection in part for his
Christian Indians.

We judge that he received his impulse in this work during
his visit to England. He was there associated with Rev.
George Whitefield, who had a decided preference for such
hymns. Moreover, he met there most of the hymn-writers of
the time, some of them intimate friends of the Countess of
Huntingdon. What influences must have surrounded him as
he preached in the church at Northampton, where Philip
Doddridge had ministered, or in John Wesley's foundry ! He
was entertained by John Newton of Olney, and by Thomas
Gibbons, the biographer of Isaac Watts. It is certain that he
preached in the pulpits of Martin Madan, Samuel Stennett,
Edward Perronet, Benjamin Beddome and other well-known
composers of hymns. The interest of the Indians in this
subject may be presumed to have been known in England, as
in 1767 Mr. Knap sent over to Doctor Wheelock some copies
of his collection of tunes—one for Samuel Kirkland, and
another for David Fowler, who were then among the Oneidas.
He had named a new tune " Lebanon," in honor of the school.
After Occom's return, and especially in 1772, he was studying
hymns and hymn-books, a number of which he had doubtless
brought from England, as they were used in the preparation
of his own. Among these were the collections of Watts,
Wesley, Whitefield, Lady Huntingdon, Madan, Mason, Cen-
nick and Maxwell. Several collections were issued while he
was there. His interest seems to have been known, for a

composer wrote him thus: "Understanding that you know music, I here present you with upwards of six score tunes amongst which are several of the Modernest and some of the Pleasantest that are used in the Methodists."[8] Probably he received other such gifts. Thus his interest in hymnology had been kindled by acquaintance with some of the masters.

The title of his book declares that it is "Intended for the Edification of sincere Christians of all Denominations." In the preface, also, he says: "I have taken no small Pains to collect a number of choice Hymns, Psalms and Spiritual Songs from a number of Authors of different Denominations of Christians, that every Christian may be suited." How great an expectation he had that his book would come into general use, we do not know. He certainly issued it partly for his Christian Indians. The plan of removing them to Oneida was then in his mind. As he purposed to adopt and teach the English language, uniting the several tribes who still spoke their Indian dialects, he may have thought the hymn-book would aid him. The first edition was issued in 1774, the year of the attempted removal; the second in 1785, the year of its accomplishment; and the third in 1792, the year of his death, three weeks after the event was known in New London. Many copies of the first two editions must have been taken by the Indians, for they used this collection both before and after the removal to Oneida.

The first notice we have of the book is in the *New London Gazette*, April 1, 1774, which makes the announcement that "Mr. Occom's Collection of Poems will be published on Wednesday next"—the 6th. of April. In the issue of the same paper, April 8th, it is advertised as just published—"A choice Collection of Hymns and Spiritual Songs." The difference between the title under which it was announced and that of the title-page is to be noted. We are, at least, prepared to

---

[8] *Conn. Hist. Soc., Indian Papers*, Lett. Thos. Kribb to Occom, Feb. 8, 1768.

find, on a critical examination of the contents, that some of the hymns were his own composition. All the editions, which are extremely scarce, have the same title; but the third lacks the preface, and has a few unimportant "addítions," probably made by the printer.[9] Occom's name was afterwards associated with some editions of Joshua Smith's collection. An edition of this, perhaps the first, was printed in 1784 at Norwich, Conn., by Thomas Hubbard, and later the name of "Samson Ockum" appeared on the title-page with Joshua Smith.[10] A critical examination of this book shows that many hymns in it were taken from Occom's earlier collection. Some were, doubtless, then known as his composition. So far as we know he had nothing to do with the publication of this book, many editions of which were issued after his death.

After the Brothertown Indians had made their second removal from New York to Wisconsin, one of their number, Thomas Commuck, issued the "Indian Melodies."[11] In this he gathered the tunes and hymns which were then in use among them, the harmony being furnished by Thomas Hastings. He states, in his preface, as one reason for issuing the

[9] (1) New-London; .. Timothy Green,.. M,DCC,LXXIV. 12º pp. 119. Congregational Library. Mass. Hist. Soc., New London Library, and Brinley Coll., No. 6022, $34. (2) New-London ; .. Timothy Green, .. M,DCC,LXXXV. 12º pp. 112. Conn. Hist. Soc., Hartford Theol. Sem., and Brinley Coll., No. 6023, $26. (3) New London ; Timothy Green and Son, M,DCC,XCII. 16º pp. 112. Watkinson Lib. Hartford. Brinley Copy, No. 6024, $22.

[10] *Divine Hymns or Spiritual Songs for the use of Religious Assemblies and Private Christians.* Norwich, T. Hubbard, 1784. [Brinley Coll., No. 6038.] Other editions were issued at Norwich by Wm. Northrop, the 8th in 1797, the 9th in 1799 [Union Theol. Sem.], the 11th in 1803 [Union Theol. Sem.], and the 12th in 1811 [Watkinson Lib.] A so-called 6th edition was printed at Albany in 1804, said to be by "Joshua Smith, Samson Ockum and others." [Union Theol. Sem.] Other editions were printed at New London in 1800, at Portland in 1803, and at Suffield in 1805. [Watkinson Lib.]

[11] *Indian Melodies, by Thomas Commuck, a Narragansett Indian. Harmonized by Thomas Hastings, Esq.* New York : Published by G. Lane & C. B. Tippett, for the Methodist Episcopal Church, 200 Mulberry street. James Collord, Printer, 1845, oblong, pp. vi, 7–116.

D. g. g. +

A CHOICE
COLLECTION
OF
H Y M N S
AND
Spiritual SONGS;

Intended for the Edification
of sincere Chriſtians, of all
Denominations.

~~~~~~~~~X~~~~~~~~~

BY
SAMSON OCCOM,
MINISTER OF THE GOSPEL.

~~~~~~~~X~~~~~~~~

BOTH young Men and Maidens, old Men and
Children—Praiſe the LORD.
PSAL. CXLVIII. 12, 14.

~~~~~~~~~~X~~~~~~~~~~

N E W - L O N D O N:

PRINTED and SOLD by TIMOTHY GREEN,
a few Rods Weſt of the COURT-HOUSE.
M,DCC,LXXIV.

INDIAN MELODIES

OCCUM. L. M.

MONTAUK. S. M.

OLD INDIAN HYMN. C. M. Double.

book, "That no son of the forest, to his knowledge, has ever undertaken a task of the kind;" and he "begs to be excused for stepping a little aside from the path generally traveled by authors," who "wind up by declaring that if such and such an object has been secured they feel amply repaid for all their toils," and admitting frankly "that notwithstanding all other ends which may result from the publication of this work, his object is to make a little money." How he came out in this purpose, we do not know; but he has done a service in preserving some melodies which the Christian Indians had long been accustomed to sing. All the tunes bear Indian names. Those which are most characteristic are Quapaw, Montauk, Delaware, Ottoe, Wabash, Kickapoo, Susquehannah and Piankashaw. The "Old Indian Hymn" already referred to is a minor, as Indian tunes were apt to be, and may very likely have been a favorite long used among the Indians of New England.

An examination of the hymns in Samson Occom's collection reveals the fact, hitherto, we think, unknown, that there are a considerable number which are not found in earlier books, and are not noted, or are unassigned by hymnologists. The conclusion is that he was himself the author of such. Was not this probably the reason why the book was announced as "Mr. Occom's Collection of Poems"? The collection contains one hundred and eight numbered hymns, with some doxologies and graces. Of these the greater part are known as by Watts, Wesley, Madan and others. He undoubtedly took them from hymn-books which were at hand. As to the remainder, some, which are unclaimed by authors so far as we are aware, do not seem to exhibit his style of composition, while others have distinctly his earmarks in certain expressions. We give the first lines of a number of these, which must be assigned to Occom, unless other authorship is proven : " Lord, I confess my sin is great," " Weary of struggling with

my Pain," "The Prodigal's return'd," "Laden'd with guilt
sinners arise," "Awake sad heart, whom sorrows drown,"
"Christ Jesus is the chiefest Good," "Now his the ever-rolling
Year," "Behold that Splendor, hear the Shout," "Most gracious God of boundless Might," "O Sight of Anguish, view it
near," "I bless the Lord, who gives his word," "Ye that seek
the Lord, who dy'd," "Welcome, welcome, blessed Servant,"
"Behold Jesus Christ in the Clouds," "Hail thou happy Morn
so glorious," "Come to Jesus, come away," "Hark ye Mortals,
hear the Trumpet," "Why was unbelieving I," "By sin my
God and all was lost," "Today Immanuel feeds his sheep,"
"Christ in that Night he was betray'd," "Farewell to my Pain
and farewell to my Chain," "Lord from thy Throne of flowing
grace," and "Blest be the God whose tender care." Six of
these hymns are found in Joshua Smith's collection. Some of
Occom's hymns have appeared in later hymn-books. It is,
of course, possible that he supplied some hymns for collections issued by others before his own, but we think not. All
his hymns must be assigned to that period of despondency
which followed his return from England. He has wrought his
experience into them. We can easily imagine that he has
expressed in some of them that peace which finally came with
his victory, the joy he felt over the prodigal Johnson's return,
and the evangelistic fervor of the awakening among his Christian Indians.

Several hymns, which are better known than those above
noted, have been assigned to this Indian hymn-writer. One
of these is on the suffering of Christ. Its first stanza is as
follows :

> Throughout the Saviour's life we trace,
> Nothing but shame and deep disgrace,
>   No period else was seen :
> Till he a spotless victim fell,
> Tasting in soul a painful hell,
>   Caus'd by the creature's sin.

This is surely Occom's composition. It is a good illustration of his style, and is found in his collection, whence it was taken by Joshua Smith. In some later hymn-books it has "our" for "the," or "I" for "we," in the first line. Another hymn with which he is credited is more familiar :

> Now the shades of night are gone,
> Now the morning light is come :
> Lord, we would be thine to-day,
> Drive the shades of sin away.

The first appearance of this hymn was in the Hartford Collection in 1799. It is also found in the edition of Joshua Smith's collection, printed at Albany in 1804, which has Occom's name on the title-page. The Prayer Book collection of 1826 gave it extensive circulation, and it is still used. This hymn is, however, quite unlike his style of thought and expression, and its authorship must remain in doubt.

The most famous of Occom's hymns is that which begins with the line "Awaked by Sinai's awful sound," and many have wondered whether he indeed wrote it. We have now this fact in the foreground that he composed quite a number of other hymns. Its appearance several years after his death does not in any wise indicate that he was not the author, for we have reason to believe that he left some hymns among his manuscripts which had not been published and which he wrote after issuing his own book. This was probably thus brought to light. A perplexity has arisen from the fact that there are two versions of this hymn, both of which appeared, so far as known, about the same time. Students of hymnology have concluded that Occom wrote one of these, beginning "Wak'd by the gospel's pow'rful sound," and that the other was an attempt of some one else to improve this, the first line being changed to read "Awak'd by Sinai's awful sound." His own book does not contain either version. Joshua Smith's collection of 1804 has the former in eight stanzas, with some

alterations, as in the first line, "Wak'd by the gospel's joyful
sound." In the Suffield edition of 1805, this modified version
is found, and there are eleven stanzas, as also in Joshua
Spalding's book, issued in 1805, "The Lord's Songs," where it
is credited to Occom. The other version was soon recognized
as better, and with some changes it passed into general use.
Possibly the first version appeared earlier than 1801, but it
was that year published in Josiah Goddard's "New and Beautiful Collection of Hymns and Spiritual Songs," printed by
Thomas & Thomas, at Walpole, N. H. We give this in full:

> Wak'd by the gospel's pow'rful sound
> My soul in sin and thrall I found,
>   Expos'd to endless woe;
> Eternal truth did loud proclaim,
> The sinner must be born again,
>   Or down to ruin go.
>
> Surpriz'd indeed, I could not tell,
> Which way to shun the gates of hell,
>   To which I 's drawing near;
> I strove alas! but all in vain,
> The sinner must be born again,
>   Still sounded in mine ears.
>
> Into the law then run for help,
> But still I felt the weight of guilt,
>   And no relief I found;
> While sin my burden'd soul did pain,
> The sinner must be born again,
>   Did loud as thunder sound.
>
> God's justice now I did behold,
> And guilt lay dreadful on my soul,
>   It was a heavy load:
> I read my bible, it was plain,
> The sinner must be born again,
>   Or feel the wrath of God.
>
> I heard some speak how Christ did give
> His life, to let the sinner live,
>   But him I could not see;

This solemn truth did still remain,
The sinner must be born again,
    Or dwell in misery.

But as my soul with dying breath,
Was gasping in eternal death,
    Christ Jesus I did see:
Free grace and pardon he proclaim'd,
I trust I then was born again,
    In gospel liberty.

Not angels in the world above,
Nor saints could glow with greater love
    Than what my soul enjoy'd;
My soul did mount on faith its wing,
And glory, glory, I did sing
    To Jesus my dear Lord.

Now with the saints I 'll sing and tell,
How Jesus sav'd my soul from hell,
    And praise redeeming love:
Ascribe the glory to the Lamb;
The sinner now is born again,
    To dwell with Christ above.

The other version of this hymn first appeared in The *Connecticut Evangelical Magazine* for July. 1802, under the title "The New Birth," and was "communicated as original." It is as follows:

Awak'd by Sinai's awful sound,
My soul in guilt & thrall I found,
    And knew not where to go:
O'erwhelm'd with sin, with anguish slain,
The sinner must be born again,
    Or sink to endless woe.

Amaz'd I stood, but could not tell,
Which way to shun the gates of hell,
    For death and hell drew near;
I strove indeed, but strove in vain,
The sinner must be born again,
    Still sounded in mine ear.

When to the law I trembling fled,
It pour'd its curses on my head,
        I no relief could find ;
This fearful truth renew'd my pain,
The sinner must be born again,
            And whelm'd my tortur'd mind.

Again did Sinai's thunders roll,
And guilt lay heavy on my soul,
        A vast, unwieldy load ;
Alas! I read, and saw it plain,
The sinner must be born again,
            Or drink the wrath of God.

The saints I heard with rapture tell,
How Jesus conquer'd death and hell,
        And broke the fowler's snare ;
Yet when I found this truth remain,
The sinner must be born again,
            I sunk in deep despair.

But while I thus in anguish lay,
Jesus of Nazareth past that way,
        And felt his pity move ;
The sinner by his justice slain,
Now by his grace is born again,
            And sings redeeming love.

To heaven the joyful tidings flew,
The angels tun'd their harps anew,
        And loftier notes did raise ;
All hail the Lamb, who once was slain ;
Unnumber'd millions born again
            Will shout thine endless praise.

The arrangement of this hymn now in use has altered this
version in many lines ; but one can easily see that what may
be called the *motive* remains.   Occom's stamp is certainly
upon this hymn.   It is in his favorite meter, the expressions
are his and the theme, so ingeniously wrought into each
stanza, was the most prominent in his ministry.   We have not

the slightest doubt that the solution of the hymnologists' perplexity is that both versions were written by Occom. He was accustomed to rewrite and make alterations, as his manuscripts show, several varying copies of the same letter or document being extant. The second version was made after the first to improve it, and perhaps there were originally more stanzas than have survived. After his death his papers were scattered. Both versions might thus quite naturally find their way into print, and one be "communicated as original" to the *Connecticut Evangelical Magazine.* There is nothing in either so superior as to be beyond the powers of Samson Occom. Some stanzas in his other hymns are better; but none of them indicates that he was a gifted poet or above the average hymnwriter of his day. The field in which he is now best known is one in which he has deserved distinction far less than in many others. He was greater as a missionary, as a wise leader among his people and as the founder of a tribe which attempted a self-government unique in our American history. Still, this hymn has served as his memorial. It has brought him to the mind of many a singer, though more perhaps have sung it in ignorance of its Indian authorship. Among white worshipers it has now grown old and is passing away. The Christian Indians of many tribes, however, esteem it still a favorite, as if it were a message of the Great Spirit through one of their prophets; and in the homes of the once famous Iroquois, to whom he carried the Gospel, they sing in a strange and failing tongue :

> Neh' ogyet' hé ni yut gaih' nih
> Nó yá nes hăh' Ná wĕn ni' yuh';
> Agi' wa neh' a goh:
> Deh'agegă há ga deh' gwat,
> Neh' dyu' i wah hă jo' na găăd
> Neh goi' wa neh' a goh.

CHAPTER XI

1717–1776

The Indian tribes of southern New England had been generally gathered from a wandering life to dwell on reservations early in the eighteenth century. Old tribes were in course of time broken up, their lands sold and the remnant absorbed in one of these communities. Maintenance by hunting was no longer possible and the Indian's interest in agriculture was confined to a few acres of corn. Some relief was granted them from time to time by the colonies; but its effect was temporary and rarely beneficial. These changed conditions made the Indian's existence more of a burden than it had been in the free life of his fathers. Corruptions were bred in his restricted associations. Intemperance, licentiousness and disease all claimed him as a victim; and the later colonial wars, in which many of their hardiest men served, left numerous widows and orphans to struggle with multiplying miseries. Yet in the midst of all the evils which were silently wasting away the race, there was at work a force making for the survival of the fittest. In every tribal center there were some who had received an education at the Indian school, or had been subjects of Christianizing influences or were naturally above the average in frugality, industry and ambition. These had come to be termed in a general way Christian Indians. Without any knowledge of scientific theories, but with the practical foresight of a statesman, Samson Occom saw what would surely befall his people, if they continued in their ancestral homes surrounded by the whites. This was the reason why he originated the plan of gathering into one tribe the better Indians and removing westward to start anew in a more favorable environment. Ere we consider the development of this design, we should review the work done preparatory thereto in the several Indian settlements.

The history of civilization in these communities dates naturally from the year 1717, when the Connecticut General Assembly passed an act, as already noted, in which reservation life had its beginning. A new interest in the Indians followed this important measure. It is evident, however, that religious work among the Indians did not get well under way until 1732. Thereafter it never lacked friends in the Connecticut colony. The government itself became the patron of Indian missions. This revived interest reached a climax in 1736, when the General Assembly at its May session passed an act directing " That at the next publick Thanksgiving that shall be appointed in this Colony, there shall be a contribution attended in every ecclesiastical society or parish in this government, and that the money that shall be raised thereby shall be improved for the civilizing and christianizing of the Indian natives in this Colony." This gave an impulse to the work by bringing it to the attention of every congregation. Although it was continued in a few places after the Revolution, that political and social upheaval wrought desolation. When the people had recovered from this conflict it was found that there were only a few Indians left in any of their reservations. The strength of the Connecticut tribes died in the cause of liberty !

One of the largest and most influential of these settlements was at Misquamicut, or Charlestown, R. I. Here in the eighteenth century the sachems of Ninegret's line reigned over the remnants of the Eastern Niantics and Narragansetts, which latter name they commonly bore. These Indians may have had occasional missionary visitations before 1721 ; but in that year the "Society for the Propagation of the Gospel in Foreign Parts"—the sectarian society of the Church of England—sent Rev. James McSparran to minister over St. Paul's church at Narragansett. The intention was that he should labor with both the English and the Indians. In Henry Caner's tract on "A Candid Examination of Dr. Mayhew's Observations," one of a series relating to the conduct of this society, there is an important paragraph on this effort:

At Charlestown in the Narragansett (R. I.) an attempt was made by this Society to establish a mission for the benefit of the English and the tribe of Indians in that neighborhood (at that time about 400) to which attempt the Indians were [so] well disposed, by the labours of Dr. Macsparran, a neighboring missionary, that the Sachem gave a piece of ground to erect a church upon and a considerable quantity of land besides for a glebe. Accordingly a church was set up and the laudable design in a promising way, when one Mr. Parks was sent thither to give a check to the attempt, who by drawing off a party and kindling a spirit of enthusiasm among both English and Indians in that town totally disappointed and frustrated the design.[1]

The facts were about as here stated. Dr. McSparran did missionary service with some success under the favor of Charles Ninegret, who gave twenty acres of land in 1727 "for the erecting thereon a house for worship, according to the form of the church of England." A small church was at that time built, though it was not until January 14, 1745–46, that the land was actually conveyed, with twenty acres more for a glebe, by George Ninegret, the succeeding sachem. It was a wooden structure, situated on the Champlin farm, north of the post-road, and about half a mile from the sachem's house.[2]

[1] "A Candid Examination, etc." [Henry Caner] Boston, 1763, p. 45. For other pamphlets on this controversy, see Brinley Catalogue, No. 6165.

[2] After the failure of this enterprise the property was held by the Champlin family by right of possession. In 1765 the Indians complained of their sachem because "about forty acres of their land granted to the Royal Society for a church of England, he suffers Col. Champlin or some of his family to keep possession of and occupy it without the least benefit to the Society, or the church or the Indians." [*N. Y. Arch., MSS., Sir Wm. Johnson*, XXIV, 251.] The Champlin place passed

This was known as "The Church of England in Charlestown;" but no church organization ever existed there, the
whites who attended being communicants of the Narragansett
church. It was only a preaching station for Dr. McSparran,
which he ceased to visit probably about 1748.[3] Indians
attended there in considerable numbers for ten years; but the
work declined when a minister came who could live among
them.

The commissioners of the "Society for Propagating the
Gospel in New England," meeting at Boston, June 1, 1732,
had before them a request for a minister in Westerly, presented in a letter from Colonel John Coddington of Newport.
It was decided to send Joseph Park, and he removed thither
with his family the following year. He was pledged to labor
under the society for five years "as a missionary to the
Indians and such English as would attend." Action was
immediately taken toward building a meeting-house, under
an agreement that the Indians should have one half of it
assigned to them and the society would defray one half of the
expense. This edifice was located about five miles west of
the Episcopal church, on the same road, and on land then
belonging to Colonel Joseph Stanton, the prime mover in the
affair. It was completed in 1734, and cost about £200.[4] Mr.
Park lived near and opened a school for Indians in his family.
The work made encouraging progress for a time, especially
under the religious influences abroad in 1740, and undoubt-

to Robert Hazard and later to James McDonald. The church gradually went to
decay and the frame was used in building a house near the spot, in the ruins of
which the ancient timbers could be seen in 1896.

[3] Updike's *Hist. of the Narragansett Church*, pp. 512, 513; *Westerly and Its Wit-
nesses*, Rev. Frederic Denison, Prov. 1878, p. 76; *Hist. Sketch of the Town of
Charlestown*, W. F. Tucker, Westerly, 1877, p. 63; *Letter Book of Rev. James
MacSparran*, Rev. Danie. Goodwin, Ph. D., pp. 34, 37, 138–141.

[4] This meeting-house stood until late in the century. It was within the present
limits of Westerly, on the James Ross place, the spot being indicated by a small
graveyard near by. Here are the graves of Rev. Joseph Park, who died March 1,
1777, and his wife, Abigail, who died October 19, 1772.

edly drew the Indians from the Episcopal church. On the 5th of May, 1742, a church was formed and Mr. Park was ordained to the pastorate August thirteenth following, at a salary of £120. During the next two years "more than sixty Indians became members" of this Presbyterian or Congregational church. Among them was one, Samuel Niles, who seems to have been named after the white minister of South Kingstown. A small schoolhouse was built for the Indians before 1745 on Colonel Stanton's land, and everything seemed to promise well for the Christianizing of the tribe.

This Congregational church, however, was divided during the Separatist excitement. In 1746 the Indians who were infected with such notions drew off, and the prospect of Mr. Park's usefulness there being gone the commissioners discontinued their support, September 17, 1748. President Stiles on one of his tours met Samuel Niles, and had from his lips an account of what followed:

May 8, 1772. This forenoon I was visited by Samuel Niles an Indian of the Narragansett. Ot 66. He told me that he was formerly a comunicant in Mr. Parks Congregᵃ Chh in Westerly where he was baptized by sprinkling. Here he was dealt with for exhorting in the Congregation, upon which he and about a hundred Indians withdrew, i. e. the chief body of the Narr. Tribe wh was xtianized. They built a new meeting house 25 ft sq and spontaneously gathered themselves, above 20 brethren in number into a chh or agreed to walk together as such. Mr. Stephen Babcock, a Deacon of Mr. Park's chh had also separated & became an Elder among the Separatists—a mixture of Baptists & Pedobaptists & was ordained I think by some bap elders. There was a Indian from Groton of the Remnants of the Pequot Tribe who came & preached at Narraᵗ and he was by the Laying [on] of hands of Elder Babcock & others ordained Elder of this Indian chh—his name was James Simon or Simon James. But about half a dozen Bʳ adhering to him, he & his adherents met in a private house—to these he administered bapᵐ & t Ld supper 3 or 4 yrs & then removed. At the same time Samˡ Niles carried on in the Meeting House & at length about 15 brethren who refused Simon united & called Samuel. But none even of the Separate Elders wd ordain him, the chh chose & appᵗ 3 breth Indians to ordain him. They began exercises about noon & cont to sunset. The 3 breth laid on Hands on Samˡ Niles & one of them, viz Wm Choise or

Cohoize or Oc-Hoyze prayed over him & gave him the charge of that Flock, during which such a Spirit was outpoured & fell upon them (as he expresses it) that many others of the Cong[n] prayed aloud & lift up their hearts with prayers & Tears to G[d]. This cont[d] a long time, half an hour or near an hour. The white pple present taking this for confusion were disgusted & went away. Afterwards they sang & were dismissed. Ever since he has ministered there in holy things, preach[g] baptizing &c. He himself was bap afores'd time & this was by plunging & I think by an Indian not an Elder. Yet he holds it indifferent & it was agreed that Bap or Pedobap principles sh'd be no Term of Communion. Accd'y Sam[l] bap both Inf & adults, latter by spk or plung, as they wish. He Has now Ninety Ind[s] Communicants in chh at Narr to whom he breaks bread once a mo. He also breaks b'd to 2 other Cong[s] one at Groton and another at Mohegan. For tho Mr. Occom preaches there & has been long ordained yet he has not administered the ordinances since his Fall. Samuel Niles cannot read. It seems extraordinary that such an one should be a Pastor. He is however acquainted with the Doctrines of the Gospel and an earnest, zealous man & perhaps does more good to the Indians than any White man could do. He is of an unblameable life as to Morals & sobriety. He has very great influence over the Indians[5]

We have further information in a report made by Rev. Joseph Fish of North Stonington to the commissioners in 1764, in which he says of the Indians, "They left Park's meeting about the time that Deacon Babcock fell off from the standing chh, about 19 or 20 years ago, & were for some time under the instruction of Babcock a separate Baptist teacher, till most of them took offense at his conduct in ordaining an Indian over y[m] y[t] wa'nt agreeable to y[e] Body of y[e] tribe, upon which some of y[e] Indian Brethren (as I am informed) not in any office took & ordained one Samuel Niles their Pastor & he has been their minister ever since, preaching, administering the Lord's Supper, baptizing and marrying."[6]

These extracts recover the history of the famous Indian church in Charlestown. It appears that about 1745 the New Light party and the Indians separated from Mr. Park's church :

[5] *Stiles' MSS., Yale College,* Diary III, 89.
[6] *Conn. Hist. Soc., Indian Papers,* Lett. of Fish.

that both were for a time under the care of Mr. Stephen Babcock, and that he then ordained James Simons over the Indians,
thereby creating a division among them which resulted in the
ordination of Samuel Niles. Mr. Babcock was himself installed
over his party, called the " Hill Church," April 4, 1750.[7] The
Indians built a rude wooden meeting-house twenty-five feet
square which stood near the center of their tract, and on this
spot the present Indian church was erected in 1859—a stone
edifice, twenty-eight feet wide and forty feet long. In their
first meeting-house Rev. Samuel Niles ministered for many
years and certainly until the year 1776. Samson Occom also
occasionally preached there on his tours; so also did Samuel
Ashbow, whom McClure heard there in 1768. It is said that
Samuel Niles was "in his day one of the most eminent Indian
preachers in America." Rev. Joseph Fish wrote of him thus :
"This Niles whom I have known some years is a sober, religious man, of good sense and great fluency of speech and [I]
know not but a very honest man. Has a good deal of the
Scriptures by heart & professes a regard for the Bible. But
his unhappiness is this he cannot read a word."[8] As above
stated he occasionally preached at Groton and Mohegan. He
was for years a councilor of the Narragansett Indians and
prominent in the defense of their land claims,[9] In the census
of 1761 his age is given as 60 years and he then had a son
and a daughter. He was succeeded in the ministry by
another Indian, John Sekatur, a useful and good man ; and he
by Moses Stanton, ordained March 17, 1823. The latter
toiled faithfully, but the tribe were fading away, and about
1844 he went to Ann Arbor, Mich., where he died. Aaron

[7] Backus' *Hist. of New England*, 1871, I, 347, 348, II, 510, 511.

[8] *Conn. Hist. Soc., Indian Papers*, Lett. of Fish. This Indian, Samuel Niles, is
sometimes confounded with the white minister of the same name who never had
anything to do with this Indian church. Denison's *Westerly and Its Witnesses*, p. 80.

[9] *A Statement of the Case of the Narragansett Tribe of Indians*, by James N.
Arnold, Newport, 1896.

THE NARRAGANSETT CHURCH

Sekatur was the last minister, ordained about 1858, and a well-known exhorter in his day. This church has long been of the Freewill Baptist order, with a leaning toward Adventist views; but only a few now remain, aged and scattered. In 1784 there were about fifty members, in 1827, ninety-three, and in 1877, about forty. Once a year, in the month of August, the remnant of the tribe gather at the meeting-house, now isolated in the midst of miles of growing woodland, and on a festival day remember the bygone years. Back of the church is their burial-ground, now almost lost to view in the brush, where rest the dead of many generations.

After the separation, for some years, these Indians were without a school. In 1764 Rev. Joseph Fish made a visitation among them, saw the necessity and influenced them to petition the commissioners of the missionary society for a schoolmaster. Edward Deake was sent and began teaching there June 3, 1765. That autumn he set about building a schoolhouse, which was to be "40 feet long and 16 wide," "one story with a Strait Roof and ye Chimney in ye middle with two Smokes." One end was to be fitted up as a tenement for the schoolmaster, with a cellar underneath. The commissioners were to furnish boards, nails and glass, and the Indians were to do the work. It was several years, however, before this structure was completed, for the commissioners declined to furnish the funds until the land was conveyed to them. This was not until January 5, 1770.[10] Meanwhile Deake went on at his own risk and the bills were afterwards paid by the society. This schoolhouse was situated on a knoll north of Cockumpaug Pond, about one half mile from the Indian church; and it is said to survive to this day in the club-house now on the spot. Rev. Joseph Fish, who was put

<hr />

[10] *Charlestown Records*, Deed from Queen Esther; *R. I. Col. Rec.*, vi, 534; *Conn. Hist. Soc. Indian Papers*; *MS. Rec. Soc. for Prop. Gos.*; and *Wheelock Papers*, Lett. Fish to Whitaker, July 30, 1766.

in charge of the work, lectured in it once a month for several years. The school prospered. In 1765 there were seventy-three Indian families on the reservation, with one hundred and fifty-one children of school age, of whom about half were pupils. A division arose among them as to the schoolmaster in the course of time, and finally, in 1776, Deake was dismissed. Many of the Indians went into the war and from that time the settlement declined. Here some of Wheelock's Indian pupils lived, and this tribe furnished more families than any other in the emigration to Oneida.

The Pequot tribe next engages our attention. Since the Pequot war they had been divided into two clans. One, under Wequash Cook, or Hermon Garret, was settled in 1683 on a tract of two hundred and eighty acres in North Stonington, three miles from the meeting-house. The other, under Cassasinamon, sometimes called Robin, removed in 1667 from Nawyonk on the seashore to a reservation of two thousand acres, called Mushantuxet, after 1705 in Groton, but now within the town of Ledyard, Conn. The former were sometimes called the Stonington Indians and the latter were commonly styled the Groton Pequots. So early as 1657 Rev. Richard Blinman of New London was invited to become a missionary among the Pequots, and though he declined the engagement he may have done some service among them. The commissioners the same year engaged Mr. William Thompson "in theire labours and Indeauors to Instruct the Indians therabouts resideing especially Robin and his companie." He began the work in 1659, laboring to some extent among both clans and being assisted by Thomas Stanton as interpreter; but after three years he discontinued it. Other early attempts were made to provide a missionary and to educate English youth as schoolmasters, for which purpose they engaged John Miner and Thomas and John Stanton. All these early efforts came to nothing. The visits of Rev. Experience

Mayhew were not followed up with zeal. It was not until the general beginning of missionary work in southern New England in the next century that any positive good was accomplished. In 1734 Mr. Peabody of Natick visited the Groton Indians, and on his advice, supported by Rev. Eliphalet Adams of New London, who began lecturing among them that year, the commissioners voted that if the Groton [Ledyard] minister would take the Indians under his care and assign them a place in the meeting-house, he should be remunerated for his services. This plan was not fully carried out, though Dr. Adams' son William, who was then supplying this church, labored for a year among the Indians. There were then on the reservation about one hundred. At this time a school was established and possibly a schoolhouse was built. Here at least Benjamin Larrabee and John Morgan taught for various terms. In 1749 Rev. Jacob W. Johnson became the minister and during his years he lectured some and exercised a general religious supervision over the Indians. The best work there was done by Indian teachers. Samuel Ashbow was both schoolmaster and preacher from 1753 to 1757, and he was succeeded by Samson Wauby. Afterwards one Hugh Sweetingham taught for a time. He who did the best work among them was Jacob Fowler, the brother-in-law of Samson Occom. His term of service began in the winter of 1770 and continued to November, 1774, when he was engaged as tutor in Dartmouth College. He also preached in a humble way there and among the Stonington Indians. Rev. Joseph Fish in writing Governor Trumbull, in 1776, to recommend Fowler for government service, said " He approved himself both skillful & faithful in his business and recommended himself to the esteem and respect of all his acquaintance by an inoffensive & exemplary behavior both in ye civil and christian life." After him Abraham Simons, another of Wheelock's pupils, taught the school until the Revolution broke it up. Fowler's salary at first was £12 a year, but he had some assistance from the Indians. The condition of these Pequots was inferior to that in some other settlements. They lived mostly within a square mile and their land was poor. So many of the men went into the Colonial wars that they were almost left a tribe of widows. No church ever existed among them, as they attended with the whites. In their schoolhouse, however, they had services for the Indians, and there Jacob Fowler, Samuel Ashbow, Samuel Niles and Samson Occom preached; the latter very near to them and the bishop of the flock. There were in this settlement in 1725, 322 souls, who were reduced to 176 in 1762. President Stiles' census the latter year gives 140 souls—16 families, seven living in houses and nine in wigwams. Rev. Jacob W. Johnson made a list in 1766, and found 164 souls, of whom eighty-eight were children under sixteen years.

The Indians of Stonington were indebted to two neighboring ministers for the best religious influences and care. These were Rev. Nathaniel Eells of Stonington, whose ministry extended from 1733 to 1786, and Rev. Joseph Fish, pastor at North Stonington from 1732 to 1781. During his early years Mr. Eells lectured to the Indians, visited them and performed such other service as they needed; but later they were especially under the supervision of Mr. Fish, whose church was only three miles away. A few were members of these churches. So early as 1738 the Indian children were gathered into a school with the whites, the commissioners allowing one shilling a week for the instruction of each. Mr. Fish in 1757 wrote the society some account of their condition, in which he said they had increased by accessions during the past six years from eight families to sixteen, seventy-one persons, of whom twenty-one were children of school age. At that time he revived his efforts among them, lecturing once a fortnight. An Indian school was also established. Edward Nedson, an In-

dian, began to teach it in his own house February 22, 1758, a
room being fitted up for the purpose. This Indian continued
faithful in this service until his death, September 1, 1769. He
is said to have been honest, prudent and useful. His widow
would not permit the school to be kept in her house thereafter, and in 1772 the commissioners voted to build a schoolhouse; but the school had seen its prosperous days. Among
these Indians also Samson Occom ministered as he went to
and fro. Some of them were well advanced in civilization.

The next Indian settlement to be considered is Niantic,
where the western branch of that tribe lived. They had a
small reservation of about 300 acres in the eastern part of
Lyme. In 1734 the commissioners at Boston considered the
establishment of a school there. The matter was referred to
Messrs. Mason and Adams, who reported adversely because
the Indians, then in a heathen state, were hostile to it on
account of the ill treatment they had received in reference to
their lands. Thereupon Rev. George Griswold of East Lyme
and Rev. Jonathan Parsons of Lyme petitioned the General
Assembly in their behalf for justice and the Indians became
more favorably disposed. A school was begun in 1736, through
the instrumentality of the colony, and Governor Talcott wrote
of it the year following, " Our School of Indians at Niantik
prospers." Then came the religious awakening. The Lyme
ministers became greatly interested in the natives, visiting
them, lecturing in their settlement, and gathering them to
their own church services. Bibles and Psalters were distributed and they were taught to read. Thirteen were received
into the East Lyme church, and Mr. Griswold was the faithful
friend of the tribe until his death in 1761. The school was
revived in 1742, and Reuben Ely became the teacher. He
was followed by George Dorr. In 1749 David Latham was
engaged and he continued in service down to the Revolution.
To him and Mr. Griswold the enlightened condition of these

Indians was due. They had no church organization or separate meeting-house. Their schoolhouse had a history. It had
been built by Gideon Quequawcom and was known as
"Gideon's mantion house." Its location was within "ye
middle hundred acres." In 1757 this was in the possession of
Joseph and Hannah Piancho, and on March 18th they conveyed it to the commissioners with the land for use as a schoolhouse. Here all their Indian meetings were held, and Samuel
Ashbow, Samson Occom and others preached. Philip Cuish
was a Baptist minister of this tribe, a pious and intelligent
man. He also did some ministerial service among this people,
and perhaps more honor is due him than we have knowledge
of. He died in 1780, and some of his descendants removed to
the Oneida settlement. This tribe had in the year 1725, 163
souls; in 1734, 150; in 1774, 104; in 1783, 80; in 1830, 17
and in 1849, 10—such was their decline. We cannot wonder
at it, for they furnished eleven soldiers for the Louisburg expedition, eighteen in the war of 1755, and a number in the Revolution. Most of the families lived in a village, which was not
far from Black Point. In 1761 President Stiles found there
eleven houses and seven wigwams.[11]

The Tunxis Indians at Farmington had a very important
part in the emigration. The English took them under their
care when they first bought the lands in that valley. A reservation was then made for them on what was called Indian
Neck, and they subsequently acquired other lands so that they
had about the middle of the eighteenth century 260 acres.
During these early years the Indian children were received

---

[11] *Stiles MSS., Yale College*, Itin. I, 425. A sketch of George Waukeets wigwam
is here given by President Stiles. Its ground plan was elliptical. The fire was in
the center and on three sides around it were sleeping places. On the fourth side
were two doors some feet apart. Seven persons could lie comfortably in it. Its
longest diameter was 13 feet, 10½ inches, its shortest 9 feet, 9½ inches, and its height
was 9 feet, 4 inches. The Indians preferred wigwams for the summer and usually
stripped them of their covering and left the poles standing from season to season.

into the town school, but education did not thrive among them. In 1732 interest in them was revived. Rev. Samuel Whitman then began labors among them, instructing them during the following winter with such success "that a number were brought to attend his ministry on Lord's days," for which he received £5 from the missionary society. He also brought the matter to the attention of Governor Talcott, who used his influence to perfect an arrangement whereby the commissioners paid for the Indian pupils in the English school. A number were then attendants. Particular interest was excited in a youth about eighteen years of age, named John Mattawan, who had shown himself desirous of obtaining sufficient education to become a minister to his people. They clothed him after the English fashion, providing therefor a "Homespun Coat, Jacket and Breeches, two Shirts, Stockings, Shoes and Hat." This was in May, 1733, and he continued under instruction, particularly of Mr. Whitman, until 1737, when he became himself the schoolmaster among the Indians, doing also some preaching. The Indians themselves built a rude schoolhouse for the purpose. The number of pupils had then increased from the "nine Indian lads" who attended in 1733, of whom Whitman wrote May 27, 1734, " 3 can read well in a testament, 3 currantly in a psalter and 3 are in their primers." Governor Talcott gave the following account of Mattawan's school in a letter, January 30, 1737-38, "Our School at Farmingtown the last sumer under the tuetion of John Tawump [?] the Indian Christian hath made very good progress, the lesser children I have ordered to be schooled at ye English schole, and boarded by the English, all at the expence of this Coloney, as they have been several winters past." [12] John Mattawan drops out of notice in 1748, and is believed to have died that year. He did a good work in laying the foundations

[12] *Conn. Hist. Soc. Coll.*, V, 39; *Conn. Col. Rec.*, VII, 102, 471, 491, 509; VIII, 6, 37.

of education and religion in the tribe. In 1751 Mr. Whitman died ; and although his successor, Rev. Timothy Pitkin, maintained an interest in the Indians and some youth attended the English school, the work for a time declined.

The original Tunxis stock had nearly died out before this work began. In the year 1725 there were only about fifty Indians in the town. But about the middle of that century they received accessions from the Quinnipiacs of East Haven and the Wangunks of Middletown. Most prominent among the former was Adam, whose children and grandchildren, under the name Adams, were strong supporters of the emigration movement. James Wowowous and David Towsey were either of the Wangunk tribe or had married among them, as they claimed rights in Middletown lands in 1762. The youth of these families obtained an education in the Farmington school. These additions revived the strength of the tribe, and they made decided advances in civilization. Some of them became exemplary Christians, among them Solomon Mossuck, who joined the Farmington church in June, 1763, and his wife, Eunice, who joined in September, 1765.

We turn on now to a later period which greatly affected the future of this tribe. The story picks up the thread of Joseph Johnson's life. After his radical reformation, as related, he entered with zeal into missionary work among the Indians. Occom had occasionally visited the Christian Indians at Farmington. In the hut of Solomon Mossuck, the foremost in such matters, he held services at many an evening hour. Possibly it was thus that Johnson was directed thither. On the 15th of November, 1772, he began work there as schoolmaster and preacher. His school was kept in a small log house situated on the Indian lands then known as the " West Woods." A number of Indian children were at once gathered. Every Sunday he assembled the tribe for worship, and some of his sermons then preached are still preserved by the Connecticut

Historical Society. He was under the pay of the commissioners at Boston and the supervision of Rev. Timothy Pitkin. His salary was £20 a year. On the 2d of December, 1773, he was married by Rev. Ephraim Judson of Norwich to Tabitha, the daughter of Samson Occom, and they established a home among the Indians. Probably it was through a visit of Olive Occom to her sister that she became the wife of Solomon Adams, a grandson of Adam the Quinnipiac. Johnson continued in this field until the summer of 1774, when he was ordained at Hanover, N. H., on the twenty-fifth of August, in the expectation of undertaking a westward mission. Many of the Tunxis Indians felt his influence. Converts were made under his ministry, and possibly some sort of a covenant organization was effected. After his departure these fires were kept alive by Samson Occom on his visits thither until most of the tribe removed to Stockbridge, Mass., or to the Oneida settlement. The people of Farmington have erected in their cemetery a monument to these early inhabitants; but the grave of one most deserving of honor is not there. Near the railway station, on the left of the road leading up from the meadows as it turns southward, on the wooded hill are some Indian graves. There probably John Mattawan's schoolhouse stood, and there sleep the Christian Indians who died in their native valley, and among them is a neglected grave whose stone bears the epitaph, "In Memory of Solomon Mossuck who died January 25th 1802. Aged 78 years."

We have already an acquaintance with the missionary labors at Montauk, L. I.—the sixth Indian settlement concerned in the emigration. After David Fowler left the Oneida mission in 1767 he was employed at Montauk as schoolmaster by the commissioners of the missionary society. His term dates from their vote to that effect, December 29, 1767. He had a salary of only £15 a year, and as his family was increasing, his father being in feeble health, it became necessary for him to devote much time to agriculture and fishing. His father's house burned also and he lost all his property. In consequence there was some complaint that he neglected the school, and in 1770 he was succeeded by David Hannibal, who was given £20 a year. Here, however, David Fowler continued to live until he took up the pioneer work of the emigration.

It will be noted that Mohegan was about in the center of these Indian settlements—a convenient place for Samson Occom to live. He was not under the commission of any missionary society; but he was in a sense the missionary of all the tribes of southern New England. He frequently, also, journeyed abroad, to Boston, Providence, New York and Philadelphia, and incidentally did much to keep the interest in the Indians alive.

We are about to leave Mohegan, and it may not be amiss to look on into its future that the reader may have its completed story. It sometimes happens, in the history of missions, that a new shoot is grafted into a stem of an older stock. So it was at Mohegan. Years passed, and the Indians of Samson Occom's generation were gathered in the tribal burial-place on the bluff overlooking the Thames. Isaiah Uncas, Wheelock's pupil, died April 6, 1770, and the sachemship became extinct. The aged councilor, Zachary Johnson, of whom so many incidents are related, died in 1789. Rev. Samuel Ashbow, who continued to live at Mohegan after the emigration and whose four sons, Samuel, Simeon, James and John, perished in the Revolution, was at length released from his labors in 1795. A few of Occom's descendants lingered thereabouts for some years. His house stood on the hillside still, a monument of the olden time, whither visitors occasionally came to view it, and among them the Connecticut antiquary, Barber, to make a pencil sketch of it. One only of the old Christian stock remained in 1827—Lucy Tantaquidgeon, the aged sister of

Samson Occom.   She was the only Indian church-member on
the reservation, and, in the phrase of Father Gleason, "a new
life was grafted in upon her."

The division of lands dating from Aug. 5, 1782, had made
it possible for many to drift away, although this tribe, more
than almost any other of New England, retained a love for the
ancestral home.   So the Mohegans had gradually diminished
and come into a condition of deplorable neglect.   In 1827,
however, Miss Sarah L. Huntington of Norwich, with characteristic missionary zeal, awakened an interest in them.[13]
A Sabbath-school was first opened in Occom's house, which
she and her friends taught.   On the Fort Hill farm, the land
being given by the daughter and granddaughter of Occom's
sister, a small chapel was erected in 1831, costing about $700,
which was mostly provided by ladies of the neighboring towns.
This event Mrs. Sigourney commemorated in her lines:

> Lo! where a savage fortress frown'd
> Amid your blood-cemented ground,
> A hallowed dome, with peaceful claim,
> Shall bear the meek Redeemer's name.

At the foot of the hill southward, which probably had been
the site of the ancient schoolhouse, a week-day school was
established, and near by a parsonage was built in 1832, with
funds provided by the United States government, which also
granted $400 annually for the salary of a teacher.   Here Rev.
Anson Gleason, who had been a teacher among the Choctaws,
settled in the spring of 1832.   A Congregational church was
formed that year, and in 1835 Mr. Gleason was ordained as
the minister.   Here he remained until 1848, known in all the
region round about as "Father Gleason."   He was a remark-

---

[13] On this movement see: *Memoirs of Mrs. Sarah L. Huntington Smith*; De
Forest's *Indians of Connecticut*, pp. 482–489; *The Bostonian*, March, 1895, p. 676
ff; Barber's *Conn. Hist. Collections*, pp. 338–340; *Contributions to the Ecc. Hist. of
Conn.*, pp. 427, 428; and a newspaper, *The Uncas Monument*, 1842.

able man in his place, of a winning personality and sincere
devotion, well adapted to such missionary labors.　His memory is revered to this day among the few remaining Mohegans.
Other ministers followed him.　A fund was given by the good
woman who established this work for its maintenance, which
others have added to, so that it now amounts to $3,500, and
the income is employed by the trustee, H. R. Bond, Esq., of
New London, in watching over the religious interests of those
Indians and whites who still worship in the remodeled chapel
on the hill.　Lucy Tantaquidgeon, who was born about the
time the Mohegans emerged from heathenism, witnessed all
the changes, struggles and labors of a century; and, preserving to an extraordinary age the pious impressions which her
mother had made upon her in childhood and her distinguished
brother had deepened in maturer life, she at last fell asleep.

CHAPTER XII

1771–1776

The Indian Charity School having been established at Hanover, its founder, Doctor Wheelock, would gladly have revived his friendly relations with the Western tribes, but it was impossible. He had long been supplanted there by Samuel Kirkland, the most successful white missionary of his time. Still, the father could not forget his children. Hoping to cultivate the good seed he had sown in the Oneida country, he proposed in a letter to Samson Occom, January 22, 1771, that he and David Fowler should remove thither with their families and become teachers among the Six Nations, promising them the same support given for that service among the seashore tribes. At the time this proposition could not be accepted; but it may have suggested to Occom, already solicitous in regard to the future of the Indians in New England, the larger plan for the emigration of all the Christian Indians. Surely the design was a development in the mind of Samson Occom and new features were added as other reasons for it were presented. As finally matured, it included the seven settlements of Indians which had come to be associated in missionary operations, viz., those at Charlestown, Groton, Stonington, Niantic, Farmington, Montauk and Mohegan. This movement is sometimes referred to as an emigration of seven tribes. It was not. There was no expectation that all of any tribe or in any settlement would remove. Only those who had been drawn together by Christian influences at first thought of it, though provision was afterwards made, necessarily, for such as desired to join them.

The earliest idea seems to have been to improve their own

condition by a removal from the corrupting influences about them.   They also needed lands of larger extent and better quality than they then possessed.   It had come about, through the clever dealings of the whites, that there were very few acres in any of these settlements well adapted to agriculture.   If they must depend upon the soil they wisely concluded that they must remove to some unsettled region and take up a new claim.   Occom, the Fowlers and Joseph Johnson were familiar with the Oneida country.   They had no doubt that lands could be had for the asking from their Indian friends.   So a prospect of new homes was inviting.   As this matter was considered further the missionary purpose was added.   Occom had long held that something beside the missionary was needed among the Six Nations—the living example of a Christian community. David Fowler had urged upon his patron the introduction of agriculture among the Oneidas.   So the scheme naturally grew to this, that they would establish in the midst of the Western Indians such a community " with a view of introducing the religion of Jesus Christ by their example among benighted Indians in the wilderness, and also of introducing agriculture among them."

Moreover, Occom believed that the Indian never would become civilized unless he was brought to depend upon the soil for subsistence.   We can easily see how his missionary experience had led him to this conclusion.   Yet this end, he thought, could not be reached unless the Indian held land which he could not alienate, for in his straits he would be unable to resist the temptation to sell himself out of house and home. Hence he proposed from the first to prevent this disintegration of his Indian colony by making such sales impossible. The sequel shows how exactly he anticipated the situation.

The last feature of his plan to be developed concerned the government of this new community.   It was evident that their old tribal relations would be broken up, and they were doubt-

less glad of it, for they had become too democratic to live
under a chief. At Mohegan and Charlestown these Indians
had protested for years against the power exercised by their
sachems. Still, their hereditary tribal instincts and customs
could not be ignored. So they decided to form a new tribe,
governed by such rulers as they might select. Their model
was the Connecticut town government, with which they were
familiar. Such a town they would establish, in which they
would be voters; and, as they purposed to live together as
"brothers," they had an appropriate name for their town and
tribe—Brothertown, which was probably suggested to them
by Brainerd's settlement of that name, now Indian Mills, Pa.
They intended also to organize themselves in church estate
and have a minister who should instruct them in religion.
How far the surviving Indian town of John Eliot influenced
Occom in this matter, if at all, it is impossible to state. He
had visited Natick and was probably acquainted with its better days. The white man's town government certainly furnished his main ideas, and from a copy of the Connecticut
statutes, which they took with them, some of their laws were
borrowed. Occom was unable to carry out his plan in all respects. Other conditions than those which he had anticipated interposed when at last Brothertown was founded. He
deserves, however, the credit of having devised a scheme
which had some original and interesting features. This Indian
town was unique in our American history.

The carrying out of this plan was due in large measure to
Joseph Johnson, the son-in-law of Samson Occom. He had
an extraordinary energy. He was young and could easily
travel to and fro, awakening interest in the subject and perfecting arrangements. Withal he was a natural diplomat,
exhibiting great tact in treating with the Oneidas and in unify-
ing the relations of the New England tribes. He brought
Occom's plan into a vigorous life.

The first move was to have a general gathering of the Indians. This was held at Mohegan, March 13, 1773, and was attended by men, women and children. We have no detailed account of this meeting; but after considerable consultation in the Indian fashion, it was decided to send representatives, one from each settlement, to look up a suitable tract of land in the Oneida country. On account of their spring work this proposed visit was delayed; but Johnson sent a messenger to Sir William Johnson to seek his advice. He gave them encouragement, and in their behalf sent a message to the Oneidas on the matter. That summer he was in the east at the seashore and there nine of the Indians waited upon him and received his promise to secure for them lands among the Oneidas, which was to be effected on his return to Johnson Hall in the autumn. Here follows the circular letter sent out by Joseph Johnson in the affair:[1]

Farmington, Octr 13th A D 1773.

This once more, we of this Tribe at Farmington send greeting to all our Indian Brethren at Mohegan, Nihantuck, Pequtt, Stonington, Narragansett and Montauk, Brethren. We love you, and wish your well-being both in this Life and that which is to come. We ask your Serious Attentions a Moment. Dear Brethren, with humility we undertake to write you, beging that ye would remember the Affair of which we so earnestly talked last Spring at the Town of Mohegan. We beg that ye would this once more take this Affair under your deliberate Consideration, let it not drop through since we have encouragements on every side. We have encouragement from His Honour, Sir William Johnson, Baronet, and things look promising. let us take Courage friends and let us step forward like men We beg that ye would by all means Send a Man out of Each Tribe, that they may go with us, and Seek a Country for our Brethren, is it not worth while. Surely it is. be so good as to Show yourselves men, for General Johnson Expects us at his house [the] last of this month, and if we do not make our appearance, he will think that we are only talkers, and not worthy of Notice. how foolish shall we feel if we be despised by General Johnson. But dear Brethren, we will not multiply words, seeing that ye are men, and it is to be hoped wise men. Consider of things, and do that which is right, by no

---

[1] *Wheelock Papers, Dart. Coll.;* and *Conn. Hist. Soc., Indian Papers.*

means be discouraged, but dear Brethren, let us put our trust in that God who ruleth in the Armies of Heaven, and doeth his pleasure among the Inhabitants of this lower World—if God be for us this is Enough, he can comfort us Even in a Wilderness. let us consider of our Condition, let us think of our Children, let us think of time to come. We mention these things to put you in Remembrance.

Brethren, if the men chosen last spring be backward to go to the Mohawk Country be so good as to Send others in their room, and Encourage one another. if Money is scarce, let us try to carry little provisions in our Packs, which will be of considerable help, let the men that go try to get the good will of the Women and let the kind women make little Yoke-hegg. We will try to help them with little Provisions when they go from here. our kind Women send a word of Encouragement and say that they will make little yoke hegg to give to the travellers.

So we must End. Wishing you all well: and we would beg that those men that shall go, come to our town be sure by the 23ᵈ day of this Month, as we purpose to Set of from here the 25ᵗʰ of October, or of this month.

Let all Christians pray for us every Day. So farewell.

We whose Names are underneath are united in those things that are contained in this Letter.

Samˡˡ adamas.

Andrew Corcemp.

Charles Wimpey.

Moses Sanchuse.

Thomas Corcemp.

Solomon Mosuck

Daniel mossuck

JOSEPH JOHNSON.

Scripsit

At the time appointed, the only messengers who went were Joseph Johnson and Elijah Wampy of Farmington. A rumor of impending war in that country discouraged the rest from going. Five Oneidas met them at Johnson Hall on the twenty-seventh of October, and in behalf of their tribe made a gift of lands to the New England Indians. A record of this transaction was given to Joseph Johnson, and is preserved among the Wheelock papers. These messengers returned in November, and Joseph Johnson himself carried their answer through the Indian settlements. The affair had thus progressed so far that a conference with the Oneidas was determined on, partly to ask for more than the ten miles square which had been prom-

ised. Samuel Kirkland had advised them that they could as
easily secure a larger tract. Again Joseph Johnson sent a
circular letter to the seven towns, December 24, 1773, urging
each to send a representative.[2] This was also signed by some
of the Tunxis tribe—Solomon Mossuck, Elijah Wampy, Daniel Mossuck, Andrew Corcomp, Solomon Adams and David
Robin. The first week of the following January four set out,
though the ground was covered with snow. Joseph Johnson
went for Mohegan, Jacob Fowler for Montauk and Groton,
Samuel Tobias for Charlestown, and Elijah Wampy for Farmington. Two of these gave out and returned; the other two
arrived safely at Kanawarohare, where, in the council-house,
Joseph Johnson delivered the following address : [3]

Kanoarohare, January the 20th, 1774.
A Speech to the Indians,

Our dear and well beloved Brethren. It is with much pleasure that
we see so many of you assembled together at this time, and upon this Occasion. We give you our great respects, and Sincere Love. We look upon you
at present as our Elder Brother as a Nation, and Beloved Brethren. We
pray you to consider of us, hearken to us as a younger Brother, not only
consider of us as two persons, but view us to be Speaking, or acting for all
our Brethren in New England, or at least for Seven towns. We pray you
to consider Seriously of our Words. Ye old men who are wise, also ye warriors, and young men, yea let children hearken that what we say may not soon
be forgotten. Brethren, in the first place we will acquaint you of the State &
Circumstances of our New England Brethren, and we will inform you of
our Proceedings & purposes. Brethren we in New England, or at least
many of us are very poor by reason of the Ignorance of our forefathers who
are now dead. Brethren ye know that the English are a wise People and
can see great ways, but some say, that Indians cant see but a little ways,
and we believe that our forefathers could not see but little ways. Brethren,
ye also know that some English loves to take the advantage of poor blind
Indians. So it was in the days of our forefathers in New England, but not
to expose the unjust act of our English Brethren I shall not say much more

---

[2] *Wheelock Papers, Dart. Coll.*; and *Conn. Hist. Soc., Indian Papers.*

[3] Copies of his addresses in Johnson's handwriting are among the *Wheelock Papers* and in the *Conn. Hist. Soc., Indian Papers.* The answers are among the *Wheelock Papers.*

about them, least I cast a prejudice against the English in your hearts, as notwithstanding many are unjust amongst the English, yet there are great many of them good men, & love the Indians from the bottom of their hearts and wishes us all a well being in this World & in the World to come everlasting Life, but all I have to say about the English at present is this, that whilst our forefathers were blind and Ignorant, yea drownded in Liquors the English striped them, yea they as it were cut off their right hands, and now we their Children just opening their Eyes, and knowledge growing in our hearts and just come to our Senses, like a drunken man, I say we now begin to look around and we perceive that we are Striped indeed, nothing to help ourselves. Thus our English Brethren leaves us and laugh. So now Brethren we leave the English, those who have acted unjustly toward us in New England, and say we leave them all in the hands of that God who knoweth all things, and will reward every one according to their deeds whether good or evil.

Brethren we seeing ourselves in such circumstances began last spring to consider together and the 13th day of the Last March 1773, a Meeting was appointed at Mohegan, that being nigh the Center, and there was a vast number of People, Men Women & Children. There we met and there we consulted together—There was present at the meeting Indians of Seven towns and it was proposed that Certain men out of every town should go out and Seek a Place somewhere for us Seven towns to settle down together in peace. Some were of a mind to go Southward as for as to Ohio, and some not so far that way. Some said we could purchase land nigher and it would not do to live so far from the English. At last it came into our minds to try to purchase some land from some of the Six nations. So a time was appointed by our great men, our Councilers & teachers that these chosen men should go forth one out of every town to Seek a place for us to settle on, and as our Spring work was coming on, our head men thought proper that those chosen men should not go till the hurrying work was over, that is after mowing & reaping, and as it pleased the Tribes to chose me for one that should come into these parts, to try to get some land upon some terms, I thought proper to send to his Honour Sir William Johnson for advice in this affair, and I wrote a letter to Sir William and acquainted him of all our circumstances and our desires & purposes, and it pleased His Honor to take notice of us and sent back a word of Encouragement which made our hearts glad, and about the time that we was to come up, his Honor Sir William Johnson was down in that part of the Country, which hindered us from coming up. There we had opportunity to speak with his Honor Sir William, 9 of our countrymen went to see Sir William, and he used us very kindly, and still gave us Encouragement. So we have been encouraged from time to time, also Sir William Johnson appointed a time for some of

our Countrymen to come up in these parts and that was last fall   It pleased
Sir William to tell us that he would help us as much as he could & advise us
in the affair.   And according to the advice of his Honor some of us came to
His house last fall, and he received us gladly to his house & showd us great
respect, two of us came up, the reason we supposed that no more came up
to his Honors house was this.   We heard that it was dangerous times.   We
heard that there was a considerable talk of war amongst the Indians in
these parts, which discouraged many of our Brethren.   But when we came
to Sir William's, he informed us otherwise, also he told us the Message
which you Oneidas sent down to him, for which he was glad, and our minds
was disposed to come even to this town to converse with you more particularly, but according to your desire & the advice of Sir William we returned
back from Sir William's after he had acquainted us of your good will.   At
that time Sir William delivered to us few lines so as we might shew it to our
New England Brethren.   In them few lines was contained the answer which
you made to Sir William's Message sent to you by Saghuagarat one of your
Chiefs, concerning the Intention of our New England Brethren of removing to this part of the World if consistent with the minds of you our Elder
Brethren, not only consistent with your minds, but also the mind of His
Honor Sir William.   Yea here in my hand is the writing drawn from the
Records of his Honor Sir William, which if you pleace ye may hear so as
things past may be fresh in your memory again.   .   .   .

   This Paper or writing I carried with my own hand through six towns of
Indians in New England, and at every town I called the People together
both Small and great, Male and female, and they received the good news
with great Joy.   I did not go to the 7th town, by reason of the inconveniency
of going by water, and also my Business called me to be at home, so I made
as much haste as possible.   However they have heard of your goodwill and
purposed to send one from that tribe but the wind perhaps was contrary so
as he could not get over to the Main.   From the town where I live at present we sent a young man down to our Brethren a few days before we sat
away to stir them up or to awake them, and to tell them that the time is
drawing nigh when we should go to visit our Western Brethren, and to discourse with them more particularly, so as we might be fully satisfied what
to do in the next place, how we shall take the next step.   But our Brethren
thought it not necessary to send great many at this time the reason is this,
because there is a great body of snow on the face of the Earth, which would
hinder them from seeing the ground.   If there was no Snow doubtless some
of our Elder Brethren would now be present at this meeting to converse
with you, but my friends we hope that ye will not be angry at us because
there is no more of us come to this place.   There was four of us, from four
different towns set away together, but two of Our Companions gave out, the

one his hip failed him, the other his back, and they returned, we dont know how it is with them. But God who is good and doeth good continually gave us health and strength, and prospered us in the way and hath safely brought us to this place, and art now allowing us an opportunity to see your faces in Comfort, and to converse with you in peace at this time. So to him we give our thanks at this time for all his goodness towards us. We rejoice that God gave us favour in the Eye of His Honor Sir William Johnson, and we rejoice that God gave us favour in your Eyes, and we are glad to hear that ye found it in your hearts to pity us and our Brethren in New England when ye heard of our Circumstances. And not only we thank you, but all our Brethren in New England give you their hearty thanks, Yea we have reason to rejoice. We thought to purchase land of you, but we are glad that it is in your hearts to give us land, yea we thank you that ye have given us so much already.

Brethren, this Silver pipe was sent to me & the tobacco pouch with it to d'spose of according to the advise of Sir William Johnson, and His Honour Sir William received us gladly at this time also and he told me to deliver the Pipe to the Chiefs at the meeting, and to let it be kept in the Council house continually, so at your assemblies ye might look on it, & smoke out of it, & remember us New England Indians. Sir William also said perhaps ye would think it odd if there was no tobacco in the pouch, so he was pleased to put some in, and sent it to you Chiefs that this day ye may smoke out of the Silver pipe. So now I deliver this pipe as a token from our Several Tribes in New England, that we are one and sincere in what we say & do. And now our Elder Brethren we have told you of our proceedings & all we desire at present is to know whether you are of the same mind as Ever, whether your Love and pity is the same. So our dear Brethren these few words we leave you to consider of at present, and then we shall tell you of little more to consider of.

The first answer of the Oneida Indians was delivered the next day. It recognized the New England Indians of the seven towns as brethren, and inquired as to the number who were intending to remove. To this Johnson replied in a second address as follows:

Our dear Brethren, what we have further for you to consider of is this, our Purposes or our Design if God willing, this I know my Elder Brethren, that we may consult together and agree to do so & so. Yet if it is not the mind of God all our Councils & purposes will come to nought, or all will be in vain. But if it please God & He open your hearts to pity us & to receive us as a younger Brother & help us indeed, we purpose and design to come

up and settle together in Peace, where you shall think fit and where it will
be most agreeable for us.   All we desire is to live in peace & to have things
Convenient.   If we cant have land enough we cant have things Convenient.
We all have little land in New England, but it is very poor the greatest
part.   So there we cant have things convenient, that is many of us, and
Some are obliged to turn their hands this way & that way to get a Liveli-
hood.   The town to which I belong is good land, and we have sufficient at
present.   We could live there this hundred years yet, if we increased.   But
we are willing at least some of us to come up and settle down together with
our Brethren in peace.   True the great drinkers & Lazy Persons are backward in coming in these parts but we are willing to leave them there.

Brethren we ought all to adoar God for his goodness to us from day to
day and we ought to bless him that he is allowing us this opportunity to
assemble ourselves together this once more in this house to consult together a little about the affairs of this World.

Brethren I am very glad that my Ears have heard those things which I
have heard from you, in your Consultations since we have been in your
town, and as perhaps this is the last time, that I shall speak to you my
Elder Brother, be so kind as to hearken to the words of your younger
Brother who would speak this once more in the Name of the seven towns in
New England.   First, I return you my hearty thanks my Elder Brothers
that ye have considered of me on my Brethren in New-England and I
rejoice that ye find in your hearts Love still remaining there, & pity towards
your younger Brethren in New England.   I thank you that ye have so
deliberately considered of those few words which we desired you to consider, and we thank you for your kind answer which ye gave to us, & to our
Brethren in New England.   We thank you that ye have taken us to be your
younger Brethren and that ye look upon us to be of the same Blood as yourselves, and we thank you that ye have received us to your Body, So that now
we may say we have one head & one heart, & may God keep us united
together indeed untill we Both grow white headed, and may we sit together
in Peace in Gods own time.   And now Brethren we thank you that according to our desire ye have been pleased to assemble yourselves together this
once more, and my Elder Brother, I have but a word to tell you of to which
I beg ye would take under your deliberate consideration.   Brother, ye was
pleased last fall to give us an Encouragement of 10 miles Square, for which
we all was glad.   But in our Consultations we thought that that was not
quite sufficient.   Perhaps we should soon clear so much, perhaps directly
or right way, then we should have to look somewhere else for our children
to live, but our Elder Brother ye know that it is a hard thing for Parents &
children to separate, and we desire to live together if it please God our
Creator, and Brethren if it please you to give us Sufficient for us and our

Children after us, if you please to give us more land it will gladen the hearts of many Poor Indians in New England. We are glad that ye have so much at your disposal. We could tell you what our Brethren in New England desire, but thus much I have to say at present.

On the following day towards evening, January twenty-second, the second answer was delivered. At the risk of being thought to make unimportant matters conspicuous, we give this in full, for it shows clearly that the New England Indians were adopted by the Six Nations, as they have since asserted in the case of "The New York Indians against the United States:"

Well Brethren, harken unto us, this day we have assembled ourselves together again, to consult together, a little about the affairs of this World.— But tomorrow is the Lords day, which he hath made, and set apart for his own Service. Brethren, we rejoice in the goodness of God, who hath preserved us all our Life-time, and hath brought us to see the light of this day of Peace, and we rejoice, that God is allowing us this opportunity of assembling ourselves together this once more, and we are glad that we are suffered to see the faces of each other in Comfort, and as we are shortsighted Creatures, we are sensable, that we stand in need of Gods help: We desire that God would direct us, and lead us to such Conclusions as will be most pleasing to Him concerning this affair which has been laid before us for our Consideration, and now our Brethren, We the Chiefs and Lords of this Place, also warriors, and all in this Assembly, are about to give you an Answer, concerning the Affair, which you laid before the Council yesterday. Brethren, we understood all that you said yesterday. But we are somewhat forgetful, our Memories cant retain for a long time what we hear: and altho we cant remember every word, yet very likely the principle, or the substance of your Speech is rooted in our Understanding, and considering Parts that is rooted and fixed in our Hearts. We well remember what you said concerning the English, and we are sorry to hear the low Circumstances into which ye are involved in owing to the Ignorance of your forefathers. We are glad to hear of your proceedings hitherto. We remember that you said you acquainted Sir William Johnson of the State and Circumstances that ye were in, also we remember that you said, that Sir William was pleased with the design, and advised you in the affair, and gave you Encouragement.—Brethren, Sir William also acquainted us of your Desires, or Intentions of removing to this part of the Country, and as soon as we was enformed of your Circumstances, we took the Message that

Sir William Johnson sent to us on your behalf under our Considerations, and Brethren we were all glad, our Great men, Lords, Warriors, and young men, yea even Women and Children rejoiced to hear that ye were disposed to come and settle in these parts. Brethren, perhaps it was the Lord that steared your minds this way. Maybe it is his will and pleasure that ye should come up here, and live side of us, your Brethren. Brethren, we that are in this Council profess to be good or Religious Men, so ye may put confidence in us, or believe what we say unto you. Be of good Courage Brethren, the Lords of this Place would have you to be of firm minds, be not discouraged for all the Inhabitants of this Place are very glad that ye are come to this Town, and we all rejoice to hear from you at this time, that your Brethren in New-England are still disposed to come up in these parts to live, and now Brethren, we receive you into our Body as it were, now we may say we have one head, one heart and one Blood, now Brethren our lives are mixed together, and let us have one Ruler, even God our Maker, Who dwells in Heaven above, who is the father of us all. Brethren, we are sensable that the Devil is never Idle, but is ever busy, and if the Evil spirit stirs up any Nation whatsoever or Person against you and causes your Blood to be spilt we shall take it as if it was done unto us, or as if they spilt the blood from our own Bodies, and we shall be ever ready to defend you and help you or be ready to protect you according to our Abilities. and now Brethren, as we expect that ye will come, and live side of us in short time, We would tell you as Brothers our principle, or Custom in these parts. Brethren, two things, we six united Nations do follow, the first and Chief is Religion, or to follow the directions given to us in Gods Word. the second is to concur with the Unchristianized Nations so far as will promote Peace, and Tranquility in our Land. Brethren, this we ought to do that Religion might grow, and flourish in these Parts. and Brethren, we shall expect that ye will assist us in advising us concerning the affairs that may be brought under our consideration when ye shall live side of us your Brothers. and Brethren, it is hoped that we both shall be disposed ever to help one another in cases of Necessity, so long as we shall live together. as for us Brethren we have already resolved to Endeavour to do all things as becometh Brothers, and so much as in us lies with Justice, and Equity so long as we shall sit together. and now Brethren, here is your Elder Brothers the Tuskaroras, we say your elder Brothers, because they came here before you, and because they came from a greater distance, these your elder Brothers, will live next to you, or side of you, and they are an understanding people, yea we are ready to say that they are become wiser than us Onoidas in considering of affairs of great importance. Brethren you see that these Tuskaroras are now white headed by reason of Age, and with these our Brothers we have sat together in Peace even from our Infancy.

Well Brethren, we hope that we shall live together in peace untill we see each other white headed. Brethren, your Ears must not be open to hear flying Stories and you must not let prejudice arise in your hearts too quick. this is the way or Custom likewise of us Six united Nations, not to regard any evil minded Person or Persons who are contrary to Peace. Brethren, we look upon you as upon a Sixth Brother. We will tell you of all your elder Brothers, the Onoidas, Kiyougas, Nanticuks, Tuskaroras, Todelehonas, these five are your Elder Brothers. But as for the Mohawks, Onondangas and Senecas they are our fathers, and they are your fathers. Brethren in the Spring we shall expect you here again, then we will shew you a place to settle on. Brethren, here is your Silver pipe and it shall be done with according to Orders. thus much we have to say at present. accept our words, tho it is but little that we have said. Brethren, we say this once more, that we are very glad to see you in our Town, and now Brethren, We the Chiefs and Lords of this Place, also Warriors and young men give our kind respects and Sincere love to our Brethren in New England that live in those Seven Towns, that are disposed to come this way. We say we give our loves to the old men, your Councilers and teachers, and to all the young men, also we give our love to all the Women old and young, and to all Children. Brethren, very likely several of our Chiefs will accompany you as far as to Sir William Johnson's and there Brothers we will confirm all our words, and rectify our Mistakes, if we have made any, there alone is the place to have all things done well, done strong and done sure. So Brethren, this is the End of our Answer.

The third answer was delivered on the Monday following, January twenty-fourth. It also is important as showing that the Oneidas purposed to grant their brethren a considerable tract of land :

Brethren, since we have received you as Brothers, we shall not confine you or pen you up to Ten Miles square : We have much Land at our disposal, and you need not fear that you shall not have Land sufficient for you, and for your Children after you. We would have you to fix your Minds here, and here alone, and when ye come to live up here, we desire that ye would not hearken to the invitations of other Nations, who may invite you to go farther back. Brethren, we say let your minds be at ease, be not troubled but come, and settle down in Peace, and live in peace for ever. Brothers, we understand that ye purpose to go homeward tomorrow ; but Brothers, dont take it hard, we think that ye must continue with us two days longer, the reason is this. Some of the Chiefs, or heads of the Six Nations, are coming up from Sir Williams with a Speech from his Honor, and we think that it will not be handsome or that it would not be so well for us to meet them in the woods. We think that it would be best for us to see them here in this Council house, also we think that it would be very proper for you to be here when Sir Williams speech will be delivered as it is concerning you, and your New England Brethren. this is all that we have to say at present.

Thus the council broke up, and Joseph Johnson and his companion set out to return home, having been at Kanawaro-hare eight days.[4] They were attended to Johnson Hall by twelve of the Oneida chiefs who in Sir William Johnson's presence ratified their pledge of eternal friendship for the New England Indians.

So far the affair had progressed favorably. Johnson returned to his school at Farmington, where he had hired a substitute in his absence. He was then busy preparing himself for approval as a minister under the encouragement of Doctor Wheelock. As the summer drew near it was arranged that Samson Occom and David Fowler, in behalf of the seven towns, should go to Oneida and view the land, and that Joseph Johnson should join them there after he had received approbation. With this purpose he attended the Commencement at Dartmouth College. The day after it, the ministers who happened to be present proceeded to his examination. The following is their testimonial:[5]

These may certify all whom it may concern that Joseph Johnson, an Indian of the Mohegan Tribe in Connecticut has offered himself before us, who were providentially together, for Examination as a Candidate to preach the Gospel, with a principal View to the Benefit of his own Nation — We have examined him as to his Knowledge and Understanding in the Doctrines of the Gospel and Experimental Religion and other Accomplishments Needful for Usefulness among his own Nation and also the Churches in a christian Land where in Providence he may be called and have opportunity

---

[4] *Wheelock Papers*, Lett. Johnson to Wheelock, May 2, 1774. Johnson's passport is dated at Johnson Hall, Feb. 5, 1774.—*Conn. Hist. Soc , Indian Papers.*

[5] *Wheelock Papers, Dart. Coll.*

to preach — We are well satisfied as to his Qualifications and heartily recommend him for ^{d} Purpose.

Dartmouth College

   in New Hampshire y^r 25 of Aug 1774

                    LEMUEL HEDGE, Pastor of Warwick

                    JEREMY BELKNAP, Dover

                    JOSIAH DANA, Hutchinson

                    ISAIAH POTTER, Lebanon

                    WILLIAM CONANT, Lime

                    SYLVANUS RIPLEY, Missionary

To this document there was also appended a recommendation by Eleazar Wheelock, president of Dartmouth College, Benjamin Pomeroy, pastor at Hebron, and Eden Burroughs, pastor at Hanover. In the afternoon the young Indian preached to a Commencement assembly. Of this occasion he says, "I preached yesterday in the afternoon at the College Hall and after the exercise was over they made general contribution and I had thirty Dollars given to me by the Gentlemen who came here commencement. I am going to set off for the Mohawk Country this Day and I shall come back as soon as ever I can." Doctor Wheelock says that this exercise was performed "to universal satisfaction," and testifies to the ability which Johnson displayed in this trying ordeal. He had only received approbation, with a view of being ordained later, which his early death prevented.

Samson Occom and David Fowler set out for Oneida on the eighth of July and safely arrived at Kanawarohare at dusk on the twenty-fourth. Here again Occom and Kirkland met. The former in his diary says, "we embraced each other with joy." The latter also in his journal records the meeting. "Mr. Occom with his brother-in-law, D^d Fowler arrived here, who are come upon a friendly visit to the Indians.' It was more than two months before the formal Treaty between the Oneidas and the New England Indians was held. Meanwhile they viewed the lands and settled its boundaries, and by friendly intercourse sought to strengthen their relations with their newly-adopted brethren. In due time Joseph Johnson arrived. On the 4th of October the Oneidas transferred to them by a deed of gift, so called, a considerable tract of land lying west of the " Property Line."

By Guy Johnson Esqr. Superintendent of Indian Affairs for the Northern Department of North America &c &c.—

Whereas, The Indians of Mohegan Naraganset Montock, Pequods of Groton and of Stonington, Nahantick, Farmington, Inhabiting within the New England Governments, Did Last Year represent that they Were Very much Streightened and Reduced to Such small Pittance of Land that they could no longer remain there and Did through the Channell of Sir, William Johnson Bar^t, late Superintendent Apply to the Six Nations for some lands to Live on Which was at Length agreed to in my Presence at the last Treaty and a Tract alloted them by the Oneidas, And Whereas Some of them have since in Company with the Oneida Chiefs view'd the said lands and Determined on its Boundary as followes desireing a Certificate of the Same and that it might be Entered on the Records of Indian Affairs, Viz. Beginning at the West End of the Scaniadaris, or the long Lake which is at the Head of One of the Branches of Orisca Creek and from thence about twelve Miles Northerly or so far that an Easterly Course from a Certain point on the first Mentioned Course Shall Intersect the Road or path leading from Old Oneida to the German Fflats Where the said Path Crosses Scanindowa Creek Running into the Oneida Lake. Then the Same Course Continued to the Line Settled as the Limits between the Province of New York and the Indians at the Treaty of Fort Stanwix in 1768, thence Southerly along the said Line about thirteen Miles or so far as that a Westerly Line from thence keeping one Mile South of the Most Southerly Bend of Orisca Creek Shall Reach the Place of Beginning so as to Comprehend the Lake first Mentioned—I Do therefore in Compliance With the Joint Request of the said Oneidas and New England Indians Declare that the Said Oneidas Do Grant to the said New England Indians and there Posterity for Ever Without Power of Alienation to any Subject the Afore Described Tract with its Appurtenances in the Amplest Manner. Also full Liberty of Hunting all sorts of Game throughout the Whole Country of the Oneidas, Beaver Hunting only Excepted. With this Particular Clause or Reservation that the same shall not be Possessed by any Persons Deemed of the said Tribes Who are Decended from or have Intermixed with Negroes and Mulattoes.

Given under my Hand and Seal at Arms at Guy Park, October the 4th 1774.

[SEAL]   G. JOHNSON

We the Chiefs Do in Testimony of the foregoing Affix the Character of our Tribes unto the Day and Year above Mentioned—

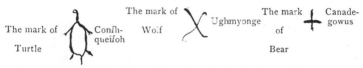

The mark of Turtle   Confh-queifoh   The mark of Wolf   Ughmyonge   The mark of Bear   Canade-gowus

Recv^d 4th Feb^ry A. D. 1785 and here Recorded

Teste
GEORGE WYLLYS, Secret.

The great practical difficulty of securing sufficient funds to carry forward the emigration had yet to be met. Joseph Johnson had already contracted personal debts in the cause. His first thought apparently had been to issue an address, "To all generous, free-hearted and Publick spirited Gentlemen," asking for aid, as a draft of such a document is extant.[6] He had petitioned the Connecticut General Assembly for assistance, and had received therefrom £6 as a contribution.[7] Having further assistance in view, he visited New York, where a friend was raised up in Rev. Dr. John Rodgers, the successor of Rev. David Bostwick, an early friend of the Oneida mission. Here Johnson preached several times, and collections were taken which relieved him of debt and provided a balance for his future maintenance. Thus encouraged, he went among the Indians of the seven towns exhibiting the deed of the Oneida lands, and preaching the emigration as one might a crusade. He wrote Dr. Rodgers thus of his success : " They are engaged to go on in prosecution of the design which I made known to you and we purpose to set off from hence [Mohegan] or from these parts the 13th of March next. I believe that there will be upwards of 60 young men from the several tribes who will go as first settlers of land granted to us by the Oneidas. However there is 58 able working men

---

[6] *Conn. Hist. Soc., Indian Papers.*
[7] *Conn. Arch., Indians.* 11, 308 ; *Conn. Col. Rec.*, XIV, 314.

on whose word I believe we can rely. From Mohegan 10. From Narragansett 20. From Montauk 13. From Nehantic 5. From Farmington $10 = 58$, & there are other tribes so deeply in debt that they cannot go this season, but fully intend to go soon as possible, i. e. Groton & Stonington. I was there last Thursday & conversed with them. Mr. Occom will preach there next Sunday, & he will propose conditions to them & their creditors, so they may go. . . . It is thought best at first that those who can endure hardships go & prepare the way & prepare a shelter for themselves to live in & to raise somewhat to eat & then move with their families, & then have the aged men & women go leaning upon their sons as it were."[8]

At the same time he wrote Doctor Wheelock to the same effect. The encouragement he had received from his patron may be inferred from the following paragraph in the Narrative of that year : "And this Prospect is yet further, I think, much increased, by the proposed Removal of the principal Indians of the Tribe at Montauck, with all the christianized and civilized Indians of the several Towns in New-England, to settle in a Body in the Heart of the Country of the Six Nations, which is expected to be effected next Summer. This is in Consequence of an Application, made under the Countenance, Assistance and Direction of Sir William Johnson, by Mr. Occom, Joseph Johnson, Jacob Fowler and others delegated by the several Tribes for that Purpose. In Consequence of which, they have obtained and well secured a Tract of choice Land, Fifteen or Twenty Miles square, where they design to settle in a Body, as a civilized and christian People, and cultivate those Lands for their Subsistence ; and also by them, as soon and as far as they shall be able, to support all Divine Ordinances and Schools among them ; and invite their Savage Brethren to an imitation of them, and a Participation of all

these Benefits and Privileges with them.   They purpose to
have, as far as may be, of their own Sons for Ministers and
School-Masters. . . . And from this Place, their Ministers may
with much less Expence, make Excursions among the Tribes
round about them, and their School will be near and convenient to receive the Children of such as shall desire a Christian Education for them."[9]   This extract truly represents the
general sentiment of approval with which the emigration was
regarded by all friends of the Indians.

When the spring opened—and it may have been on the thirteenth of March, as they had planned—the first company of
emigrants set out for their new home.   How many there were,
and what their fortunes were on the way, we cannot tell.
Joseph Johnson, David Fowler and Elijah Wampy were
among them, as were John Skeesuck, James Shattocks and
Samuel Tallman, not so well known to us.   The last was
one of Wheelock's Delaware Indian pupils, who had since
lived among the New England tribes.   Probably they carried
out their purpose of sending the younger men on in advance.
They arrived safely in the Oneida country, and immediately
set about building log huts in that wide expanse of wilderness,
making gardens and planting corn-fields.   All might have gone
as they had planned had it not been for the war-cloud which
burst in all its fury that spring over the New England colonies.
These Indians heard the sound of the patriot's gun, though they
were far away.

One of the most serious concerns which faced the colonies
in the early days of the Revolution was as to the attitude
of the Six Nations.   Many have known that the Oneidas
remained faithful to the patriots, notwithstanding the strenu-
ous efforts which were made to alienate them ; but no one has
ever given credit to the Christian Indians of New England for
this, to whom it belongs no less than to Samuel Kirkland.

[9] *Wheelock's Narrative*, 1775, pp. 15, 16.

They had reached Oneida at the opportune time, and their voices were at once raised in behalf of their white friends. It was they who inspired the "Declaration of Neutrality," addressed to the four New England Provinces by the Oneidas and dated June 19, 1775. We think, indeed, that one of their number wrote it. They certainly carried it eastward. It begins thus : "As my younger Brothers of the New England Indians who have settled in our Vicinity are now going down to visit their Friends, & to move up Parts of their Families that were left behind, with this belt by them I open the Rode wide, clearing it of all Obstacles that they may visit their Friends & return to their settlement here in Peace." [10] At that date Joseph Johnson was on his way to New York, where he presented a petition to the Provincial Congress on the twenty-first and received £10 New York currency.[11] In this he states that some had already returned to New England and three more were to follow him to New York for whom he requested a passport. These were John Skeesuck, James Shattocks and Samuel Tallman, and some days afterwards they joined him. Possibly they were the bearers of the "Declaration of Neutrality," which contained welcome news. Some, however, did not return, but held their post in Oneida. Foremost among these was David Fowler, the early teacher at Kanawarohare. Johnson also received from the Provincial Congress a message to the Oneidas. He went on to Mohegan and on the seventeenth of July set out to carry it. Again he was in New York August twenty-sixth and on the eleventh of September received a pass from the Committee of Safety— "having given proof of his attachment to the cause of American Liberty." [12] After this he returned to Oneida. He had not lost sight of his mission as a preacher among the Six Nations, and

[10] *Mass. Archives*, Vol. 144, pp. 311, 312. *Conn. Col. Rec.*, xv, 100.
[11] *N. Y. Archives*, Rev. I, 102.
[12] *Wheelock Papers.*

it was the necessity of raising funds for this work which brought him again to New England late in the autumn. In the January following he visited Col. John Phillips at Exeter, N. H., who gave him substantial encouragement. He was also at Portsmouth. The letter he bore from Rev. David McClure to Doctor Wheelock when he departed says: "His coming this way was as welcome as it was unexpected. I receive him as an old acquaintance but very happily made more valuable by distinguished grace—the good effects of which are very manifest in him. . . . It must afford you joy that this your pupil, whom once if I mistake not you was ready to weep over as lost is now walking in the truth."[13] On the sixteenth of the month he appeared before the New Hampshire General Assembly, and received from them a testimonial signed by M. Weare, the president, commending him "not only as a Friend to the Cause of American Liberty, but as a modest, discreet, sensible Man, whose Influence among the Indian Nations has been & may be very serviceable to the Colonies," to which also an address to the Six Nations was appended.[14] He was instructed "to use his utmost endeavors to brighten the chain of friendship which has for many years past subsisted between us and them." Thence he went to Hanover.[15] Doctor Wheelock wrote a letter, dated January twenty-ninth, recommending him to General Washington at Cambridge. This he presented on the twentieth of February, going thither by the way of Mohegan. General Washington sent by him the following message to the Six Nations, the original of which is among the Wheelock Papers:

Sir.

I am very much pleased to find by the strong recommendations you produce, that we have among our Brothers of the Six Nations a person who

---

[13] *Wheelock Papers*, Lett. Portsmouth, Jan. 8, 1776.

[14] The original is among the Wheelock Papers.

[15] He preached there the funeral sermon of Levi Washburn, Jan. 23rd.—Chase's *Hist. of Dart. Coll.*, p. 352.

can explain to them the sense of their Brothers on the dispute between us and the Ministers of Great Britain. You have seen a part of our Strength, and can inform our Brothers that we can withstand all the force which those who want to rob us of our Lands and our Homes can send against us.

You can tell our friends that they may always look upon me, whom the Whole United Colonies have chosen to be their Chief Warrior, as their brother; whilst they continue in Friendship with us, they may depend upon mine and the protection of those under my command.

Tell them that we dont want them to take up the hatchet for us except they chuse it; we only desire that they will not fight against us, we want that the chain of friendship should always remain bright between our friends of the Nations and us. Their attention to you will be a proof to us that they wish the same. We recommend you to them, and hope by your spreading the truths of the Holy Gospel amongst them, it will contribute to keep the chain so bright, that the malicious insinuations or practices of our Enemies will never be able to break this Union, so much for the benefit of our Brothers of the Six Nations and of us—And to prove to them that this is my desire and of the Warriors under me, I hereto Subscribe my name at Cambridge this 20th day of February 1776

Gᵒ. WASHINGTON.

Mr. Joseph Johnson.

It was doubtless also at this time that he received the address of Samson Occom to his Indian brethren urging them to maintain neutrality. It is as follows:

Beloved Brethren

I Rejoice to hear, that you keep to your Promise, that you will not meddle with the Family Contentions of the English, but will be at peace and quietness. Peace never does any hurt. Peace is from the God of Peace and Love, and therefore be at Peace among yourselves, and with all men, and the God of Peace Dwell with you. Jesus Christ is the Prince of Peace, he is the Peace Maker, if all Mankind in the World Believed in Jesus Christ with all their Hearts, there wou'd be no more Wars, they would live as one Family in Peace. Jesus Christ said to his ·Disciples just before he left them, Peace I leave with you, my Peace I give unto you, not as the World giveth give I unto you, and again, a New Command I give unto you that ye Love one another. Now Consider, my Beloved Brethren who is the Author of these Bloody wars. Will God Set his People to kill one another? You will certainly say No. Well, who then makes all this Mischief? Methinks I hear you all say, the Devil, the Devil,—so he is, he makes all the Contentions as he sows the Seeds of Discord among the Children of men and makes all the Mischief in the World.—Yet it is right for the Peaceable to Defend themselves when wicked People fall upon them without Reason or Cause, then they can look up to Heaven to their God and he will help them.

I will now give you a little insight into the Nature of the English Quarrils over the great Waters. They got to be rich, I mean the Nobles and the great, and they are very Proud and they keep the rest of their Brethren under their Feet, they make Slaves of them. The great ones have got all the Land and the rest are poor Tenants—and the People in this Country live more upon a leavel and they live happy, and the former Kings of England use to let the People in this Country have their Freedom and Liberty ; but the present King of England wants to make them Slaves to himself, and the People in this Country don't want to be Slaves,—and so they are come over to kill them, and the People here are oblig'd to Defend themselves, they dont go over the great Lake to kill them. And now I think you must see who is the oppresser and who are the oppressed and now I think, if you must join on one way or other you cant join the oppresser, but will help the oppressed. But let me conclude with one word of Advice, use all your Influence to your Brethren, so far as you have any Connections to keep them in Peace and quietness, and not to intermeddle in these Quarrils among the White People. The Lord Jesus Christ says, Blessed are the Peacemakers, for they shall be called the Children of God.

This with great Love is from

Your True Brother

SAMSON OCCOM [16]

Joseph Johnson, being thus commissioned by the highest authorities to carry messages of peace to the Indians, and as he says in a letter being " heartily engaged to go and preach the glad tidings of the gospel of Jesus Christ to my western Brethren," turned his footsteps again westward. Here he disáppears from view as many another Indian has on the trail. He was detained at Mohegan by the illness of his wife, and it must have been early in the summer ere he set out. David Fowler, who was still in the wilderness, wrote encouraging words to Samson Occom on the 14th of August, of the neutrality of the Indians and the health of their company.[17] We con-

---

[16] *Conn. Hist. Soc., Indian Papers.*
[17] *Ibid.*

jecture that Johnson was then among them or in that region on his mission.   On some unknown day within a few months, this remarkable young missionary, then only twenty-four years old, in whom there was ability most honorable and courage illustrious, was laid to rest in an unmarked grave.   The only obituary we have met with is in the postscript of a letter from Rev. David McClure to Doctor Wheelock, in which he says, "The Churches this way who had a taste of Mr. Johnson's ministerial Gifts feel for the public in the loss of that zealous, pious and very promising Indian Preacher."[18]   So ended the life of that pupil in the Indian Charity School, who was thought at one time to prove the futility of attempts to educate native missionaries.

[18] *Wheelock Papers*, Lett. North Hampton, May 8, 1777.

CHAPTER XIII

1734—1783

The part which the Christian Indians of New England took in the American Revolution should win them lasting honor among patriots. In that conflict their settlements were wasted, their habits demoralized and the flower of their youth perished. The future of those who had emigrated to Oneida would certainly have been different had it not been for the devastation of that war. Most of the younger men returned at once and enlisted as soldiers. The names of many such are known. William Williams testified in 1783 that eighteen of the Mohegans had died in the service, and, remembering that the tribe was not large, this was a great loss. Only a few remained on their Oneida lands with their families. Among these were David Fowler, Elijah Wampy, Andrew Corcomb, John Adams, James Cusk and Samuel Adams. Their houses were of no very pretentious sort ; but they were the only ones for miles around. In one of them doubtless Heinrich Staring was confined by his Indian captors during the Revolution, as related by Pomroy Jones.[1] Hardships were certainly their lot, and dangers from the enemy surrounded them. At last there came a time when their position was untenable. The enemy under the command of General St. Leger approached to besiege Fort Schuyler. Probably some of his marauding bands of savages who knew the location of these friendly Indians threatened them, but the circumstances are unknown to us in

---

[1] Jones' *Annals of Oneida County*, pp. 254-259.

detail. Occom says they were driven off by the enemy and were obliged to leave all their effects in their haste. The Oneidas and Tuscaroras went to Albany and were there supported by the government; but the Brothertown Indians were homeless. All they had possessed in New England had been sold when they emigrated. Whither should they go? Eastward they took their course. So in time they arrived at Stockbridge. It was natural for them to feel that they were there among friends, for the Housatonic tribe was at this time the most advanced in civilization of any in western Massachusetts. Land was plenty where they might build huts and cultivate their Indian corn. Here, then, these refugees settled down in West Stockbridge and Richmond, intending to return to Oneida as soon as it was safe. Some of them, having nothing else at hand to do, became soldiers of the Revolution. Their friends in the old settlements, among whom Samson Occom still ministered, assisted them as they could. Jacob Fowler was not with them. He was no longer needed as Indian tutor at Dartmouth College, there being no Indians to teach, and in 1776 he had entered the government service as a messenger to the Western tribes. In September of that year he traveled thither with others to a distance of six hundred miles and returned in the dead of winter. On occasions afterwards he carried more than one important despatch to and from the "war-office" of Governor Jonathan Trumbull at Lebanon. David Fowler, however, was there—the mainstay of the refugees—industrious, wise and faithful as in his younger days; and in his care we leave them for a little to give some account of these Indian friends at Stockbridge with whom to this day they have been so intimately associated.

The beginning of missionary labors among the Housatonic Indians was due to the interest which the "prudent, industrious and temperate" character of their chief, Konkapot, had kindled in the minds of Revs. Stephen Williams of Long-

meadow and Samuel Hopkins of West Springfield.[2] Through
them this fact was communicated to the commissioners of the
" Society for Propagating the Gospel " at Boston, who wished
them to visit Housatonic. Before they could comply it
chanced that Konkapot and the second chief, Umpachenee,
came to Springfield, May 22, 1734, to receive a captain's and
lieutenant's commission, respectively, for loyal services to the
Massachusetts Colony. A conference with them was held to
ascertain whether they would receive a missionary. The
result was so encouraging that Mr. Williams, with Rev. Nehe-
miah Bull of Westfield, visited them in July, when the tribe
decided to welcome religious instruction. Mr. Williams went
to Boston and reported to the commissioners, whereupon they
voted, August 16, 1734, to empower him and Mr. Bull to
engage a suitable man for the work. John Sergeant, then a
tutor at Yale College, was secured and he spent two months
with them that autumn. There were then, as reported to the
commissioners, only about six families at Skatehook (Sheffield)
and the same number ten miles north at Wnahktukook (Stockbridge). It should not be inferred, however, that this included
all of the tribe. More were scattered about in the neighborhood, and eventually their numbers were augmented by
Brainerd's Indians and some from the southward at Kent and
Sharon. Between these two Housatonic settlements, at Great
Barrington, on the twenty-first of October they began to build
a log house, in which Sergeant set up a school on the fifth of
November. Rude huts round about sufficed for the Indians.
Timothy Woodbridge of Springfield was then engaged as
schoolmaster. Here the school was kept for two winters, the
same being carried on in their Indian settlements during the
summer. The work made rapid progress. On the 1st of July,

---

[2] On the history of this tribe see: *Historical Memoirs, Relating to the Housantun-
nuk Indians,* Samuel Hopkins, Boston, 1753; *Stockbridge Past and Present,* Miss
E. F. Jones; *Muhhekaneok, A History of the Stockbridge Nation,* J. N. Davidson;
and Biographies of John Sergeant, Jonathan Edwards and Stephen West.

1735, Sergeant entered upon his mission and was ordained at Deerfield, August 31st, the Indians being present and publicly receiving him as their minister.[3]   He had scarcely begun his good work before he saw the necessity of more permanent civilizing influences.   This end he planned to attain by establishing a town, in which the Indians could live on their own lands and be continuously under his ministry.   He also thought it would be well—in the words of Governor Belcher, who endorsed the scheme, " that some English Families be interspers'd and settled among the Indians, for to civilize will be the readiest way to christianize them."   Accordingly under the authority of the General Court, the Indians surrendered their other lands, and a township was secured by buying off the few white settlers, to which the Indians removed in 1736. This town, six miles square, was incorporated in May, 1739, as Stockbridge.   Sergeant built a house there in 1737 ; and the same year "a Meeting-House of thirty Feet broad and forty long together with a School-House " were begun at the expense of the Colony.   He soon acquired the native language and preached with marked effect.   Parts of the Bible, prayers and Watts' Catechism were translated for their use.   Indian boys, who were maintained on the Hollis foundation, were instructed, and by his success he was led to project an Indian boarding-school.   A building was erected in 1749 for its accommodation, but on account of Sergeant's death, on the twenty-seventh of July, the school fell into other hands and after a few years it failed through poor management.   In 1750 the town con-

3 Gospel Ministers | Must be fit for | The Master's Use, | and | Prepared to every Good Work, | if they would be Vessels unto Honour ; | Illustrated in | A Sermon | Preached at Deerfield, August 31. 1735. | At the Ordination of | Mr. John Sargeant, | To the Evangelical Ministry, with a special Reference—to the Indians at Houssa-tonnoc, who have lately | manifested their desires to receive the Gospel. | By Nathaniel Appleton, M. A. . . . . Boston: . . . S. Kneeland & T. Green.   MDCCXXXV. 8° pp. (2) XIV, 33. [Conn. Hist. Soc.] Another edition was printed at Edinburgh in 1736.

tained fifty-three families of Indians, who had twenty houses built in the English fashion. Of the 218 individuals in these families, 129 had been baptized, forty-two of whom were communicants. At this time all of David Brainerd's Indians at Kaunaumeek, where he had labored for a year from April 1, 1743, had removed to Stockbridge.

One feature of John Sergeant's work it is important to notice —he baptized such natives as renounced heathenism several years before a church was formed with which they could fellowship. In this he followed the example of John Eliot. His interpreter, when he first visited them in 1734, Ebenezer Paupaumnuk, was examined by Mr. Bull, and baptized the seventeenth of October. Captain Konkapot and Lieutenant Umpachenee, with their wives, were baptized in November, 1735, and within a year after his ordination about forty infants and adults had received baptism. This fact has led some to conclude that a church was then formed; but we think there was no such organization until 1738. Baptism was practised as the sign of a renunciation of heathenism and preparatory to church estate when the time should come. In the spring of 1738 four white families, of a character approved by Sergeant, had become residents. The commissioners' manuscript records note under June third the report of Captain Williams, that there was "likely to be a church gathered at Housatonic in a short time"; and their first Lord's Supper was celebrated on the fourth of June. We conclude, therefore, that the church had been formed during the week previous to that date.[4] There were eleven communicants, some of whom were Indians. Peter Pauquaunaupeet was chosen a deacon. During his ministry Sergeant baptized 182 Indians and admitted about sixty to the church. His successor, Rev. Jonathan Edwards, ad-

---

[4] The claim has always been that this church was organized in 1734. *Muhhekaneok*, pp. 4, 5; *Stockbridge, Past and Present*, p. 42; and Dr. Field in Barber's *Historical Collections of Mass.*, p. 97.

mitted about twenty-five and Rev. Stephen West nearly as many.[5]

The defect in John Sergeant's scheme of Indian civilization was in the introduction of families of whites into the town. This operated, as it always has, to the injury of the weaker race. Samson Occom at Brothertown contended against this feature. So soon as the lands at Stockbridge were divided, and so held that the Indians could sell their claims, they did so. The whites thus gradually crowded them out. In the church also there was more or less distinction between the natives and the English, and finally in 1775 the Indian portion of the congregation was committed by Dr. West to the care of John Sergeant, the son of their first minister, who had previously taught school there.[6] He received the salary which had been allowed for the mission by the Scotch Society. Some writers have said that at this time sixteen Indians took letters from the old church and formed a new organization. We think this is an error, and that the Indian church was formed ten years later in anticipation of their removal to the Oneida country. A separate church at Stockbridge was not needed. Indeed, there is evidence that some of the principal Christian Indians retained their membership in the mother church, participating in their sacramental occasions under the leadership of John Sergeant. He was practically an associate minister,

---

[5] Dr. Field's MSS. in the Conn. Hist. Soc.

[6] John Sergeant, the elder, was born in Newark, N. J., in 1710, being the son of Jonathan and Mary Sergeant. His father had removed to New Jersey from Branford, Conn. He graduated from Yale College in 1729 and became a tutor there in 1731. He married, August 16, 1739, Abigail, eldest daughter of Colonel Ephraim Williams of Stockbridge, and they had three children, Erastus, John and a daughter who married Colonel Mark Hopkins of Great Barrington and was the grandmother of the famous president of Williams College. After John Sergeant's death his widow married General Joseph Dwight of Great Barrington, by whom she had three children. John Sergeant, the younger, was born at Stockbridge in 1747. After the Indians had been some years at New Stockbridge he removed his family thither, and there died Sept. 7, 1824.

having charge of the Indian portion of the church. In many respects he was well adapted to this service. Although he was an infant when his father died, he had imbibed from his mother an interest in the missionary cause, and especially in the Indians to whose welfare his father had been so devoted. He knew the language perfectly, and the natives naturally looked upon him as their friend in his father's stead. Thus, having been prepared by some theological instruction under Dr. West, he entered with zeal upon the service. The period of his labors at Stockbridge was full of troubles for the Indians. Their lands had gradually slipped away from them. Some were reduced to poverty. Many of the older members of the church, who seem to have been Christian Indians of remarkable piety, had passed away, and the younger generation were less inclined to education and religion. Yet amid all these trials John Sergeant sought with faith, earnestness and wisdom to maintain the Christian character of the tribe.

As the American Revolution was a serious blow to the Brothertown Indians, so it was to the Stockbridge tribe. It was to be expected that they would be loyal to the patriot cause, and they were. Many of them enlisted in the company of Captain William Goodrich, of which Jehoiakim Mtohksin was second lieutenant, and marched from Stockbridge on the 23d of April, 1775. Later others joined this company, among them Hendrick Aupaumut and Jacob Konkapot. It was stationed at Watertown. There were thirty-five Stockbridge Indians in this one company. Timothy Yokens, who was first sergeant, afterwards became captain of a company of Indian rangers who did honorable service. The tribe sent a full company to White Plains, under Captain Daniel Nimham, of whom thirty were killed and others died of disease. Twenty blankets were sent to their families at Stockbridge, partly in recognition of this service—" five to the widows of the Indians lately slain at White Plains." Most of the killed were young

men.   This action occurred August 31, 1778, and a petition to
the General Court of Massachusetts, dated September twenty-
second, says, "many lately fell in battle."   General Washington
wrote that Captain Hendrick and others were with the army in
1778, and that the tribe suffered severely during that campaign
and lost a chief and several warriors. A newspaper of the time
gives an interesting account of the adventures of five of these
Stockbridge Indians, who were sent on a scout under Abraham
[Konkapot] and brought in six prisoners.[7]   A number were
in the company of Captain Enoch Noble, which marched to
Bennington in October, 1780.   There was, indeed, scarcely an
able-bodied man in the tribe who was not at some time in the
service.   Some of them served throughout the war in the Con-
tinental army.   "At the close of the war," it is said, " General
Washington directed a feast to be prepared for the Indians in
consideration of their good conduct, and an ox was roasted
whole, of which the tribe partook, the men first and then the
women and children."[8]   We can scarcely appreciate at this
day the demoralizing effect of the war upon this tribe.   Widows and orphans were left without means of support.   Nearly
half of their young men had perished.   They were reduced in
ambition, and the salutary effects of religion were dissipated.
Yet in this we see one of the practical results of their civilization,—they recovered quickly from these evils and set their
faces toward the future in new hope.

The sachemship of the Stockbridge Indians devolved in
1777 upon Joseph Quanaukaunt [Quinney].   He had for his
councilors three conspicuous young men, who had a great influence upon the subsequent life of the tribe. The first was Peter
Pauquaunaupeet [Pohquonnoppeet,   Pohquannopput,   Poh-
qunohpeet, Poquanopeet, Pohquenumpec, and Ponknepeet.]
He was a son of the first Indian deacon of the same name.

[7] *Penn. Journal*, Sept. 3, 1777, in Moore's *Diary of the Revolution*, pp. 474, 475.
[8] Jones' *Annals of Oneida County*, p. 888.

Having been instructed in the school there, he was sent in 1771 to Dartmouth College, where he spent most of the time in study until 1780, when he graduated. Sergeant wrote of him in 1771, " He is not so quick to learn as some, but appears to relish what he does get, is of a steady turn of mind and of a good family." The custom then was to prefix " Sir " to the names of seniors, from which fact he derived the name he bore throughout his after life—" Sir Peter." After his graduation he returned to Stockbridge and taught the school for a time. It is said that " he was possessed of good talents and sustained an unblemished character." This Indian we shall meet again. The second of these councilors was Hendrick Aupaumut. We have reason to think that he was a descendant of Hendrick, the celebrated Mohawk chief, who in 1750 came to Stockbridge with about ninety of that tribe to obtain an education. This chief is said to have been related to Joseph Brant and Molly, his sister, the Indian wife of Sir William Johnson. He was killed in the war of 1755. Hendrick Aupaumut was educated in the Stockbridge school. He enlisted in the Revolutionary War and won distinction, being at one time in command of a company, probably of scouts. The name he afterwards bore was derived from this service— " Captain Hendrick." This Indian also appears in later events. He became one of the most conspicuous Indians in the tribe, their chief, and an emissary to the far West on several occasions. The third councilor was John Konkapot [Kunkapot, Concopot, Kunkerpot, Konkpott], a son or grandson of their first Christian chief. He also was taught in the Indian school and entered Dartmouth College, where he was at the commencement of the Revolution. The name usually given him by Doctor Wheelock was John Stockbridge. In a petition which he presented to the General Assembly of Massachusetts, June 7, 1781, asking for six months' pay as the teacher at Stockbridge, he says " he early entered into the

service of the United States and suffered loss, that he has
since applied himself to learning and has been some time in
college, since which he has been employed in keeping school." [9]
He probably enlisted early in the war, and he was certainly
one of those who marched to Bennington in 1780. In his
later life he was sometimes called "Captain John" in consequence of this military service. These three councilors, it will
be observed, were fairly well educated. The second was a
member of the Stockbridge church. All had knowledge of
public affairs. In short, they came into power at a time when
such leaders were needed to revive the strength of the tribe,
and lead them forth into the future.

Such were the Stockbridge Indians at the time the Brothertown refugees settled near them. It was never the latter's
intent to remain there longer than was necessary—their homes
were in the wilderness. As to their experiences while there
we have only glimpses of them. In 1780 they presented a petition to their old friends in Connecticut which we submit in
evidence of their condition :

To the Honorable the General Assembly of the State of Connecticut now
Sitting at Hartford
This may Certify that We who removed from the New England States
to the Oneida, and resided on a tract of land granted to us from our Brethren the Six Nations, have been lately driven from our Settlements by the
Enemy and sustained grate damage leaving our Effects—by which means
[we] are now reduced to the necessity of Seeking a redress—particularly are
[we] desirous of being instructed in the great things of religion, and [having]
our Children trained up to enjoy a School and religious Privileges—and as
Daniel Simon of the Narragansit Tribe of Indians of a College Education,
properly authorized and ordained to Preach the Gospel, has been both keeping a School and Preaching among us the most of the Time Since the first
of May last, upon his own expence and Charge—and we are unable to pay
him and being desirous of his Continueing among us—and all Funds of
Money for the Spread of the Gospel among the Indians are Stop'd—and
therefore we are obleg'd to apply to any State where ever God in his Providence may open the Hearts of his People to us, with a Charitable design,

Praying that your Honors would Consider us—they of the State to which we formerly belong'd and were particularly our Brethren from whom we have heretofore received many favours—we have twenty two Childrun which we are exceedingly desirous Should be instructed the insuing year—and Should be thankfull for Simon even three Months Schoolling—as we Shall all reside in the neighborhood of Stockbridge till these troubles be over—we therefore would earnestly pray them to encourage Daniel Simon our Brother by donation or any other way therefore we have made known our request wishing the Healths and Prosperity of your own Persons—which we will ever pray

West Stockbridge, Octr th — 1780

GIDEON COMRUY [?]
ELIJAH WIMPEY
JAMES CUSK
ANDREW CORCOMP
JOHN ADAMS

P. S. By request I certify the foregoing representation to be just & true, & would recommend them to the Charity of those who are able to afford them Relief.

Stockbridge

13 Octob^r 1780 SAM^l. KIRKLAND [10]

On this petition the upper house granted £30 from the public treasury, but the lower house did not concur. The result of the ensuing conference was probably the issuing of a brief for collections in the churches, though no copy of this document is known to have survived. The fact is recovered from a later petition, May 8, 1783, asking for the redemption of £77-15-11 in bills collected. In this they thank the General Assembly for "the repeated Kindness and Favours conferred upon them by their best Friends and Brothers, the Inhabitants of their Native and Beloved State. Particularly in the late Instance of a Brief granted by a former General Assembly for a Contribution in Several Churches within the State." This document was signed by Elijah Wampey, David Fowler and Samuel Adams, and accompanied by letters from Samuel Kirkland and Stephen West to Dr. Nathan Strong of Hart-

---

[10] *Conn. Archives, Indians,* II, 226.

ford.[11]   Their request was granted by the payment of £33-1-8
for the bills.   We learn from these documents that there were
in all forty-four of them at West Stockbridge.   This probably
includes the few who were within the present borders of Richmond, where David Fowler lived.   Kirkland says, "They are
really distressed objects."   They had experienced sickness and
many were reduced to poverty.   Evidence is also thus obtained that they were preparing to return to Oneida, and this
removal the funds collected for them made possible.

Who was this Daniel Simon [Simons] who had been their
teacher and minister?   He was a Narragansett Indian, and
one of Wheelock's Indian pupils of the Lebanon school,
already mentioned in that connection.   With his brother
Abraham he had gone with the school to Hanover.   There
he studied for some years, graduating in the class of 1777.   A
letter is preserved among the Wheelock Papers in which he
complained to his benefactor that he was compelled to work
so much of the time that he could not study—he already knew
how to work and wanted to learn something else—"What
good will the charity money do the poor Indian" if he has to
pay his way?[12]   He was in college at the breaking out of the
Revolution, and was the Indian who is said to have heard the
guns of Bunker Hill by putting his ear to the earth—a fact
which others at the time confirmed.   After his graduation
he continued at Hanover studying theology under Doctor
Wheelock, and he was approved as an Indian preacher by the
Grafton Presbytery, January 29, 1778. On the seventh of October, following, he wrote the president a letter as follows: "I
have been preaching some about the country since I left college.   Do not engage long at a place on the account I am
young in the ministry.   I am at present keeping school at
Stockbridge, where I have thirty and forty in my school, and

---

[11] *Conn. Archives, Indians*, II, 227–229.
[12] *Wheelock Papers*, Lett. Sept. 1771.

sometimes fifty. I began my school on the first of May and engaged for five months; have preached some in the towns round about and supplied the pulpit of the great and good Mr. West, in his absence, two Sabbaths. But Mr. West and I am not familiar, by reason I find, that I am in or near the centre of Gravity. It is not allowed for a sinner to pray here, because all things are ordained of God, and neither can the sinner change the counsel of the Divine Being by prayer. But I may say this, that some people's God is my devil."[13] The commissioners' records show that Simons undertook this work of teaching with the approval of John Sergeant, but he did not continue in it long. On the first of May, 1780, he seems to have begun a similar work among the Brothertown Indians at West Stockbridge. He may have continued with them to 1783; but in that year he became a missionary among the Indians at Cranbery, N. J., succeeding Rev. John Brainerd. It is said that he was not long after suspended from the ministry for intemperance.[14] He was never an ordained minister. Certainly his relations with the Brothertown Indians terminated in 1783, though others of his family became useful and faithful members of the Oneida settlement.

We are now approaching the close of this distressing period in the history of the Christian Indians of New England. It remains only to point out the fact, which the reader may have conjectured already, that it was the influence of these Brothertown refugees which led the Stockbridge tribe also to project a removal to the Oneida country. A friendship was formed between the tribes during those six years, which has continued to the present time. The refugees did not suffer the enthusiasm over the emigration to die out. It was uppermost in their minds. They had left pleasant homes in those fertile

---

[13] Chapman's *Alumni of Dart. Coll.,* p. 22.
[14] *Ibid.*

valleys of New York, to which they would return like the children of Jacob to Canaan. During the Revolution others in
the old settlements were preparing to join these pioneers by
selling their lands, which in several instances required legislative action. It has been claimed by some that the Stockbridge Indians had secured a tract of land from the Oneidas
before the Revolution. Some have even thought that a few
of them removed thither. This is an error. It probably arose
from the impression that they were included in the grant of
1774 to the seven settlements, usually called thereafter the
"New England Indians." At that time the Stockbridge tribe
had no thought of emigration, notwithstanding the fact that
they had disposed of the greater part of their lands. The
way was opened for them, however, by their friends, who had
a very extensive tract themselves, and were assured that a
similar grant would be made to the Indians at Stockbridge
who had succored them. So it happened. When the Brothertown Indians in 1783 returned to their Oneida homes, a
number of the Stockbridge tribe accompanied them. It was a
return of that hospitality which they had themselves received.
Then these Stockbridge chiefs held a council with the Oneidas
and were duly adopted by them after the Indian custom, receiving the promise of a tract of land six miles square. We
have not been able to find any written agreement or conveyance of this grant, though one was probably made. Indian
affairs were then in a very unsettled state. It is certain, however, that the promise was then given them, and they returned
to Stockbridge to prepare for a removal. Most of them came
thither in the spring of 1785, but they did not all remain
through the following winter. Others came in 1788. Samuel
Kirkland wrote, March 10, 1784, " The Oneidas expect in the
course of two years to have more than a thousand Indians in
this vicinity who will be disposed to attend the word of God."
This undoubtedly refers to a prospective increase from the

Stockbridge and New England tribes. Some of the chiefs of the former were present at the Treaty held at Fort Herkimer in June, 1785, and the Oneidas then spoke of them as their "younger brethren." All these earlier grants were superseded at the Treaty of Fort Schuyler in September, 1788, when the Oneidas, in their cession to the state of New York, made this reservation that: "the New England Indians (now settled at Brothertown under the pastoral care of Reverend Samson Occom) and their posterity forever and the Stockbridge Indians and their posterity forever are to enjoy their Settlements on the Lands heretofore given to them by the Oneidas for that purpose, that is to say a Tract Two Miles in Breadth and three miles in length for the New England Indians and a Tract of Six Miles square for the Stockbridge Indians." At first some of the latter tribe seem to have settled within the bounds of the grant to the former, much more extensive in the agreement of 1774 than as reduced in 1788. Afterwards their tract six miles square was located for them, and it was partly within the town of Vernon, Oneida county, and partly within the town of Stockbridge, Madison county, as now described. The Stockbridge Indians, in memory of their old home in Massachusetts, named their settlement New Stockbridge. In the year 1785 they numbered 420. There they lived for many years, until 1818, when some of them removed to White River, Indiana. At that time they began to sell their lands, and this continued until they were all established again beside their friends, the Brothertown Indians, on the east side of Winnebago Lake, in Wisconsin.

No single tribe of New England Indians has a more interesting history than this, whose wigwams once dotted the banks of the swift-flowing Housatonic. Its chiefs won their first distinction from the white man in recognition of their friendly service. Intelligent, brave and industrious they have always been, and on the battle-fields of every war which has roused the patriot to arms their warriors have fallen. Among them the best of missionaries and the greatest of divines have lived and taught. If weaknesses have been theirs, they have been those of the race, and they have paid the penalty in hardships and wasting death. On the hunt and in the wilderness they have tasted adventure. Romance has been woven into their story—a thread of gold in a worn and fretted garment. So this nation, having followed the trail of civilization for more than a century and a half, has come to an honorable old age and leans upon the staff among the sachems of the West.

CHAPTER XIV

1783–1789

Peace was at length restored in the colonies which had achieved their independence. Then the first of many companies of emigrants to cross the Hudson River and thread their way along the Mohawk westward, in 1783, was composed of New England Indians. Their leader was David Fowler. He and some others had visited their deserted huts at Brothertown in the summer of 1782; but now it was safe for them to remove their families thither. We have no record of their experiences during that season. Some at least returned late in the autumn to Stockbridge to escape the winter in that vast and cheerless wilderness.

The first delegation from the old settlements set out May 8, 1784.[1] It now devolved upon Samson Occom, as in command of the reserves, to push forward the Indian families as they could be made ready, and in this service he was engaged more or less for several years. On the date above named a number of families set sail from New London in the sloop *Victory*, commanded by Captain Hayley. Occom notes in his diary their fortunes of wind and weather as they coasted along toward New York, where they arrived at 6 o'clock in the evening of the tenth. The nights had been spent at anchor in safe waters. The ninth was a Sabbath and, the sea being calm, the reverend elder of this company of Indian pilgrims conducted a service on the deck, expounding a part of the twenty

[1] *Occom's Diary*, Dart. Coll.

fifth chapter of Matthew, wherein he might have found sundry lessons appropriate to this novel situation. The only persons known to have been in that congregation were Jacob Fowler and Esther Poquiantup his wife, Anthony Paul and Christiana Occom his wife, with four young children, and the mother " Widow Paul" with her son John. Others were with them, but their names are unknown. Occom and Jacob Fowler left the ship at New York to call on Dr. Rodgers and others with a view of obtaining further financial assistance in the emigration. On the twelfth they went on board an Albany sloop, Mr. Waters, master, having as fellow passengers " a number of very agreeable gentlemen" who were members of the New York General Assembly. To them on the voyage they unfolded their plan, in which the gentlemen were much interested. Thus early Occom began an acquaintance with the members of that body, over whose legislation in Indian affairs he had considerable influence. At Albany they overtook their people. Occom made application to the chief men of the town for assistance, but provisions were no longer allowed to Indians, as had been the case during the Revolution. They were permitted to put up at the hospital and the people were very kind to them. Occom was invited to speak to the prisoners and complied. On the twenty-second the Indian company started forward on their way to Schenectady, Occom remaining to preach on the Sabbath, as he did twice in the Presbyterian meeting-house. Collections amounting to eight pounds were taken up in behalf of his people. From Albany he turned back, leaving Jacob Fowler to guide the emigrants to their new homes.

The expense of this party was considerable, and Occom had given his own personal note for their passage from New London to Albany. All that he collected on the way was not sufficient to meet this. Such were the troubles he had in removing his people to Oneida. This, too, was the reason he did not at once go with them. His service was necessary in New England

on his own account and on theirs.   He reached Mohegan on
the seventh of June, and until the autumn preached here and
there in the furtherance of this work.   On the twenty-second of
September he set out for Oneida to visit his people.   He went
first to Farmington, where he stopped with Daniel Mossuck,
one of Wheelock's Indian pupils who is here met with for the
last time and probably died there soon afterwards.   There were
then only eight Indian families remaining in their old home
on Indian Neck.   Here he also found George Pharaoh and
his family from Montauk moving up to Oneida.   Somewhere
between there and Stockbridge he visited "Bro. Phineas," possibly a Fowler, and there heard of the death of his daughter
Talitha—"a mournful addition to his troubles."   At Stockbridge he found that almost all of the Indians had scattered,
all who had not gone to Oneida.   So he went on his way to
Richmond, New Bethlehem, Albany, Saratoga, Stillwater and
the Mohawk River.   He preached wherever he had opportunity
and there was scarcely an evening that he did not gather the
people in some pioneer cabin, to teach them and sing his
spiritual songs.   This will illustrate what he called his "peregrinations," which made him known to all near and far and
won him the honorable title—"the missionary of the wilderness."   Ere he arrived at Brothertown he met his friends
David and Jacob Fowler and Elijah Wampy.   In company
with David he set out for Brothertown.   Here we will let him
tell his own story:

Monday Octr 24 [1785]: Some Time after Breakfast Brother David
Fowler and I sot of to go thro' the Woods to our Indians new Settlements,
and presently after we sot out it began to Rain and it Rain'd all the way
not very hard,—and it was extreemly bad muddy riding, and the Creeks
were very high, and some Places were Mirely, and we were over taken with
Night before we got in, and some places were very Dark where Hamlock
Trees were, our Eyes did us but little good.   we travild about a mile in the
Dark and then we arriv'd at Davids House.   as [we] approach'd the House
I hear^d a Melodious Singing, a number were together Singing Psalms
hymns and Spiritual Songs.   We went in amongst them and they all took

hold of my Hand one by one with Joy and Gladness from the greatest to
the least, and we sot down awhile, and then they began to sing again, and
Some Time after I gave them a few words of Exhortation, and then Concluded with Prayer,—and then went to Sleep Quietly, the Lord be praised
for his great goodness to us.

Tuesday Octr 25. Was a Snowy Day, was very uncomfortable weather.
I kept still all Day at Davids House and it was crowded all Day, some of
Onoydas came in — In the evening Singers came in again, and they Sang
till near ten o.c. and then I gave them a Word of Exhortation and concluded with prayer, so we ended another Day—

Wednesday Octr 26: Snow is about ancle Deep this Morn'g and all
slosh under the Snow and the Land is ful of water every where, and the
Brooks are very high—it is not clear wheather yet — in the evening we had
a little Singing again — This morning I rench'd my Back, only puting on
my Stockings, and was put to some difficulty to go out all Day.

Thirdsday Octo^r 27: Cloudy but moderate, my back continues as it was
yesterday.

Fryday Octr 28: it was warm and pleasant Day but cloudy the bigest
part of the Day — in the evening they sung (in Abra^m Simons House, a
mile from David Fowlers) [Erased]

Fryday Oct^r [29] David intended to gather his corn but it look'd very
much like for Rain, and so [he] defer it to another Day.—the young Folks
went in the evening to Abraham Simons a mile of from David Fowlers to
sing, but I did not go my back continued out of order.—

Saturday Octr 29: David gather'd his corn, he had a number of Hands
tho it was cloudy in the morning, and little Rain, and in the after noon he
husked his corn, and the Huskers Sung Hymns Psalms and Spiritual
Songs the bigest part of the Time, finish'd in the evening—and after supper
the Singers Sung a while, and then dispersed.

Sabbath Octr 30: Had a meeting in Davids House, and a Number of
Stockbridgers came to meeting to the distance of six miles, they had eleven
Horses and there was a number of foot People, and there was a Solemn
Assembly, the People attended the word with affection many of them — I
spoke from Mathew iv. 10: in the after Noon from — xxxii : 1 : in the evening
we had Singing a long while and then gave them a word of Exhortation
and concluded with Prayer —

Monday, Tuesday and Wednesday nothing hapen'd remarkable only
Rainy and Snowy weather, and I was much confind my wrentchd Back —

Thirdsday Novr 3. 1785. Towards Night we attended upon the antient
ordenance of marrage, the first that ever was selebrated by our People in
their New Settlement in this Wilderness. The cupple to be married and
the Young People formed in a Neighbouring House and came to the House

of Weding in a Regular Procession according to their age and were seated accordingly — and the old People also seated themselves Regularly, and A great Number of Stockbridgers came from their Town to attend the Weding, but many of them were too late —

When I got up, I spoke to them Some Time upon the nature of Marriage, the Honourableness and Lawfulness of it, whereby we are distinguished from the Brutal Creation: Said Some of the first marrage in Eden & of the Marrage where Christ and his Disciples were invited and the Honour he did to it by working the first mericle he wrought in the World in turning water into Wine and then we prayed, after Prayer I orderd them to take each other by the Right Hand alternately and then I declared them in the Face of the Assembly to be a Lawful Husband and Wife, according to the Law of god [2] — and then pray'd. prayer being ended Marriage salutations went round Regularly, and concluded by Singing a Marriage Hymn — and then the People sat down, and Jacob Fowler who was appointed Master of Serimonies at this Marriage, gave out some Drink a Round the Company and then Supper was brought, sot in order on a long Board, and we sot down to eat, and had Totty well sweeten'd with wild Sugar made of Sugar Trees in the Wilderness: and after supper we Spent the Evening in Singing Psalms Hymns and Spiritual Songs,—and after that every [one] went home Peaceably without any Carausing or Frollicking.

Fryday Nov[r] 4: The Young People put on their best Clouths, and went to a Neighbours House, all on Horse back, and they appear'd agreeable and Decent, and they had no carousing, they had some Pleasant chat and agreable conduct, some Singing of Psalms Hymns and Spiritual Songs. Some Time in the after Noon they dined together, and after Dinner every one went Home Quietly.—so the Weding ended, and it was conducted, caried on and finished with Honour and great Decency—and the Lord help this People to go on Regularly in all their concerns—

Sab: Nov[r] 6: Brother Jacob Fowler and I went of early in the Mor[g] for Stockbridge Indians, that lately settled at old Onoyda. got there some Time before meeting. Went to Sir Peter Pauquunnuppeets House. he is a Collegian brought up and Educated at Dartmouth College, and he received [us] with all kindnest Friendship,—about 11 went to meeting and

[2] The following is Occom's marriage service: " You do take this woman to be your Married Wife and do in the Presence of God and before these witnesses Promise and covenant to be a loving and faithful Husband unto her until God shall separate you by death. You do in like manner take this man to be your Married Husband and do in the Presence of God and before these Witnesses Promise to be a loving, faithful and obedient wife unto him till God shall separate you by Death. I do then before God and these witnesses Declare you to be Husband and Wife. Therefore what God has joined together let not man put asunder."

many of our People from our new settlements came to meeting, to the distance of six miles — I spoke to them from Joshua 24 : 22 : and Esther 7 : 2 :
in the Evening we had another meeting, and we had solemn Day and evening, the People attended with great attention and Solemnity, after I had
done speaking, we sat down and the singer rose up and they sang Some
Time, and then dispersed, every one to his quarters and Sister Hannah and
Sister Esther and I Lodgd at Widow Quinnys where the meeting was —

Monday Novr 7 : Some Time after Sun Rise I sot of with Brother Roger
and his wife to our Place ; and stopt at Roger's and I took Breakfast with
them, they live near three miles from the rest of the People, and after eating
I went on to the Town, got there about 12 and found them all well—In the
Evening we met on our Temporal and Religious concerns—we met once
before but we did not come to proceed any Business—But now we proceeded to form into a Body Politick—we Named our Town by the Name of
Brotherton, in Indian Eeyamquittoowauconnuck—J. Fowler was chosen
clarke for the Town. Roger Waupieh, David Fowler, Elijah Wympy,
John Tuhy, and Abraham Simon were chosen a Committee or Trustees for
the Town, for a year and for the future, the committee is to be chosen
Annually.—and Andrew Acorrocomb and Thomas Putchauker were chosen
to be Fence Vewers to continue a year. Concluded to have a Centre near
David Fowlers House, the main Street is to run North and South &
East and West, to cross at the centre. Concluded to live in Peace, and in
Friendship and to go on in all their Public Concerns in Harmony both in
their Religious and Temporal concerns, and every one to bear his part of
Public Charges in the Town.—They desired me to be a Teacher amongst
them. I consented to spend some of my remaining [days] with them, and
make this Town my Home and center—

Tuesday Novr 8 : got up early and sot of for Stockbridge Indians. got
there Some Time before meeting. this is a Day of fasting and Prayer with
the People here and they desired me to assist them. the Design of this
fast is to confess their sins before God, and to repent and beg the Pardon
of all their sins and desire the Blessing of God upon them, and to Prosper
them in their New Settlement, and also bless them in their Religious Life—
and I preached to them, in the fore Noon from Jonah 3 : 8 : in the afternoon from Prover 23 : 26 and it was a solemn Fast Day, many were deeply
afected, all attended like criminals before the Barr : in the Evening they
met again and they advised and gave councel to one another to conduct well
and be careful in all their conduct the ensuing winter as they were about to
disperse for the winter, that they may get together in the spring in Love and
Peace—and after advice, they spent Some Time in Singing of Spiritual
Songs, and when they had done, I gave them a word of Exhortation, advising them to use their Natural Powers and conduct as becomes Rational

Creatures, and break off from all outbreaking of sin, and especially to break off from that abominable sin of Drunkeness and give themselves to watching and Prayer, and so conclude with Prayer,—and the People dispersed in Peace. I Lodged at Sir Peter Punquunnuppeets.

Wednesday Nov 9: Breakfasted with Capt Hindreck & soon after Eating I sot off for Home, got to our Place about 12 and found our Folks well—

Thirdsday Fryday and Saturday look about a little to see the land and it is the best land I ever did see in all my Travils. John Tuhy Planted Just about one acre of ground, which he cleared last may, and this Fall he took of 20 Bushels of good Corn, 56 Bushels of Potatoes, about 200 Heads of Cabage, and about 3 Bushels of Beans, and about 2 Bushels of Pusnips and Beats together, besides Cucumbers and Watermelons, of the Same ground, and it was not Plowd nor dug up with a Hoe, only leaves and Small Bushes were burnt on it and great many Logs lay on it now—and I was told last week among the Stockbridge Indians that in their clearing some spots of land where it has been improved in years past, they Plowed up and dug up good many Potatoes, where they had been Planted perhaps 10 or 12 years ago. One man got 3 skipples and he planted them, and he has raised a fine passel of them, and Brother David Fowler told me, and his wife and others confirm'd it, that he had one Cabage Stomp stood three summers and it headed every year, the last it stood, it [had] three Heads.—

Sab. Nov 13: Preachd at David Fowlers and many of the Stockbridgers came to meeting, and there was good attention and I believe some felt the Power of the word,—in the evening we had some singing—

Monday Nov 14: Was geting ready to return homeward.

Tuesday Nov 15: got up very early in the morning, and we were fitting to go off, and little after sunrise we sot off. Brother David and his wife, Daughter, and James Waucus went together. Elijah Wympys two Daughters and others—some Stockbridgers there were Eight Horses of [off] amongst us, and many foot men and we got thro the woods just as the Sun was going down. I put up at Mr Fols's—

The reader will note in this portion of Occom's Diary the record of some important events. Here is the account of the founding of Brothertown, November 7, 1785, and their organization into a "Body Politick." Here are the names of the most prominent Indians of the tribe. Here the early location of the center of their town is stated to have been near David Fowler's house. We have, also, the name of this unique town in the Indian language, as Occom wrote it—Eeyamquittoowau-connuck. On the eighth of November we note the Fast Day

of the Stockbridge Indians—who were then six miles westward
from David Fowler's house—and its solemn import, a day of
prayer for God's blessing on their new town.   Here we meet
again with "Sir Peter" and "Capt. Hindreck," who became
Occom's firm friends.   It seems that these Indians of New
Stockbridge were to disperse for the winter.   Some, indeed,
of both tribes tarried in the settlements along the Mohawk
until the following spring.   Here already we see how it happened that Occom ministered to a church composed of both
tribes.   The Stockbridge missionary, John Sergeant, had not
come with his people; they were as sheep without a shepherd.
We shall have occasion to refer to these points again.

Occom's journey homeward was another missionary tour.
He had an acquaintance along the road.   The following are
some of his lodging-places: Esquire Waubret's; Captain
Foof's [?]; Esquire Kimball's at Bowmen's Creek; Peter Van
Wormer's, a mile from Mohawk river, where he met Mr.
Romine, a Dutch minister; Mr. Otis' in Gallaway; Mr.
Smith's, where he met Mr. Coffin, a Universalist preacher,
with whom he "disagreed altogether without debate"; Mr.
Kalley's, where he married Jonathan Bunyan Cotes and Polly
Doulin; Mrs. Post's, near Schenectady; Mr. Holms'; Balls-
town, where he baptized Theophilus Hide, a dying man, and
married Sanford White and Hannah Hide; Pittstown; Hoo-
suck, at Mr. Porter's; Williamstown; Richmond; and so to
the house of Mr. Sergeant at Stockbridge.   That winter he
was at Mohegan, engaged in his work here and there.   The
volume of his diary is missing which describes his return in
the spring of 1786 to Oneida.   We find him on his way at Fort
Hunter on the twenty-sixth of June, and at German Flats on
the fourth of July.

Tuesday July 4, [1786] Went to see my folks at Mr Tygut's and
Wednesday was there yet.—
Thirdsday July 6 in the morning Some Time we sot of to go thro the

Woods, near 12 we reached at Chunangusde. we turned out our Horses and my mare run away and we were obligd to stay there all Night, we could not find her—

Fryday July 7 : we went of prety early, and got to our Settlement Some Time in the afternoon, and we were glad to see one another, but many of our People were gone away to seek after provisions, for food is very scarce—

Saturday July 8 : Anthony and James Fowler Waucus went after my mare—

Sabb. July 9 : we met together at Abraham Simon's. There was but few of our folks and good many Stockbridgers were with us. I spoke from Rom viii and there was good attention amongst the People—

Monday July 10 : In the evening Anthony and James came back without my mare. They found her in a mire, Dead, Sunk almost all over, there is the end of her—

Fryday July 14 Andrew Corricomb had a son Born.

Sabb July 16, Preachd at Brother David Fowler's. Spoke from Matt, Jesus Cried and from Romans, if god be for us &c most of our People were there and a great number of Stocbredgers, and there was great and solemn attention—

Sabb July 23 went from Roger Wauby's to the Town of Stockbridgers, and many of our People went and we had a large Assembly. Mr Dean[3] and four with him came to meeting they live about six miles of, and I spoke from Matt vi : 9 : and Psalm 133 : 1, and the People attended well. we had a shower just as meeting was concluded and we sot till it was over and that was soon, and then we pusht on homeward. I got [to] Jacob Fowler's about sun set, and I was some what woried—

Sabb July the 30 About 9 I went to Brother Davids & there I preachd,

---

[3] James Dean of "Dean's Patent"—the best Indian interpreter of his day and conspicuous in all treaties. His life in detail would make an interesting volume. He was the son of John and Sarah (Douglass) Dean, and was born in Groton, Conn., Aug. 20, 1748. It is said that his parents devoted him to the life of a missionary, and when he was nine years old sent him, with an uncle, to reside at Onohoquaga. He there lived with "Good Feter," probably, and became a master of several Indian languages. In September, 1762, he was brought home by Rev. Eli Forbes, and subsequently engaged as an interpreter for Mr. Moseley. He entered Dartmouth College, and graduated in 1773. Thereafter, until 1775, he was employed by Doctor Wheelock, but then went into the government service, among the New York tribes. After the war, he took up his residence in the Oneida country, became a distinguished citizen, and died at Westmoreland, N. Y., Sept. 10, 1823.—Chapman's *Alumni of Dart Coll.*, p. 14 ; Chase's *Hist. of Dart. Coll.*, p. 87 ; Jones' *Annals of Oneida County*; Sprague's *Annals*, I, 493, 494 ; *Wheelock Papers* and *MS., Rec. Soc. for Prop. Gos.*

and many of the Stockbridgers were there and four young Onoyda men were there, and were drest compleat in Indian way. they shined with Silver, they had large Clasps about their arms, one had two Jewels in his Nose, and had a large Silver half moon on his Breast; and Bells about their Legs, & their heads were powderd up quite stiff with red paint, and one of them was white as any white man and gray eyes, his appearance made me think of the old Britains in their Heathenism. I spoke from Hosea xiii : 9 : & Eclesi xii. 1 and there was great attention among the people. after meeting the singers sung some Time and then we all dispersd—

Monday July 31 a number of us went to the Flats. we got there before night and I put up at Mr Conrod Fols. Tuesday was at the place all Day—

Wednesday, Augst 2 Sun about two hours high we sot [off] again for home, and we got home just about Sundown, all well, and found our Folks well. Thanks be to god.—

Sabb. Augt 6. Preached at Jacob Fowlers in fore Noon, and there was but few People, it was rainy morning. In the after Noon we went to David Fowlers, and there was a large number of People. Several of the Stockbridgers came. I spoke from Rom 11 . 28. 29: & Luke xvi. 13—and the People attended well. in the evening I returned again to Brother Jacob.—

Tuesday Augt 8 : Some Time in the morning I went to Fishing at Orisco Creek, and I catchd 5 Doz^n and five Salmon Trouts,—and Just at Night I removd to Brother David Fowler's to Stay a while.—

Saturday Augt 12 In the after Noon I Sot out for Stockbridgers, stopt awhile at Roger Waubys took Dinner there, and after eating, went on, got to the Place Some Time before Night. Lodged at Sir Peter Paukqunuppeat.—

Sabb. Augt 13 : About 10 we began the holy Exercise at the House of Jacob Cunkcuppot, and there a large collection of People, some white people,—I spoke from Jerem xxx 14. in the after noon from Luke x. 42 and the People attended with great solemnity, and with some affection ; and it was a Rainy afternoon. I Lodgd again at Sir Peters.—

Monday Augt 14 : got up very early, and sot of for Brotherton,—Stopt at Roger Waubys, and took Breakfast and soon after eatg I went on again : got at Brother Davids abot 10 : & found them all well—

Wednesday Augt 16 : Towards Night, the Young People came together at Jacob Fowlers to receive Instruction; and I gave them a Short Discourse from Proverbs iv. 13 : and they attended exceeding well, they behaved becomingly, and were Solemn, and there was Some affection, with Tears. after I had Spoke and Prayd I orderd them to sing, and they sung three Times, with great Decency and solemnity, and as they were going out, Elyjah Wimpy first gave me thanks, and all manifested thankfulness ;

The Lord Bless them, and give them teachable Hearts, that they be Wise unto eternal salva[tion].

Sabb Augt 20: Went to David Fowlers Some what early, and about 10 began the Holy Service, and there was a large Number of People many Stockbridgers came and there were four out of Mr Deans Family, and more whatman,—I Spoke from Luke ii: 10: 11 and Psalm xxxi: 1 and there was great and solemn attention in the Assembly; after meeting our People Stay'd Some and [sung] Psalms—near sun set I went down to Brother Jacobs, and to bed soon and rested quietly once more—

Wednesday Augt 23 Towards Night the Young People came to Jacob Fowlers to receive instruction; and I spoke to them from Prover^b[blank] a little whi[le] and then we Prayd, and after Prayer I Exercised with my Christian Cards with them, and they were agreable to them, and they [were] Awd with the Various Texts of Scripture, and I believe they will not forget the evening very soon. there was one Stockbridge Girl came on purpose, and there was one English Girl, and they also chose each of 'em a Text; and they concluded with singing several Tunes, and the whole was caried on with Decency, & Solemnity—

Sabb. Augt 27 Had a meeting at Abraham Simons on acount of his wife's Sickness; he was not at Home, he has been gone five weeks tomorrow.— There was a great Number of People, a number of Stockbridgers was there, and tow white Men from the New Town. I spoke from Gene. xxii. 12 and in the after Noon from John iii. 16 & I believe we had the Presence of God with us, there was uncommon attention, and great solemnity and many Tears flowd down the cheeks of many; after meeting a Number of Singers went to Jacob Fowlers and sung a while, and then we Prayd & so every one went Home Soberly & quietly—

Wednesday Augt 30 Soon after Breakfast thirteen of us sot out into the Woods, they went after Ginshang Roots, and I was going to Mr James Dean's, we travild together about 3 Miles, and there they incamped made up great Fire, and soon after I went on. sister Hannah Fowler went with me, and then we went thro' a Hedious Wilderness for three or four miles. we had only markd Trees to go by, and there was but very poor Track—we arrivd to Mr Deans Some time in the afternoon, found them all well, and we were receivd with all kindness, and at sundown Brother David came runing in pufing and Blowing and all of a fome with sweat. he had treed a couple of Racoons and he [came] for a gun, and went right back and one young man; and some Time in the [evening] he came in with one Racoon—

Thirdsday Augt 31 about 11, we took leave of the Fa[mily] and went to New Stockbridge—got there some Time in the afternoon. we calld on Sir Peter Pankquunnupeat & I put up there,—

Fryday Sepr 1: Some Time in the after noon we had a meeting, and I spoke from Psalm, 32 : 9 and there was very good attention—I[n] the evening they got together to sing, and after singing, we had exercise with Christian Cards, and it was new [to] them and very agreable. they attended with great solemnity, but all did not Draw that intended to draw. it grew late, and so we broak up.—

Saturday Sepr 2 : I was at the Place all Day long. I visited some Families, as I did yesterday, in the evening we met together again to go thro' the Exercise we began the last Night with my Christian Cards, and it was very agreable. some were much affected, we concluded with singing a Psalm—

Sabb : Sepr 3. About 10 we began the Divine worship of god and there was a great number of People for this wilderness, some white People— I spoke from Matt xi. 12 and I Kings xix. 13 and I be[lieve] the Lord was present with us. I [had] some sense of the great things I [was] delivering and I believe many felt the Power of the word; for there was great solemnity, and Awful Atention thro the Asembly, many Tears flowd from many Eyes.—as soon as the meeting was done I went Home with our People, we got Home Just before sun set; and our singers got together and they sung some Time, we had some newcomers at the singing meeting.—Last Satur day 13 : of our People came to our Place to settle, a Family from Mohegan & a Family from Montauk and some from Narroganset and one from Farmington—

Wednesday Sepr 6 : towards Night I attended upon our Young People, and ten Stockbridgers came to the meeting old and Young, and many of our old People came too. We began with singing, and then Prayd, after Prayer the Young People rehearsed the Texts and Verses they had Chosen at our second meeting, and they were very Solemn, and when they had done I began a Discourse with them, from I Timothy, vi. 19 and it was a solemn Time with the People, many were much affected. Concluded with Prayer and Singing.—

Sabb Sepr 10 In the morning we went [to] Abraham Simons to meeting, began about 10 and there was a great number of People, many from Stockbridge, and we had to white men at the meeting, they were going to Niegara from Johns Town, and there was a solemn attention thro' the Assembly. I spoke from Matt. ix, 12. In the after noon we went to David Fowlers, and I Spoke from Job xxi. 14, 15 and there was greater attention many affected deeply, after meeting the singers stopt and sung Some Time and concluded with Prayer and so we parted—

Monday Sepr 11. I went down to the German Flats. Young Elijah Wympy & I went together : we got thro Just before sun set, and I put up at my good Friends Mr Conrod Fols, was some woried and went to bed soon but had uncomfortable Nt of it there were so many vir^n

Tuesday Sepr 12. got up very early, and it was very Lowery and so did not set out so soon as I intended. took Breakfast, and about 10 I sot out for Springfield, and just before I got to the Place I mist my way. got to south west of the Place [a] good ways and towards Night it began to be sowerry, and just at Night, I calld at a certain House, to as[k] the way, and it began to rain, and asked me whether I Might stay there and I thanked him told [him] I wou'd and so I stayd; tooke supper with them—and went to bed soon, and had comfortable rest—

Wednesday Sepr 13 Got up very early and got ready and they would have me stay to take Breakfast with them but I told them I wou'd take it another Time.—The man's Name is Mr Nicholas Lowe, they were very kind to me. the man had heard me at New York above 20 years back. So tooke good leave of them and went on my way. got to the Place about 9 and call'd on Mr Winters but they were not at Home, the Women were at Home, and they got me Breakfast, they were exceeding kind.—and from thence I went to Mr Griffins, and was there till near sun sit, and then I went to Mr Stansel's, where a meeting was apointed, and there was a large Number of People collected together, and I spoke from Rom. ii. 28-29: and the People attended with all gravity and [I] believe some felt the Power and Love of God.—I stayd at the same House, it is a Dutch Family and there is one young man in this House, Very Remarkable in Religion, he is a living christian. I believe is not ashamed of his Lord and Master. he was converted last Winter, and he is much opposed by the most of the Family. Yet he keeps on—he and I Lodgd together this night, after we had a long conversation in the Family; I was Treated well by the whole Family. Rested comfortably—

Thirsday Sepr 14 and Fry^d was at the place. went to see some Families. Lodgd once at Mr Dicks and once at Mr Crippins—

Saturday Sepr 16: Just after Dinner we went to one Mr Nicholas Pickards where the Christian People were to have a Conference meeting. the People collected Some Time in the after Noon, and they began by Prayer and sung, and they began to relate their Experiences, and there were 12 men and three women, that related the work of god on their souls and it took them till near Mid Night, and it was the most agreable meeting that ever I was at. there were several Nations and Denominations & yet all harmonious. there was no Jar amongst them, but Peace and Love. there experiences were acording to the Doctrines of the Gospel.—I Lodgd at the same House & was very kindly entertained. the man is a Dutchman & his [wife] is Ireish woman, and both I believe were sincere Christians—

Sabb Sepr 17: Near 10 we went to meeting at old Mr Pickards in his New House only coverd over head, and there was a Prodigious Number of People and I spoke from Acts xi. 26. in the after Noon from the last Psa and the last verse—after meetg went to Deacon Childs, and in the Evening a

number of young People came to the House to receive Instruction, and I
spoke to them from some passages of Scripture, and after that we had
Exercise with my Notes, and there was great solemnity amongst them. they
were most all Dutch People they stayd late—

Monday Sepr 18: It was a Rainy Day, and I did not sit out. towards
Night I went to Mr Pickards from Mr Crippens. Mr Nicholas Pickard
went with me, the old gentleman and his wife received me with all kindness,
and in the evening the Young People came together again for Instruction,
and I spoke to them the words Remember thy Creator &c and after that we
had Exercise with my cards again, and the People were much solemnised.
We sot up somewhat late again. I rested comfortably once more—

Tusday Sepr 19: Got up early, and got Breakfast and then sot off, and
got to Mr Fols just after sun set. went to Bed soon—

Wednesday Sepr 20 sot of Some What early. old E. Wimpy went
with me and we got thro before Night. we overtook a num[ber] of Stockbridgers just come from there old settlement. found our Folks well—

Sabb Sepr 24 Had a meeting in David Fowlers Barn, and there was a
large number of People collected. great many from old Town,—the bigest
Assembly we have had since I came to this Place. I spoke from I Corin
vii 29. 30. 31 : & Acts xvi. 28, and I believe we had the presence of god
with us. many were deeply affected there was flow of Tears from many
Eyes,—in the evening the singers went to Jacob Fowlers to sing, and I
went there too, and they sung near two Hours and then [I] gave them a
word of Exhortation and prayd, and things were done decently and in order,
and so we parted once more in Peace and Love. I went backe to Brother
Davids and soon went to bed quietly once more. The Lord be Praised—

Monday Sepr 25 Sot of about mid Day for old Town. David went
with me in order to the Lake to Fishing,—Lodgd at Widow Quinnys,—

Tuesday Sepr 26, I did not feel well, and it looked like for Storm, and so
we returnd backe got home some time before noon—

Fryday Sepr 28: in the morning went to Stockbridgers, and toward Night
Preachd a Discourse to them. I spoke from Gala vi. 15 and there was
great solemnity in the congregation—Lodgd at Sir Peters—

Sabath, Octo^r 1: Had our meeting in Jacob Concoppots and there was a
Prodigious large congregation for the wilderness, some white People—I
spoke from Psalm 58: 15: in the afternoon from Ezek xxxii: 11 and we
had an Awfull solemnity in the assembly, there was a shower [of] Tears.
I felt Bowels of Compassion towards my poor Brethren ; in the Evening
the Stockbridgers met at Sir Peters, and they rehearsed what they heard in
the Day, and they were Very Solemn ; at the end of their rehearsal, Sir
Peter Pohquunnuppeet made a confession of his wanderings from God, and
Asked the Peoples forgiveness, and he was very Solemn, and the People
received him in their charity—

Wednesday Octr 4 : had a meeting with our Young People, and there was many old People also,—I spoke from Prover xxii. 1 and there was uncommon attention amongst the People, Especially the Young People—

Saturd morning Sep^r [Oct] 6: after the reading a chap^r I took notice of some Passages and spoke to the Family, and there was a solemn attention, and then I attempted to Pray, and I had an awful sense of the Miserable situation of mankind, and the goodness of God which melted down my soul before God, and there was much affection in the Family.—

Sabb Octo^r 7 : Had a meeting in Brother Davids & there was but a little number of People by reason of the uncommon Floods in all the creeks, and on the Land. most of the Bridges were carried off, for it had been Raining several Days last week ; and it Rains yet ; Some Stockbridgers came to meeting for all the dreadful traviling. there [were] five women and four men. I spoke from I[sa] xl. 22, and I think I had an Awful sense of the Deplorable state of [the] sinful race of Adam, and some sense of the greatness and goodness of God, and there was an Awful attention and flow of Tears—in the afternoon I spoke from Gene xxiv. 58: and there was again a moving among the People : I hope they will not soon forget the Day.—In the evening they sung at Davids, and after singing I spoke to the Young People in particular, and they were greatly bowed down before the word. Some were deeply affected, and it was some [time] before we broak up the meeting, and they went home with solemnity.—

Wednesday Octr 11 : towards Night had a meeting with the Young People, and we had Exercise with Christian Cards out of the old Testam^t and there was an uncommon affection amongst them. I believe there was scarcely one but what was some what moved, and old People were moved too.—We sung a little after the Exercise — and so parted —

Sabb Octr 15 Had a meeting in Brother David Fowlers and there was a great Number of People, and we had a solemn Meeting. I spoke from Matt 5.

Monday Octo^r 16: a number of us, I think sixteen, all men went to New-Town to have a Treaty with the Oneidas. We had calld them to our Town but they chuse to have us come to their Town, and we drove one creature to them to kill. we got there after sun sit went directly to the Councell House, David and I Lodgd there, and there rest were ordered elsewhere. I had but poor rest all Night, they have too many Vermine for me —

Tuesday Octo^r 17 : Some Time in the after noon, were calld to appear before the Councell and we were permitted to speak for ourselves,—and we related the whole of our transactions with them about the Land they gave us — for they had a notion to take it back again last summer, and only allow one mile square which we utterly refused, and we had not got thro that Day, and we were dismisst. in the evening we all went together in a certain House to sing and Pray together & after prayers David and I [went] Back to the Councell House to Lodge —

Wednesday Octo^r 18 Near mid Day we were calld again to the Councell, and we resumed our relation and soon finishd and then we went out, and were calld again soon, and they begun to rehearse [what] we had deliverd, and they said it was all good and True, and then they made a New offer to us, to live in the same spot of Ground, but [not] to be bound by any Bound, but live at large with them on theer Land, which we refused, and we told them we chuse to [be] bounded, and they had bounded us allready, all most all round, and we wanted only to be bound alround where we were. and they took it under consideration.—

Thirdsday Octr 19: We wer calld again, and, about 11 o c: we received the News of the Death of our oldest man in our Town, old uncle Cornelius, Dead the evening before, and so we were obligd to Drop our Business, and went homeward; I stopd at old T [own]. Lodged at Sir Peter Pohqun —

Fryday Octr 20. I went off early, to our Town about 10: Towards Night we all [went] to the House of mourning, and I deliver [ed] a short Discourse from —— xxxix.4.5. and from thence [we] went to the grove, and we finished Buriing after sun sit and I went home —

Saturday Octr 21 : soon after Breakfast, sot of for old Town. Sally Skesuck and I went together. got there before Noon. I sot a while in Widow Quinne's and then went to Sir Peters — and was there a while, and there came a man, and brought a Maloncholy word concerning Sally as she was returning and had Just got out of the Town the Mare got a fit of kicking up her heels, and crowded up against a fence, and she fell Backward, and broak her right Arm ; I went directly to see her and found her in great Misery. we Splinted up her arm and so left. in the evening went again to see her, and she was in great Pains, and I tryd to bleed her. but I coud not make out.

Sabb Octr 22, at usual Time went to meeting and our Folks had Just come and most of them went back to try to carry home Salley. the assembly was not so large as usual by reason of the above mentioned accident. And I spoke from I Corn x. 21. in the after noon from Matt iii : 11 and there was most sole[mn] attention thro the Day. I Baptized Sir Peters wife and child.—In the evening a Number of 'em met at Sir Peters, and there were 9 : or 10 manifested their exercises of mind. They never were so awakend about their souls affairs as they are now, there never was so many men brought to such consideration as they are now. they confest they have been and [are] vile sinners, and determine by the help of god to turn from their evel ways and seek God. They say they [that] it is by hearing me Preach to them ; one old woman said she had some thoughts about Religion, and was Baptizd some nine years ago, and she thought it was well enough with her till she heard me. she thinks now she never has met with anything, and she thinks it is a gone case with her. I gave her encouragement to press forward if at eleven Hour with her. She may yet come in. we broke up and I went to bed soon.—

Monday Octr 23 A little past Noon four of our men came to old Town on their way to New Town, and I sot of with them directly, and we got there Just before sun sit, and the Councell was then sitting, and were orderd to a certain House, and in the Dusk of the evening we were calld, and after we sot there good while they read their Speech and Conclusion, and it was if [we] did not accept of their offer they would take the Land back again and we woud not accept of their offer, it was [to] take the Land at large without any bounds.—

Tuesday Octr 24 : our men went to Canaserake to Fishing, and I sot of for home. Stopt at the old Town, and intended to pass along, but they desired me to Stay to have a meeting in the Evening, and I consented ; in the evening they collected together I believe most all the old People, and many Young P. I Expounded upon II Corin. xiii : 11 and there was deep attention with flow of Tears. after I had done two or three spoke in their own Tongue reharsl ing what I had deliverd, and the Chief man asked me as I was about to leave them, how they should go on in their religious concerns, and I told them as they were not formed into Church State, they shoud enter into Christian Fellowship and put themselves under Watch care of one another, and cary on the public Worship of god in Singing Praying and reading of the word of God, and some Exhortation, and some Explination of the word of God and maintain Family Worship constantly—

Wednesday Octr 25. Some Time in the morning I left old Town and went to our Town, got there a little before noon, and found Davids Family well, but one child was unwell, but not very sicke.

Saturday Octr 28 : Our People pretended to have a convearence meeting, but one man who was most concernd in the meeting did not come, and so they did nothing. they concluded to cut the Road thro to the Flats. Just at Night two white men came to our Town from Spring Field, about forty miles from here. they came on purpose to give us a Christian Visit. we expected them and accordingly they came, and we were Glad to see each other. In the Evening we had a meeting, and there were Some Stockbridge Brethren with us, and there was great moving and some making [up] and there was some crying out. held the meeting late.—

Sabb. Octo^r 29 : Many Stockbridgers came to meeting. about ten we began the Exercise, and there was great Assembly. I spoke from Matt xxiv : 14 : and we had a solemn meeting, many were affected—in the evening we had another meeting, and there was great moving and some making up, and many were affected, but I believe there was more Natural affection than Gracious, afn [afternoon] there was considerable Noise. we were late before we left the Place.—

Wednesday Nov[r] 1, I had a meeting with the Young Peop[le] at David Fowlers, and they repeated the verses upon the Texts they chose the last Time they met, and it was a Solemn Time with us, many Tears were Shed. Several indeed are [under] Deep Convictions, and been so for Some Time—

Saturday Nov[r] 4 : near noon I sot of for New Stockbridge. Stopt a while at Brother Roger Waubys and took dinner there, and after eating past on· got to the Place towards Night. put up at Cap[t] Hind[recks]. in the Evening we had a meetg. I dropt a few words, and many discoverd their Spiritual Exercise and it was a solemn Time. many confest and lamented their past conduct, and determind to live a Regular life in Time to come &c—

Sabb. Nov[r] 5: People began to [be] collected together, and there was a great Number of P. we began the Exercise about ten. I Spoke [from] Joshua xxiv : 15, and I believe the Lord acompanied his word by his Divine Spirit. the People were Bowd before the word,—after speaking I Baptized [Blank]. in the Evening we met again. I did not say much, and there was a number again that discoverd their concern and resolutions, and it was a solemn Season, and we held the mg late. Lodged at Cap[t] Hindricks again—

Monday Nov[r] 6: We had another meeting quite early, and there was much affection. I Spoke to them about the Nature of Baptism very close, and I Baptized [Blank]. Some Time towards noon I left New Stockbridge. Stopt a little while at Roger Waubys and so past on. got to Brother Davids Some Time in the after Noon,—in the eving we had a meeting, and it was a comfortable meeting :—

Tuesday Nov[r] 7 was geting ready to return homeward. Visited some Families—

Wednesday Nov[r] 8. Visited again and was busy geting ready—

Thirdsday Nov[r] 9: sot of early. Sir Peter Puhquennuppeet, Catty Quinney, Betsey Fowler and Elizy Corricomb went with me, and we were obligd to Lodge in the Woods. we coud not get thro' and it rain'd some. we found a good Hutt, and made out to make fire, and we lodged quite comfortable. I had good rest—

Fryday Nov[r] 10: got up some Time before Day, and as soon as it was break a Day we tacled our Horses and went on. we got to M[r] Folss Just after sun rise. took breakfast at Mr. Fols's: and about 8 : we sot off again. Stopt a little at Esq[r] Franks, and near 12 we went on again. Got to Spring Field some Time in the Evening. we put up at Brother Crippens and we were Gladly receivd and we were glad to see them—

Again Occom spent the winter at Mohegan. On the 26th of May, 1787, he began his next journey to Oneida, arriving at Fols' on the evening of July first. Here he met John Tuhie, who gave him intelligence concerning the state of his people. Among other things which he then learned was that several of them had died since he left. On the fourth instant, as he was preparing to journey through the wilderness to Brothertown, David Fowler and his wife, with " Sister Esther, Brother Jacob Fowlers widow," came in. Here, then, another of Wheelock's pupils drops out of our story. The circumstances and exact time of Jacob Fowler's death are unknown. He probably died shortly before Occom's arrival in the spring of 1787. But we know he lived a worthy life to the last, and died beloved among his people. He had done some service to his honor as a schoolmaster in the Oneida mission, the teacher and preacher at Mushantuxet, the Indian tutor at Dartmouth College, and the faithful messenger of " Brother Jonathan " during the Revolution. He is doubtless buried in an unmarked grave in their early cemetery on the hill at Brothertown.

Here we resume the story as told in a volume of Occom's diary in the Connecticut Historical Society:

Thirsday Jul. 5 [1787] arrivd here Yesterday, this Day went nowhere but kept at Christiana all Day.—

Sabb. July 8: about 9 went to Brother Davids, and prety many People collected together. Both Towns got together, and Some White People, from Clenton. we began about 10, in Brother Davids Barn. I Spoke from Mathew [Blank] in the after Noon from Deuto x. and the People attend[ed] with great solemnity and some affection. towards Night went back to Daughters and Lodged there —

Thirdsday July 12 : Some Time before Noon I sot of from our Town, and went to New-Stockbridge. Stopt a while at Brother Roger's and took Dinner there, and soon after went on again. got to the Place about 2, put up at Capt Hindrick's and Lodged. the People were exceeding glad to see me : but many of them were gone a fishing after Salmon.

Fryday July 13: Some Time after Breakfast went to see a woman that had been some Sick. Peter Pohquunnuppeet went with me, and I had some conversation with her about her eternal concerns. she seemed to be reseignd. she said she was willing God should dispose of her as he Pleases. Prayed with her, and then went back to Capt Hindrecks, and towards Night went to meeting, and there was but few Collected, and I spoke to them from xxxiii Psalm 12 verse, and there was very good attention. after I had done speaking Capt Hindreck rehersed what he could remember in his own Tongue and he made the last Prayer and so the People were dismissed, and I went home with Capt Hindreck and Lodged there again.

Saturday July 14. Some [time] in the morning went to see Joseph Pye, alias Shauqueathquat, and had very agreable conversation with him, his wife, sister & another old woman about their Heart Exercises, and they asked Some Questions and I answered them, and after a while I went back.

Sabb July 15 about 10, we began the Divine Service, & there was a large number of People, many English were with us. I Spoke from I Corin 2 : 2 : and Luke vii. 48 and the People attended with great solemnity, and gravity. after meeting went back to my lodgings, and Just before Sunset went to meeting again, and Capt Hindreck, and Peter Peet reharsed in the Indian Language, the Discourses I Deliverd in the Day, because many old People coud not readly understand what I deliver'd in the English, and in the Evening went back to Capt H^s and Sir Peter, Jo Queney and John Quenney came to my Lodgings and they asked many Questions, and we had very agreable Evenings Conversation and it was Rainey Night. went to Bed somewhat late and had comfortable repose.

Monday July 16. Went to see several Families. —— —— This Evening after we had got to Bed, sot up quite late too, widow Quenney Knocked at the Door, and she just look'd in, and spoke & she went back : and I ask'd what was the Matter, and Capt Hindreck said, that Cathrine Quenney was taken very Strangely at once, her Breath was most gone all of a Sudden, and Capt Hindreck and his wife got up and went to see her, and I lay still, and told them, if she continued so, let me know, and the Capt came back directly, and desired me to go over, and I got up and Drest me and went over, and when I got into the House, I went right to her Bed Side, and sot down. she lay very still only Breathe with struggle, and sigh'd once in a while : and I asked her whether she was sick : she said no. what then is the matter with you, and she said, with Tears, I want to Love God more, and serve him better ; and I said to her, if She really Desired and asked for it she shu'd have her desire granted, for it was a good Desire, & gave her some further advice and counsel, and she desir'd me to Pray with her, and I asked her what we shou'd pray for. she said, that she may have more Faith, that she might serve with her whole Heart and so we pray'd, and after that I went back to my lodgings, and went to bed again quietly and had comfortable rest.—

Tuesday July 17 : Soon after Prayers I went over to see Catey and she was yet a Bed and I asked how [she] did. She said well, and asked how her mind was. She said, she found more love and Peace, and she wanted to serve God with all [her] heart. Said, she slept none or but little all Night, and her Body felt very weak, but her heart felt well: she desired me to pray with her. I asked her, what she wanted to pray for. she said for Wisdom and more Faith: and soon after Prayer I went to my Quaters, and about 10 my son in Law, Anthony Paul came to me and little Jo Wauby, and we went to the Lake. Stopt a little while at Mr Aucut's and were well treated, he is from Connecticut,—and so we past on. got [to] Colo^l Lewee's Just after sun set, and Lodged, but I had but small Portions of sleep. Flees Plagued me all Night.

Wednesday, July 18: was at Lewees. We cou'd not find a connoo till afternoon, and then we went to the Lake, about 3 quaters of a mile, and wee made up a Fire where the Black Creek runs into the New Town creek, and there we spent the Night. some Five in the after [noon] I went to Salmon Creek near 3 miles, where the Block House was once. I had been there 26 years ago, there was then a number of sod'ers, but it is all grown up with Large Stadles. there I saw a Family over the Creek, I suppose moving to the West, but I did not go over to see them. towards Night went back to our Fire, and we catch'd some Fish—we made up great Fire, and after a while went to sleep, but I was cold.—

Thirdsday July 19, got up early and Pray'd and then got some Victuals and soon after we sot off to go to Salmon Creek. soon got there. I rode and the Boys went by water in a little Connoo. We went to fishing, but had no Luck, and so went back to our Fire. soon got there and went to fishing in the creek, and catch'd [a] few fish. Just at Night, we got ready to return home Lodged again at Colo^l Lewees, but I had no comfort, I had too many Bed Fellows.—

Fryday July 20, got up quite early and went of soon: Stopt a while at Mr Alcuts in New Town. took Dinner there. soon after we went on again, got to New-Stockbridge some [time] in the after Noon—sun about two hours high, at Night we had a meeting, there was not great many People, and I spoke to them from [Blank] and there was good attention. after meeting went to Bed soon and had a comfortable rest—

Saturday July 21. Lay a Bed somewhat late, and Some Time before noon I left the Place, and went to Brotherton. Stopt a little while at Brother Roger Waubys and soon past on, got to my Daughter Christianas some Time before Night: and at Night went to Bed soon and had good rest—

Sabb July 22. about 9 went to Brother Davids to meeting, and about 10 began the service, and there was a large Assembly. I spoke from I Cor:n

iii. 11 & Matt xxv. 46 and there was uncommon attention among the
People, many were melted Down to Tears, some were alarm'd. I felt the
Power of God's word myself. after meeting went to Brother David's
House, for we met in his Barn. Just at Night went to my Daughters.—

Thirsday July 26, towards Night I went to Abraham Simons, married
him to Sarah Adams, they did not make any widding yet there was good
many People. Lodged there—

Saturday July 28. Some Time in the morning David Fowler and his
wife, and I sot of to go to Deans Ville [Dean's Patent], and we went by
way of Clenton, got to Clenton Some Time in the afternoon, and it was a
Rainey Day, and very bad way, many Mirery holes. stopt a few minutes at
Capt Foots, and so past on. got to Mr James Dean's about sun set, and I
was kindly receiv'd, and I Lodg'd there. Brother David and his Wife went
to Mr Jonathan Deans and Lodged there.

Sabb July 29. about 9 went to Mr Felps's to meetg and there was considerable Number of People, and I spoke from the words, he that soweth
to the flesh &c and let the word of Christ Dwell in you &c, and there was
very good attention. after meeting went back to Mr James Deans, and
Lodged there again—

Monday July 30: after Breakfast we sot of for Brotherton. got home
about Noon. towards Night I went to my Daughters and found them
well—

Thirsday August 2. towards Night I went to Widow Esther Fowlers,
and we had a mg [meeting] there, and there was not a great Number of
People, our People are much scattered on account of the scarcity of Provisions. I spoke from Luke ix. 62 and there was an affectionate attention
among the People. I Lodged at the same House—

Saturday. Augt 4: Went to New-Stockbridge, got there before Night.—I
put up at Sir Peter Pohequenuppeets.

Sabb. Augt 5. about 10 went to meeting, and there was a goodly number
of People,—I Spoke from Theol. 3: 20 and the People attended well, the
People met again toward Night and Capt Hindreck and Sir Peter Rehearsed
what I had delivered in the Day. Baptised 2 Children one for Sir Peter by
the Name Mary, and [the] other was for Joseph Quiney by the [name of]
Joseph.—

Monday Augt 6. was at the Place all Day.—

Tuesday Augt 7. Some Time in towards noon I went to Brotherton.
Stopt a little while at Rogers and 10 past on. got to Brother David abt 2:
and was there a little while, and down the Hill, got to my Daughter's some
Time in the after Noon, found them well—

Thirsday Augt 9. Just at Night went to meeting at Sister Esther Fowlers and there was but few People, it was Raney. I spoke from Matt xiii,

2 &c, and there was great solemnity among the People. I Lodged at the Same House.—

Sabb Augt 12. went to Davids and about 10 we began the holy service and there was a great Number of People and I Spoke from Deut xxxiii. 27 and the People attended well. Lodged at Brother Davids. Monday morning went to my Daughters.

Wednesday Augt 15: I had a Number of People come to clear a bid of ground for me from New Stockbridge and from this Place—the Names of the Stockbridgers, Capt Hindrick [Blank]

Thirdsday Augt 16 they worked again, and they Laboured exceeding well, this is the first Labour I ever had from my Brethren according to the Flesh, and it was a Voluntary offer and I accepted of it thankfully. I never did receive anything from my Indian Brethren before. Now I do it out of Principle. It is high Time that we should begin to maintain ourselves, and to support our Temporal & Religious Concerns. towards Night, we went up on the Hill and a meeting at Brother Davids. there was a considerable of People & I spoke from Psalm cxix: 97 and the word fell with great Power, many were deeply Bowed down :—after I had done, the People sung some Time. I Lodged at Brother David's and many of the Stockbridgers stayd here too and we went to rest soon.—

. Fryday Augt 17 many of the Stockbridgers took Breakfast at Davids, and then they went home. I soon went after them. I got to the Place before Noon & put up at Capt Hindricks. towards Night we had a meeting, and there was not many People, and I Spoke from John xv. 12. and we had a comfortable meeting. the Word was weighty in the minds of the People. Mr Kirkland was present and one Mr Olcut was there also.—

Saturday, Augt 18 in the afternoon towards N^t the People got together & Capt Hindrick Rehearsed what I deliver'd the Day before, and there was a solemnity among the People—

Sabb Augt 19, about 10 we began the service and there was a large N^o of People, and I Spoke from Deut xxvi. 16. 17. 18. 19 and Reval. xxii. 17 and it was a solemn Day with us, as soon as the meeting was over, I had my Horse got up and I sot a way for Brotherton with our People; got home to Davids about sunset and there Lodged—

Thirdsday Augt 23 I had 6 Stockbridgers to help me to clear Land,— and sun about an Hour high we had a meeting at Widow Fowler, and there was but a small number of People and I spoke from Hos vi: 3 and there was very good attention.—I Lodged at the Same House—

Sabb. Augt 26 about 9 went to meeting upon the Hill at Brother Davids, and about 10 began the Divine worship and there was a large number of People, & I spoke from Rom. i. 16 & iii. 1. 2: and there was a solemn attention amongst the People.—at the end of the afternoon sermon, I Baptized my Son in Law Anthony, and my Daughter Christiana owned her Baptism and renew[ed] her covenant with god, and I Baptized their children: their Names are, Samson, James, Sarah, Phebe—these were the first that were Baptized in this New Settlement, and I hope and Pray that it may be only the beginning of multitudes in this Wilderness, till the Whole Wilderness shall Blossom as the Rose—

Thirds Day Aug^r 30 Just at Night went [to] Widow Fowler's and had a meeting, but there was but very few People. I spoke from the words, O that my People woud consider—

Saturday Sepr 1 I went to Deansville, one Dr Petre went with me, he is a garman Doctor. we got there Some Time before Night, took Tea at Mr James Dean's, and before sun set I went to Mr Jona^n Dean's, and there I Lodged and the Doctor Lodged there also.

Sabb. Sepr 2. about 11 we began the worship of god. and there was but a small number of People and I spoke from John xv, 23 & xiv. 23 and People attended with solemnity all Day. Lodged at Mr James Deans where the meeting was. Esq White and I Lodged together, and had a comfortable rest—

Monday Sepr 3: I got up early and went to Mr Phelps's and there I took Breakfast. Some Time in the morning went back to Mr James Deans, and leave and went home. got to Brotherton about 1 in the afternoon.—

Thirday Sepr 6: towards Night went to Sister Esther Fowlers and had a meeting, and there was but few People, and I spoke from I Peter i: 15: and the People attended solemnly to appearance. as soon as the meeting was over I went back to my Daughters and it was very Dark, but had Torches to give us light thro' thick Woods—

Sabb Sepr 9: went to Brother David's to meeting, we begun the service about [Blank] and there was considerable number of People, and I spoke from Acts xvii, 28 & 30 and we had a solemn meeting, many were deeply affected. Several Onoydas were there—toward Night I went back to my Daughters and went to bed soon—

Thirdsday Sepr 13 this Day we had appointed as a Day of fasting and prayer. We met at David Fowler's and there was a considerable number of People, and I spoke from Luke xv and it was a solemn Day. there were some that made confession of their wanderings from god, many were bow'd before the Majesty of Heaven and I believe [the] Day will not be forgot soon.

Sabb Sepr 16 had our meeting at Brother David Fowlers, and ther was a great Number of People, 3 men came from Stock—left Mr Serjan's meeting, and there were some white People, and the People attend with Awful Solemnity. I spoke from Daniel [blank] and Psalm cxix. 1, after meeting went [to] George Peters and took supper there and after went back to Davids & lodged there.

The continuation of this narrative is from a volume of the diary in Dartmouth College Library :

Thirdsday Sepr 20. 1787. Just at Night had a meeting at Widow Fowlers, and there was not many People, and I gave them a few words of Exhortation, from Luke vi. 8 and the People attended with great solemnity, and some affection. after meeting I went to Brother Davids & Lodged there—

Fryday Sepr 21 Some Time in the morning went to New Stockbridge. David Fowler Ju^r went with me. we got there about 2, called on Mr Sergeant and he appered good condition'd, and so to Sir Peters, and directly from there we went to meeting and there was considerable number of People, and I spoke from Mark v. 9 and there was very good attention. This meeting was Designd chiefly for the young People.—soon after meeting went back to Sir Peters, and tooke some refreshment, and soon after Sun Set went to meeting again, and there was great Number of People and there was Several that related there exercises of mind.—three men, three women relate their Exercises, a Young man, and a maried woman, manifested their desire of Being Baptized and some Children were to be Baptized also.—Mr Serjant made some objection against two Being Baptized, but the Professors gave their fellowship to their Desire.—& so we broke up our meeting some late in the Evening. I [went] to Peters and their I Lodged, and had good rest—

Saturday Sepr 22 was all Day at the Place—

Sabb Sepr 23 : about 10 we went to meeting, and there was a large number of People. many of our People from Brotherton came also, and some White[s] were there, and Mr Serjant read a Discourse to the Indians in their Tongue and read it also in English. he read his Prayer also in Indian, and he prayed partly in English—In the afternoon I tryed to Preach. I spoke from Acts x. 34. 35 and there was very great solemnity. Some were much affected.—and I Baptized at this Time Eight persons two adults & the rest children : The Name of the Young [man] is Solomon and the woman [Blank]. Soon after meeting I went to Sir Peters—In the evening we had another meeting. one of the men reharsed what [I] had deliver'd in the Day. after meeting went back with Sir Peter and Lodged there again—

Monday Sepr 24, I took Breakfast with Mr Sergeant and soon after Breakfast I returnd to Brotherton. Betsy Fowler rid behind me and got to the Place near Noon. Stopt but few minutes at Brother Davids and past on to my Daughters

Tuesday Sepr 25 : eleven Stockbridgers came to our Place to help, and some of our men came also.—

Wednesday I had help again till after Noon—

Thirdsday Sepr 27 in the Evening had meeting at Widow Fowlers, there was but few People and I Spoke from [Blank] and there was a solemn attention. after I had done speaking two of our People spoke a [few] words, one after another, & when they had done a white man got up and Spoke, and he spoke with a feeling. he gave an account of a remarkable reformation in Vergena—He came from Stockbridge—after meeting I went up to Brother David Fowlers & Lodged there.—

Saturday Sepr 29 about 1 in the after Noon, my Son in Law, Anthony Paul and Daughter Christiana and Betsey Fowler sot of for Whites Bourrow, but we were overtaken with Night at one Mr Blanckets and there we Lodged, and were exceedingly well entertained, and we had a little Exercise with a Christian Card,—we went to Bed in good season, and I had a comfortable Rest—

Sabb Sepr 30 Got up very early and Prayd together and then we Sot of. we had near four Miles to go and it was extreamly Bad riding, Dreadful miry—We got to the Place just as Esq White was about taking Breakfast, and we sot down with them—and soon after Breakfast we went to meeting to another House and there was a large N. of People, and I spoke from Isaia 43:21: and there was great attention in the Assembly. I believe they felt the weight of the word,—after meeting; I went home with Mr Weatmore, and tooke Dinner with them. in the after Noon meeting was removed to this House on account of a funeral that is to be attended in this House, for an Infant just Born Dyed in this House last Monday. it liv'd about two Hours after it was Born, and they have kept the corps to this Day for they expected me here this Day. this is the first Death that happend in this Place since it has been settled. it has been settled three years, and it is now a large Settlement. this after Noon I spoke from Isaia 38:1 and it was a Solemn Time, indeed many were deeply affected, there was a shower of Tears. soon after meeting we carried the little corps to the grave it was but a few Rods from the House. after Burying returned to the House—in the Evening went to Mr Livingworths and spent the evening there—about 10 went back to Mr Weatmores and Lodged there—

Monday Octo^r 1 got up early. took Breakfast with Family. after Breakfast went to Esqr Whites, and got ready, and about 9 we sot off for Home. Lieu^t White & Mr Leavett went to our Place—as we past a long, took Notice of the Settlement, and it is a fine Spot of Land, and a very large Spot too, and the People has made a rapped Progress in cultivating the Land. if the People were as ingag'd in Religion as they are in their Temporal Concerns this Settlement would be very much like the Garden of Eden, which was the Garden of God. the Lord be with them and Bless them that they may indeed be a Peculiar People unto God, that

they may be Lights in this Wilderness—We Stopt a while at Clenton,—
and we got Home just as the sun was setting.—

Thirdsday Octr 4: in the Evening had a meeting in Widow Fowlers, and
there was but few People, and I Spoke from [Blank] and we had a comfortable Season—

Sabb Octr 7 : had a meeting in Brother Davids and there was not many
People, and I Spoke from [Blank] and we had a solemn meeting : Lodg'd
at Brother Davids—

Tuesday Octr 9: about 1 in the afternoon I sot of for Clenton, got there
Some Time before Night. Stopt a little while at Mr Jones's to see his wife,
had been sick some Time and she was very poorly, and went from there to
Capt Foot's and in the Evening the People collected together and I spoke
to them from John xxi: 22 and there was great solemnity amongst the
People. I believe some felt the weight of the word—the Beginning of last
March there was no House in this Place, a perfect Wild Wilderness. Now
there are 20 Families and there were seventy odd Persons in the meeting
this evening, and have made great appearance in their improvements.
these are chiefly from New England and Youngerly People—

Wednesday Octr 10 Stayd here till after Dinner, and then went to a certain House between this Place and Whitesbourough about half way. the
mans Name is Blanchet. I got there Some Time before Night, and had a
meeting, and there was a considerable Number of People, and I Spoke
from Psalm cvii, 31 : and the People attended exceeding well.—this was
all a wild Wilderness in the beginning of last spring & now the People are
settling al along from Whitesbourgh to Clenton—in few Years this will be
settled thick as any part of the Globe the Land is so good, it draws all
sorts of People and Nations are flocking here continually—

Thirdsday Octr 11. some Time [after] Breakfast I sot of for home—
Stopt a while at Capt Foots in Clenton and took Dinner. went on again,
got to my Daughters—and in the evening we had a meeting [at] Sister
Esther's, and was not many People and I spoke from Psal cvii. 31 and
there was an uncommon attention, many were deeply affected.—

Fryday Octo^r 12 some Time in the morning I sot of for N. Stockbridge
and had a meeting there in the Evening, and I spoke from [Blank] and
there was good atention. Lodgd at Sir Peters—

Saturday Octo 13: About 2 in the afternoon I went to Deanville [Dean's
Patent] got to the Place about sun set. Peter went. found Mrs Dean
exceedingly distrest with uncommon Difficulties in her Pregnancy, and
Peter and I went to Mr Jonathan Deans and Lodged there, and 2. o. c. in
the Night I was called up to the other House, and Bleed Mrs Dean and I
went directly, and found her much distrest and took Blood from her foot,
and Bled exceeding well—and her distresses begun to mitigate directly, and

I stayd the rest of the Night and she was somewhat comfortable—I was calld up again before Day to write to Doc^r for them, for they were sending to Albany for one, and were sending for Mr Dean too for he had been gone some Time to Spencertown—

Sabb Octo^r 14: about 10 the People got together, and there was a large number of People, many White People from other Places and many Indians from Both our Towns. I spoke from Matt v, 20 & 5 and there was a solemn attention all Day. Soon after meeting Peter and I went to Clenton. got there a little after Sun Set. We put up at Capt Foots and the People Collected directly and there was quite a large number, and I spoke from [Blank]. we lodged at the Same House & had comfortable rest—

Monday Octo^r 15: Soon after Breakfast went to mill, and was there Some Time, before we coud get Grinding—we got to our Place about 1: and Sir Peter past on to his Place—

Thirdsday Octo^r 18: Went to Stockbridge to a wedding Just before SunSet, attended upon Marriage. the Young man was one the Sachem's son and the Young woman was of noted Family, and there was a vast concourse of People of many Nations. it was Said there were ten different Languages among the People and the People behaved decently, but the Onoydas began to behave unseamly and in the Night they had a terrible froleck even all Night—

Fryday was all Day at the Place—in the evening we collected together at Capt Hindrecks. I spoke from Matt 6: 22: 23 and there was a solemn attention. after I had done Capt Hindreck rehearsed the Same. Lodgd at the Same House—

Saturday Octo^r 20: some Time in the afternoon I returnd to Brotherton. Mr Warmsly went with me. we stopt at Roger Waubys and there took Dinner; soon after Dinner I went on and Mr Warmsly went back. I got to Brother Davids before Night and I Lodgd at Davids—

Sabb. Octo^r 21: about 10 the People got together & [there] was a large Number of People, Some white People and I spoke from John xiii. 17 and the People were very solemn and many were affected. Lodged at the Same House—

Monday Octo^r 22, in the evening had a meeting in Sister Fowlers, and there was not many People and I spoke from [Blank] and the People attended well. Lodgd at the same House.

Tuesday Octo^r 23. People from Stockbridge came to help me—the[re] were 5 of them and they workd two Days.

Thirdsday Octo^r 24: we were calld suddenly to appear before the chiefs of the Onoyd, that had Just come to our Place—and we eat our Breakfast in hast, and went direcly to Widow Fowlers and there the chiefs meet with us, and it was about our Lands. But there was such confusion I woud not say a word about it. it was a party Scheme, contrivd by a few of our People. they [have] been agreing with the Onoydas for a Piece of Land without the knowledge of the Headmen of the Place. Some of the contrivers of this mischief were much intoxicated and they drove on the Business with all fury in no order, it was like Whirlwind. Some Time towards Night we broke up and every one went his way: in great confusion of mind.—I went to Brother Davids and there Lodgd with a sorrowful mind.—

Fryday Octo^r 25 was at our Places all Day

Saturday Octo^r 26 Towards Night Just as I was going away to Clenton, Brother Chrippen and B^r Swane came to my son in Laws, and we had a little conversation. these Brethren are from a Place called Springfield, Joing to Cherryvaley; so I left them, and went on to Clenton. got there about sun set put up at Capt Foots, found them all well.—

Sabb. Octo^r 27 about half after 10 we began the exercise, and there was a large Number of People, some from other Places, & several Stockbridgers were with us, and there was very great attention both before noon and afternoon. I spoke from John. I know you that the Love of god is not in you, in the afternoon from Mark viii, 36, 37. as soon as the meeting was done I went of to Brotherton, the Stockbridgers went with me. we got there about Sun Set. we eat a few mouthfulls and went to meeting at sister easter's and there was not much moving. there seemed to be some party spirit in the meeting.—

Sabb. Novr 4 Preached at New Stockbridge & Spoke from [Blank] and there was very serious attention al Day

Monday Novr 5: went back to Brotherton—

Sabb. Novr 11: Preachd at Brotherton once more and Baptized Brother David Fowler's Children six of them, and we had a solemn Day of it. in the evening we had another meeting, and it was a comfortable meeting—

Monday Novr 12 this Day intended to set out for home but it begun [raining] in the morning, and so stopt for the Day—

Tuesday Novr 13: Got up very early and got ready, and we sot out Sun about an Hour and half high. Betsy Fowler, Jerusha Wympe and Henry Stensel a young Dutch man went with me. we had exceeding fine warm Day. got thro' the woods before sun sit. I put up at Conrod Folss. Jerusha and Betsey went to Mr Smiths about 2 miles further.

Occom did not return directly to Mohegan after this visit; but in company with David Fowler, representing the Brothertown Indians, and Peter Pauquaunaupeet those of New Stockbridge, went on a journey to solicit aid for the maintenance of Occom as their minister. Of this ecclesiastical relationship we shall write presently. They drew up an address stating their case to use on this mission:

To all Benevolent Gentlemen, to Whom these following lines may make their appearance.

We who lately mov'd from Several Tribes of Indians in New England, and Setled here in Oneida Country.—And we also Muhheeconnuck Tribe, who lately came from Housotonuk alias Stockbridge, and have settled in Oneida, And finding it our indispensible Duty to maintain the Christian Religion amongst ourselves in our Towns, And from this Consideration, Some of us desired our Dear Brother, the Revd Samfon Occom, to give us a visit, and accordingly, he came up two years ago this Fall, and he was here a few Days; and his preaching came with great weight upon our Minds. And he has been here two Summers and Falls since. And we must confess to the Glory of God, that God has made him an Eminant Instrument amongst us, of a Great and Remarkable Reformation. And have now given him a Call to Settle amongst us, and be our Minister that we may enjoy the glorious Doctrines and ordinances of the New Testament. And he has accepted our Call.—But we for ourselves very weak, we c'd do but very little for him. And we want to have him live comfortable.

The late unhappy wars have Script us almost Naked of every thing, our Temporal enjoyments are greatly lesstened, our Numbers vastly diminished, by being warmly engaged in favour of the United States. Tho' we had no immediate Business with it, and our Spiritual enjoyments and Priviledges are all gone. The Fountains abroad, that use to water and refresh our Wilderness are all Dryed up, and the Springs that use to rise near are ceased. And we are truly like the man that fell among Thieves, that was Script, wounded and left half dead in the high way.—And our Wheat was blasted and our Corn and Beans were Frost bitten and kill'd this year.— And our moving up here was expensive and these have brought us to great Necessity—And these things have brought us to a resolution to try to get a little help from the People of God, for the present; for we have determined to be independent as fast as we can, that we may be no longer troublesome to our good Friends,—And therefore our most humble Request and Petition is, to the Friends of the Kingdom of Jesus Christ, [that they] would take notice of us, and help us in encourageing our Dear Minister, in Communicating Such Things that may Support him and his Family.—This is the most humble request and Petition of the Publicks true Friend & Brothers

	ELIJAH WIMPEY
New-Stockbridge	DAVID FOWLER
Novr 28: 1787	JOSEPH SHAUQUETHGENT
Brotherton	HENDRECH AUPAUMUT
Novr 29: 1787.	JOSEPH QUAUNCKHAM
	PETER POHQUENUMPEC [4]

Conn. Hist. Soc., Indian Papers.

The principal places they visited on this tour were Newark, New Brunswick, Trenton and Princeton in New Jersey, and they spent about a month in and about Philadelphia, returning by the way of New York. Some funds were collected, but much less than they had hoped. It was the thirty-first of March, 1788, before Occom reached home. He there resumed his work until the twenty-sixth of May, when he started again for Oneida, arriving at Brothertown July eighth. We have not a complete account of that visit, and a lost volume of the diary leaves us without details until May 11, 1789. On that date we find him at Albany moving his family and other New England Indians to their new homes. It is known, however, that he spent his time as in the preceding years. We regret most the loss of the account of his own departure from the Mohegan home, where he had so long lived. It must have cost him some sorrow. Most of his furniture he was obliged to leave behind in the care of his sister, Lucy Tantaquidgeon, or his younger sons. On the wall hung the painting of him which had been made in England and presented to him. His books he could not carry, and perhaps we owe to that fact the preservation of so many of them, as in time they became scattered. His bookcase or secretary was left, and its two parts are now separated, one being in the Connecticut Historical Society rooms. So he left Mohegan, the home of his fathers, which he more than any other Christian Indian has made famous. Although he visited New England in the September following and stood again in his familiar and noted house on the hillside, he had finished there his work. The company he then led forth contained all who could then be persuaded to emigrate, and so this Indian Moses brought his people into their promised land. The journey was doubtless made on a schooner from New London to Albany, where they took wagons to Schenectady and in bateaux followed the course of the Mohawk river until they reached the trail through the woods to Brothertown.

It is evident that Occom's journeys to and fro afforded him
an excellent opportunity of ministering to the infant settlements along the route of westward emigration, then setting in
with a strong current. No one could do it better. He had
no sectarian prejudices, and was content to preach in any
sort of a place to any kind of an audience. Everybody knew
him. All received him gladly into their homes. He married
couples, baptized children, visited and doctored the sick, and
attended funerals. In the evenings when no neighborhood
meeting could be held, he gathered the young people about
the pioneer's fireside, and entertained and instructed them
with a game which he had devised, called "Christian cards."
These were versified passages of Scripture printed on card-
board, which he gave out to the company and as they were
read he offered some comments upon them. He seems to
have had an Old Testament and a New Testament pack; and
the art was in the appropriateness of the card to the person,
at which religious dealing the Reverend Occom was doubtless
expert, though he does note instances when one "did not
get the card which he intended." Occasionally he met with
those who were fond of singing, as he was himself. Then from
the copy of his own "Hymns and Spiritual Songs," which he
carried in his pocket, he would lead the company in praise.
Of course there was a novelty in his being an Indian minister,
which furthered his popularity in the cabin of the woodsman
as it had among the nobility of England; but he was never
conscious of any such distinction. He won respect and
affection wherever he went in the settlements because he
honored his own mission. Some were New England people
who were glad to hear a sermon once more. Many were
shepherdless sheep in the wilderness. All were interested in
the outside world they had left, and were ready to welcome a
visitor who had news to impart of any sort to while away the
evening hour. There were formal occasions, too, even among

pioneers, when a minister was needed to add dignity to the event. Such was the first "training day" at Clinton, the first of September, 1789, when the military, making a "fine appearance," waited on the Indian minister at Colonel Timothy Tuttle's newly built frame house and escorted him to the place of assembly, where he delivered to them an "exhortation" and prayed, as they had been wont to order the day in New England. Sometimes there was a novel aptness in his sermon texts which must have captured his auditors, as when at the New Lebanon Springs he chose the words, "Now there is at Jerusalem a pool," or when in a back settlement he spoke on "A three days' journey into the wilderness." The most amusing incidents of his travels are recorded in the utmost seriousness. The track of his humor is covered like the trail of an Indian ; there is not a trace of a smile in any of his writings. An accident several years before had made him lame, and he could not walk far. So he went from place to place, riding such a horse as he could own, one of which must have revived the memory of his traditional ill-fortune by expiring in a quagmire. So in winter and in summer, as it chanced, through rivers, intervales and forests, he pursued his mission.

Meanwhile, however, Occom was doing his utmost for the religious welfare of the Brothertown and Stockbridge Indians. The latter, in 1785, when the main body arrived, had no minister nor any prospect of one, for Sergeant did not accompany them. Their town was west of Brothertown, and six miles only, says Occom, from Fowler's house on the hill. This was not inconvenient for the New Stockbridge Indians. So they fell naturally and without any improper persuasion on Occom's part into the plan of worshiping on alternate Sundays in Fowler's barn and in some house at Stockbridge. He thus combined the tribes in one parish, to which he ministered for two seasons before Sergeant made his first visit to his people. By this time he had established himself in the

favor of those who had formerly been under Sergeant's care,
and had removed as a church into the wilderness or had
brought letters from the old church intending to form one.
These and some of the Brothertown Indians united, in 1787,
in extending a call to Occom.[5] This was in the month of
August and before Sergeant arrived. At this time the Stockbridge minister had no intention of removing to the new
settlement. He knew the Indians could not support him, and
grants from the English and Scotch societies had been cut off.
The two ministers met on the twenty-first of September, as related
in Occom's diary, and on the following Sabbath they shared the
services of the day. Then Occom with representatives of
both tribes made the above-mentioned journey to see what
support he could obtain in his ministry. That autumn, however, the situation was changed by the incorporation of a new
society in Massachusetts, called " The Society for Propagating
the Gospel among the Indians and others in North America."
Sergeant went to Boston and applied to the society for aid.
He was accepted and ordained as an evangelist with a view of
continuing his mission among the Stockbridge tribe. This
caused a division among his people, some adhering to him
and others to Occom. Such was the origin of these two
churches. Sergeant gives some account of the matter in a
letter to Rev. Peter Thacher, secretary of the new society,
dated May 19, 1788, from which we quote: " The dispute
began upon this question, whether they had better take Mr.
Occom or myself for their minister, as he was about to settle
in a neighboring town, expecting to have him part of the time,
and could support him easier than myself. In their division
of the tribe on the question, there were 30 for Mr. Occom
and 50 for myself. Since my new appointment half of the
30 have openly left Mr. Occom. I have n't time, Sir, to
mention some unkind measures Mr. Occom has taken to

---

[5] This document and the reply are in the *Conn. Hist. Soc., Indian Papers.*

support his wish, but only mention that the bigger half of my people are so prejudiced against Mr. Occom that I sincerely believe if I were to leave them they would be most unhappy. . . . In the division of the old professors belonging to the Stockbridge church 10 were for Occom and 16 for me." [6]

Samson Occom removed permanently to Brothertown in 1789. The Stockbridge minister was then among his people, though it is said he did not remove his family thither until the year 1796.[7] An attempt was made July 26, 1789, to adjust these differences in a meeting at New Stockbridge, but without success. So they concluded, as Occom says, "That every one should have full liberty to chuse and act in accordance with the light and understanding he has in his religious concerns." Sergeant, having good assurances of outside support, had the advantage; but Occom had been first on the field and had been regularly called to be their minister. Joseph Pye and Joseph Quinney, who had been conspicuous in calling Occom, finally went over to Sergeant's church; but "Sir Peter" and Captain Hendrick remained faithful to him. Thus Occom ministered at Stockbridge and at Brothertown— after 1788 in the schoolhouse—until his death. By the division of the Suffolk Presbytery, he became a member of the Presbytery of Albany. This fact led him to bring his church into that ecclesiastical fellowship, which he did with their approval, being instructed by them, September 8, 1791, "to spend a portion of his time among the Brothertown Indians and explain to them the discipline laid down in the Confession of Faith and render an account of his diligence therein." [8] Still he seems, from the beginning, to have considered his church of the Presbyterian order. Only a few months before

---

[6] *MSS. of the Society,* Am. Bd. Com. For. Miss. Sergeant was certainly commissioned by this society in 1788, two years earlier than the time noted in the printed volume, *Soc. for Prop. the Gos.,* 1887, p. 40.

[7] Jones' *Annals of Oneida County,* pp. 888, 889.

[8] *MS. Records of the Albany Presbytery.*

his death, in 1792, he wrote as follows: "The People I attend upon, have willingly and cheerfully adopted the Confession of Faith of the Presbyterian Church of the United States in America—they Joyfully put themselves under the Care and inspection of our Presbytery, and thankfully receive the Gospel Fellowship open'd for them and will from this Time Look upon themselves [as] one with the Presbyterian Family. Sir, This Church is the first Indian Presbyterian Church that ever was formed by Indians themselves, for we had no white man to assist us when we formed." [9]

After Occom's death, through the instrumentality of Rev. Samuel Eells, missionary in that region in behalf of the General Association of Connecticut, the Stockbridge portion of his church was united with that of Mr. Sergeant. A meeting for this purpose was held at New Stockbridge, September 24, 1793. Mr. Eells then had a statement of the case from the minister, the church, and the principal Indians of the tribe not members. He declared his opinion that both ministers were "good men." In view of the circumstances, however, he thought it best to unite the Stockbridge Indians under Mr. Sergeant's ministry, which he accordingly did.[10] This was a wise union for that portion of Occom's church, but it left the members of the Brothertown tribe to become the prey of such religious factions as might spring up among them through the influence of the itinerant preachers of the time. Thereafter they had only such ministers or exhorters as were raised up among their own people. So ends the story of Occom's religious ministration among his people.

[9] *Wheelock Papers.*
[10] Eells' account—*MSS. Conn. Home Miss. Soc.*

CHAPTER XV

1785–1792

The famous author of "The Pioneers" has put into the mouth of Nathaniel Bumppo, his hero in adventure, the following impressive utterance: "When I look about me at these hills, where I used to could count sometimes twenty smokes, curling over the tree tops, from Delaware camps, it raises mournful thoughts, to think that not a redskin is left of them all: unless it be a drunken vagabond from the Oneidas or them Yankee Indians, who they say be moving up from the sea-shore, and who belong to none of God's creatures, to my seeming, being, as it were, neither fish nor flesh—neither white man nor savage. Well, well! the time has come at last, and I must go." [1] It was too bad, surely, Leather-stocking, that the Indian, who had been crowded out of New England and could no longer be a savage there if he would, should attempt to make a new home in the wilderness and live there like a civilized man! But one thing was worse—this, that the white man would not give him a chance to try it in peace.

Samson Occom, more than any other North American Indian, had considered the problem of civilizing his people. He knew their weaknesses and appreciated the difficulties. His experience in the Mohegan Land Case, his large acquaintance with Indian affairs in many tribes and his repeated conferences with those whites who were most engaged in such matters, had brought him to see the situation in all its lights and ponder

---

[1] *The Pioneers*, Cooper, Chap. XLI.

much over it.   If any native has merited the dignity of being
called an Indian statesman, that man was Samson Occom.
To recapitulate his views : he believed in the efficacy of Christian missions, and in education, particularly in industrial
affairs ; but he seems to have thought that the civilization of
the Indian depended in large measure upon his relation to the
land upon which he lived.   So long as he roamed at large in
the forest, he thought the native would remain a savage.   It
was necessary to gather them apart from the white men and
on land which they could not sell, where they could be taught
industrial pursuits and obtain a living from the soil.   Moreover, he believed in maintaining, so far as possible, a tribal
unity, establishing a form of self-government under the protection of the state, and preserving the Indian blood in its
purity, especially from a mixture with the negro.   These principles he sought to embody in the Brothertown tribe and the
town they founded.

We have already a considerable acquaintance with the individuals who were most prominent in this movement—Occom,
his brothers-in-law, David and Jacob Fowler, and his son-in-law,
Joseph Johnson, of one family by marriage, two of them ministers and all pupils of Rev. Eleazar Wheelock.   But other
educated Indians were participants in this affair.   Abraham
Simons, Emanuel Simons, James Niles and John Matthews,
among the founders, were also pupils at the Indian Charity
School.   Others educated there in part were interested, and
their kindred or descendants removed to Brothertown, as, for
instance, Samson Wauby, Samuel Niles, James Simons, Hannah Poquiantup, Hannah Garrett, Mary Seketer, Sarah Simons,
and Hannah Nonesuch.   Samuel Tallman was there before
the Revolution.   Samuel Ashbow, the Mohegan preacher, was
there for a time.   Benjamin Toucee, a son of David, an early
Farmington friend of the movement who died before its
accomplishment, had been a student at Dartmouth College.

In fact, nearly every one of Wheelock's pupils, who was of
the New England tribes and lived to that day, was concerned
in the founding of this Indian town.   It was a natural fruit of
Wheelock's work which he did not live to see and of which he
never dreamed.   Other conspicuous members of the Brothertown tribe had been pupils in the schools of the seven settlements of Christian Indians.   Such were Elijah Wampy, Samuel and John Adams, and Andrew Acorrocomb of Farmington ;
John Tuhie, Roger Wauby, and John Skeesuck of Charlestown ; and Samson Poquiantup and James Sampson of Groton.
Moreover, Occom had a large circle of family connections who
became residents at Brothertown.   His daughter Olive married Solomon Adams, son of the above-named Samuel, and
Anthony Paul married his daughter Christiana.   Ephraim
Pharaoh of Montauk was his brother-in-law.   He was related
to the Wauby, Samson and Poquiantup families.   Indeed,
before his death in 1792, he was surrounded with a people
whom he could call his own in a special sense, and they
included the most intelligent and religious portion of the tribe.
It was well that this was so, for in Occom's last days he had a
battle to fight in behalf of the landed rights of his people, and
in this his kindred gave him faithful support.

The Oneidas' grant of 1774 had conveyed a large and valuable tract of land west of the "Line of Property," and extending
along it about thirteen miles north and south.   These lands
were given to the New England Indians and their posterity
"without power of alienation," and they could "not be possessed by any persons deemed of the said tribes who are
descended from or have intermixed with negroes or molat-
toes."   Occom and his friends considered this as a deed of
gift by which they had full title to the said lands.   Scarcely
had they located there, however, when the Oneidas, at the
instigation, it was said, of the whites, set up the claim that the
New England Indians had not fulfilled the conditions of the

grant and it was void. This was in 1785. We cannot imagine what those conditions were unless the lands were to be occupied at once, which had certainly been bravely attempted. Meanwhile, of course, circumstances had changed, and the Oneidas undoubtedly wanted to reclaim the tract. Early in 1786 a council was held, and they proposed to give the Brothertown Indians, in lieu of their claim, 640 acres, whereon those who had already emigrated could live.[2] This was promptly declined. On the sixteenth of October, at another council, an account of which is given in Occom's diary, the Oneidas repeated their offer, and wanted them to "live at large" on their lands. Again on the twenty-third they urged their case and threatened to take back all the lands if the Brothertown Indians did not accept their offer. Occom was unmoved, and the intelligent majority supported him. A few, however, were ready to yield. This was the beginning of the factional disputes which so embittered Occom's last days. So matters stood until the 22d of September, 1788, when the Oneidas, by a treaty made at Fort Schuyler, ceded all their lands to the state of New York, excepting their own reservation, and one for the Brothertown and another for the Stockbridge Indians.[3] This reduced their extensive tract to one "two miles in breadth and three miles in length." The Oneidas agreed to this in the negotiations; but the state of New York would not thus disregard the conveyance of 1774, which Occom had recorded in the office of the Secretary of State in Connecticut, and upon which he planted his feet to stand for their rights. So the General Assembly of New York, having a desire to do justice to the New England Indians, in "An Act for the Sale and Disposition of Lands" passed February 25, 1789, provided that the Surveyor General should

---

[2] *N. Y. Arch., Letts. on Indian Affairs*, James Dean to Gov. Clinton, June 7, 1786,
[3] *MS. Rec. Supt. Brothertown Indians*; *Proceedings of the Com. af Ind. Affairs* Hough, I, 122, 230, 241-243.

lay out for them "all that part of the tract of land, formerly
given to them by the Oneida Indians, which is included in
the cession lately made by the Oneida Indians to the people
of this State," and south of the lands which by the same act
were confirmed to Samuel Kirkland and his sons.[4] This
tract was six times larger than the reservation in the treaty,
and when it was finally surveyed, in 1795, was found to
contain 24,052 acres. Thus Occom's wisdom and courage
were rewarded. Doubtless also this result was partly due
to Governor George Clinton, who was very friendly toward
Occom's purposes, and did all he could to further them, even
after this Indian was in his unmarked grave.

The act of 1789 had also provided that this tract should be
called Brothertown, and should remain for "the cultivation,
improvement and use" of the New England Indians, "but
without any power of alienation or right of leasing the same
lands or any part thereof, for any longer term than ten years
and without any power of granting such leases where there
shall be any subsisting lease including the same lands." Here
was another source of trouble. Occom had not been able to
prevent New England Indians of the baser sort from attaching
themselves to the Brothertown tribe. Some came who belonged to other tribes than those to whom the land had been
given. These built their huts on the tract, claiming equal
rights with the founders. They did not recognize the tribal
authority, and as yet the state had not constituted any town
government. Since the voluntary organization of 1785 the
tribe had not met to choose officers.[5] The original five
trustees still acted—Roger Wauby, David Fowler, Elijah
Wampy, John Tuhie and Abraham Simons. However, on
the 10th of October, 1790, a town-meeting was held, Occom
being present. After an unsuccessful attempt to choose new

---

[4] *Laws of N. Y.*, Reprint, III, 70.
[5] *Conn. Hist. Soc., Indian Papers*, Lett. Occom to Ezra L'Hommedieu.

trustees, it was decided that the old board should continue until the March following, and should consult and act for the good of the town meanwhile. They met in November, but Elijah Wampy was found to be opposed to the plans of the others, who were Occom's particular friends. Wampy drew up a petition, which was signed largely by the interlopers, and this was sent to the General Assembly, a Martha's Vineyard Indian named Puichaker being their messenger. The act of 1789 was understood to allow leasing for a period of ten years, and the Wampy party began at once to make such leases to the whites who were coming in as settlers.[6] New farms were then taken up by these Indians, which also in some cases were leased to the whites. This was extremely demoralizing. It put a premium on fraud, and was disloyal to the purposes of the town. Had it not been for the mercifully slow progress of white immigration, the greater part of the tract would have been leased out. Occom was distressed, but not utterly discouraged. He also wrote a petition which he carried to the General Assembly by the authority of the other trustees. There he was known to many and had influence. His "perigrinations" were in evidence. The result was the passage of "An Act for the relief of the Indians residing in Brothertown and New Stockbridge," dated February 21, 1791.[7] In this bill the ideas of Occom as to Indian town government were to some extent embodied. It provided for an annual town-meeting, the first Tuesday in April, at which all male Indians twenty-one years of age should choose a clerk to preside and keep the records, a marshal and three trustees, the latter "by and with the consent of the Mayor of the City of Albany for the time being." These trustees were given

---

[6] Some of these leases are extant. We have one from James Toxcoit to Abraham Oaks, and have seen several others.

[7] *Laws of N. Y.*, Reprint, III, 212. The Assembly by a resolution, February 24, 1791, advanced £15 for the payment of Occom's expenses in appearing in behalf of the Brothertown and New Stockbridge Indians.

power to lay out lots as they should think necessary to the
Indian families; to lease a tract not exceeding 640 acres, the
rents thereof to be applied for maintaining a minister and free
school; to bring actions for trespass against any whites; and
to adjudicate cases of trespass or debt among the Indians
themselves, and levy for the judgment in a sum not to exceed
twenty shillings.

Meanwhile the leasing of home lots had been going on, and
before Occom's return about 2,000 acres had been taken by
the whites. A fine grove of pine and a cedar swamp, particularly valuable to the Indians and designed for town use, had
been disposed of. Occom was not wholly opposed to ten-year
leases; but as their lands had never been surveyed he thought
such action was premature and should always have the consent of the town authorities. When the time appointed in
the above act for organizing the town government came, they
were so demoralized that they could not elect trustees as provided. Here was a new difficulty. The time having passed
they thought nothing could be done. Again Occom appealed
to the General Assembly, and that body, April 12, 1792, re-
enacted the former measure, appointing the first Tuesday in
May following for town organization, and authorized the
forcible ejectment of the whites.[8] In this act the trustees were
called peacemakers, and the title was certainly appropriate.
Neither measure, however, had distinctly invalidated the ten-
year leases. The whites crowded in and urged on the Wampy
party in opposition. Occom became unpopular with the
white settlers. The Oneidas had not forgiven him for maintaining his rights against them so successfully. He had also
incurred the displeasure of John Sergeant and his friends
among the Stockbridge Indians. He was surrounded by
enemies. Only those who had entered into his long-cherished
plans, the intelligent, substantial and more religious Indians

---

[8]*Laws of N. Y.*, Reprint, III, 379.

of Brothertown, who saw that he was fighting in their behalf, and David Fowler foremost among them, adhered to his leadership. His experiment in Indian town government had not been so far a signal success. Now in his sixty-ninth year —an old man before his time, who like a hemlock had endured many storms and outlived its usefulness—his courage may have failed him. A greater Moses than he had become discouraged at the rebellious hearts of his people. So in the winter of 1791, hoping to find some peace among the Stockbridge branch of his flock, he removed over the hill westward to Tuscarora. His work was done, and there he died on the fourteenth of July, 1792.

Let us follow to its conclusion this land war of the Brothertown Indians, before we consider the circumstances of Occom's death and burial. The excitement was somewhat allayed by the loss of their leader, but the leasing went on. In the course of two years the Indians came to see that Occom was right. Even Elijah Wampy seems to have repented of his action. Three peacemakers were chosen—David Fowler, John Tuhie and John Paul—and these set about considering what could be done. The whites, too, were troubled, having only ten-year leases and some uncertainty as to them. They appointed a committee consisting of Asa Hamlin, James Cowing, Jr., Ithmar Coe, Simon Hubbard and Solomon Kellogg, who petitioned for legislative action February 14, 1794.[9] In their statement of the case they said that two hundred farms had been located on the tract, and one hundred and fifty families were settled on them. A sawmill and grist-mill had also been erected. But from insecurity of title they could make no improvements, and had no church or schools. On the seventh of October the Indian peacemakers addressed a complaint to Governor Clinton against Bender Webber, Charles Wilbor, Isaac Curtis, Nathaniel Lowring and Samuel Lewis, stating

[9] *N. Y. Arch., Assembly Papers, Ind. Aff.*, 1783-1810, 95, 97.

that they were trespassers on their lands. This petition was signed by the peacemakers, and Samuel Adams, Roger Wobby, David Fowler, Jun., Jeremiah Tuhie, Samuel Scipio, Samuel Brusheill, Elijah Wimpey, John Skeesuck, Christopher Skeesuck, and Elijah Wimpey, Jun.[10] A letter which accompanied the petition recited their grievances, and had, in addition to the above names, the following signatures: Obadiah Scippio, George Paul, Joseph Woby, Isaac Wobby, Oliver Peter, Solomon Cochegan, George Crosley, James Waucus, Ephraim Pharaoh, Frederick Peters, Nhamon Wobby, Henry Davies, Amos Hutton, and Thomas Pechorker. These were the principal men of Brothertown. Governor Clinton took immediate action, and ordered Colonel William Colbrath, the sheriff of Herkimer county, to eject the trespassers, which had been authorized by the act of 1792.[11] Esquires Hugh White and Moses Foot, who were among the principal men in the county, interceded for them. The result was, that the ejectment was delayed and the General Assembly took the whole matter into consideration.[12] The decision was favorable to the Indians. It was a conspicuous example of justice, the most so of any we have met with in the history of Indian land claims,—a lasting honor to the state of New York. The verdict was embodied in " An Act relative to Lands in Brothertown," passed March 31, 1795.[13] This constituted Samuel Jones, Ezra L'Hommedieu and Zina Hitchcock commissioners to examine into and settle all matters relating to Brothertown lands. They were authorized to set off a tract of not less than six thousand nor more than ten thousand acres for the use of the Indians, dividing the same into lots, and apportioning them to the several families, notwithstanding any leases to whites resident thereon. The remainder of the lands

[10] *N. Y. Arch., Letts. on Indian Affairs,* 1785-1825, 2.
[11] *N. Y. Arch., Assembly Papers, Ind. Aff.,* 1783-1810, 263.
[12] *Ibid.,* pp. 245, 251, 263, 265, 269.
[13] *Laws of N. Y.,* Reprint, III, 585.

were to be sold to the lessees, the mean price being not
less than sixteen shillings per acre, allowing for improvements, if they were removed. They were authorized to
take mortgages in payment. These commissioners performed
their duties in the summer of 1795, making a census of
the Indians by families, giving the age of each, and as-
signing lots. A survey was made by Garret Cluett.[14] Of
the 24.052 acres in the tract, 9,390 were set off in 149 lots to
the Indians, and the balance sold to the white lessees. They
received in cash £97, 2s, and in mortgages at six per cent.,
payable on demand after the first Tuesday of July, 1805,
£15,217, 4s. The state afterwards took the mortgages, and
the whole amount was invested as the Brothertown fund.

One difficulty was encountered by the commissioners. They
found it hard to decide as to the Indians who were entitled to
land, and recommended in their report, February 18, 1796,
the passage of an act relating to the matter. This was done
on the fourth of March following.[15] Thus ended the contest
of the New England Indians for their rights in the land given
to them more than twenty years before.

Samson Occom died in the battle; but the victory was his.
For years the income of this fund was expended by their superintendents for the benefit of his people. It provided many
industrial advantages, secured to them the privileges of education, ministered to their necessities, and its benefits followed
them in their second emigration, and are traceable to this day.
Thus he who had led them forth into their promised land, to
whom more than any other the maintenance of their claim was
due, blessed his people after he had departed from them.

The last days of Samson Occom's life, as we have stated,
were passed at Tuscarora. He had located a home lot at

---

[14] *Map and Field Book, Surveyor General's Office*, Albany ; *Rec. Supt. Brother
town Indians.*

[15] *Laws of N. Y.*, Reprint, III, 655.

Brothertown several years before he removed his family thither from Mohegan. His parishioners, he notes in his diary, came in August, 1787, to clear some land for him. This lot was undoubtedly No. 10 in the survey of 1795, which was then assigned by the superintendents to Anthony Paul in accordance with their plan of retaining the locations of early settlers in their families. Occom built there a log house, sufficient for the humble needs of his family. Most of his children had grown up. Benoni, Theodosia and Lemuel may have come with him to Brothertown in 1789. Andrew Gifford, a youth of fifteen years, and Sally, his youngest, certainly did, the latter dying before her father. It will be remembered that the center of the town in 1785 was located at David Fowler's place on the hill, lot 105. This was the actual center in very early days—the location of 1775. Roger Wauby was three miles west of this—outside the bounds of the later town.[16] Elijah Wampy was half a mile to the northwest; Abraham Simons a mile to the northeast; John Tuhie east at the foot of the hill and next south of Occom. The younger men afterwards took up lots in the valley, Elijah Wampy, Jr., and David Fowler, Jr., being located on lots 15 and 16, where the village of Deansville now has its center. Therefore, as David Fowler's place was the early location where they first worshiped, being the eastern section of Occom's Stockbridge and Brothertown parish, it was supposed, before the place was visited by the writer, that there they established a burial-place in accordance with their tribal notions, as well as the custom they knew so well in New England. Death went with them into the wilderness. On the nineteenth of October, 1786, their council at Oneida was interrupted by news of the death of " Old Uncle Cornelius " [Hannable ?], the oldest man in the town. The next day, toward night, they assembled at the house of mourning, where Occom says, " I delivered a short discourse . . . and

---

[16] *N. Y. Arch , Assembly Papers, Ind. Aff.,* 1783–1810, 105.

from thence [we] went to the grove, and we finished burying after sunset." During his absence the following winter
there were several deaths—Jacob Fowler being one. When
Abraham Simons died they also buried him in "the grove."
Evidently they had then a tribal burial-place, presumably near
the center. Occom's young daughter died. She would have been
buried there. While he was away on his mission to the General Assembly in the spring of 1791, one of his grandchildren
died, probably one of the Paul family. Samuel Kirkland
makes this entry in his diary under March 15, 1791 : " I have
now returned from Brothertown, where I have attended the
funeral of a grand child of Mr. Occom—the whole village assembled on the occasion—it has been a very solemn & affecting meeting—discoursed from Mark 10 : 27." Already then,
before Occom's death, even if the tribe had no common burial-
place, the large circle of his kindred, numbering not less than
thirty in 1792, so loyal to his ministry and leadership, would
have claimed a sacred acre from the forest for their dead.

   The house which David Fowler built in 1775—the first in
that wilderness—has long since been torn down by the fingers
of time. Some of the timbers of his hallowed barn remain in
a later structure. The farm is now owned by Mr. Andrew H.
Wier, who bought it of Mr. Alonzo G. Miller. The white man
draws water from the well the Indian pioneer dug. On this
place, only a quarter of a mile southward from the house, in
the edge of the wood, which was a "grove" a hundred years
ago, there is an Indian burial-ground. The woodsman's sled
has broken off the tops of some rude headstones. Brothertown Indians are still living who remember when the tribe
made their burials in that spot, and they say this continued
down to about 1812.[17] Its distance from the more populous

[17] There were four other Indian burial-places in Brothertown later. One was at
the foot of the hill where the present cemetery is ; another was near the center of
Deansville, north of the highway and between the railroad and the river, called the

district in the valley eastward, finally led to its abandonment. This digression will prepare us to appreciate the conditions in 1792, and locate the burial-place of the Brothertown minister. The exact date of Occom's removal from his old home to Tuscarora is not known. A young Stockbridge Indian, John Quinney, who was at Orange Dale Academy, wrote him, January 26, 1792, that one Samuel Littleman had arrived there on the twenty-first, and had informed him that his minister "was about to move with his family to our village, which he had long wished for."[18] This letter was addressed to Occom at Muhheconnuck. He removed, therefore, about the middle of January, and into a house about a mile from Tuscarora village, probably owned by some of his friends. Perhaps he did not intend to remain there permanently. A little land would have been sufficient for his purposes, for he had returned to his old trade of manufacturing woodenware.

There are two accounts of Occom's death. One is given us in Prime's History of Long Island, and in Sprague's Annals. It professes to have been "prepared from the recital of his wife." We quote it in full:

For some time he had a presentiment that his death was near. As he accustomed himself, in his earlier life, to the manufacture of pails and cooper-ware, he still devoted what strength he had, when leisure permitted, to the same employment. One day he observed to his wife, that he must finish a churn soon, that he had commenced, or he might not live to do it. He went out to his work, a little distance from the house, finished the churn and started to return. His wife observed him crossing a run of

"Dugway" burial-place; the third was near John Tuhie's place and the fourth on the the farm of Asa Dick. There may have been others. Our interviews with aged Indians—Elias Dick, James Simons, J. C. Fowler, Rebecca Johnson, and Hannah Commuck—leave no doubt as to the fact that all the early burials were on the hill. They name a number whose deaths occurred in their youth, and variously estimate the graves there from seventy-five to one hundred. Here, doubtless, Jacob Fowler was buried, and all who died in Occom's time. David Fowler and Hannah Garret were among the last.

[18] *Conn. Hist. Soc., Indian Papers.*

water near the house upon a pole; looking towards him again, a few minutes after, she saw that he had fallen and going to him she found him dead.[19]

The other account was printed in the *Connecticut Gazette* of New London, August 2, 1792, and was doubtless sent by messenger to Occom's kindred at Mohegan. It is as follows:

Died at New Stockbridge, in the vicinity of Oneida, in the 69th year of his age, the Rev. Samson Occom, in a very sudden and unexpected manner. About a week before he died he complained to his wife of a very uncommon and distressing pain in his vitals, which occasioned a faintness, but it was soon over. A few hours before his death the same disorder came on again, but as before soon left him—after which he eat as hearty a dinner as usual, told his wife he would ride to one of his neighbors and get him to accompany him to a cedar swamp in search of some timber he was wanting. His wife in vain remonstrated against it; he went, and just before they came to the swamp he told the man he must rest, asked for water, desired the man to call for help, which he did, he then took off his coat and as the man returned, he said, I have done—and appeared inclined to sleep—asked his friend to ease him down, which done, he folded his hands across his breast and expired in a few minutes. On Sunday the 15th inst. his remains were decently interred—previous to which the Rev. Mr. Kirkland preached his funeral sermon from Matt. xxiv: 44. Upwards of 300 Indians, from different tribes, attended. Mr. Occom was of the Mohegan tribe of Indians and removed with a number of that tribe a few years since to Oneida.[20]

The latter being a contemporary account, and more natural in its circumstances, is very likely the true one. Neither of them, however, states the place of burial. Rev. John Sergeant was absent from New Stockbridge at the time, or his diary might inform us on this point. But the manuscript journal of Samuel Kirkland gives the following account of the event, under date of July 16th:

Last Saturday evening, about 10 o'clock, a messenger came to me with the news of Mr. Occum's death at Tuscarora. This was very sudden and unexpected. I was requested to preach his funeral sermon on Lord's day at 3 o'clock P. M. I agreed to be there seasonably, after attending divine

[19] Prime's *Hist. of Long Island*, p. 112; Sprague's *Annals*, III, 194.
[20] Conn. Hist. Soc., *Conn. Gaz.*, Aug. 2, 1792. Cf. *Conn. Courant* and *Am. Mercury*, July 30, 1792.

service in the morning early at Kanonwalchäle. The Indians were so alarmed at the sudden death of Mr. Occum that they began to collect at Tuscarora from the various settlements very early in the morning. By a mistake of the messenger they were led to conceive that the first meeting would be held there instead of at Kanonwalchäle ; as many of the Indians came the distance of ten miles. After an exhortation and prayer at the house of the deceased, we moved about a mile to a bower near the center of the town, for the sake of convenience, there being no house sufficiently large to contain one half of the Indians who were assembled on the occasion. I discoursed from Math. 24. 44 in both the Indian and English languages, that all might understand me on that solemn occasion. The Indians appeared to be struck with unusual awe and reverence of Him who is the Lord of life and death. In the evening attended a conference with a small number till near midnight.

Several later references are made in Kirkland's journals to Occom's death, which indicate that a profound impression was left among the Indians. During the following week, he had "various conferences with Indians of different tribes and parties, principally on the subject of Mr. Occum's death as an alarming and instructive providence." On the following Sabbath, he preached at Kanonwalohäle sermons from Psalm 90 : 12, and Phil. 1 : 21–24, appropriate to the event. The assembly "seemed to melt into tenderness with many sighs and tears." At the request of the Stockbridge Indians, in the absence of Mr. Sergeant, he preached at Tuscarora a week later. He says there was a large gathering of Brothertown, Oriske, Stockbridge, Oneida and Tuscarora Indians. "Many came with a view and in expectation of hearing not only a general, but a particular and minute character given of Mr. Occum. The divisions, however, among the Indians were such that I thought it not prudent to attempt it and indeed was advised to omit it. Discoursed from Job 33 : 12, 13."

As to Samson Occom's burial, there seems to be but one interpretation to be put upon Kirkland's account. If the burial had been at Tuscarora, they would have borne the body, after the service, to the grave, and he would have included a mention of it. They moved to the bower only to find a convenient auditorium.   Evidently the body was not then to be buried.   Many were there who had reason to mourn the death of this renowned Indian—the minister, his friend, of whose mission he had been an inspiration in youth, the Oneidas, to whom he had carried the gospel thirty years before, the pupils who had been taught in his wigwam at Montauk, the subjects of his fervid ministry in the Indian settlements of New England, and, above all, his own beloved and misguided people; but his own kindred were there—a goodly company of them, and the burial was their service.   A Mohegan was never willingly allowed to rest away from his own—from their homes and their graves !   So it must have been that they returned to the house of mourning from the place where they had found a cathedral under the arches of the woodland.   As the summer's sun was declining in the west, at their customary hour, the body of this Indian Moses was lifted, not by angels, but by the strong arms of his faithful friends, the purest blood of the New England aborigines, and borne up the hill, by the way they had often gone, and laid beside his own dust—a king like those of the Scriptures to rest in the inheritance of David !

The unmarked grave was thus in the keeping of Samson Occom's brother beloved and loyal friend, David Fowler. Time has dealt ruthlessly with that consecrated acre.   Doubtless the last fifty years would have swept away all traces of its existence had it not been that the descendants of David Fowler and Hannah Garrett, before they joined the westward pilgrimage of the race, long after their deaths, raised a white marble slab to their memory, whereon the wanderer in that woodland may read :

DAVID FOWLER
died March 31, 1807.   Aet
72 years

HANNAH wife of
DAVID FOWLER died
Aug. 1811.   Aet. 64 years

BURIAL PLACE OF THE CHRISTIAN INDIANS

CHAPTER XVI

INDIAN TOWN GOVERNMENT

1785–1842

The town government, which the Brothertown Indians had known in New England, afforded an opportunity for individual independence which was very pleasing to the Indian nature. Those who had come to Oneida had been emancipated from the sachem's tyrannical authority. Quite naturally, they went to the extreme of individualism, and from this arose many of their early troubles. In time, however, they settled down, and their town went on as well as is generally the case in new communities.

Some of these Indians from Farmington, as they were about to remove, petitioned the General Assembly for a copy of the statutes of Connecticut, on the ground that they were expected to observe laws of which they were ignorant.[1] Their request was granted, and doubtless this was the volume which they carried into the wilderness and used as the basis of town regulations. We know that their intent was to establish the ancient Connecticut town. At their first meeting, even in 1785, they chose " fence-viewers " when there was not a pair of bars for many miles around. Their early purpose, however, was modified on account of their troubles by the authorities of the state of New York. The act passed by the General Assembly, March 4, 1796, set off their one hundred and forty-nine lots from the town of Paris, and provided finally for Indian town government. It authorized the appointment, by

[1] *Conn. Arch., Indians,* II, 195.

the governor and council, of three commissioners, known as the superintendents of the Brothertown Indians, who were to determine what persons were entitled to rights, permanently assign lots, divide the land of deceased Indians among their heirs, advise as to the expenditure of the income of the invested funds, maintain a school among them, prevent the illegal sale of spirituous liquors, and exercise a general supervision over their affairs. The appointment of an attorney was also authorized to defend their rights in the courts. Accordingly, the following were chosen superintendents, March 26, 1796 : William Floyd, Thomas Eddy and Edmund Prior, and Joseph Kirkland became their attorney.[2] William Floyd visited them in June, 1796, to examine into their condition and needs. The record-book, which contains the legislation relating to the Brothertown Indians and the subsequent proceedings of the superintendents, is still preserved by the tribe at Brothertown, Wisconsin.

So much of their government, therefore, was taken from the Indians, but in its main features the town was ordered by the voters therein. The above act authorized the appointment by the governor and council of five Indians as " Keepers of the Peace," or " Peacemakers," who should hold office during the pleasure of the council. They, or any three of them, were empowered to hold a court at Brothertown on the first Monday of each month, and hear and determine all disputes or controversies concerning debts and trespasses, where the sum due or damages sustained did not exceed five pounds. All violations of the town by-laws were to be tried in this peacemakers' court, and a proper fine imposed, to be collected by

---

[2] The following also served as superintendents during the town's existence : Henry McNiel, Thomas Hart, Bill Smith, George Brayton, John Murray, Jr., Ashahel Curtis, Uri Doolittle, Joseph Stebbins, William Root. Nathan Davis, Elijah Wilson, Austin Wygatt, Samuel L. Hubbard and Samuel Comstock. William Hotchkiss was their attorney about 1812. An act of May 25, 1841 abolished this office, and reduced the superintendents to one.

due process, failing which, upon complaint of the peacemakers, the attorney cou d imprison for thirty days. They were also constituted commissioners of highways, which were to be four rods wide, with power to lay out, alter or direct the repair of the same. An annual town-meeting was to be held the first Tuesday in April, at which the senior peacemaker should preside, and in which all males twenty-one years of age and upwards should be voters. They were to elect a town clerk, two overseers of the poor, two marshals, and so many overseers of highways as should be thought necessary. On their own authority they also elected fence-viewers, a pound-keeper and tithing-men, whose duty it was to give notice to all evil-doers in the form of a complaint. Moreover, in this town-meeting they were to enact such rules, regulations and by-laws as should be deemed expedient in ordering their affairs. In the exercise of this latter privilege we shall see best the character of Indian legislation.

The senior peacemaker appointed under this act was David Fowler, who served until his death in 1807. Two of his associates also held office until they died—John Tuhie in 1811 and John Skeesuck in 1807. The others were Isaac Wauby, afterwards known as "Elder Wauby," and Samuel Scipio. On the fifteenth of May, 1796, the first regular town-meeting was held in the schoolhouse, though the date thereafter was the first Tuesday in April, as provided. Officers were then chosen, and David Fowler, Jr., the babe born in Samuel Kirkland's hut in 1767, was elected town clerk, an office which he held until 1802. The "Town Records of Brothertown," which he and his successors kept with commendable care until there were not enough Indians remaining in the town to fill the offices, are an interesting memorial of Indian civilization altogether unique in American history.

The laws which were made from time to time in this Indian town-meeting had largely the character of ordinances. They

related to fences, highways, damage by dogs, stray cattle and
the like matters.   The duties of town officers also were defined.
It was ordered that any one elected to an office and declining to
serve, without reasonable excuse, should pay a fine of two and
a half dollars, while those who neglected their duties were to
pay twice that sum.   As to women, the widows were to work
on the roads, or at any other public business, half as much as
the men.   It was further declared, " That it shall not be lawful
by the authority of Brothertown that any woman shall be permitted to speak that has causes depending in the Brothertown
courts without asking some particular question or she shall
apply to some suitable man to speak in her behalf."   They
made stringent laws against immorality, profanity, drunkenness, theft, extortion, idleness, neglect of children, and marriages with persons of negro blood.   A person who should
display signs of intoxication at town-meeting was punished as
a great offender.   In many cases the penalty was a confinement in the stocks, though we do not know that they employed
this mode of punishment.   Dancing or frolicking on Saturday
or Sunday nights was forbidden.   It was unlawful to harbor
or conceal a fugitive slave, servant or apprentice.   The following are samples of the laws by which they sought to secure
the order and decorum of Puritan New England in their
Indian community.

There shall be no travelling, servile labouring or working (works of necessity and charity excepted) shooting, fishing, sporting, playing, horseracing,
hunting or any unlawful exercise or pastime, by any Person or Persons on
the first day of the week commonly called Sunday

If any person shall permit any playing with Cards or dice in his house, or
bet win or lose any sum of money at such play and shall be thereof convicted, [he] shall forfeit and pay a sum not to exceed five Dollars or under
fifty cents for every such offence, one half to the complainant and the other
half to the People of Brothertown.

If any of said inhabitants shall Divulge any Report about any of said
inhabitants either Male or Female, and shall not have sufficient proof to
support what he, she or they hath Divulged and reported, then the Divulger

or Divulgers shall pay a fine of ten shillings for every Breach of this bye-law if found so convicted.

If any of the inhabitants shall abuse any one of the aforesaid inhabitants in their Houses or at any other place either by foul language or assault, he or they shall be immediately summoned to be and appear before the Peace-makers of said town, then and there to be adjudged before them as the Case may be in their judgment to decide the matter, to be deemed just and equitable.

Some of these laws were in substance those of New Eng-land at the time. As there was great laxity among the whites of the new settlements round about them in many things which the Indians endeavored to prohibit, it was not strange that some of these were a dead letter. But they made honest and earn-est efforts to enforce most of them, and in some measure they succeeded. The peacemaker's court held their first session the first Monday in September, 1797, and thereafter at inter-vals for forty years. Their extant records show that every manner of complaint was tried before them. They fined offenders with vigor. There is, indeed, no reason to think that the town was not well-governed. More and more, as the years went by, they became accustomed to their town govern-ment and the supervision of the superintendents was less and less needed. This does not mean, of course, that Brother-town was free from the common vices of Indians, but it was as much so as other frontier settlements of whites. There was some drunkenness and the consequent ills. Notable cases which made a great impression were the murder of Eunice Peters by her husband, George Peters, at Rome, February 24, 1800, and the killing of Joseph Tuhie by John Tuhie, 2d, May 1, 1817.[3]

One object of the emigration had been to make of these Indians an agricultural people. How did they succeed in this respect? The assignment of 1795 located most of the fami-lies on their original claims. These they had cleared to a

---

[3] Jones' *Annals of Oneida County*, pp. 43, 44, 96.

considerable extent. Barns had been built. They had in a
short time stock of all kinds and enclosed fields. On the
twenty-sixth of September, 1799, Brothertown was visited by
Timothy Dwight. He had a strong inclination to see civilized
Indian life, and had been told that it might probably be seen
at Brothertown. He gives us the following account of their
condition :

> The settlement is formed on the declivity of a hill, running from north to
> south. The land is excellent, and the spot in every respect well chosen.
> Here forty families of these people have fixed themselves in the business of
> agriculture. They have cleared the ground on both sides of the road about
> a quarter of a mile in breadth and about four miles in length. Three of
> them have framed houses. One, named Amos Hutton, has a good house
> well finished, and a large barn well built. Several others have barns also.
> The remaining houses are of logs, and differ little from those of the whites
> when formed of the same material. Their husbandry is generally much
> inferior to that of the white people. Their fences are indifferent, and their
> meadows and arable grounds are imperfectly cleared. Indeed almost every-
> where is visible that slack hand, that disposition to leave everything unfin-
> ished, which peculiarly characterizes such Indians as have left the savage
> life. I have observed that the house and barn of Amos Hutton were both
> well built. We had an opportunity to see the interior of the house, and
> by the neatness which everywhere appeared, both in the building and furni-
> ture, were assured that his wife was an industrious and thorough housewife.
> Mr. Kirkland informed me that this man lives well, that he keeps always
> one and sometimes two yoke of good oxen, two or three horses, and three
> or four cows ; that he is an exact paymaster; and that although no debt
> against an Indian is recoverable by law, he is readily trusted for anything
> which he is willing to buy. He is probably the fairest example of industry,
> economy, and punctuality, which these people can boast. Most of them
> will leave their own business to labour for the white inhabitants. They are
> universally civil in their deportment. The men and boys took off their hats,
> and the girls courtesied, as we passed by them. They speak decent English,
> and much excel the ordinary Dutch people in the correctness of their pro-
> nunciation. One of them tends a saw mill, built by the state for this settle-
> ment.[4]

President Dwight evidently did not traverse the entire town
or he would have seen, especially on the hill westward, many

4 Dwight's *Travels*, Lond., 1823, III, 168 ff.

cleared and well-tilled acres. The road to which he refers was that now running north and south through the village of Deansville, named by the Indians Federal Street. Amos Hutton lived on lot No. 5, toward the northern limit. There were certainly others as skilled in farming as he, and notably David Fowler. Dwight's census of families is too small, for in 1795 lots were assigned to thirty-nine families and in 1799 there were about sixty. More joined them about 1800. In 1813 they numbered 302. In 1819 there were said to be sixty families and twenty-two widows whose lots were leased to whites for their benefit. The condition of their fields should be judged in view of the fact that this was a new settlement. Many had not been accustomed to agriculture, and they had not been able to accomplish all they would for lack of means. With praiseworthy zeal they had undertaken what was for the Indian a great work. The first request made of their superintendents in 1796 was for "four pair of oxen, twelve cows, one hundred and twenty bushels of corn, three barrels of pork, six ploughs, six chains, three sets of harrow teeth, three sets of cart irons and one hundred sheep." [5] In 1805 the town voted to give a premium on the raising of grain, and to encourage those who would build houses and barns. It was determined in 1818 that one who cleared thirty acres out of fifty was to have twenty-five more for farming purposes. Examinations into their progress were made from time to time by the state of New York. From these it appears that in 1813 they had 2,000 acres of land cleared and under cultivation, and they were "considerably advanced in agricultural knowledge." They then had ninety cows, thirty horses, sixteen yoke of oxen, ninety-three young cattle, eighty-eight sheep and a great number of swine. They had a grist-mill, two saw-mills, sixteen framed houses, eighteen framed barns, twenty-one ploughs, seventeen sleds, three carts and three wagons.

[5] *Supt. Rec.*, Lett. Floyd to Eddy, June 19, 1796.

Four of their number were carpenters, two blacksmiths, four
shoemakers, two tailors and five weavers. During the preceding year they had manufactured 320 yards of woolen and 600
yards of linen cloth, and they had produced 11,300 bushels of
grain of various kinds and raised 3,400 bushels of potatoes.
The report of 1825 shows that during the year they had manufactured 1,495 yards of woolen, 890 yards of linen, 302 yards
of wool and cotton and 188 yards of cotton and linen cloth,
which was 700 yards more than they had made the year before.
This thrift in weaving had been brought about by premiums
paid from their annuity on domestic manufactures.[6] Industry
and sobriety were also rewarded by payments in nails, glass,
and other articles used in their improvements. At that time
it was said that "the greater part of them are men whose
lives and characters would disgrace no community being temperate and industrious." They were living in good and convenient houses which were kept clean and neat. Their farms
were well fenced, they had good roads and their crops were
larger than they needed to use. Dwight saw them at an early
day and compared them with the white settlers round about—
the best blood of New England. He recites some interesting facts as to certain ones among them, whose skin had
begun to change to whiteness, notably Samuel Adams who
"is almost become a white man." We should think that the
signs indicated leprosy were it not that he distinctly denies
this. Perhaps his witness exaggerated somewhat. This was
certainly a symptom of the white man's civilization which the
Indians had not looked for.

The chief public improvement which interested them in
early years was the town roads. They began at once to
widen the Indian trails which crossed their tract. One of
these led eastward through the town of Paris, or over "Hanover Hill" as the Indians termed it. That which was most

[6] *N. Y. Arch., Assembly Papers, Ind. Aff.*, Vol. 41, p. 93.

used, and doubtless older, was one from Utica through the present village of Clinton. It entered their tract by two ways, one going west from the ford of the Oriskany, between lots 4 and 5, and there uniting with the other which ran through lot 1 from the northeast corner. From the point where these joined, the road went southward until between lots 7 and 8, where it bore to the southwest, and in lot 11 led westward up over the hill to lot 105, where David Fowler lived. Thence it ran between lots 118 and 119 to Tuscarora. This was the original approach to their town, and it was put in condition for their travel before the town government was organized. There was also a road branching off from it in lot 11, and leading southward through their tract, dividing again between lots 15 and 16. One of these went southwest, out at lot 133, and the other went southeast, across the Oriskany, southward and out at lot 45. Their main street was from lot 5 to lot 16. In 1796 this was moved by the peacemakers farther east and ran at the foot of the hill, being the present highway north and south, through Deansville. We have thus the earliest roads through the town. The road from David Fowler's, eastward, down the hill to lot 13 was laid out about 1804, though it was in use earlier. That same year the road from Deansville west to Augusta was laid out. The one from lot 5 northwest dates from 1802, that across the southwest corner from 1809, and that from lot 7 southwest to lot 118 probably from the discontinuance of the old road up the hill.

As already stated, the town of Brothertown as constituted in 1795 contained 9,390 acres, the balance of their tract being sold to the whites. About a third of this is now located in the town of Kirkland and the remainder in Marshall. It was supposed to comprise 149 lots, but in a later survey made by Peleg Gifford in 1828, at the direction of Thomas Dean, only 148 lots were found, containing 9,587 acres. Most of these were fifty-acre lots. Those of Elijah Wampy and David Fow-

ler were the largest, the former having 169 and the latter
155 acres. This later survey has been used as the basis of
various maps.[7] As shown in the "Atlas of Oneida County,"
Samson Occom's house was located on the western end of lot
10, marked as the residence of J. Whitney, and on the old road.
The first schoolhouse of 1788 stood south of it on lot 11.
Occom, therefore, lived within the present limits of the town
of Kirkland, where also David Fowler was located and the
ancient cemetery.

The first mill erected in Brothertown was the sawmill to
which reference is made by President Dwight. It was built
only the year before his visit, and was located on the west end
of lot 24, bordering on Oriskany creek, two acres of which
the town bought for £10 from Thomas Isaacs.[8] A grist-mill
was built in 1801 on the creek between lots 16 and 20. This
was tended by various Indians appointed for the purpose,
among them Asa and Paul Dick. The latter received fifteen
dollars a month in 1808 for the service. Some time before
that a second sawmill was erected in the south part of the
town.

The act of 1796 provided that a schoolhouse should be built
and a school maintained therein. The early structure which
bore that name must then have been in a decrepit condition.
A new one was therefore begun by the superintendents in the
summer of 1796, and completed in the autumn. It stood, the
records state, "near where the old one stands on John Tuhis
land." A detailed description is extant. It was twenty-four feet
by thirty, built of timbers sawed four or five inches thick and
dove-tailed together, with a white oak floor and shingled roof.
Outside it was covered with planed boards standing upright

---

[7] See *A Map of the Lands Called Brothertown*, by Gerrit Cluett, 1795, Chart No.
62, Field book No. 27, Sec. of State of N. Y.; Survey of 1828, by P. Gifford, Surveyor General's Office, No. 136; and *Atlas of Oneida County, N. Y.*, D. G. Beers &
Co., 1874.

[8] *Supt. Rec.*, pp. 55, 63; *Town Rec.*, April 2, 1799.

and painted. The chimney rose on the east. The door was in the middle of the south side, and it was well provided with windows, having twelve lights of glass each. The cost was £167, 5s. Elijah Wampy, Jr., was the first schoolmaster, but after three months he was discharged, and Hannah, the daughter of David Fowler, succeeded him. In 1819 they reported forty scholars, and in 1825 about eighty. Another schoolhouse was built in 1809 in the south part of the town, and a third later near Asa Dick's, where Grace Tocus was at one time the teacher. The building of 1796 is said to have been destroyed by fire, and another erected farther south in the center of the settlement. As they voted in 1816 to sell the schoolhouse lot, this doubtless happened shortly before that date. Both edifices were designed also as a court-house and place for religious assemblies. Their town-meetings were held in them, and the sessions of the peacemaker's court. Here on Sunday they gathered to hear such preaching as could be had, the signal being a blast on the shell. A larger building was suggested by the superintendents, with a view of a more extensive education for Indian children; but in 1805 the town voted that it was inexpedient. There was at this time, and for many years thereafter, no store of any kind in Brothertown. All their trading was done at John Post's well-known establishment in Utica. He received in exchange the ginseng, of which they gathered large quantities, and other produce which they had to market.

The religious affairs of Brothertown did not move very smoothly after the death of Samson Occom. Samuel Kirkland visited them repeatedly, and his manuscript journals contain sundry references to them. He made the following entry: "April 13, 1793. The poor people [at Brothertown] have been rent and torn to pieces by certain [seventh] day baptist teachers, or exhorters, who have been among them during my absence and confinement. Lastly they have been assailed by the Methodists and by persons who do not support the best characters among that sect. The few remaining steady Indians are much concerned and know not which way to turn themselves nor what measures can be devised to preserve the nation from those divisions and animosities which will eventually prove their ruin." The Separatist notions, which, it will be remembered, had prevailed among some at Charlestown, seem to have lingered among them. The day after the above entry Kirkland preached at Brothertown, and he made the following record of his service: "Sighs and groans were now and then heard from various parts of the assembly; but no crying out, as I was told there had frequently been with many. These would fall flat on the floor without receiving any apparent injury. This they ascribed to the power which they supposed came upon them, and carried them quite beyond themselves. I conversed with several on the subject and used so much tenderness and candour as not to provoke them or excite their jealousies. I soon found that they had but confused ideas themselves of what they thought this power to be. When I had explained to them the natural and genuine fruits and operation of the Holy Spirit in bringing souls home to Christ, they did not incline to ascribe it altogether to his operations or influences, but would say it was something above or beyond the power of man and the person upon whom the power thus came must be highly favoured of God." When Kirkland preached there again on the twenty-third of May, his service, he notes, was attended by all parties, Methodists, Baptists, Separatists and Presbyterians. In 1793 Brothertown was visited by our old acquaintance, Rev. Samuel Ashbow, then about seventy-five years of age. We quote again from Kirkland's journal, December 16, 1793: "Was told by several Indians of the steady class that some of their tribe of the Baptist and Separate persuasion, particularly Ashpo, had lately arrived from N. E. Stonington and Mohegan in Connecticut; that they depended much on hearing me in order to judge for themselves if I was a gospel preacher. . . I publicly proposed to Elder Ashpo (as they call him) to make the last prayer, but he declined. After service several of the Indians applied to him for another religious exercise, in which he should improve his gift, as they phrase it. Their object was that he should speak while I was present. He objected on account of the day being far spent etc." Elder Ashbow agreed, however, to meet the Indians in the evening and Kirkland gives a report of the meeting: "Had an account of the meeting last evening. They had four speakers or exhorters, the last of whom was a woman. They continued together till midnight, but were all disappointed in Mr. Ashpo, the old gentleman, who instead of flame and zeal and an elevated voice spake with great deliberation, low voice and said little more than to repeat over a considerable part of my sermon with some comments on particular passages, and concluded by speaking highly of learning. After this young David Fowler rose and spake with great vehemence till he almost foamed at the mouth, but communicated no information or instruction. The whole of his harangue was a repetition of some extravagant words and phrases." On the next Sabbath, also, Kirkland preached there, but by mistake or design the people assembled in two different places and he was obliged to preach without the attendance of the Baptists. Samuel Ashbow had always held such views as are here attributed to him, though at one time under Doctor Wheelock's influence he cast them aside. He remained at Brothertown only a short time, returned to Mohegan and died there. David Fowler, Jr., seems to have imbibed his views, though his father was one of the "steady" kind, which included the members of Occom's scattered flock. A congregation of Baptists with Separatist tendencies was the outcome of this year of divisions. The Methodist party was small and scarcely survived the mention of their name in Kirkland's journal, for he notes in July that "The methodist meeting is entirely broken up." The missionary continued to preach at intervals to the steady class, but they had no stated minister thereafter. Thus it happened that there was developed among them a Baptist party, which was strong for many years. These in the course of time were divided, some being Freewill Baptists, of whom Elder Isaac Wauby and Elder Benjamin Garret Fowler were ministers, and others being close communion Baptists, to whom Elder Thomas Dick ministered. Perhaps this division prevented the building of a meeting-house, as the superintendents proposed. The town voted October 2, 1808, "That the Meeting House to be built in Brothertown is to stand west of the school house where the barn stands ; the said meeting house is to be thirty by forty feet square, two stories high with a steeple and a bell." This building, however, was not erected. The town voted June 24, 1811, "That Elder Isaac Wauby and his Church should oc- cupy the school house in Brothertown on the last Sunday of June for the purpose of Public worship; and that Thos. Dick and his church shall occupy the same House for the same pur- pose the Sunday thereafter, and each without any molestation whatsoever, and so on alternately until some further arrange- ment shall be made by their agreement or otherwise." Elder Wauby removed with a party to White River, Indiana, and there died about 1824. His successor was Elder Fowler. The report on Brothertown affairs in 1825, says : "They have two preachers of the gospel among them of their own number, who are pious and exemplary men, regularly devoted to their calling."

The superintendents came early to the conclusion that it was best to have a white man act in the capacity of teacher, and as their agent in the management of their business. Some time was spent in looking for a proper person. Thomas Eddy of New York, one of the superintendents, was a Quaker, and withal very greatly interested in the welfare of the tribe.

A missionary movement among the Quakers about this time had awakened a zeal for such labor. In 1796, John Prince, James Cooper, Joseph Sanson, Isaiah Powland, Enoch Walker and Henry Simmons, Jr., "steady and judicious men," came to Oneida, where some of them began labors among the Indians. Eddy naturally looked to his brethren for one to fill this office. In 1798 he and his associates settled upon a Quaker named John Dean, then residing in New York. When word came to the Indians that a Quaker was to become their schoolmaster, they had some fear of his religious views. A petition was sent to Governor Jay representing "that they did not wish to be made proselytes by any people, but wished to have the liberty of acting according to the dictates of their own consciences both in religion and the teaching of their children." The superintendents disclaimed any other purpose than to assist the Indians, but said that John Dean was the only person of suitable character they had been able to prevail upon to reside among them. It was, therefore, decided that Dean should engage in the work at a salary of $300 per annum. The letter which he carried from Thomas Eddy to the peacemakers, and which says "he goes to be schoolmaster," is dated December 31, 1798. It has been said that he was commissioned in 1795 by the Society of Friends to labor as a missionary among the Brothertown Indians.[9] We find no evidence that he was among them in any capacity at that time. He seems to have been a stranger when he was engaged. Possibly he was commissioned as a missionary, and labored among the Oneidas, or some neighboring tribe, as other Quakers did. At all events, he set out as above noted for Brothertown, and arrived there early in January. His family, we think, were not removed thither till the following summer. That spring a small house was built for him "near the schoolhouse," and the superintendents then set off ten

---

[9] Durant's *Hist. of Oneida County.*

acres of land for this purpose. This was the Dean residence for some years, and, as it was near the schoolhouse it was, probably, on lot 11. John Dean was then well on in life. He is said to have been a good farmer, and much respected for his steady, sober conduct. His wife was "a reliable woman and in good respect for her industry and good management." President Dwight makes the following reference to him : "A Quaker who is a well-appearing man and of a good character, has come to Brothertown with his family, and resided here some time for the benevolent purpose of teaching the Indian children to read and write. He told me they learn as readily and rapidly as the children of whites. Their schoolhouse was built for them by the state and serves them as a church."[10] How long John Dean was actually engaged in teaching is uncertain. Some of the Indian children were boarded with him, at the town's expense, so late as 1811. He is said to have died in 1820, aged eighty-eight years. His son, Thomas Dean, was associated with him by the action of the superintendents, March 26, 1801, and soon thereafter became the schoolmaster. He was then twenty-two years of age, and wise beyond his years. Like his father, he was a Quaker; but the Indians had ceased to fear any proselytism to that faith. He possessed those qualities of character which enabled him to control them without offending their independence; and, from the first, even more than his father, he won their confidence and affection. In 1809 he married Mary Flandrau, of New Rochelle, N. Y., and settled down to devote his life to the welfare of the people whom he had adopted. He became not only their schoolmaster, but the agent of the superintendents. The Indians came to look upon him as their white father. He was their surveyor to lay out their roads, their lawyer to advise them in the sale of their lands, draw up conveyances and agreements, and hold trusts for the

[10] Dwight's *Travels*, III, 169.

benefit of certain individuals and families. He interested himself in the industrial affairs of the tribe, encouraging them in building, manufacturing and the improved tillage of their farms. There are, doubtless, to this day, at Deansville, which was named after him, and throughout the region, descendants of a nursery of apple-trees which he set out, and which were distributed among their farms. To him are largely due the later stability and success of the tribe. In 1824 he leased for ten years part of lot 16, which had been assigned to David Fowler, Jr., and three years later, a law having been passed permitting the sale of Indian lands, he bought four fifths of this lot for $640, from the Fowler heirs. The remaining fifth he bought in 1830. On this lot the Dean mansion was erected, and there he resided until his death, in 1842, at the age of sixty-three years.[11] During his maturer years he did his greatest service for the Brothertown Indians. The emigration fever had again possessed them. A vast region in the new and distant West invited them, and they were surrounded by the whites. Thomas Dean then saw the wisdom of another removal to Wisconsin. In their behalf he undertook to open the way, journeying to Washington with Randall Abner, their representative, and to the westward in this arduous service. His efforts were successful. In their appreciation of his many years as their father and friend, the Indians at first named their new settlement Deansborough. Company after company were made ready for their pilgrimage. One by one the aged, who tarried still, were laid in their graves. At last, when Thomas Dean came to his death, there were only a few of his people in the neighborhood to attend upon his burial. The Indian town of Samson Occom had melted away.

His children were as follows : I. Philena Hunt, m. Prof. Marcus Catlin of Hamilton College. II. Phebe, m. Col. Alexander H. Redfield of Detroit, Mich. III. John, b. Aug. 16, 1813; Ham Coll., 1832; Mem. Leg. of N. Y., 1846, and Com. of Customs, Treas. Dept., Washington. IV. Hannah, d. 1847. V. Elias Flandrau, physician, Phila., Pa.

CHAPTER XVII

1809–1898

The ultimate emigration of the Brothertown Indians to another location in the far West was foreseen by Samson Occom before his death. He looked about him on the beautiful hills and valleys of the Oneidas, and with prophetic gaze saw them thickly peopled by the whites. Doubtless he had many a conversation on the subject with his friends, and prominent among them was Hendrick Aupaumut, the chief of the Stockbridge tribe. He it was who became the forerunner of the New York Indians in their subsequent removal westward.

So early as the year 1791 this chief, accompanied by several of his nation and Good Peter, the aged father of the faith among the Oneidas, went on an embassy to the Miami tribe. The ostensible purpose of this visit was the introduction of Christianity; but he seems also to have done some prospecting, with a view of locating a large tract of land on White river, now in Indiana, to which the Stockbridge tribe somehow had acquired a claim. A council was held there in 1802 with the Delawares who had removed thither, Hendrick Aupaumut being chief of the Stockbridge delegation.[1] A friendly compact was then made between them. For two years thereafter Captain Hendrick was engaged in perfecting this relationship in behalf of the Oneidas and their wards, the Indians of New Stockbridge and Brothertown. In the spring

---

[1] *A Report to the Secretary of War*, Dr. Morse, App., pp. 110, 111.

of 1809 the latter were invited to send delegates westward
with him. They did so, by a vote of the town on the fourth of
April, and John Tuhie, John Skeesuck, Henry Cuship and
Jacob Fowler were appointed. The speech delivered by them
July third and the reply, read in their town-meeting, August
twenty-ninth, are recorded in the town records. This passage
is conspicuous in the reply: "Grand-children, Brothers and
Friends : Be it known to you that you have the same privilege as we have to this land, we can not point out a particular
spot for you to live on ; but you may take your own choice
wherever you should be suited on undivided land along this
river, there you may build your fire-place."[2] Captain Hendrick
did not at once return to New Stockbridge, but remained some
time in the White River country.[3] During this period Tecumseh
became powerful, and his brother, Elskwatawa, the " Shauwasee
prophet," preached the extermination of the whites. The
Stockbridge chief was then of great service to the government
in opposing this excitement, and to General Harrison in the
Indian war which followed. He had once fought in the Revolution, and in this war, as in that of 1812, he was no less a
brave warrior.[4]

It had been determined at Brothertown in 1812 to begin a
settlement at White River. These wars deterred them, and
many of their number enlisted in the United States service.
Some never returned. Finally, when peace had been restored,
the town voted, January 13, 1817, to choose five men to go
there " in pursuit of a tract of land heretofore sought for by
their [our] delegates sent there in the year 1809, and to get a
title to it." The Stockbridge tribe also were preparing to

---

[2] *Town Records*, pp. 58-60 ; Jones' *Annals of Oneida County*, pp. 267-270.

[3] *Sergeant's Journals*, Am. Bd. Com. For. Miss.; Dr. Morse's *Report*, App., pp.
108, 109.

This remarkable Indian afterwards removed with his people to Wisconsin, living
an honorable life to the last, and died at South Kaukauna in the summer of 1830.
Muhhekaneok, Davidson, pp. 19, 20, 27 ; *Wis. Hist. Soc. Coll.*, II, 433.

remove. Two families went in 1817 and more the next season. On the twenty-fourth of July, 1818, Rev. John Sergeant assembled the tribe in anticipation of this pilgrimage. The old church then dismissed and formed into a new body eleven of their number, for whom he transcribed the Confession of Faith and Covenant in English, adding in their own language a Covenant especially adapted to their circumstances.[5] On the fifteenth of August following, some having gone and more being then ready to depart, another meeting was held, at which the chief, Hendrick Aupaumut, in a "large speech" presented to them from the old church a copy of Scott's Bible " to read on Lord's Days and at other religious meetings." So they said farewell, and were gone to return no more.

Some Brothertown families went with this latter company, which soon overtook the first. Among these were Elder Isaac Wauby and some of his followers, Thomas Isaacs, and Samson Occom, a grandson of the minister, who is said to have descendants living in Wisconsin. Aged Indians now survive who remember this affecting farewell—the first of this pilgrim people to set out toward the setting sun.

A great disappointment awaited them. Ere they reached their destination, they heard that the United States government by a treaty with the Miamis had bought a large tract of land, including that on which they had intended to settle.[6] A few of the Brothertown tribe returned, but most of them went on. Earnest efforts were made by these tribes in an appeal to the government to regain their lands, but they were

---

[5] This Covenant was signed by Deacon Joseph Quinney, John M'Toksin, Robert Konkpot, John Bennet, Betsey Bennet, Esther T., Margaret Q., Hannah K., Catharine M., Dolly N., and Mary K.—*Sergeant's Journals; Report of the Select Com. of the Soc. for Prop. the Gos. among the Indians and others in North America,* Cambridge, 1819, p. 14; Dr. Morse's *Report,* App., p. 112; and *Muhhekaneok,* Davidson, pp. 20 ff.

[6] Dr Morse's *Report,* App. pp. 114–118.

of no avail. The trials of these emigrants discouraged them and sickness wasted their numbers. Elder Wauby died. Several years afterwards the remnant found their way to Green Bay. Thus the first attempt to establish a new town in the West came to naught.

As this hope was dying out a new movement was being inaugurated. In the year 1816, that most remarkable missionary and strange man of a royal likeness, Rev. Eleazar Williams, appeared among the Oneida Indians. The attempt already made suggested to him, to Rev. Jedediah Morse and especially to the land companies who wished the Indians to vacate their reservations in New York, the removal of all these Indians to a Western home.[7] Williams hoped to form a confederacy of Indian towns under one controlling head, and though this purpose failed, his efforts greatly furthered the emigration movement.

The account of the negotiations of delegates from the New York tribes with the Menomonees and Winnebagoes at Green Bay, Wisconsin, in 1821, is a tedious story. They were conducted under the authority of the United States. Captain Hendrick Aupaumut was prominent in the business. The result was the purchase of a large tract from these Wisconsin tribes, said to contain 2,000,000 acres, the consideration being $2,000, one quarter of which was then paid. The date of this treaty is August 18, 1821. On the twenty-third of September, 1822, another treaty was made, by which the New York Indians acquired " all the right, title, interest and claim " to another tract, for which they agreed to pay $3,000. The price was all the land was worth at the time. The Brothertown Indians were represented in these treaties; but they formally united in the affair in 1824, when on the sixth of April the town voted " that a purchase shall be made of land at Green

---

[7] *The Lost Prince,* by John H. Hanson ; *Wis. Hist. Soc. Coll.,* II, 415–449 ; *Muhhekaneok,* pp. 21 ff. ; Dr. Morse's *Report,* pp. 24–27, App. 75–89 ; and Jones' *Annals of Oneida County,* pp. 861–863. 889, 893.

Bay." The following Indians were then appointed to act in the matter with their agent, Thomas Dean: William Dick, Rhodolphus Fowler, Paul Dick, Benjamin G. Fowler, Thomas Dick, Randall Abner, John Johnson, Daniel Dick, David Toucee, George Scippio, George Sampson, and Samuel Scippio. Some of these went to Wisconsin with Thomas Dean, and they bought a tract on Fox river, eight miles wide and thirty miles long, paying therefor $950, out of their annuity, which was nearly the amount of the payment then due on the above-named agreement with the Wisconsin Indians.[8] Thus they had by representation at the treaty, by town vote, and by an actual payment allowed by the state of New York, acquired valuable lands. On the twenty-fourth of August, 1830, at the laying out of lands for the New York Indians, they were represented by William Dick, Rhodolphus Fowler and John Johnson.[9] The remnant from White River removed thither at once, and others made ready to go. This required time. They had to sell their lots at Brothertown and arrange their affairs. Meanwhile, the Menomonees and Winnebagoes had repented of their bargain, as the Oneidas did of their grant to the New England Indians. They denied the claim of the New York tribes. The United States government investigated the subject; and notwithstanding the above treaties, which had been several times ratified and acknowledged, proceeded in the Stambaugh treaty, made at Washington, February 8, 1831, to acquire from the Wisconsin tribes a title to all their lands. When this treaty came before the United States Senate, that body refused to ratify it without providing that three townships east of Winnebago Lake be granted to the Stockbridge, Munsee and Brothertown Indians, in addition to 500,000 acres lying west of Fox river, and giving them compensation for the improvements on the lands they then occu-

---

[8] *N. Y. Ach., Assembly Papers, Ind. Aff.,* Vol. 41, p. 93; and *Report of 1825.*
[9] *Wis. Hist. Soc. Coll., McCall's Journal,* XII, 191.

pied. The township of the Brothertown tribe was to contain 23,040 acres and they were allowed $1,600 for their improvements. Even an Indian could see the difference between this and the 153,600 acres they had bought and paid for. The boundaries of the tract west of Fox River were changed and the Indians protested. What could they do? Some of them were on the ground and they wanted to settle down. Their brethren in New York were anxiously awaiting the fixing of a location. So finally the agreement was accepted and the treaty was proclaimed July 9, 1832.

This was the status of their land affairs until the treaty of January 15, 1838, concluded at Buffalo Creek, N. Y. Let it be remembered that the New York Indians then had a title to 500,000 acres as above stated, in addition to the reservations on which they lived. The possession of this tract was the object of the treaty of 1838.[10] We have no place here for details; but the issues depending upon this transaction have been of importance to the New York Indians ever since. Upon them their so-called " Kansas claim " has rested. This famous case of the " New York Indians *vs.* The United States " has been on its tedious journey through the courts these many years, and now in this memorable year of justice, A. D. 1898, has come to a final decision in the Supreme Court in favor of the Indians.[11] How strange is this dénouement of history!

[10] *U. S. Statutes at Large*, Vol. VII, *Indian Treaties*, pp. 550 ff.

[11] The history of this case would fill a volume. It is Congressional Case No. 151; United States Court of Claims, No. 17.861; Supreme Court of the United States, Oct., 1896, No. 415. The Court of Claims decided in favor of the Indians in 1890. This decision was finally reversed and the Indians appealed to the Supreme Court. The argument was made by Hon. Joseph H. Choate, Dec. 7 and 8, 1896, and it was reargued later on a constitutional question. The Supreme Court decided in favor of the Indians, who then moved for judgment in the Court of Claims. An attempt was then made to reduce the amount of the claim by excluding the New York Indians in Wisconsin; but the Court of Claims on the mandate of the Supreme Court entered judgment, Nov. 14, 1898, in favor of the claimants for $1,961,400. Provision for this payment will be a duty of the Fifty-sixth Congress. All of the nine nations and tribes of New York are beneficiaries. James B. Jenkins, Esq., of Oneida, N. Y., has been

The half million acres which was the stake in 1838 came to the New York Indians in consequence of the agreement of 1822; this was made valid by the payment of the $950 by the Brothertown Indians; they obtained this money from the fund arising out of the lands which Samson Occom so bravely fought to retain; and he was the first native missionary of New England to carry the gospel to the Six Nations.

The New York Indians certainly deeded by the above treaty of 1838, the 500,000 acres of their Green Bay lands. In return they were to receive "as a permanent home for all the New York Indians then residing in the State of New York or in Wisconsin" a tract of land directly west of the state of Missouri "to include 1,824,000 acres," "to have and to hold the same in fee simple to the said tribes or nations by patent from the President." It was further provided that the tribes should agree to remove thither "within five years, or such other time as the President may from time to time appoint," or forfeit their interest to the United States; but the government was to appropriate $400,000 to aid them in this removal. The Indians claimed that the United States government never performed its part of the agreement, that no time was appointed for their removal, that no appropriation was made therefor, that the Kansas lands were never conveyed to them, and that they have been sold to white settlers. An attempt was made in 1846, without the President's appointment, to remove two hundred and one Indians from New York. These were conducted by the Indian agent to the Little Osage River in Kansas and there left unprovided for—to starve and die during the following winter. Thirty-two only of the survivors remained there and their lands were taken from them by settlers. As shown in the statement of their case, this is all the government has done to fulfil its agreement in payment

interested in this case for many years as attorney for the Indians, and to him the credit of the final decision is largely due.

for the Green Bay lands, which are said to have been sold under various acts of Congress at an average price of $1.34 per acre.

As to the historical relation of the Brothertown tribe to the New York Indians, by which they participated in all these treaties, there can be no doubt. Since the grant to the New England Indians in 1774, as heretofore related, they have been by Indian customs and treaty wards of the Oneida Indians. In all the early negotiations they were concerned. They specifically by a town vote, April 4, 1824, reaffirmed their union with the New York Indians in making the purchase of 1822. Thereafter they were recognized in all these transactions by the Wisconsin tribes and the United States. As to the treaty of 1838, the Brothertown Indians are named among the tribes participating and concerned in the Western grant.

The Brothertown Indians, as the remnant of the New England tribes, have had a peculiar plea for consideration and justice. They alone of all the scattered nations, which our forefathers were wont to term "the lost tribes of Israel," can trace their ancestry back to the days of the founders of this Republic. In their civilization the seeds of the saintly John Eliot's sowing are still bearing fruit. They are the descendants of Wheelock's Indian Charity School—the spiritual children of Samson Occom. Their ancestors fought with Uncas, "the white man's friend," in the Pequot War, went out with his three sons against King Philip and came to the rescue of the English after the massacre of Bloody Brook. The rolls of all the later Colonial wars contain the names of soldiers from whom they can prove a lineal descent. Their great grandfathers fought in the Revolution, and so many of them perished that it was, by the testimony of William Williams, the death blow to their ancient tribal strength. In the war of 1812 their grandsires were engaged. and they themselves, out of their diminished numbers, furnished nearly threescore and ten soldiers in the Civil War. Where in this broad land can such a Society of the Colonial Wars be found? Whatever the merits of their claim may have been, which it is not for the historian to judge, the survivors of the New England Indians have a title to the respect of the American people.

The first emigration of families from Brothertown, N. Y., to Green Bay was in the year 1831. Individuals and deputations only had before this made journeys thither to secure the land and take possession. With this removal in view they petitioned the General Assembly of New York for permission to sell their lots, which was granted by an act passed April 16, 1827. The superintendents were thus authorized on the application of any Indian to convey his land in fee simple, receiving one fourth of the purchase money in cash and leaving the balance secured by a mortgage to be paid in instalments. The seller and the peacemakers were to acknowledge all deeds which were to be duly recorded. The proceeds of all common lands were to be expended in the removal of the poor and the residue, if any, in building a schoolhouse in their new home. All who removed were still to receive their portion of the annuity. This provision in regard to the Brothertown fund was carried out until, by an act passed May 25, 1841, those who had then removed to Wisconsin received their portion of the principal. Thus the obstacles in the way were cleared. The Indians began at once in 1827 to dispose of their lots. All matters relating to their emigration were placed in the hands of a committee chosen annually, and the affair was conducted with discretion. Probably no Indian tribe of North America ever emigrated under more favorable circumstances. They had acquired experience and knowledge of government. They had the means necessary for a good start in a new country. Some of them were well-to-do. The distance was great and they could not transport all their household effects. Fortunately, however, they had a waterway in the Erie canal from Utica to Buffalo and thence they could conveniently reach Green Bay by the great lakes.

The company of 1831 was composed of nearly forty persons, chiefly the large families of William and Elkanah Dick and Randall Abner. Thomas Commuck and his wife Hannah, Isaac Scippio and David Johnson also went in this party. Of these the following were living in 1895 : Barbara Dick, Delila Dick Brushil, Hannah Abner Commuck, Rebecca Abner Johnson, and Elias and David Dick. They made their settlement at Kaukauna on the Fox River, and built their log houses. The land was not the best adapted to farming and they did not intend to remain there. The treaty which gave them a township farther south on the east shore of Winnebago Lake was then pending and was ratified the following year. Hence they had not long to remain, and they moved to their final location in 1832 and 1833. In 1832 a larger company reached the new settlement, consisting of forty-four persons, as nearly as can now be ascertained. These included the families of Alexander, Daniel and Thomas Dick, William Johnson, Simeon and John Adams, Ezekiel Wiggins, Abraham Skeesuck, Nathan Paul and John Seketer, besides several men, Jeremiah Johnson, George Skeesuck, Charles Seketer and James Wauby. By the town records they were expecting to start on the twenty-fifth of June. They probably set out about that time, as they were four weeks going from Buffalo to Green Bay and arrived there early in August. The vessel in which the lake voyage was made was *The President*. Another party went in 1834, in which were Elder Thomas Dick and his wife Debora, Patience Fowler, the widow of James, and her children, widow Hannah Dick, James Niles, Jesse Corcomb, Isaac Wauby, Emanuel Johnson, Joseph Palmer and such families as they had. They made the voyage in a schooner named *The Navigator*. In 1835 there went James Simons, Samuel Skeesuck, Alonzo D. Dick and his family and Solomon Paul.

They went in the steamboat *United States*. One of the largest
companies went in 1836, in which were Rhodolphus Fowler and
his children, Simeon Hart, Lothrop Dick, William Crosley,
John Johnson, Ira Hammer, David Wiggins, George Scippio,
John Matthews, Henry Fowler and Erastus Fowler, some of
them with families. Some of these met a tragic death by the
capsizing of a boat on Fox River, where six men were drowned.
After this they went in smaller parties as they conveniently
could, including widows Esther Sampson and Amy Johnson,
Charles Anthony, Henry Skeesuck, Hezekiah Fowler, John
Wauby, Rowland Johnson, Isaac Dick, Alexander Fowler,
Laton Dick and Thomas Hammer. Elder Benjamin G. Fowler went in 1846, most of his flock having preceded him.
Thus most of the tribe were reunited in their new home. In
anticipation of a distribution of the principal of their fund a
census was made of those remaining in New York in 1843,
and it shows the names of ninety-six persons. Of these a
large number went to Wisconsin during the five years following. As an enumeration made in 1837, in connection with the
treaty, gives their number as three hundred and sixty, there
must have been in Wisconsin in 1843 about two hundred and
fifty. Probably the number at its greatest was not far from
three hundred. Some few never removed and some who did so
afterwards returned and died in their old home. They decreased,
however, rapidly ; and when after the late war one of the
tribe, Lyman P. Fowler, visited the old Oneida town, he found
himself among strangers. He brightened the memories of the
past by visiting the home of Thomas Dean's daughter—a
gracious woman whom the Indians called Lady Catlin ; but
he could scarcely identify the landmarks of his youth. The
remnant in the town had melted away and everything about
was changed. He sorrowfully climbed the hill on the shoulder
of which Samuel Kirkland's college is now situated, and
stopped half way up—as many another returning pilgrim has

done—at the residence of Professor Edward North, and there related the fact that in the old Indian town of by-gone days he had seen on a fence-post near their burial-place an Indian skull. In 1893, when the writer visited Deansville in search of the grave of Samson Occom, he could find only one Indian in the town ; and he was the aged " Billy Paul," a descendant of both Samson Occom and David Fowler, spending his lingering years in the white man's poorhouse !

The township granted to the Brothertown Indians by the treaty of 1832 extended four miles north and south on Winnebago Lake and eight miles east and west. Two roads were laid out in straight parallel lines leading north and south, the westernmost about a quarter of a mile from the lake, called the " Base Line Road," and another eastward called " Turkey Street." A so-called " Military Road," built by Colonel Scott for the use of troops, ran north and south between these, and on this the village of Brothertown is now located. The town was not laid out in lots until 1839, in which year they received the honors of citizenship in the United States. An act of Congress, passed March 3, 1839, provided that their land could be divided and held in fee simple.[12] Commissioners were then appointed. The old town voted, May 6, 1839, that the Green Bay lands should be divided that season, that one share should be given to adults and one-half share to minors and that the latter should also be apportioned to females who had married outside of the tribe. Thomas Dean was sent to attend upon this business. The land proved to be of the best character for their agricultural purposes. It is claimed by them that the bounds of their grant were unlawfully altered and the only reason they can give for this is that it was

---

[12] The deeds reciting this act were on parchment and were signed by John Tyler, Prest. There were two hundred and forty lots in all and each Indian had a fifty-acre lot and a fraction of twelve and one half acres. At the present time twenty-five families hold lands there and some of them are on their original claims. The early mill locations were held by David and William Fowler until their leases expired.

"too good land for Indians." At first they named their town
Deansborough, though a certain locality was called Pequot.
It was also known as Manchester. The name is now Brother-
town, in remembrance of their old home.

The county called Calumet was formed the year after their
admission to citizenship, by an act approved January 6, 1840.
The first election was held in the house of Elkanah Dick.
John Johnson, Daniel Dick and David Fowler were chosen
county commissioners and the other offices were filled by
David Johnson, O. D. Fowler, Simeon Hart and John Johnson, Jr. The first session of the county commissioners was
held in the house of David Fowler, March 11, 1840. John
Johnson was elected chairman, and Daniel Dick, clerk. William Dick was treasurer, and James Wauby and Alexander G.
Dick were constables. The county was divided into two
assessment and election districts. At this time the value of
real and personal property in the county was $68,320, upon
which a tax of nine mills was assessed. This early county
organization gave place, a few years later, to one in which the
whites participated. Some of the tribe have attained honors
in public office. William Fowler, Alonzo D. and William H.
Dick have served as members of the Wisconsin legislature.

In early days they formed no new ecclesiastical organization. After the coming of their elders, Benjamin G. Fowler
and Thomas Dick, they had preachers of their own. David
Fowler was for years a deacon among them. About 1840, a
Methodist church was organized and a small meeting-house
built. The congregation was successively ministered to by
neighboring clergymen, especially from Duck Creek, named
Poe, Frink, Clark and Halsted. Thomas Commuck was their
first postmaster, and he and Randall Abner were justices of
the peace and performed their marriages. The "Indian
Melodies" which Commuck issued was never very exten-
sively used by them, though copies are preserved and highly

regarded in their homes. Its author was himself a singer. He was an eccentric man, of remarkable memory, and a literary turn of mind.[13] Since the days of the first emigration they have used the English language. It is remembered among them, however, that sometimes a group of old ladies— Pually Mossuck, Martha Paul and Lucy Waukeet—would carry on their private gossip in the musical tongue to which they had been born.

During the early years of the town they made encouraging progress in agriculture. Their farms were cleared and substantial buildings were erected. Among their number were those who were skilled in the trades. The work on the first steamboat which was built on Lake Winnebago, under the superintendence of Peter Hoteling and called "The Manchester" and later the "Fountain City," was done largely by Deacon David Fowler. Gradually, however, a change has been going on. When the parents died, the younger generation sought brighter prospects in other employments. Some are engaged on railroads and some on the lakes. Others turned to trade. The foreign elements began to come in, mostly Germans, and buy out the Indians. Some emigrated farther west, to Minnesota, Kansas, Nebraska and even to California. At the present time there are probably not more than one hundred and fifty of the tribe within the town, which has a population of fifteen hundred. Their village, located about half a mile from the lake, comprises about twenty houses, a store or two, the church, a schoolhouse and their town hall. In one of these stores, Edgar M. Dick, a lineal descendant of a bloodthirsty Narragansett, will cut your hair, and, with more consideration than his ancestor had, will leave the scalp. They have the reputation of being a respectable and worthy people. In morals and religion they com-

---

[13] See *Sketch of the Brothertown Indians, Wis. Hist. Soc. Coll.*, IV, 291; and *Sketch of Calumet County, Ibid.*, I, 103, by Thomas Commuck.

pare favorably with the whites round about them. For more than sixty years since they located in that wilderness, not one of their number ever saw the inside of the state prison. The visitor among them will readily recognize the peculiar traits of Indian character. Reserve and caution distinguish them. Some are as keen in discernment as their ancestors were on the war-path. The place is an interesting field for the ethnologist, for the types of the ancient tribes of New England are still to be observed among them. The Narragansett is there with his athletic figure and easy poise, the Mohegan with his intelligent face and the Montauk with his sturdy frame. An admixture of both white and negro blood is clearly visible, but it is known to have taken place in alliances before they left New England. Children of the same parents exhibit the greatest variety, in features, in shades of color and expression of countenance, though all are distinctly Indian. The tribe still maintains a unity in an organization, a relic of their Indian town, and they have duly chosen " Headmen." In 1895 these were James Simons, Edgar M. Dick, Lathrop Fowler, Oscar Johnson, John E. Hammar and Theodore Dick. This office conveys no more authority than the tribe choose to give. It has been perpetuated in large measure by the necessity of their land claim.

Among these survivors of the Christian Indians of New England it is believed that their numbers are slowly decreasing. " Here we have taken our stand," wrote Thomas Cummuck, " and are resolved to meet manfully that overwhelming tide of fate which seems destined in a few short years to sweep the Red Man from the face of existence." The chill winds which blow between the lake on their west and the greater Michigan on their east, are favorable to that terrible disease, consumption, which has always carried many to the grave. Their burial-place near at hand has gathered most of the founders. Only a few remain, whose memories, amply

EDGAR M. DICK

LATHROP FOWLER

OSCAR JOHNSON

HEADMEN OF THE BROTHERTOWN INDIANS

proven on many points to be most retentive and accurate, reach back to the times and scenes of their Oneida home. Elias Dick, whose frame in its stalwart days would have done honor to a Narragansett sachem; Hannah Cummuck, in whom the trials of many years have ripened an autumnal glory; Rowland Johnson, distinguished in dignity and gentleness; and Rebecca Johnson, the storehouse of all the facts and traditions of their tribal history—these, who have contributed invaluable details to this narrative, will long be remembered by their white friend.

Here speaks the sage of Brothertown, John Collins Fowler, a grandson of the faithful David of early times: "The Indian, whatever his present state, can be civilized and made a useful citizen of this great Republic; but his nature is different from that of the white man. He is easily tempted by the fire-water, which has been his curse since men have known him. The white man is energetic, ambitious, over-reaching. The Indian is content with little, sluggish, and he cannot hold on to what he gets. It is not for the Indians to have anything. They should never live in the same community with the whites, for they will soon be stripped of all they have and left by the roadside. Ah! yes, my people are dying away, and we shall soon be gone."

The Montauk Indians of Samson Occom's day had a belief in the existence of souls after death, and that the spirits of good Indians go to the westward, where they exercise themselves in dancing and pleasurable singing forever in the presence of the western God. Westward they have been going ever since the Pilgrims landed. Some day may they find there the land of plenty and of peace. Ere another century has passed may those words be true which the Oneida sachem Onondega uttered to a Commencement audience at Dartmouth College a century ago, "The light begins a little to break away from yonder wilderness toward the setting of the sun."

APPENDIX

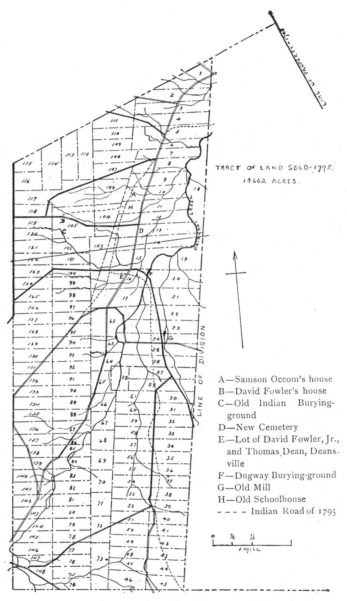

TRACT OF LAND SOLD - 1795.
14662 ACRES.

A—Samson Occom's house
B—David Fowler's house
C—Old Indian Burying-
ground
D—New Cemetery
E—Lot of David Fowler, Jr.,
and Thomas Dean, Deans-
ville
F—Dugway Burying-ground
G—Old Mill
H—Old Schoolhouse
- - - - Indian Road of 1795

MAP OF BROTHERTOWN
P. Gifford, Surveyor, 1828

APPENDIX

FAMILY HISTORY

OF THE

BROTHERTOWN INDIANS

ABNER,—Pequot tribe, Stonington, Conn. In 1762 an Indian called "Abner," aged 45, was living in a wigwam at Mushantuxet in Groton.. He had six children. James Abner, who with his wife Mary was living at Lantern Hill, Stonington, in 1788, was doubtless a son and the father of Randall.

Randall Abner, born June 4, 1789, at Stonington, married Sarah Tocus. They moved to Stephentown, N. Y., and thence in 1819 to Brothertown. He received lot 86, in 1823; was a peacemaker from 1823 to 1831; removed to Wisconsin in 1831 and to Kansas later, where he died in 1852, æ. 63, and she Apr. 9, 1869, æ. 73. Chn.: I. Hannah Abigail, b. Aug. 21, 1814, m. Thomas Commuck. II. Rebecca, b. Mar. 2, 1816, m. (1) Simeon Adams, (2) John W. Johnson. III. Randall, who went to Nebraska. IV. Joseph, who was lost at sea. V. Silvia, m. Daniel Skeesuck. VI. Lucy, m. (1) Stowe, (2) Coffin. VII. Marietta, m. John Welch. VIII. Roxy. IX. James. X. Denison, who went to Kansas. XI. Grace.

ADAMS, ADAM, —Tunxis tribe, Farmington, Conn. A Quinnipiac Indian, nicknamed "Adam," of East Haven, "bought of a squaw" land at Farmington, which he divided Nov. 3, 1756, between his sons, John and Samuel Adam. He signed as "Jacob Adam," but Oct. 10, 1776, he is "Thomas Adams late deceased." He was the head man of the Quinnipiac Indians who exchanged rights at New Haven for lands at Farmington, removed thither and were adopted by the Tunxis tribe. In 1770 he was aged and infirm and soon after died.

John Adams (1Adam). New Haven, 1756, and of age, married Sarah —— and moved to Farmington. He was a councilor and landowner;

a soldier in the French wars and the Revolution; was at Stockbridge, Mass.; and a founder of Brothertown, where he soon died. Chn.: I. John, b. 1755. II. Sarah, m. Abraham Simons. III. Simeon. IV. Samuel.

John Adams (2 John, 1 Adam) was an early settler at Brothertown, where he received lot 126 in 1795. He married later "Widow Sarah Davies," born in 1748, owner of lot 6, and died before 1804, without issue. His lot was then assigned to Eliphalet Adams (Marthers), subject to the dower of Widow Sarah.

Simeon Adams (2 John, 1 Adam) was a soldier in Capt. Elisha Lee's company in 1776. He moved to Brothertown before 1799, and had lots 99 and 124 in 1804. He died about 1829, his heirs being his brother Samuel's children.

Samuel Adams (2 John, 1 Adam) married Mary, daughter of David Fowler, and settled at Brothertown. He had been a soldier in the Revolution, enlisted in the War of 1812, and was killed at Black Rock. She was living at Brothertown in 1817. Chn.: I. Thankful, m. Stevens. II. John, who with his wife Sally removed to Wisconsin in 1832, and died at Dickenson's Mills. III. Simeon, who m. Rebecca Abner, moved to Wisconsin and died there. IV. Hannah, m. Solomon Paul. V. Emeline, m. Lothrop Dick. Edwin C. Adams, alias Edwin Edwards or Edwin Hathaway, an orphan, was brought up in this family. He m. Lovina Matthews, and moved to Brothertown, Wis. Their son, Arthur Adams, was in Co. G, 36th Wis. Vols., and died in Andersonville prison Sept. 2, 1864.

Samuel Adams (1 Adam) was born in 1734, and married Hannah Squamp of the Wangunk tribe, by whom he had rights in the Mattabesett lands at Middletown, Conn. Both were well educated. He was a soldier in Capt. John Patterson's company in 1756, and in Capt. Timothy Northam's company, 1st Regt N. Y. troops, in 1762. He was a councilor and landowner at Farmington; an early settler at Brothertown; was driven out by the war, and went to Hancock, Mass. He returned to Brothertown and in 1795 received lot 7. where he had built his first hut. He died about 1800. Ch.: Solomon, and perhaps others.

Solomon Adams (2 Samuel, 1 Adam) received part of lot 52 at Farmington from his father, March 21, 1782. He married Olive, daughter of Rev. Samson Occom, was a soldier in the Revolution, and died about 1783. His widow held "a part of the 5th lot west of the Indian tract and the house thereon," whence she afterwards emigrated to eastern New York. Chn.: I. Philena, m. (1) James Waucus, (2) Thomas Crosley. II. Damaris, m. Jacob Thomas. III. Ellen, New Marlboro, Mass. These sold their father's rights at Farmington in 1801. Probably also there was a son David, who received lot 134 at Brothertown in 1797, and died without issue.

ANTHONY,—Narragansett tribe, Charlestown, R. I. A number of Indians bearing this name were living there in 1750. John Anthony married Sarah, the widow of George Ninegret. A Charles Anthony resided there in 1763, and thence the Brothertown emigrant came.

Charles Anthony was a later settler at Brothertown. He married Lorinda Brushel, who inherited rights in several lots sold 1828–1835. He was town marshal from 1828 to 1832. They moved to Wisconsin about 1837, and died there. Ch.: Lowana.

BRUSHEL, BRUSHIL, BRUSHILL, BRUSHEILL,—Mohegan tribe, Mohegan, Conn. This family was not of the early Mohegan stock. The name is not found in lists made so late as 1782. In recent times some of that name have lived at Mohegan, and Sam Brushel, who died there in 1882, aged 37, claimed to have royal blood. Probably an Indian of another tribe married a Mohegan woman and was adopted.

Abigail Brushel appeared at Brothertown in 1796, a widow, and received lot 46, which was sold in 1829 for the benefit of "Widow Abigail." She had sons Samuel and Sampson, and probably Mary, John, Lemuel and Timothy were also her children. Mary had lot 47 in 1804; John lots 38 and 39 in 1804; Lemuel lot 44 in 1797; and Timothy lot 73 in 1796. Lemuel died about 1827 without issue. Timothy died on a man-of-war and his widow and son Samuel inherited his lot.

Samuel Brushel (^{1}Abigail), born in 1772, and his wife Esther, born in 1774, received lot 25, in 1795. She died and he married Abigail Skeesuck. The lot was sold for their benefit in 1828. Chn.: I. Thomas, m. Hannah Cujep. II. Nancy, m. Hart. III. Henry. IV. Lucinda, m. Welch, removed to Wisconsin, and died. V. Samuel, m. Nancy Welch. VI. Lydia, m. Aaron Toucee.

Henry Brushel (^{2}Samuel, ^{1}Abigail), born June 24, 1814, married Nancy Welch Brushel, his brother's widow. They moved to Wisconsin, where he died Sept. 24, 1864, and she April 7, 1864, aged 55. Chn.: I. Samuel, a soldier in the Civil War, who died after his return. II. Frances. III. Almira. IV. Nancy E., d. Feb. 15, 1865, æ. 25.

Sampson Brushel (^{1}Abigail), born in 1774, had lots 127 and 34 at Brothertown. He married Betsey Ceipet, by whom he had Lorinda, who married Charles Anthony, and possibly a son Benjamin. They died at Brothertown.

CEIPET, CEBIT, SEEPET, SEABPEET. Benjamin Ceipet and Hannah his wife received lot 35 at Brothertown in 1804. He died about 1807 and she about 1828. They left a daughter Betsey, a son Daniel, and possibly other children.

CHARLES. There were families of this name at Montauk, L. I., Farmington, Conn., and Charlestown, R. I. An Indian so named, probably of the latter place, married Rhoda, daughter of James Niles, who as a widow settled at Brothertown and received lot 32 in 1804. She married later Daniel Wauby. Two youth, John and Mary Charles, living with John Tuhie in 1795, were doubtless her children, the former inheriting as an heir of James Niles. She also had a daughter Olive who moved to Wisconsin. John Charles, born in 1789, is thought to have been the father of Oliver Charles, grandson of Rhoda and heir in 1843. Josiah Charles, whose relation to the above is unknown, received lot 102 at Brothertown in 1804, married Jerusha, daughter of George Peters, and died about 1828. Their only child Eunice m. (1) David Toucee; (2) William Crosley.

COCHEATT, COCHEAKS, QUOCHEETS,—Pequot tribe, Groton, Conn. This was a prominent family at Mushantuxet, the earliest of the name being Daniel, who, in 1762, aged 60, was living there in a wigwam, having a family of six. A descendant, Charles Cocheatt, was a late comer at Brothertown, having lot 82 in 1831. He married Sophia Crosley. Chn.: Joseph, Josiah, Hannah, and Malinda.

COCHEGAN, COCHEGION,—Mohegan tribe, Mohegan, Conn. Solomon Cochegan, born about 1735, was an early settler at Brothertown, living on lot 114, which was given to his widow Hannah, aged 60, after his death in 1794. They had a daughter Mehitable, who with an infant child Johanna, lived with them, and a son Solomon, who received lot 61 in 1797, and was probably the father of Hannah and Lucy Cochegan, heirs to lot 114 in 1834.

COMMUCK, CUMMUCK, COMMACH,—Narragansett tribe, Charlestown, R. I. In 1766 an Indian named "Commach" was living there, and Patience Cummuck, the only other of the name, may have been his wife. A son or grandson, Joseph Commuck, became a councilor in 1802, and both he and his wife died a few years thereafter, leaving two young sons, James and Thomas.

Thomas Commuck (1 Joseph), born Jan. 18, 1804, at Charlestown, received a fair education in his youth, which was increased by habits of reading throughout his life. He emigrated to Brothertown before 1825, and received the west half of lot 85 in 1831, to be sold that he might remove to Wisconsin. He married, July 31, 1831, Hannah, daughter of Randall Abner. They were first settlers in the Green Bay home. He was the first postmaster of Brothertown, Wis., a Justice of the Peace and prominent in the affairs of the tribe. Besides several historical papers he printed the " Indian Melodies." He died Nov. 25, 1855. His widow is still living at Brothertown, Wis., and enjoys a vigorous old age in the home of Edgar M. Dick. Chn.: I. Alzuma, b. Nov. 14, 1832, m. Toxuse. II. Thomas Mirvan, b. Nov. 26, 1835, a soldier in the Civil War, who died in Iowa in 1892. III. Sarah Prentiss, b. Apr. 12, 1838, m. Orville A. Hart. IV. Worthington, b. Aug. 31, 1840, d. Feb. 1, 1863, in Libby Prison— a soldier in Co. E, 21st Wis. Vols. V. Victoria, b. June 11, 1842. VI. Helen, b. Aug. 4, 1844, m. Frank La Belle. VII. Theresa, b. Sept. 29, 1846. VIII. Bertha, b. Sept. 8, 1848. IX. Alice E., b. June 12, 1851; m. Rhodolphus M. Fowler. X. Omer Pasha, b. May 25, 1854.

COYHIS, COYS, COHOIZE, COGHOOISZE, — Narragansett tribe, Charlestown, R. I. Toby Cohoize, born in 1673 and living in 1763, was doubtless the father of Ephraim, the councilor of 1747, then aged 44. Ephraim had a son Ephraim, who also became councilor and fought in the French wars. The latter had a son William, under 16 years of age in 1761.

William Coyhis (² Ephraim, ¹ Ephraim) married Mary ——, a white woman, and moved to Brothertown about 1800. He had sons to whom lot 72 was assigned in 1804, on condition that they support their white mother, who was a widow, her husband dying in May, 1804. He was town clerk from 1802 to 1804. Of his sons. John only grew to manhood and received lot 72 in 1824.

John Coyhis (³ William, ² Ephraim, ¹ Ephraim) married Martha, daughter of Asa Dick. He received part of lot 52 in 1814, where both lived and died. Chn.: I. Isaac C. II. John R., m. Sophia Sampson. III. Benjamin J., who moved to Wisconsin. He m. (1) Laura, d. Jan. 14, 1875, ae. 58; (2) Rosella S., d. Sept. 9, 1880, ae. 29.

CROSLEY. This family is said to have been of the Pequot tribe at Stonington, Conn. George Crosley, born in 1748, was an early settler at Brothertown, living on lot 2. In 1795 he had a wife Lornhamah, born in 1754, and six children. His second wife was Elizabeth Fowler, widow of Obadiah Scippio. He lived to old age, held several town offices and died at Brothertown Chn.: I. Grace. b. 1776, m. Joseph Tocus. II. Thomas, b. 1783. III. Nathan, b. 1785, d. at B. IV. Katharine, b. 1787, m. William Dick. V. Elizabeth, b. 1790, m. John Hammer.

Thomas Crosley (¹ George) received lot 76 in 1804, and married Philena, daughter of Solomon Adams and Olive Occom, and widow of James Waucus. He was town clerk from 1809 to 1812. He also held lots 96 and 97. Chn.: I. William. II. Sophronia, m.

Doxstater. III. Lucenette (Lureanett), b. 1807, m. Alonzo D. Dick. Lurea Dick of Manchester, Wis., certified in 1844 that her mother was Dimiss Kuish, a granddaughter of Philip Kuish. If so, Thomas Crosley married a second wife.

William Crosley ([2] Thomas, [1] George), born about 1805, with his sister Sophronia, inherited his father's lot in 1828, removed to Wisconsin in 1836 and there died in 1866. He married (1) Hannah, dau. of William Dick, 1st, (2) Aurilla, dau. of Thomas Dick, (3) Eunice Charles Toucee, dau. of Josiah Charles and widow of David Toucee, who died in 1880, ae. 66. Chn.: I. John, m. Parmelia, dau. of Hezekiah Fowler. II. Caroline, m. Daniel Jakeways. III. Grace Ann. m. Albert D. Cottrell. IV. Serepta, m. Elias Dick.

CUJEP, CHUCHIP, —probably of the Pequot tribe, Groton, Conn. In 1795 Prudence Cujep, widow, aged 39, received lot 104 at Brothertown. She had a son Henry, aged 12. Probably her husband emigrated with her and died before 1795. She married 2d, Gideon Harry, and died at Brothertown, where her gravestone has the epitaph—"In memory of Prude Harry, Daughter of Sampson and Eunice Pouquenup, Feb. 24, 1828." Hannah Cujep, who married Thomas Brushel, may have been the widow of Henry.

CURRICOMB, CORCOM, CURRACOMP, CORRECOMPT, ACCORRECOMPT, —Tunxis tribe, Farmington, Conn. This was a prominent Indian family of the original Tunxis stock. Andrew Correcompt owned several tracts of land at Farmington. He served during the French wars in Capt. Aaron Hitchcock's company in 1756, in Col. Nathan Whiting's company in 1760, and in Capt. Samuel Dimock's company, N. Y. troops, in 1762.

Andrew Curricomb ([1] Andrew), born in 1747, was prominent in the emigration plans, and an early settler at Brothertown. After the Revolution, in which he is said to have served while at West Stockbridge, Mass., he returned to Oneida with his family. He settled on lots 120 and 121, which were divided among his heirs in 1818. His wife's name was Abigail. Chn.: I. Elizabeth, b. 1768, m. Benjamin Toucee. II. Anne, b. 1770, m. James Wiggins. III. Abigail, b. 1778. IV. Eliakim, b. 1780. V. Thomas (?) b. July 14, 1786. VI. Jesse, b. 1791. VII. Moses, b. 1794, d. about 1815. Elizabeth and Anne were probably children by a first wife. Eliakim married Martha Onion and received lots 57 and 58 in 1804. He removed about 1828.

Jesse Curricomb in 1818 inherited lots 120 and 121, with his brother Eliakim. David Toucee and the heirs of Anne Wiggins, and he had lot 142 assigned to him in 1824. His wife's name was Phebe, who died before 1834, when her husband and son John removed to Wisconsin. The son was drowned in Fox River.

CUSK, ASKUSK, ACKUST,—Tunxis tribe, Farmington. Conn. "Cusk, Indian," deeded to his son James Cusk a house and land at Indian Neck, Farmington, in 1761, where the son afterwards lived. He was interested in the emigration in 1775, but never removed permanently. For a time his home was at Saratoga, N. Y.

DAVIES. Henry Davies, of a tribe unknown, was an early settler at Brothertown, and lived on lot 6, which after his death in 1794 was given to his widow Sarah, who married a second husband, John Adams.

DESHON. Felix Deshon, of the Pequot tribe, at Mushantuxet, was prominent in tribal affairs in 1774, but he did not remove to Brothertown until 1804, when he received a part of lot 113, where he lived until his death, about 1816.

DICK.—Narragansett tribe, Charlestown, R. I. This family was neither large nor prominent in the mother tribe to which tradition unanimously assigns it. Tribal lists give only the name of "Widow Mary Dick," and the connection shows that she had children attending Edward Deake's school. We conjecture that William and Isaac Dick, afterwards of Brothertown, were her sons. The relationship of Paul and Thomas Dick to these brothers is undetermined. They may have been also sons of Mary Dick, or elder sons of Isaac. One fact, however, is perplexing. Lots were assigned in 1799 to Isaac and Paul Richards, which are put down in 1804 to Isaac and Paul Dick. The name Richards is not found among the tribe. We suppose that the superintendents at first thought that the name "Dick" was a nickname.

William Dick was born in Charlestown about 1755, married Hannah Potter, probably a daughter of Daniel and Mary Potter, removed to Brothertown about 1799, and was from the first a prominent man there. He settled on lot 135, assigned to him in 1804, and died about 1814. Chn.: I. William. II. Elkanah. III. Laton. IV. Lothrop, m. Emeline Adams. He had lot 124, went to Wisconsin in 1836, and was drowned in Fox River. V. Patience, m. James Fowler, and as a widow removed to Wis. with her children in 1834. VI. Lucena, m. George Sampson. VII. Elizabeth. m. Rhodolphus Fowler. VIII. Abigail, m. David Johnson. IX. Grace. X. Hannah, m. William Crosley. XI. Thankful, m. Skeesuck. The widow, Hannah Dick, with her daughters, Abigail and Thankful, went to Wis. in 1834.

William Dick (1 William) was born at Charlestown, R. I., Feb. 16, 1786, and died at Brothertown, Wis., Feb. 28, 1869. He married, Dec. 6, 1806, Catharine, daughter of George Crosley, who was born Jan. 3, 1787, and died at Brothertown, Wis., Sept. 7, 1866. He lived on lot 131, was town clerk for five years and a peacemaker from 1822 to 1831. The success of the emigration to Wisconsin was largely due to him and his brother Elkanah. He removed with his family in 1831. Chn.: I. William H. II. Nathan Crosley. III. Laura. IV. Jemima, m. Jeremiah W. Johnson. V. Sarah, m. Skeesuck. VI. Barbara, m. Rowland Johnson. VII. Delila, m. Benjamin Brushel. VIII. Desdamona, m. Alexander Fowler. IX. Dorcas.

William H. Dick (2 William, 1 William), married Juliett Peters, was a prominent man in Brothertown, Wis.,and at one time treasurer of the county. In 1851 and 1871 he was a member of the Wisconsin legislature, and discharged his duties with credit to his nation and himself. Ch.: Hannah A. Dick.

Nathan Crosley Dick (2 William, 1 William) born at Brothertown, N. Y., Feb. 8, 1820, married Eunice, daughter of Emanuel Johnson. He died at Brothertown, Wis., in 1884, and she in 1885. He was a worthy citizen and influential in the county. Chn.: I. Orlando D., m. Almira J., dau. of Clark D. Sampson, served during the Civil War in Co. A, 2d Wis. Cav., and in Co. K, 17th Wis. Vols., and died Aug. 9, 1881, æ. 42. II. Franklin M., was in Co. D, 35th Wis. Vols., and died at Vicksburg, July 22, 1864. III. Edgar Morris. IV. Asa D., was in Co. K, 4th Wis. Cav., and died at Cairo in March, 1864. V. Minerva N. VI. Grace.

Edgar Morris Dick (8 Nathan Crosley, 2 William, 1 William) was born at Brothertown, Wis., Oct. 28, 1843. He received a common school education, but further plans were interrupted by the war. He enlisted in Co. F, 21st Wis. Vols., and was wounded at Perryville. Formerly he was a farmer, but is now conducting a mercantile and barber business at Brothertown, where he is respected for his integrity and consistent life. He has identified himself with the Prohibition party, in which he thoroughly believes, and was their nominee for Congress in that district in 1890. The Brothertown Indians have chosen him one of their Headmen. He married Abba Loretta, daughter of Osamus D. Fowler, who was born Sept. 29, 1843, and died Dec. 12, 1896.

Elkanah Dick (1 William), born at Charlestown in 1789, settled at Brothertown, N. Y., on lot 31, held several offices in the town, and removed to Wisconsin in 1831. He married (1) Sarah Ann, dau. of Benjamin Toucee, by whom he had seven children. (2) Eliza Skeesuck. His first wife died in New York, and he in Wisconsin, in 1870. Chn.: I. Elias Jacob, m. Serepta Crosley, by whom he had (1) Jason, (2) Hannah. II. Benjamin, enlisted in Co. G, 36th Wis. Vols., and died at Andersonville, Aug. 25, 1864. III David. IV. Hubbard, was in Co. A, 17th Wis. Vols., and died at Lake Providence, La., April 3, 1863. V. Susan. VI. Elizabeth, m. Laton Fowler, and was drowned in 1875. VII. Laton.

David Dick (²Elkanah, ¹William) was born at Brothertown, N. Y., Oct. 24, 1824, and married Elizabeth, daughter of Joseph Fowler, who died Aug. 15, 1863, aged 35. He served in the war in Co. H, 5th Wis. Vols. Chn.: I. Theodore, who is one of the Headmen. II. Duane. III. Keyes. IV. Jenette, d. young.

Laton Dick (¹William) was born July 14, 1797, and died at Brothertown, Wis., July 31, 1880. He married Abigail, daughter of James Fowler, and lived on lot 78, assigned to him in 1828. He was a peacemaker in 1837, but later removed to Wisconsin with his family. Chn.: I. Emma. II. Emma. III. Frances.

Isaac Dick was a brother of William Dick, and came to Brothertown, N. Y., about 1799, settling on lot 37, which was assigned to him in 1804. His wife was Cynthia Brown, and he then had a family of adult children. He died about 1812, and his lot was sold in 1835 for his children. Asa, Martha, Isaac, Hannah and Betsey, reserving three rods square for the burial lot. Some think Paul Dick was also a son. Chn.: I. Jacob, b. 1787, received lot 60 in 1812, and died before 1825. II. Asa. III. John, received lot 92 and died before 1818. IV. Martha, m. John Coyhis. V. Isaac. VI. Hannah, m. James Kindness. VII. Elizabeth, m. Ira Hammar.

Asa Dick (¹Isaac) came to Brothertown, N. Y., with or shortly after his father, from Sandy Creek, near Lake George, and lot 36 was set apart for him in 1804. The present village of Dickville was named after him, and there he died Sept. 13, 1843, aged 47ʸ, 3ᵐ, 22ᵈ. He was the most prominent man in the town in his day, and attained honors among Indians and whites, being known as " Esquire Dick." In 1820 he was chosen peacemaker, and was the last to fill that office. Pomroy Jones says, " He was a man of enterprise, lived in a good style, had a good two-story dwelling, painted white, but in the latter part of his life he extended his business beyond his means, and after his death his estate was found to be insolvent." His house is still standing and is occupied by Mr. Edward Peck. He bought the lots of many Indians who wished to emigrate to Wisconsin, and would probably have realized his expectations had he lived. His wife was Nancy, daughter of Daniel Skeesuck. Chn.: I. Harriett, m. Alexander Fowler. II. Amanda. III. Isaac. IV. Aurilla. V. Margaret. VI. Orrin. Several children also died young.

Isaac Dick (¹Isaac), born in 1804, married Hannah, daughter of Jacob Fowler, held several town offices, and removed to Wisconsin about 1843, where he died April 10, 1854. Chn : I. Laton, d. in Wis. II. Harriet E., d young. III. Ellen, m. Oscar Johnson.

Paul Dick came to Brothertown, N. Y., from Charlestown, and received lot 129 in 1799, as Paul Richards, and subsequently lot 94. His wife was Hannah, daughter of David Fowler, who died at Brothertown. He removed to White River, Ind., and died there. Chn.:

I. John. II. Alonzo D. III. Alexander. IV. Adeline, m. Abraham Skeesuck. V. Sophia, m. Peter Cooper, an Oneida Indian.
VI. Eunice, m. James Wauby.

John Dick (¹Paul) married Hannah Hammar, who died at Brothertown, N. Y. He owned part of lot 66, sold in 1841, was a peacemaker in 1832, and served until the tribe had nearly all emigrated,
when he followed them. He was an exhorter and was called "Elder
Dick." Ch.: John W., d. 1846, æ. 7.

Alonzo David Dick (¹Paul) was born at Brothertown, N. Y., and
died at Chilton, Wis. He emigrated in 1834, and became an
honored citizen. His wife, Lureanett, daughter of Thomas Crosley,
died Sept. 12, 1854, in her 46th year. Chn.: I. Jane, m. Osamus
D. Fowler. II. Harriet, d. 1849, ae. 13. III. Cornelia. IV. Almira.

Alexander Dick (¹Paul) married Samantha, daughter of John
Seketer, received lot 81 in 1827, removed to Wisconsin in 1832, and
to Kansas in 1852, where they died. Chn.: I. John P. II. Harriett, m. Joseph Scanandoa, an Oneida Indian. III. Lucius C., was
in Co. K, 4th Wis. Cav. He married Sarah ——, who died Jan. 13,
1868, aged 23. IV. Charles W., was in Co. K, 4th Wis. Cav. V.
Jacob, was in Co. A, 2d Kan. Vols.

Thomas Dick was born in Charlestown, R. I., and removed to
Brothertown. N. Y., before 1802, settling on lot 27, which was assigned to him in 1804. As an elder of the Baptist persuasion he
conducted services there for many years, was a peacemaker from 1808
to 1813, and held other town offices. In 1834 he removed to Wisconsin, being then about 80 years of age, where he and his wife
Debora died. Chn.: I. Daniel. II. Thomas. Perhaps there were
others.

Daniel Dick (¹Thomas) married Jerusha, daughter of Joseph
Wauby; lived on lot 74, assigned to him in 1817, being then aged
21; held several town offices, and removed to Wisconsin in 1832,
where he and his wife died. Chn.: I. Zephaniah. II. John W.,
was in Co. G, 36th Wis. Vols., and died after his return home.

Thomas Dick (¹Thomas) married Cynthia, daughter of Joseph
Wauby; lived on lot 63 at Brothertown, and removed to Wisconsin
in 1832, where he was killed by the Menomenee Indians. His widow
died Nov. 24, 1871, ae. 73. Chn.: I. Aurilla, m. William Crosley.
II. Margaritta. III. Jacob.

FOWLER,—Montauk tribe, Montauk. L. I. James Fowler, the earliest of the name known to us, was born at Montauk about 1700,
married Elizabeth ——, born in 1707, and in 1761 had a family of
six children. Of these, Mary married Rev. Samson Occom, and
Phœbe married Ephraim Pharaoh. David and Jacob Fowler were
sons, and another is believed to have remained at Montauk. The

father died about 1774, and his widow removed to Brothertown, where she was living with her son David in 1795, at the age of 87.

David Fowler (¹James), born in 1735, was one of the founders of Brothertown, N. Y., where he settled in 1775. The details of his life are narrated in this volume and need not be repeated here. He settled on what was afterwards lot 105, which with lot 119, was assigned to him in 1795. He was the most conspicuous figure in town affairs, a trustee in 1785, and senior peacemaker from 1796 to 1807. He amassed some property, lived well and was universally respected until his death, March 31, 1807, at the age of 72. His wife, Hannah Garret, whom he married in 1766, died in August, 1811, aged 64. Chn.: I. David. II. Hannah, b. 1768, m. Paul Dick. III. Elizabeth, b. 1770, m. (1) Obadiah Scippio. (2) George Crosley. IV. Benjamin Garret, b. 1774. V. Lurheana (Rhenea), b. 1776. VI. Mary. b. 1781, m. Samuel Adams. VII. James, b. 1784. VIII. Jacob, b. 1788. IX. Rhodolphus, b. 1791.

David Fowler (²David, ¹James), born in June, 1767, in Kirkland's cabin, married Phebe Kiness about 1791, and was given lot 16 in 1795, which, in 1824, was leased for ten years to Thomas Dean, and sold to him in 1826, after David Fowler's death. He served as town clerk several years, and was conspicuous in religious matters. His widow removed to Wisconsin, where she died March 13, 1863, aged 89. Chn.: I. Martha, b 1793, m. Emanuel Johnson. II. James, b. March 11, 1795. III. Theophilus, d. at Brothertown, N. Y. See Jones' *Annals of Oneida County*, p 96. IV. Pually, m. Timothy Jordan, a Stockbridge Indian. V Tryphena. m. Dick.

James Fowler (³David, ²David, ¹James), married Sarah, daughter of John Mason Simons; lived on lot 103, assigned to him in 1817; inherited part of lot 111 from Emanuel Simons in 1828, and was killed in a quarrel at Utica, about 1832. His widow emigrated with her family to Wisconsin. Chn.: I. Henry. drowned in Fox River. II. Phebe J., b. 1819, m. L. S. Fowler. III. Erastus, drowned in Fox River.

Benjamin Garret Fowler (²David, ¹James) married (1) Temperance Pharaoh, who died at Brothertown, N. Y. (2) Elizabeth Skeesuck, widow of Arnold Skeesuck. He lived on lot 62, assigned to him in 1795, which was sold in 1836. He was marshal of the town for several years, and a peacemaker from 1808 to 1811. In religious affairs he was a leader, and ministered as an elder of the Freewill Baptist order. He removed to Wisconsin with his family, and died Dec. 12, 1848. aged 74. His gravestone bears the tribute: " He spoke the language of his Master, ' little children, love one another.' " Chn.: I. Benjamin Garret. II. Joseph. who married and had a daughter, Elizabeth. the wife of David Dick. III. Lura, m. Nelson Paul.

James Fowler (²David, ¹James) married Patience Dick, and lived

on lot 100, assigned to him in 1804.   He was a peacemaker in 1812,
and for several years thereafter.   About 1830 he died suddenly while
at work in his field, and his widow moved with her family to Wisconsin in 1834.   Chn.: I. Abigail, m. Laton Dick.   II. David, b. Feb.
8, 1813.   III. William.   IV. Russell, burned to death.   V. John
Collins, b. Sept. 19, 1817.   VI. Simeon Adams, b. May 27, 1819,
d. at Brothertown, Wis., Nov. 20, 1880.   VII. Smith, d. in Iowa.
VIII. Laton, m. Elizabeth, dau. of Elkanah Dick, who died Sept.
15, 1873, æ. 51.   IX. Patience, lost in the woods when 12 years
old.   X. Roxanna, died April 30, 1891, æ. 66.

David Fowler (3 James, 2 David, 1 James) married Elizabeth, daughter of James Simons, who was born Feb. 2, 1819, and died Sept. 8,
1885.   He was a prominent man in town and tribal affairs, and died
in honor at Brothertown, Wis., Feb. 10, 1890.   Chn.: I. Harriet
Adelaide, b. May 9, 1844, m. Jan. 24, 1864, to John Niles, and has
children, (1) Frederick T., (2) Frances S., (3) Herbert T., (4) Walter E., (5) Hermon A.   II. Victorine, d. March 8, 1861, æ. 19.
III. Patience, b. Dec. 25, 1846, m. John W. Dick, and d. in 1885.
IV. Lathrop.   V. Theodore M., d. March 21, 1852.   VI. Elizabeth
A., b. 1850, d. 1889.

Lathrop Fowler (4 David, 8 James, 2 David, 1 James) was born at
Brothertown, Wis., Feb. 29, 1848, and attended the common schools
until at the age of 18 years he went to the business college at Fond
du Lac.   He is a carpenter by trade, which he follows in addition to
farming.   In 1866 he became a member of the I. O. G. T., and has
been honored by important offices in district and grand lodges.   He
is an ardent and consistent prohibitionist, a patriotic citizen, and a
friend of all means for the civilization of the Indians.   He is one of
the Headmen of the Brothertown tribe.

William Fowler (3 James, 2 David, 1 James) was born about 1815,
and married Mary Brushel.   He lived at Brothertown, Wis., until
he enlisted in Co. E, 21st Wis. Vols.   He was killed at Perryville,
Oct. 8, 1862.   Chn.: I. James D., b. 1840, was a soldier in the
38th Wis. Vols.   II. Emeline, m. William Welch, and d. Jan. 1,
1865, æ. 22.   III. Ella, d. 1865.   IV. Melvina, m. Rufus Skeesuck,
and d. in 1892.   V. Lisetta, m. Miles M. Johnson, and d. in 1876.

John Collins Fowler (8 James, 2 David, 1 James) was born at Brothertown, N. Y., Sept. 19, 1817, and removed to Wisconsin in 1834,
where he has since lived on his farm to an honored old age.   He
married Phebe, daughter of James Niles, who died several years since.

Jacob Fowler (2 David, 1 James) married Amy, daughter of Sampson Potter; lived on lot 141, assigned to him in 1815, and was for
years a tithingman and marshal in the town.   He went to Wisconsin, but returned later, and died in his old home.   His wife died at
Brothertown, Wis., Feb. 10, 1862, ae. 69.   Chn.: I. Alexander.

II. Hezekiah. III. Lucius Syrenius. IV. Hannah, m. Isaac Dick. V. Lorenzo David. VI. Alzina.

Alexander Fowler (³Jacob, ²David, ¹James) married (1) Harriet, daughter of Asa Dick, who died at Brothertown, N. Y., Aug. 22, 1845, æ. 23, (2) Desdemona, daughter of William Dick. He was the last town clerk, and finally removed to Wisconsin. Chn.: I. George L., d. in 1845, æ. 4. II. Amy L., d. Dec. 7, 1870, æ. 20.

Hezekiah Fowler (³Jacob, ²David, ¹James) married Fanny F. Skeesuck, and removed to Wisconsin, where she died Aug. 17, 1857, æ. 45. He held part of lot 11, in Brothertown, which was sold in 1834. Chn.: I. Parmelia, m. John Crosley. II. Irene. III. Adaline, d. Feb. 18, 1845. IV. Adah, d. Feb. 11, 1845. V. Israel, was in Co. A, 3d Wis. Vols., and died at Chancellorsville, May 3, 1863.

Lucius Syrenius Fowler (³Jacob, ²David, ¹James) was born at Brothertown, N. Y., May 10, 1819, and died at Brothertown, Wis., Feb. 23, 1886. He married Phebe J. Fowler, who died Feb. 4, 1885. They went to Wisconsin in 1834. Chn.: I. Almanza E., d. Dec. 24, 1868, æ. 26. II. Frances A., d. Sept. 4, 1859. III. Lurenette, d. Jan. 15, 1862.

Lorenzo David Fowler (³Jacob, ²David, ¹James) married Mary V., daughter of Emanuel Johnson. Chn.: I. Rhodolphus, d. in 1850, æ. 15. II. Theophilus, d. in 1852, æ. 17. III. Cordelia, m. Solomon Niles.

Rhodolphus Fowler (²David, ¹James) married Elizabeth, daughter of William Dick; lived on lot 113 in 1817; was town clerk and peacemaker, and removed to Wisconsin in 1836, where he was drowned in Fox River. Chn.: I. Lura, m. Simeon Hart. II. Osamus David, b. 1816. III. Lewis. IV. Almira, m. Rowland Johnson. V. Lyman Palmer. VI. Orrin Gridley. VII. Wealthy, m. Orrin G. Johnson.

Osamus David Fowler (³Rhodolphus, ²David, ¹James) married (1) Rosetta, dau. of Eliphalet Matthews, who died July 29, 1854, ae. 35, (2) Jane, dau. of Alonzo D. Dick, who died April 5, 1861, ae. 28. He was a prominent man in Brothertown, Wis., and died Aug. 4, 1874, æ. 58. Chn.: I. Abba Loretta. II. Ellen A., d. June 30, 1845. III. Lewis F., d. March 11, 1849. IV. James L., d. Nov. 8, 1855. V. James Lawrence, by the second wife.

Lyman Palmer Fowler (³Rhodolphus, ²David, ¹James) married Aurilla, daughter of Asa Dick. He served as a soldier in the Civil War, and died at Brothertown, Wis. Chn.: I. Oscar. II. Emelia A., d. March 18, 1851.

Orrin Gridley Fowler (³Rhodolphus, ²David, ¹James) married Ruth Skeesuck, who died at Brothertown, Wis., Aug. 15, 1870, aged 40. He was in Co. K, 4th Wis. Cav., and died at Ship Island,

Miss., May 13, 1862, æ. 49. Chn.: I. Emma E., d. 1867, æ. 17. II. Wealthy J., d. 1864, æ. 13.

Jacob Fowler ([1]James) was born in 1750, and married Esther Poquiantup, who survived his death at Brothertown, N. Y., but removed or died before 1795. He was the first town clerk, chosen in 1785, but his records, if he kept any, are lost. They had an only child, who died in 1772, at Mushantuxet, and perhaps others later. The further details of his life are given elsewhere.

HAMMAR, HAMMER,—Narragansett tribe, Charlestown, R. I. James Hammer and Margery, his wife, were living at Charlestown, in 1761, having two sons under sixteen years of age. One of these, it is thought, was John Hammar. the founder of the Brothertown family. The mother was called "Widow Margery Hammar," in 1763.

John Hammar, with his family, came to Brothertown, N. Y., before 1804, when lot 109 was assigned to him. He was then about 50 years old. His wife's name is unknown. A lot was afterwards assigned for her support "while a widow." Chn.: I. John. II. Joseph, who had lot 116 in 1814. There was also a Thomas Hammar, who married and went to Wisconsin, having children Duane, Rufus, Lucinda, Louisa, Lowana, Eveline and Carrie; but his relationship is unknown.

John Hammar ([1]John) was born about 1780. married Elizabeth Crosley, and died about 1823. His widow was living in 1843. Chn.: I. John Crosley. II. Ira. III. Samuel. IV. Louisa, m. David Wiggins. V. Rue, m. Hodge.

John Crosley Hammar ([2]John, [1]John) married Esther, daughter of William Johnson. Chn.: I. Alexander. was in Co. A, 2d Wis. Cav. II. Irene. III. Lucretia. IV. John Emery. b. Sept. 8, 1851. He is one of the Headmen of the Brothertown Indians. V. Francis M.

Ira Hammar ([2]John, [1]John) married (1) Elizabeth Dick: (2) Elizabeth Johnson. He moved to Wisconsin in 1836. and died in 1872. Chn.: I. Olive. II. Jarns. was in the 35th Wis. Vols., and died after his return. III. Wesley. IV. Amelia. V. Franklin. VI. George. was in Co. K. 4th Wis. Cav. VII. John, was in the 38th Wis. Vols., and died after his return.

Samuel Hammar ([2]John. [1]John) married Polly Johnson. and lived on lot 132 at Brothertown. Chn.: I. Louisa. II. Lorry. III. Henry, was in Co A, 1st Wis. Vols., and died at Chaplin Hills, Oct. 15, 1862.

HARRY.—Narragansett tribe. Charlestown. R. I. This was a numerous family in New England. Christopher. or "Kit" Harry had several sons in 1761. one of whom was Christopher, born in 1747. This son was a soldier in the Revolution, moved to Brothertown before 1795, and received lot 27. He soon returned to Charlestown, became a councilor of the tribe, and died there. He was an early friend of Christian education among his people. His wife's name was Clowe, and they had a son Augustus, who also became a councilor. Gideon Harry, perhaps the youth, who, with his parents Gideon and Judah Harry joined the Stonington church, April 18, 1742, came to Brothertown, and in 1796 was given lot 1. He married there Prudence Poquiantup Cujep, and had a son Gideon, who removed to White River.

HART.—Probably of the Pequot tribe, Stonington, Conn. One of that name was a late comer at Brothertown, and married Nancy Brushel. They had a son, Simeon Hart, born in 1810, who married Lura, daughter of Rhodolphus Fowler. He was town clerk from 1832 to 1835, removed to Wisconsin in 1836, and died July 1, 1847. Chn.: I. Orvill Amon, m. Sarah P. Commuck, was in Co G, 36th Wis. Vols., and died after his return. II. Rolett B., d. 1851, æ. 13. III. Sarah E., d. 1838, æ. 2.

HUTTON,—Narragansett tribe, Charlestown, R. I. Samuel Hutton, living at Charlestown in 1745, was doubtless the father of Amos Hutton, an early settler at Brothertown, living on lot 5 in 1795. President Dwight visited him in 1799, and says he had "a good house, well finished, and a large barn, well built." He was an "example of industry, economy and punctuality." In the list of 1795 he is said to have been 38 years of age, and his wife, Elizabeth, 53. They died at Brothertown, he about 1810, leaving no children

ISAACS.—Thomas Isaacs, of a tribe unknown, aged 20, and Thetura, his wife, aged 18, were given lot 24 at Brothertown, in 1795. He was interested in the White River emigration, and removed thither. The sawmill stood on his lot, which was deeded to Thomas Dean in 1828.

JOHNSON,—Mohegan tribe, Mohegan, Conn. This family was of the oldest Mohegan stock. In 1723 Manahawon Johnson was living at Mohegan, and probably he was the Manghaughwont who signed with the tribe in 1714. The name "Johnson" was taken from a white family. This man had three sons, and perhaps a fourth. Zachariah, or Zachary, became a famous councilor of the tribe, and died in September, 1787, at an advanced age. Joseph's story is told elsewhere. He had children, Joseph and Amy. Ephraim became a councilor of the tribe in 1742.

Joseph Johnson (¹Joseph) born in April, 1752, married Dec. 2, 1773, Tabitha, a daughter of Rev. Samson Occom. The details of his life are related in this volume. They had two sons, William, born Sept. 2, 1774, and Joseph, born in 1776. After their father's death, the sons lived at Mohegan, and shared in the distribution of lands in 1790. Joseph went to Brothertown; received lots 133 and 134 in 1797; and married Sarah —— in 1799. They returned, about 1820, to Mohegan, and died there.

John Johnson is said by his descendants to have come from Charlestown, but the name is not found in Narragansett lists. A "widow Johnson" was living at Mushantuxet in 1766, and her husband may have come from Mohegan, and her children have moved to Charlestown. John Johnson married, before his emigration to Brothertown, a white woman, whence came the white blood, distinctly visible in this family. She died about 1780, and he married an Indian named Eunice, who returned to New England about 1843, and died there. He came to Brothertown about 1800, receiving lots 55 and 56 in 1804. These were sold in 1828 for the benefit of Emanuel, William and John Johnson, "sons of John Johnson, deceased." He was an intelligent, Christian Indian, prominent in town affairs, and a peacemaker from 1817 to 1821. He worked at the shoemaker's trade. Beside the three sons he had daughters, Esther and Elizabeth.

John Johnson ([1]John) born in 1774, married (1) Abigail Poquiantup (?); (2) Mercy Thomas. His first wife was killed by falling from a cart. He settled on lot 138, assigned to him in 1804, was a peacemaker from 1808 to 1821, and was titled "Esquire Johnson," in honor of his service. In 1836 he removed to Wisconsin, where he died May 10, 1860, aged 86. Chn.: I. Abigail, by 1st wife, m. James Niles. II. John W. III. Henry, m. Avis Sampson. He was in Co. E, 21st Wis. Vols., and died at Perryville, Nov. 6, 1862. IV. Colen Bardit, m. Electa Scippio. V. Elizabeth, m. Ira Hammar. VI. Anna Thomas.

John W. Johnson ([2]John, [1]John) was born at Brothertown, N. Y., Dec. 28, 1818, and died at Brothertown, Wis., Feb. 27, 1881. He married twice, his second wife being Rebecca Abner, the widow of Simeon Adams. She is living at an advanced age, and is one of the most intelligent of women, with a remarkable memory and knowledge of tribal history. Chn.: 1st wife: I. Gazelle M., d. April 20, 1846. II. Jeremiah E., d. Nov. 28, 1851, æ. 18. III. Emanuel P., d. Oct. 27, 1857, æ. 19. By 2d wife: IV. Samuel. V. Wayland L., d. April 4, 1870, æ. 17. VI. Rozetta C., b. Sept. 1, 1857, m. Stevens, and d. March 10, 1878.

William Johnson ([1]John) married Charlotte Skeesuck, and they removed to Wisconsin in 1832, where they died. Chn.: I. Esther, b. Nov. 10, 1813. m. John Crosley Hammar. II. Nancy. m. Jonathan Schooner. III. William, m. (1) Charlotte Wiggins (2) Mandy Dick. IV. Orrin G. V. Elisha. VI. Abigail, m. George Skeesuck. VII. Huldah.

Orrin G. Johnson ([2] William, [1] John) married (1) Wealthy J. Fowler, who died Aug. 6, 1849, æ. 22; (2) Mary, daughter of Peter Crowell. He was a lay preacher, removed to Minnesota, and died there in 1880, aged 65. Amasa, Horenzo, Orsil and Maie, his children, all died young.

Emanuel Johnson ([1] John) married Martha, daughter of David Fowler, lived on lot 61, and removed to Wisconsin in 1834, where he soon died. Chn.: I. Eunice, m. Nathan C. Dick. II. Jeremiah W., m. Jemima Dick, went to Wisconsin in 1834, and died there. They had sons—Ovando F. was in Co. C, 35th Wis. Vols., and died Aug. 4, 1864; William H. was in Co. A, 2d Wis. Cav. III. Rowland. IV. David. V. Mary V., m. L. D. Fowler. VI. Phebe. VII. Martha.

Rowland Johnson ([2] Emanuel, [1] John) was born at Brothertown, N. Y., Feb. 22, 1816. He married (1) Nov. 18, 1840, Almira, daughter of Rhodolphus Fowler, who died July 31, 1850, æ. 31; (2) Barbara, daughter of William Dick. He removed to Wisconsin, was an honored and influential citizen, and died in 1897. Chn.: By 1st wife: I. Oscar. II. Henry, d. young. III. Hiram, d. 1853. By 2d wife: IV. Loren M., was in Co. A, 2d Wis. Cav., and died after his return. V Melville, who served in Co. K, 4th Wis. Cav., and resides at Brothertown, Wis.

Oscar Johnson ([3] Rowland, [2] Emanuel, [1] John) was born at Brothertown, Wis., March 28, 1842, was educated in the common school, and worked on the farm until 1861, when he enlisted in Co. B, 5th Wis. Vols. He served his country throughout the war, and was wounded at Sailor's Creek, April 6, 1865. He married, Dec. 22, 1867, Ellen Jane, daughter of Isaac Dick, and has a son, Harley A. Johnson. He is one of the Headmen of the Brothertown Indians, and an honored citizen.

David Johnson ([2] Emanuel, [1] John) removed to Wisconsin in 1831, being one of the first settlers. He married Abigail, daughter of William Dick, who died June 8, 1859, aged 57. He died in 1896. Chn.: I. Gracy, d. young. II. Lewis, was in Co. I, 5th Wis. Vols.

KINDNESS, KINESS.—Pequot tribe, Stonington, Conn. The only one of this name in tribal lists is John Kindness, who signed a document in 1788. Thomas Kindness, who may have been a son, removed to Brothertown about 1815, settled on lot 78, and was killed shortly afterwards in a brawl by Nathan Paul. His wife's name was Phebe. Chn.: I. James. II. Thomas, m. Christiana Paul. III. Prudence. IV. Phebe, m. David Fowler.

James Kindness ([1] Thomas) married Hannah Dick, who died Nov. 30, 1861, æ. 54. He was town clerk from 1825 to 1830, and from 1835 to 1841. Chn.: I. Laton. II. Ira. III. Isaac. There were others of this name at Brothertown, doubtless descendants of Thomas. George Kindness was in the Civil War. Lewis Kindness served in Co. I, 5th Wis. Vols., and James H. Kindness in a Kansas regiment.

MATTHEWS, MARTHERS,—A John Matthews of the Narragansett tribe is mentioned in our history. He is thought to have removed to Brothertown as an early settler, and died there. Eliphalet Marthers was an orphan, and possibly a son of John. as he was adopted by Abraham Simons, the latter's cousin, or by his widow, Sarah Adams Simons. In 1795 he was 13 years old, and then bore the name Adams which he changed to Marthers about 1804. In 1828, part of lot 126, assigned to him in 1804, was sold, for the benefit of " Eliphalet Adams otherwise Eliphalet Marthers an Indian." He became prominent in tribe and town. was a peacemaker for twenty years, and was called " Esquire Matthews." He married Elizabeth Crosley, who died at Brothertown, N. Y.; removed to Wisconsin about 1839. and died Sept. 5, 1851. Chn.: I. Rozina, m. C. D. Sampson. II. Lovina, m. E. C. Adams. III. Rozetta, m. O. D. Fowler. IV. Sarah. V. John. VI. Ransom. VII. Seth. VIII. Joel.

John Matthews (¹Eliphalet) married Adelia, daughter of George Sampson, removed to Wisconsin in 1836, and died Feb. 24, 1883, ag'd 70. Chn.: I. Eliza. II. Amanda. III. Esther.

Ransom Matthews (¹Eliphalet) married Maria, daughter of George Sampson, and died at Brothertown, Wis., June 13, 1866, in his 49th year. Chn.: I. Arsula, b. Sept. 14, 1844. II. Matthew, d. 1873, ae. 13.

MOSSUCK, MOSUCK, MAUSSUCK, MAUSSAUK.—Tunxis tribe, Farmington, Conn. Solomon Maussauk, born in 1723, was an early convert at Farmington, and he and his wife Eunice were church members. He owned lands there, and bought lot 51 in the " south east division" in 1765. More of his story is given elsewhere in this volume. His son, Daniel Mossuck, was a pupil at Lebanon, was interested in the emigration, became a Revolutionary soldier in Capt. William Judd's company of the Third regiment " Connecticut Line," and died at Farmington. Luke Mosuck of Brothertown, N. Y., is said to have been his son. He was born at Farmington in 1769 removed to the Indian town before 1795, and received lot 61. As this was forfeited in 1797, he probably returned to New England, but his son Daniel held lot 65 in 1824, and another son, Newton, received part of lot 116 in 1827. The latter moved to Wisconsin in 1834, and was frozen to death on Winnebago Lake.

NILES, NYLES,—Narragansett tribe, Charlestown, R. I. In 1747, and for years afterwards, James Niles, aged 34, a kinsman of Samuel Niles, the Indian preacher, was a councilor of this tribe. In 1763, he and his wife Jerusha had two daughters and a son, James Niles, the latter afterwards a pupil at Lebanon. This son was interested in the emigration; became a Revolutionary soldier in the Second Connecticut regiment in 1780, and a Rhode Island regiment in 1781; removed to Brothertown about 1796, and received lots 41 and 42. These were divided among his heirs in 1829. He married Barbara Poquiantup, who died before him. Chn.: I. James. II. Lucy, m. John Seketer. III. Mary, m. Nathan Pendleton, a mulatto, and died, leaving two sons, Joshua and Peter, who by the tribal laws were denied rights in the Brothertown lands. IV. Rhoda, m. (1) Charles; (2) Daniel Wauby. V. Phebe, m. Joseph Wauby.

James Niles (² James, ¹ James) married Abigail Johnson, received lot 93 in 1804, and removed to Wisconsin in 1834, where he died Sept. 7, 1863, in his 83d year. Chn.: I. Phebe, m. John Collins Fowler. II. Andrew, m. Fanny A., dau. of Lorenzo Fowler, and died Sept. 18, 1864, æ. 23. III. John, m. Harriet A., dau. of David Fowler. IV. Samuel, d. 1853, æ. 17. V. Solomon, m. Cordelia, dau. of Lorenzo Fowler, and was in the 38th Wis. Vols. during the Civil War.

OCCUM,—Mohegan tribe, Mohegan, Conn. We sum up the early history of this family given elsewhere in these pages: "Tomockham alias Ashneon" had three sons—"Joshua Ockham," "Tomocham Junr" and "John Tomocham." The latter signed in 1738 as "son of the aforesaid Tomockham." He probably married Elizabeth, a descendant of Oweneco, known as "Betty Aucum widow" in a Norwich deed of 1745. She was a member of the Montville church. John Occom, head of a family about 1765, was doubtless her son. "Tomocham Junr" probably was the "Thomas Occom" who signed as such in 1749, and was a soldier in Capt. Ebenezer Leache's company in 1755. If so, he was living in 1764, and unmarried. "Joshua Ockham," was a councilor of Ben Uncas in 1742, and died before May 17, 1743, leaving a widow Sarah, and the following children: I. Joshua, b. about 1716. II. Samson, b. 1723. III. Jonathan, b. 1725. IV. Lucy, b. about 1731. Lucy married John Tantaquidgeon, and died in 1830 at Mohegan. She had the following children: I. Lucy, m. Peter Teecomwas, and had Eliphalet, Cynthia, who married a Hoscott, and Sarah, who married Jacob H. Fowler. II. John, was a Revolutionary soldier, removed to Brothertown, received lot 139 in 1816, and was living there in 1843. III. Jerusha. IV. David. V. Bartholomew. VI. Parthenia. Joshua Occom married Eunice ——, a Pequot Indian. He was a soldier in Capt. Joshua Abell's company in 1755. His name is in a list of 1765, but she is called "Widow Eunice" in 1769. She died about 1809. They had the following children: I. Ann. II. Joshua, died before 1782. III. David, who was a soldier in Colonel Parsons' regiment in 1776, and died in the service. IV. Eunice, d. April, 1787. Jonathan Occom was a soldier in Capt. Ebenezer Leache's company in 1755, and in Capt. Zachaeus Wheeler's company in 1758. He survived the French wars, and in 1775 enlisted in Capt. John Durkee's company of General Putnam's regiment, serving throughout the war. He returned to Mohegan, received 20 acres of land in the distribution of 1790, and was living there in 1804. In lists he is called "a single man" and a "brother of Samson."

Samsom Occom needs no further notice here. His children were as follows: I. Mary, b. 1752. She was living in 1769, but nothing is known of her afterwards. II. Aaron, b. 1753, married Ann, a daughter of Samuel Robin of the Wangunk tribe, and died in the winter of 1771, at Mohegan, leaving a son Aaron. III. Tabitha, b. 1754, m. Joseph Johnson. IV. Olive, b. 1755, m. Solomon Adams. V. Christiana, b. 1757, m. Anthony Paul. VI. Talitha, b. 1761. We think she married a Cooper. She died at or near Farmington in May, 1785, leaving at least one child. VII. Benoni, b. 1763, married and had one child, but in 1808 he was living at Mohegan and had no family. VIII. Theodosia (Dorothy), b. 1769, and was living in 1789 at Mohegan. IX. Lemuel Fowler, b. 1771, and was drowned at Mohegan in 1790. X. Andrew Gifford, b. 1774, went to Brothertown, and had a lot there which he leased April 12, 1792. He married, and his death occurred before 1796, when "Widow Patience Occum" was given lot 41. They had a son, Samsom Occom, who lived at Brothertown, received part of lot 19 in 1827, and removed, it is said, with his wife Elizabeth to White River. Some Indians say he joined the Stockbridge tribe. writing his name Yoccom, and has descendants among them. XI. Sally, b. 1784. Occom called her his "child," but she may have been a grandchild. She went to Brothertown, and died there.

OCCUISH, CUISH, KUISH, KEWISH,—Niantic tribe, Niantic, Conn. Philip Occuish, born in 1716, was converted in 1740, and became a prominent Christian Indian. He had some education and was a Baptist minister, conducting services sometimes in his own house. In 1761 he had four boys and three girls, and his widowed mother, aged 70, lived with him. He was living at Niantic in 1784, and Occom wrote of him as "Old Brother Philip Cuish." His wife Sarah died April 16, 1787, in her 67th year. Their sons, or grandsons, Joshua and Abraham Occuish, removed to Brothertown, N. Y., and Philip Occuish had lots 100 and 103 assigned to him in 1799. As lot 103 was afterwards given to Joshua Occuish, perhaps he was a son. He and his wife Elizabeth were at Brothertown in 1804. They removed about 1817. Their children were: I. John, who received part of lot 145 in 1831, and was living there in 1843, having a son John and probably a daughter Melissa. II. Dimiss, who married and died before 1814, leaving a daughter Lurea, the wife of Alonzo D. Dick. III Elijah, who had part of lot 116 in 1827. IV. Anna, who married and had a son John. Abraham Occuish removed to Brothertown before 1804, received lot 131, and died before 1813.

PALMER,—The tribe of this family is unknown. Joseph Palmer was at Brothertown, N. Y., in 1818, having lot 92. He married Martha Waukeet, a Niantic Indian, removed to Wisconsin in 1834, and was murdered by a Stockbridge Indian July 3, 1836. The murderer was sentenced to be hanged, but escaped from the jail. In 1854 the widow lived at Manchester, Wis., and testified that she had two sisters, Mary Paul and Lucy Waukeet, living at Niantic. She married later Solomon Paul, and died Jan. 26, 1874, æ. 72. Chn.: I. Prudence. II. Lucy, m. Charles Wiggins. III. George. IV. Benjamin, was in Co. D, 14th Kan. Vols., and died after his return home.

PATCHAUKER, PESHAUKER, PECHORKER. PAUHETER,—This family is said to have come from Martha's Vineyard. Thomas Patchauker was an original settler at Brothertown, N. Y., and was chosen fence-viewer in 1785. He was then a widower, and died in 1795, his lot number 14 being then assigned to his daughter Jane. Chn.: I. Jane, b. 1760, m. Isaac Wauby. II. Thomas, enlisted in the navy, married and his wife Abigail lived on lot 65 till her death about 1804. She left a son Jeremiah, b. 1801.

PAUL,—There were families of this name at Charlestown, R. I., Mohegan, Conn., and Montauk, L. I. The only one which emigrated to New York was of the Narraganset tribe. In the company of 1784 were Anthony and John Paul, with their families and widowed mother. We think her name was Mary, and her husband was James Paul, living at Charlestown in a wigwam in 1766. George Paul was also a son.

Anthony Paul was born in 1758; married, about 1777, Christiana, daughter of Rev. Samson Occom; lived for a time at Mohegan, cultivating Joseph Johnson's land; emigrated in 1784 to Brothertown, receiving lot 10 in 1795, formerly owned by Occom; and returned eastward about 1797, locating near Lake George, where both died. Occom baptized his children in 1787, the first in the town. Chn.: I. Samson. II. Sarah, b. 1780. III. James, b. 1782. IV. Phebe, b. 1784, living at B. in 1843. V. Benoni, b. 1787. VI. Jonathan,

b. 1791. Probably also a daughter Christiana, who married Thomas Kindness.

Samson Paul (¹Anthony), born in 1778, married (1) Hannah, daughter of Samuel Brushel, (2) a white woman. Lot 136 was given to him in 1799, but he moved to Lake George and died there. By his first wife he had a son Nelson, and a daughter Elizabeth, who married Ezekiel Wiggins.

Nelson Paul (²Samson, ¹Anthony) lived at Brothertown, N. Y., and married Lura, daughter of B. G. Fowler. Chn.: I. Charles, was in 1st Wis. Vols. II. William, "Billy Paul," the last of his people in the old town. III. Rhodolphus. IV. David Occom, who with his brother Rodolphus was in a New York regiment during the Civil War. V. Hannah.

John Paul, a Revolutionary soldier in Durkee's regiment, emigrated in 1784, and died in the winter of 1794. He located on lot 4, which was assigned to his widow Penelope in 1795. She died in 1811. Chn.: I. Anne, b. 1785. II. Nathan, b. 1788. m. Sarah, dau. of Daniel Skeesuck; lived on lot 136, assigned to him in 1812; was imprisoned three years for killing Thomas Kindness; and removed to Wisconsin in 1832, where he died. III. Mary, b. 1790. IV. John, b. 1792. V. Isaiah, b. 1794.

George Paul was born in 1772; probably removed to Brothertown in 1784, and received lot 23, in 1795. He married Lucy ——, and they both died before 1828, when Solomon, Moses and Bathsheba were heirs. Chn.: I. Amy, b. 1794. II. Solomon, b. 1796, removed to Wisconsin in 1836. He m. (1) Hannah, dau. of Samuel Adams, who d. May 11, 1843, æ. 35; (2) Martha Waukeet, widow of Joseph Palmer, who d. 1874. Ch.: George. III. Moses, m. Rachael Scippio. IV. Bathsheba, m. George Scippio.

PETERS, PETER,—Montauk tribe, Montauk, L. I. In 1761 John Peter and his son John were living at Montauk, the latter having four children. The son was interested in the emigration, and was probably the husband of Elizabeth Peters, born in 1737, who was a widow in 1795, and received lot 106. She had children then at Brothertown, as follows: I. George, b. 1761. II. Oliver, b. 1765. III. Rhoda. IV. Frederick, possibly also William.

George Peters was an early settler at Brothertown, N. Y., and married Eunice, daughter of Elijah Wampy. He settled on lot 118, which he received with lot 125, in 1795. He had an evil temper and was intemperate. At Rome, N. Y., Feb. 24, 1800, he killed his wife, for which crime he was hanged, Aug. 28, 1801. See Jones' *Annals of Oneida County*, p. 43. Chn.: I. John, b. 1787, and living at B. in 1811. II. Jerusha, b. 1790, m. Josiah Charles. III. Elisha, b. 1792.

Oliver Peters received lot 29 in 1795. His wife's name was Anne. Chn.: I. Nathan, b. 1791, living at B. in 1814, and may have been the father of Amos, whose sons, Melancthon, William and Martin, are named in 1843. Melancthon was in the 1st Wis. Vols., and William was in Co. E, 21st Wis. Vols., and was killed at Dallas, Ga., June 29, 1864. II. Jeremiah, b. 1795. III. Aurilla, m. John Baldwin, had lot 3 in 1825, and inherited part of 106 in 1828 from her grandmother, Elizabeth.

William Peters and his wife, Bridget, lived on lot 148, assigned to them in 1804. He died about 1828, and the lot was given to his widow, to revert at her death.

PHARAOH,—Montauk tribe, Montauk. L. I. Indians of this name were living at Montauk in the seventeenth century, and several families are named in 1761. Ephraim Pharaoh married Phebe Fowler, both born in 1747, and was an early settler at Brothertown, N. Y., living on lot 17. He also received in 1795 lot 132, for the support of his daughter, Priscilla Hannable, a widow. He died before 1825, when his lot went to his widow. Chn.: I. Priscilla, b. 1772, d. about 1813. II. Temperance, m. B. G. Fowler. III. Phebe, b. 1785.

Benjamin Pharaoh was a brother of Ephraim, and was born in 1762. He also was an early settler and, with his wife, Damaris, lived on lot 124. Chn.: I. Nancy, b. 1788. II. Benjamin, b. 1790. III. Ephraim, b. 1794.

POQUIANTUP, PCUQUENUP, PAUHQUNNUP, UPPUIQUIYANTUP,—Pequot tribe, Groton, Conn., or Niantic tribe, Niantic, Conn. This was a prominent family of Christian Indians, and seems to have had one branch at Groton and another at Niantic. Occom names Joseph and Isaac at the latter place, and Isaac was his cousin. He had an aunt, "Hannah Justice," there, who may have been Isaac's mother. His language also indicates that he was related to the family at Groton. Hannah Poquiantup, Wheelock's pupil, was from Niantic. In 1766 Samson and Esther Poquiantup, with a family, were living at Groton, Esther being of the Mohegan tribe. She became a widow before 1787, and removed to Brothertown, N. Y. Her epitaph in the Deansville cemetery reads: "In Memory of Esther Pouquenup, who was a member of the Mohegan Tribe of Indians. Died Jan. 22, 1822, a practical and exemplary Christian, Aged 96 years & 3 months." One daughter, Esther, married Jacob Fowler. There was also a daughter Eunice. The epitaph of Prude Harry, in the Deansville cemetery, says she was the "daughter of Sampson and *Eunice* Pouquenup," a statement which we cannot reconcile with the above facts unless there was a son Samson. Aaron Poquiantup, a single man, with whom his mother's family were living, received lot 130 at Brothertown, in 1795. His epitaph at Dickville says he was "a member of the Nahantic tribe of Indians, R. I." He was town treasurer, 1808 to 1810, and his lot was sold for his benefit in 1832. He died Dec. 2, 1835, ae. 58, and his wife Lovinia died Aug. 14, 1835, ae. 45. Solomon Poquiantup, probably his brother, received lot 137 in 1804.

POTTER,—Narragansett tribe, Charlestown, R. I. Sampson Potter emigrated to Brothertown about 1804, and received lot 147 in 1813. He was probably a son of Daniel and Mary Potter, of Charlestown, in 1783. Amy Potter, who married Jacob Fowler, and Hannah Potter, who married William Dick, were probably his kindred. Sampson died about 1832, when his lot was sold for the benefit of Jason, Katura and Sally Potter, and Rasselas Scippio, his heirs. Jason married Carlin Cook, and they had a son Henry in the 32d Wis. Vols., who was frozen to death on Winnebago Lake.

ROBBINS, ROBBENS, ROBIN,—Tunxis tribe, Farmington, Conn. This family originally came from Middletown, and belonged to the Wangunk tribe. David Robin, of Farmington, was interested in the emigration in 1773, but probably died before 1777. His wife Hannah owned land there at that date. She removed to Brothertown, N. Y., with her daughter Rhoda, and received lot 116. Rhoda died about 1814, and her mother in 1827.

ROBERTS,—In 1797 lot 102, at Brothertown, was assigned to Abigail, the wife of Thomas Roberts. It was forfeited later, and lot 101 was given her in 1821, part of which was sold in 1833 for Abigail Roberts, and the balance in 1842 for Abigail Fowler, probably a daughter. Both are named in the list of 1843.

SAMPSON,—Pequot tribe, Groton, Conn. In 1762 " Sampson, a likely Indian," aged 33, was living in a house at Mushantuxet. He had eight children, one of whom was James. He died before 1787, when his wife is called " Widow Sampson." She was an earnest Christian Indian. James removed to Brothertown, N. Y., with his wife Sarah and their children about 1797, when lot 10, formerly owned by Samson Occom and Anthony Paul, was assigned to him. He died about 1815. Chn.: I. George. II. Abel. III. Eveline. IV. David, who received part of lot 112 in 1828, and died in N. Y. V. James, d. in N. Y. VI. Fanny. VII. John, who received part of lot 113 in 1828.

In the census list of 1843, the following names are found which probably represent the families of David, James, or John Sampson— Moses, Catharine, George W., Emily, Rufus, Alonzo, Avery, Avis, and Mills W. Clark D. Sampson was also a descendant. He married Rozina Matthews, removed to Wisconsin, and died in 1884, aged 65 They had sons, James J. and George, in Co. E, 21st Wis. Vols., the latter dying March 6, 1865, and a daughter, Almira J., the wife of O. D. Dick.

George Sampson (¹James) married Lucena, daughter of William Dick; received part of lot 112 in 1817; was a peacemaker from 1821 to 1824, and died at Brothertown, N. Y., in 1839. His lot was then disposed of for his daughters. Chn.: I. Delia (Adelia) m. John Matthews. II. Maria, m. Ransom Matthews. III. Jane, m. John Foss, a white man. IV. Sophia, m. John Coyhis.

Abel Sampson (¹James) married Esther, daughter of John M. Simons; received lot 115 in 1819; and died at Brothertown about 1830. His widow removed to Wisconsin in 1844. Chn.: I. James. II. Melinda (Malvina). III. Welthea A. IV. Grizel H. V. Ralph W. VI. Eliza E.

SCIPPIO,—This family came from Montauk, but the name is not found in early lists of that tribe. Two brothers, Samuel and Obadiah, were among the first settlers at Brothertown, N. Y.

Samuel Scippio, born in 1764, and his wife Charlotte, born in 1767, with five children, were living on lot 21 in 1795. He was a peacemaker from 1796 to 1807, and from 1812 to 1820. He died shortly after the latter date. His widow, "Loty Scippio," was living in 1843. Chn.: I. Sarah, b. 1787, m. Anthony. II. Isaac, b. 1789, received lot 50 in 1813, which he and his wife Julia sold in 1829, removing in 1831 to Wisconsin, where they died. III. Jacob, b 1791, received lot 97 in 1813, married Clarinda, daughter of Elijah Wampy, who inherited from her father in 1828, and removed later to Wisconsin. They returned East during the time of cholera, and were never heard of more. IV. Esther, b. 1793. V. Abraham, b. 1795. VI. Richard, who received lot 64 in 1824. VII. Phebe, m. Denny, of the Oneida tribe.

Obadiah Scippio was born in 1766. He married Elizabeth, daughter of David Fowler, removed to Brothertown, and settled on lot 13. He died about 1806. His widow afterwards married George Crosley, removed to Wisconsin, and died there. Chn.: I. Dennis, b. 1791, and living in 1816. II. George, b. May 18, 1795, married Bathsheba Paul, removed to Wisconsin in 1836, and was drowned in Fox River. III. Celinda, m. James Simons. IV. Cynthia. V. Rachel, m. Moses Paul. VI. Calvin.

SEKETER, SICKETOR, SECUTOR, SEQUETTASS,—Narragansett tribe, Charlestown, R. I. This family was very influential in colonial times. John Secutor, a son of David Seketer, sent his daughter, Mary Sequettass, to Wheelock's school in 1763, and in 1767, his son, John Secutor, was a pupil. The son was interested in the emigration plans, and may have gone to Brothertown, but he did not become a permanent settler. He was later a councilor of the tribe, and died at Charlestown. His son John and daughter Mary, however, removed to Brothertown, N. Y.

John Seketer (²John, ¹John) was at Brothertown in 1807, when he was chosen marshal. In 1813 lot 32 was assigned to him, and, in 1814, part of lot 52. He was a peacemaker from 1820 to 1822. In 1832 he sold his estate and removed to Wisconsin. He married Lucy, daughter of James Niles, who died about 1830. Chn.: I. Samantha, m. Alexander Dick. II. Charlotta, who removed with her father and married John Wilber, a white man. III. Charles, who married Abigail, daughter of Thomas Wiott, and died in N. Y., leaving sons Milo C. and John D. IV. Grace, m. Samuel Skeesuck. V. Sarah.

SHELLEY,—Pequot tribe, Stonington, Conn. Several families of this name were living there in 1788, from one of which Bradley and Simeon Shelley were descended. The former removed to Brothertown, N. Y., about 1830, and received lot 146. The latter was there earlier and received lot 68 in 1820. This was sold in 1834, and he afterwards removed to Brothertown, Wis., where he died June 25, 1860, aged 59. His wife, Sabrina Welch, died Nov. 2, 1869, aged 65. They had six sons in the Civil War: Elias, in the 3d Wis. Vols., Henry and Simeon in Co. E. 21st Wis. Vols., Lewis in Co. H. 32d Wis. Vols., David in Co. K. 19th Wis. Vols., and John in the "Pioneer Corps."

SIMONS, SIMON,—Narragansett tribe, Charlestown, R. I. Sarah Simons was one of the most faithful Christian Indians in this tribe. In 1767 she was a widow with a family of children, and we conjecture that her husband was John Simon, named in a list of 1761. She sent five children to Wheelock's school, as elsewhere stated, all of whom were interested in the emigration, though only Abraham and Emanuel removed to Brothertown.

Abraham Simons, born at Charlestown about 1750, and educated under Doctor Wheelock, was probably one of the young men who went to Oneida before the Revolution. He returned when the war broke out, and enlisted in Capt. Prentice's company of the Sixth Connecticut regiment. After the war he returned early to Oneida, and was one of the trustees chosen in 1785. He was then married, but his wife died in 1786. He married again July 26, 1787, Sarah, daughter of John Adams. He is frequently mentioned by Occom, and is said to have led an exemplary life. He died at Brothertown, and Occom attended his funeral. Lot 12 was assigned to his widow in 1795, and was no doubt the early location of his pioneer hut. In 1797 the house stood in the highway, and she was ordered to remove it. Her age was 43 years in 1795, and she was living in 1800. Her lot passed to Eliphalet Marthers, and he sold it in 1832. Abraham and Sarah Simons had a son Reuben, born in 1790, who practised medicine in an Indian fashion at Brothertown until about 1826.

Emanuel Simons, born about 1746, after attending school for a time at Lebanon, returned to Charlestown. In 1775 he and his brother James enlisted in Capt. Edward Mott's company of the Sixth Connecticut regiment. He was then married and had a family. About 1800 he removed, with his children then grown, to Brothertown, where he died in 1806. He received lot 111 in 1804, which was divided among his heirs in 1829. Chn.: I. John Mason. II. James. III. Dennis, d. unm. in Wis. IV. Cynthia, m. Joseph M. Quinney of the Stockbridge tribe.

John Mason Simons ([1]Emanuel) came with his father to Brothertown, and was chosen marshal in 1801. He received lots 107 and 108 in 1804, and is said to have died in 1822. His estate was divided in 1833, doubtless after the death of his wife Lucy. Chn.: I. Esther, m. Abel Sampson. II. Sarah, m. James Fowler. III. Emeline, m. Jaques. IV. Moses, d. young.

James Simons ([1]Emanuel) was born at Charlestown, R. I., March 7, 1790, came as a youth to Brothertown and received lot 98 in 1812. He served as a soldier in the War of 1812, and was by trade a plow-maker. He married Celinda (Sylinda) daughter of Obadiah Scippio, who removed to Wisconsin in 1835, whither her son James had preceded her. The father was killed by an accident in 1825. Chn.: I. Elizabeth, m. David Fowler. II. James.

James Simons ([2]James, [1]Emanuel) was born at Brothertown, N. Y., Jan. 21, 1821, and died at Kaukauna, Wis., Jan. 25, 1898. He removed to Wisconsin in 1835, and during his later years lived at Kaukauna, where a son survives him. He was a carpenter by trade and also cultivated a farm. At the time of his death he was one of the Headmen of the Brothertown Indians, and was greatly respected as an intelligent and honorable citizen.

SKEESUCK, SHEESUCK, SCHESUCK, SKEEZUC, SKIEEZUP.—Narragansett tribe, Charlestown, R. I. John Skeesuck was one of the early settlers at Brothertown, and he came from Charlestown. He was born in 1746, and his name occurs in a list of 1763. Probably Elizabeth Skeesuck, a widow with three sons in 1761, was his mother, and we think his father was John Skeesuck, a soldier in 1755.

John Skeesuck was interested in the emigration plans, and was

Johnson's companion in 1775. He was a Revolutionary soldier in Col. John Topham's regiment of Rhode Island troops in 1775, and probably saw later service. He removed to Brothertown after the war and located on lot 26. He was a peacemaker from 1796 to 1807, and probably died in office. His wife's name was Anne, born in 1747. The following were certainly their children, and there were probably others older: I. Christopher, b. 1776, who received lot 22 in 1804, was town clerk from 1804 to 1809, and died at Brothertown, leaving a son John, his only heir, in 1831. II. Sarah, b. 1780. III. John, b. in 1782, received lot 77 in 1804. IV. Charlotte, b. 1790, m. William Johnson.

John Skeesuck (2Christopher, 1John) was born in 1782, married Hannah Galin, inherited lot 22 from his father and lot 26 from his grandmother Anne. Lot 83 also was assigned to him. They had a son Henry who removed to Wisconsin.

Daniel Skeesuck came from Charlestown to Brothertown about 1800. One of this name is in a list of 1763, and was a councilor of his tribe in 1774, continuing as such to 1791. We do not know whether he or his father was the Indian who settled in Brothertown. The emigrant was well advanced in life, however, and we think he was a brother of John Skeesuck. He received lots 43 and 48 in 1804, and at the same time lots were assigned to Simon and Bennet Skeesuck, probably the sons of John or Daniel. The estate of Daniel Skeesuck was divided in 1828, the following heirs receiving shares—Samuel Skeesuck, Sen., Daniel Skeesuck, Sally, the wife of Nathan Paul, Nancy, the wife of Asa Dick, Eliza and Martha Skeesuck, and Abigail Brushel. Eliza and Martha Skeesuck are said to have been daughters of Arnold Skeesuck, which indicates that Arnold was a son of Daniel.

Samuel Skeesuck (1Daniel) was born at Charlestown in 1772. He married Mary Seketer, born in 1775, a sister of John Seketer, and they were at Brothertown in 1795. She died in New York, but he removed to Wisconsin in his old age. Chn.: I. Daniel, m. Sylvia Abner; received lot 80 in 1827; removed to Wisconsin and in 1852 to Kansas, where both died, leaving a daughter Mary. II. Abraham, m. Adeline, daughter of Paul Dick; received lot 70, which was sold for him in 1829; and removed to Wisconsin in 1832. They had children, Mary, Lester and Lyman. III. Samuel, m. Grace, daughter of John Seketer; received lot 69 in 1821, and removed to Wisconsin. Their children were Solomon, called Sykes, who was in the Civil War and died after reaching home, Dorcas, and John who was in Co. H, 5th Wis. Vols., and died at Brothertown, Wis. IV. Fanny, m. Hezekiah Fowler. V. Lucy, m. Henry Welch.

Arnold Skeesuck, probably the son of Daniel, received lot 49 in 1804, which was sold in 1836, Eliza, Arnold and Abigail having shares. He died at Brothertown, N. Y., about 1820, and his widow married B. G. Fowler. Chn.: I. Arnold. II. Samuel. III. David. IV. Eliza. V. Martha. VI. Abigail (?). George Skeesuck, whose mother was Thankful Dick, is thought to have been also of this family. He married Abigail Johnson, and removed to Wisconsin. They had a son, Rufus, in Co. I, 5th Wis. Vols.

Arnold Skeesuck (¹Arnold) married Hannah Walker, a white woman, removed to Wisconsin, and died March 1, 1877, aged 60. She died June 4, 1873, aged 60. Chn.: I. Sylvester was in Co. A, 2d Wis. Cav. II. Madison was in Co. D, 35th Wis. Vols., and died at Port Hudson, May 22, 1864.

Simon Skeesuck came to Brothertown about 1800, and settled on lot 51, assigned to him in 1804. In 1824 this was given to his son, Daniel, on condition that he support his mother if she becomes chargeable. It was sold for "Daniel Skeesuck, 1st," in 1835. The wife of Simon Skeesuck is said to have borne the name Hannah, and their son, Simon, was in the 3d Regiment Wis. Vols., and was killed.

TOCUS,—Joseph Tocus is said to have come to Brothertown from Charlestown. He received lot 59 in 1813, and married Grace, daughter of George Crosley. They sold in 1834, and removed to Wisconsin. Later, he went to Kansas and died there. She was well educated, and taught a school in the Indian town. Thomas Tokus, of the Brothertown tribe, was a soldier in the Civil War, but his relationship is unknown.

TOUCEE, TOWSEY, TOWCEE, TOWSEE,—Tunxis tribe, Farmington, Conn. David and Sarah Towsey were the results of early instruction at Farmington, and became influential Christian Indians. He was a soldier in Capt. John Patterson's company in 1755 and 1756, and in Col. Nathan Whiting's company in 1762. In 1769 he sold his land at Indian Neck, being then "of Stockbridge," and in 1774 he was at Kingsbury, near Fort Edward. He maintained, however, his tribal interest, and was sometimes at Farmington. In 1772 he wrote Doctor Wheelock, asking him to take his two sons for instruction. Benjamin was at Hanover in 1777. David Towsey died about 1778, and his widow removed to Brothertown, receiving lot 45 in 1796. As it was afterwards forfeited, she doubtless returned to New England. Chn.: I. Benjamin. II. Joseph, b. 1769.

Benjamin Toucee (¹David) was born in 1765 at Farmington, attended school there and at Hanover, and was a Revolutionary soldier in Capt. Hull's company from West Stockbridge, Mass., being then aged 17. He married Elizabeth, daughter of Andrew Curricomb, and they removed to Brothertown, settling on lot 20, assigned to him in 1795. Both died there, and his lot was sold for his children in 1828. Chn.: I. Aaron, b. 1793, received his grandmother's lot in 1817, which was sold for him in 1828. He married Lydia Brushel. II. Sarah Ann, m. Elkanah Dick. III. David, born at Brothertown, Aug. 9, 1800, was bound out to the Misses Kirkland when eleven years old. In 1824 he received part of lot 87. He married Eunice, daughter of Josiah Charles, and they removed to Wisconsin, where he died about 1844, and she in 1886.

TOXCOIT, TOXCOIET,—James Toxcoit of the Narragansett tribe, born in 1744, was an early emigrant to Brothertown, where he leased his lot in 1791 to Abraham Oaks. In 1795 he received lot 19. His wife's name was Barsha, born in 1753. They both died at Brothertown.

TUHIE, TUHUY, TUHI, TUHIGH, TOHOY,—Narragansett tribe, Charlestown, R. I. In the census of 1761 is the name John Tohoy, then above 16 years, and the son of Joseph and Jane. We have reason to think that this was John Tuhie, born in 1744, who was interested in the emigration, and removed to Brothertown after the Revolution. Lots 11 and 18 were assigned to him in 1795, the latter for the support of Elizabeth Cognehew, a widow, aged 60. He was a prominent man and a peacemaker from 1796 to 1811. His epitaph reads " John Tuhie Esq. Died December 14, 1811. Aged 65 years." His wife, Sarah, outlived him, and became blind. They had a son, Jeremiah, and also brought up John and Mary Charles. Jeremiah Tuhie was born in 1768, married Jerusha.Charles, born in 1772, came to Brothertown in 1788, and settled on lot 8. Chn.: I. Eliza. II. John, who had a cousin Joseph Tuhie, whom he killed in a quarrel. See Jones' *Annals of Oneida County*, p. 44.

WAMPY, WIMPEY, WEAMPY, WEAMPEE,—Tunxis tribe, Farmington, Conn. Elijah Wampy, born in 1734, was one of the well known Indians of his day. He was educated in the Farmington school, owned land there, and bought more, served as a soldier in 1757, and became conspicuous in tribal affairs. He was one of the leaders in the emigration plans, and removed to Oneida in 1775. During the Revolution he was at Stockbridge, but returned as soon as it was safe to do so, settling on lot 117, where he lived until his death. Incidents of his adventurous life in the wilderness were related among the early settlers for years. He was foremost in the Brothertown land troubles, having an ambition for authority, which was never gratified. He died, probably, about 1802. His wife, Jerusha, died before 1795. We think she was a second wife, and his first was Eunice Waucus, who died at Farmington. Chn.: I.

Eunice, d. 1767, æ. 3. II. Elijah. III. Eunice, 2d, m. George Peters. IV. Sarah. V. Hannah. VI. Charles, who received lot 63 in 1804. VII. Esther. VIII. Jerusha, m. Charles. The heirs to lot 117, in 1831, were Elijah, Esther, Jersuha and Clarinda.

Elijah Wampy (1 Elijah) was born in 1765, and married widow Elizabeth Peters, born in 1761, whose daughter, Mary Peters, was living with them in 1795. He lived on lot 15, and died at Brothertown about 1812. In 1828, his only living child was Clarinda, born in 1791, who married Jacob Scippio, though he had a son, Elijah, born in 1794.

WAUBY, WOBBY, WAPPY, WOBI, WOYBOY,—Narragansett or Pequot tribe. Roger Wauby, born in 1734, belonged to a family originally of the Pequot tribe. Some of that name lived at Mushantuxet. He had land rights at Stonington, and his name is found in their lists. In 1765, however, he was living among the Narragansetts, and he signed with them in 1767. He was related to Samson Wauby, Wheelock's pupil—probably a brother. Occom called him "Brother Roger," and we think they were related through Occom's mother. He was one of the foremost in the emigration scheme; became a Revolutionary soldier in Capt. Samuel Prentice's company of the Sixth Connecticut regiment; and, after the war, removed to Oneida, becoming one of the founders of Brothertown. His first location was found to be west of the town, and he moved to lot 3. He is said to have lived a consistent Christian life, and was a devoted friend of Samson Occom. He died before 1819, when his lot was assigned to his son, Isaac. His widow, Mary, was living in 1808. Chn.: I. Isaac. II. A daughter, who married a Paul, and whose sons, Andrew and John were living with him in 1795. III. Daniel, who married Rhoda Charles, daughter of James Niles, received lots 30 and 31 in 1797, and died before 1817. His widow held lot 30 during her life, and it was sold for Oliver Charles in 1843. IV. Joseph.

Isaac Wauby (1 Roger) born in 1762, lived on lot 28. He married Jane, daughter of Thomas Patchauker, who was probably his second wife. He had a fair education, and became an exhorter of the Freewill Baptist order, being known as "Elder Wauby." About 1812 he became a naturalized citizen, the first of his people to secure the honor. He moved to White River, Ind., where he died. His widow returned to Brothertown, and in 1825 held part of lot 3. Ch.: Jehoiakim, b. 1791.

Joseph Wauby (1 Roger) was born in 1776, and married Phebe, daughter of James Niles. They lived on lot 33, in 1804. In 1831, part of lot 3 was sold for Isaac, James, John and Silas Wauby, and Jerusha Dick "heirs of Joseph Wauby deceased." A daughter, Cynthia, married Thomas Dick. His son, Isaac, married Mary Jakeways and they moved to Wisconsin in 1834, where he died about 1870, and she Dec. 3, 1888, aged 78. Their children were Amon, Sarah, Aaron, who was in Co. D, 35th Wis. Vols., and died at Morganzia, Aug. 14, 1864, and Lewis, who was in Co. A, 2d Wis. Cav., and died after his return from the war. Joseph's son, James, married Eunice, daughter of Paul Dick, and removed to Wisconsin.

WAUCUS, WAUKAS, WOWOUS, WOWOWOUS, WAWAWIS,—Tunxis tribe, Farmington, Conn. This was one of the original families of the tribe. In 1688 Wawawis was one of the two chosen Tunxis chiefs. He died before 1727, when his four children, Peathus, Achatowset, James and Eunice released the land he had owned, commonly called Indian Neck. James Wowowous had a son, James, born in 1728. He attended the early schools at Farmington, became a soldier in Capt. John Patterson's company in 1755 and 1756, and in Capt. Timothy Northam's company, 1st Regiment N. Y. troops, raised in Connecticut in 1762. His wife's name was Rachel. In 1771 he is "James Wowous of Farmington, now of Stockbridge." He was engaged in the emigration scheme, went to Oneida before the Revolution, but died before 1778, when "Rachel Wowous" sold their Farmington lands. They had children, Susannah and James, and perhaps others.

James Waucus (³ James, ² James, ¹ Wawawis) was born in 1768 and became a pupil in Joseph Johnson's school at Farmington. He married Philena, daughter of Solomon Adams, and settled at Brothertown on lot 9. In 1795 his wife's sister, Damaris, who afterwards married Jacob Thomas, was living with them. The sisters sold land at Farmington in 1801. He died about 1806 and his widow married Thomas Crosley. Olive Sampson was heir to lot 9 in 1837.

WAUKEET, WAUKEETS, WAUKETE, WALKEAT,—Niantic tribe, Niantic, Conn. This was an old and prominent Indian family. Joshua Waukeet was the only one who removed to Brothertown. He received lot 60 in 1804, and died there, leaving a widow Susannah, living in 1812. Martha Palmer, Mary Paul, and Lucy Waukeet, sisters, who went to Wisconsin from Niantic, were of this family.

WIGGINS,—Among the settlers at Brothertown, N. Y., in 1795, was James Wiggins Titus. He dropped the last name later. He married Anne, daughter of Andrew Curricomb, and they lived on lots 122 and 123. Chn.: I. Martin. II. Mary, b. 1793. III. Samson. Perhaps, also, Ethan Wiggins was a son.

Martin Wiggins (¹ James), born in 1791, lived at Brothertown, N. Y. He is believed to have been the father of David and Ezekiel. The former married Louisa Hammar and they lived at Brothertown,

Wis. Their son Leander married Henrietta Brushel, was in Co. E, 21st Wis. Vols., and died at Chaplin Hills, Oct. 8, 1862. Another son was in Co. A, 2d Wis. Cav., and died in the service. Ezekiel Wiggins married Elizabeth, daughter of Samson Paul, and they removed to Wisconsin. Their son Martin married Mary Ann Denny, an Oneida Indian, and they had a son Martin in Co. E., 21st Wis. Vols., who died Nov. 30, 1862.

Samson Wiggins ([1] James) was born about 1796, and received lot 143 in 1824. He married and had the following children, for whom his lot was sold in 1833: I. Eli, who was in the 18th Wis. Vols., and died at Brothertown. Wis. II. James. III. Samuel IV. Charlotte, m. William Johnson. V. Seth. VI. Hiram, who was in a N. Y. regiment in the war.

WIOTT, WYATT, WIUTT, WIAT,—Thomas Wiat, aged 24, was at Brothertown in 1795, and received lot 135. In 1828 his land was sold for Thomas and Caroline Wiott. He died before 1831. Chn. : I. Thomas, who received lot 149 in 1827. II. Daniel. III. Abigail, m. Seketer. The son Daniel received lot (88) in 1821, where he and his wife Rachel lived. They had a son Romance, or " Matt," born in 1826, who was brought up by Cynthia Dick, removed to Wisconsin, but returned to New York later, and worked on the Erie Canal. He was in Co. K, 26th N. Y. Vols., in the war. At the last accounts he had gone to spend his old age in the town where so many of his people are buried in forgotten graves.

INDEX